"A wonderful, concise encyclopedia of ADR wisdom essential to all—private parties, public parties, advocates, and neutrals."
—*Benjamin R. Civiletti, chairman, Venable, LLP; former Attorney General of the United States*

"At last lawyers and clients have a book that comprehensively describes how ADR might be used effectively in disputes with the United States Government. Senger's sage advice—if followed—will lead to speedier and fairer outcomes and will save resources for all concerned."
—*Robert H. Mnookin, Williston Professor of Law; chair, Program on Negotiation at Harvard Law School*

"*Federal Dispute Resolution* is one of those unusual books that offers at the same time sound and practical advice for the novice and insight for the dispute resolution expert on the unique challenges of disputes involving the Federal government. The author's advice on how the lawyer and client should prepare for and advocate within mediation is likely to become a classic on this topic."
—*Nancy H. Rogers, dean and Moritz Chair in Alternative Dispute Resolution, Ohio State University Moritz College of Law*

"Jeffrey Senger makes a very persuasive case for ADR, especially in the context of government contracting, where continuing business relationships are critical and government policy encourages its use. He has drawn a well-marked roadmap designed to help counsel and their business clients drive down litigation costs, save management time and resources, and preserve key customer relationships by using an ADR process to resolve complex commercial and government contract disputes." —*Jay B. Stephens, senior vice president and general counsel, Raytheon Company*

"Written by an insider, *Federal Dispute Resolution* is must-reading for anyone who has a dispute with the Federal government or wishes to play a role in resolving one." —*Linda R. Singer, principal, ADR Associates, LLC; president, Center for Dispute Settlement*

Federal Dispute Resolution

Federal Dispute Resolution

Using ADR with the
United States Government

Jeffrey M. Senger

Foreword by Frank E. A. Sander

Published in Cooperation with the American Bar Association
Section of Dispute Resolution

JOSSEY-BASS
A Wiley Imprint
www.josseybass.com

Published by Jossey-Bass
A Wiley Imprint
989 Market Street, San Francisco, CA 94103-1741   www.josseybass.com

Jossey-Bass books and products are available through most bookstores. To contact Jossey-Bass directly
call our Customer Care Department within the U.S. at 800-956-7739, outside the U.S. at 317-572-3986
or fax 317-572-4002.

Jossey-Bass also publishes its books in a variety of electronic formats. Some content that appears in
print may not be available in electronic books.

The publisher and the author make no representations or warranties with respect to the accuracy or
completeness of the contents of this work and specifically disclaim that any views expressed herein are
necessarily the views of the American Bar Association or its Section of Dispute Resolution.

Library of Congress Cataloging-in-Publication Data
Senger, Jeffrey M., date.
    Federal dispute resolution: using ADR with the United States government
/Jeffrey M. Senger.—1st ed.
        p. cm.
    Includes bibliographical references and index.
    ISBN 0-7879-6858-7 (alk. paper)
    1. Administrative procedure—United States. 2. Dispute resolution
(Law)—United States. I. Title.
    KF5417.S46 2003
    342.73'066—dc21

                                              2003013874

Printed in the United States of America
FIRST EDITION
HB Printing   10 9 8 7 6 5 4 3 2 1

Contents

Foreword

The publication of this book is eloquent testimony to the increasing sophistication of the alternative dispute resolution (ADR) field. Who would have thought twenty-five years ago that an entire book could be devoted to so specific a subject as federal ADR? Yet, stimulated by several key federal statutes and executive orders, along with extensive implementation at a number of federal agencies, the subject has gradually proliferated, so that now a sophisticated guide to the field is very much needed.

Of course, federal ADR is, above all, ADR. Thus, it is not surprising—indeed, it is most welcome—that this book deals usefully with a number of generic ADR questions, such as matching disputes to particular mechanisms and how to prepare for and conduct a mediation. These materials should therefore be of interest to anyone who seeks a form of dispute resolution other than litigation.

Some of these points raise nice questions for debate. For example, the author says that a counterindication for mediation is where a party claims not to have sufficient information to assess the case's worth and that therefore more discovery is needed. Others might argue—and Jeffrey Senger does so in this book—that this is a key role for skilled mediators: to examine precisely the asserted need for further discovery (that is, to mediate first the need for further discovery).

There are, of course, some questions unique to governmental ADR. If there is one paramount complaint voiced by individuals who are engaged in mediations with the federal government—or indeed with any government—it is the maddening difficulty of getting officials with sufficient authority—in law as well as in spirit. Sometimes particular statutes or regulations explicitly restrict the settlement authority of lower officials. The scope and wisdom of these laws ought to be reexamined. But equally exasperating is the tendency of some government officials to pass the buck upstairs and refuse to take responsibility for innovative, creative settlements. This critical question, discussed in this book, needs continuing attention if federal government ADR is to thrive.

This book is of wide-ranging scope. Senger is to be particularly commended for including some important, but not often dealt with, topics such as evaluation of programs. Increasingly, in a tight economy, legislators and other funders are demanding proof of effectiveness. This suggests the need for careful clarification of goals at the outset, plus well-thought-out collection of data in the implementation.

In conclusion, it must be remembered that this is but a first effort on this subject. I hope that some topics (like negotiated regulations) that were not addressed in this book for space reasons will be added to future editions.

Cambridge, Massachusetts   FRANK E. A. SANDER
Bussey Professor
Harvard Law School

Preface

Alternative dispute resolution (ADR) has the potential to change fundamentally the way the federal government does business with its citizens. People both inside and outside the government have found it has substantial advantages over more traditional adversarial processes. Participants report that ADR is often quicker and cheaper than administrative adjudication and federal litigation. Perhaps even more important, people find that ADR gives them greater control over how they resolve their disputes, more opportunities to be creative, increased feelings of satisfaction, and improved relationships with each other.

The field has grown dramatically in recent years, creating the need for a comprehensive guide to using ADR in matters involving the federal government. This book is designed for those who are interested in learning more about how ADR can help parties resolve government disputes. It does not require special knowledge of ADR or the law, and it is designed to be useful for both beginners and experienced ADR practitioners. It is written for both public and private sector audiences. Thus, it should be helpful to those who have disputes with the government as well as those who represent the government in these matters. Neutrals who participate in ADR with the government (or would like to) should find it valuable. Finally, teachers and students will find materials that can be useful in ADR courses.

Each chapter is self-contained, allowing readers to move through the book in any order they wish. Chapter One introduces the subject with a discussion of the benefits of ADR in the government, the history of federal dispute resolution, and the laws and regulations that govern the field. The next four chapters provide a detailed, practical guide to the use of ADR in disputes involving the federal government. Chapter Two covers how to select disputes for ADR, discussing those cases where it is most and least effective. It also addresses the advantages and disadvantages of each of the ADR processes used in the government. Chapter Three discusses how to select the best possible neutrals to lead ADR processes, covering the factors to consider in this regard. It also provides a guide to how federal government practitioners select and hire neutrals. Chapter Four provides a step-by-step description of how to prepare for ADR. It covers considerations for both clients and attorneys. Chapter Five explores ideas on how to advocate effectively in ADR. It describes how to be persuasive at each stage of the ADR process.

The second half of the book addresses specific topics of interest in the field.[1] Chapters Five and Six cover the two types of cases where ADR is used most frequently in the government: workplace and contracting disputes. These chapters describe the special laws, policies, and practices in these areas. Chapter Eight addresses confidentiality, a subject of considerable interest and some controversy. It describes the law in this area and provides practical advice for handling confidentiality concerns. The final two chapters examine ADR programs in the government. Chapter Nine addresses design, management, and training concerns. It will be useful for those who lead ADR programs, as well as those who want to understand how ADR programs work in the government. Chapter Ten provides guidance on how to evaluate the effectiveness of ADR programs, a topic of importance as the field seeks to become even more established in the government.

The book also contains six appendixes. Appendix A sets out the Administrative Resolution Act of 1996, which calls for federal agencies to promote the use of ADR and promulgates laws governing the field (this is the amended version of the original act passed in 1990). Appendix B is the order from the attorney general that established the ADR program at the U.S. Department of Justice. Appendix C contains the Alternate Dispute Resolution Act of 1998, which provides for ADR in the federal district courts. Appendix D is the presidential order that requires federal agencies to promote the use of ADR. Appendix E is a document that gives advice on confidentiality in administrative ADR that was drafted by the Federal ADR Council, a group of high-level agency officials. Finally, Appendix F is a report to the president from the Interagency ADR Working Group that describes the ADR activities of the federal government.

Acknowledgments

Many people both inside and outside the federal government have contributed to this book. I am particularly grateful for the assistance of Pete Steenland, with whom I worked closely for four years on most of the topics discussed in the book. My colleagues from the Department of Justice have been very helpful, including Steve Altman, Loretta Argrett, Linda Cinciotta, Rachel Cramer, Janice Hebert, Virginia Howard, Deborah Kant, Aloma Shaw, and Ron Silver.

The federal Interagency ADR Working Group, an organization of ADR specialists throughout the federal government, has developed materials that have informed a number of parts of this work. Members of the group who have provided specific comments on this book are David Batson, Rob Burton, Andrew Colsky, Cathy Costantino, Deborah Dalton, John Dietrich, Geoff Drucker, Kirk Emerson, Howard Gadlin, Doug Gallegos, Elena Gonzales, Will Hall, Phyllis Hanfling, Martin Harty, Eileen Hoffman, Judy Kaleta, Chris Kopocis, Jody Lee, Martha McClellan, Joseph McDade, Leah Meltzer, Rick Miles, Linda Myers, Patricia Orr, Tony Palladino, Daniel Rainey, Cherie Shanteau, Pat Sheridan, Rick Southern, and Rich Walters.

People from other branches of the government, academia, and the private sector who have contributed are Lisa Bingham, Frank Carr, Jack Cooley, Jon Gould, Phil Harter, Chris Honeyman, Tony Lofaro, Bobbi McAdoo, Joe McMahon, Wallace Meissner, Carrie Menkel-Meadow, Michael Moffitt, Charles Pou, Karen Powell, Richard Reuben, Frank Sander, Andrea Schneider, Donna Stienstra, and Mark Umbreit. The Dispute Resolution Section of the American Bar Association has been helpful, particularly John Bickerman, Gina Brown, Jack Hanna, Sameena Sabir, and Kyo Suh. I also am grateful for the assistance of my publisher, particularly Rachel Anderson, Beverly Miller, and Alan Rinzler.

Washington, D.C.   JEFFREY M. SENGER

For my mother and father,
whose love and support I have cherished all my life

| Introduction

Disputes with the federal government may be inevitable, but litigation is not. Traditional government methods of dispute resolution, including adversarial processes such as trials, have inherent limitations. They are expensive, sapping resources from both citizens and their government. These methods are time-consuming, demanding participants' attention and energy for months and even years. They often force people who need to work together to engage in combat instead, driving them further apart rather than bringing them together. Even when parties prevail in these processes, they can find the victory has come too late or at too high a price. Moreover, controversy may not end just because one side has won and the other has lost. Court rulings often fail to resolve the underlying problems that caused the complaints to be filed in the first place. It is no wonder that citizens and government officials alike are increasingly searching for other ways to resolve conflict.

Alternative dispute resolution (ADR) often is a better way to solve problems in a wide variety of government matters.[1] In ADR, the parties meet with a neutral professional who is trained and experienced in handling disputes. With the guidance of the neutral party, they talk directly with each other about the problems that caused the dispute and ideas for resolving their differences. The neutral party assists them in identifying their underlying interests, developing creative options for meeting their needs, and crafting a resolution that will work for the future. Experience has shown that this approach is frequently quicker, cheaper, and more satisfying for everyone involved than adjudication.

These ideas have gained bipartisan support in all branches of the federal government. The U.S. Congress has noted, "Administrative proceedings have become increasingly formal, costly, and lengthy resulting in unnecessary expenditures of time and in a decreased likelihood of achieving consensual resolution of disputes; [ADR] can lead to more creative, efficient, and sensible outcomes; . . . the availability of a wide range of dispute resolution procedures, and an increased understanding of the most effective use of such procedures, will enhance the operation of the Government and better serve the public."[2]

Former Chief Justice Warren Burger commented, "The notion that ordinary people want black-robed judges, well dressed lawyers and fine courtrooms as settings to resolve their disputes is incorrect. People with problems, like people with pains, want relief, and they want it as quickly and inexpensively as possible."[3]

Former attorney general Janet Reno has said of ADR, "We have an extraordinary opportunity. The legal profession has an opportunity to help bring this Nation together; to build understanding, rather than to divide it; to build community, rather than to fragment it; to be the peacemaker and the problem solver, as never before in the history of the profession. . . . In this next millennium of the practice of law, we may know a more peaceful Nation and a more peaceful world."[4]

Because of ADR's success, the government's use of it has grown greatly. At the Justice Department, for example, parties used ADR in five hundred cases in 1995. Seven years later, annual ADR use had grown to close to three thousand cases. The Equal Employment Opportunity Commission (EEOC) now uses mediation in about five thousand workplace cases annually, and the U.S. Postal Service mediates twice that many each year. The Environmental Protection Agency has eight full-time ADR staff members and pays private mediators millions of dollars in mediator fees each year. All told, more than four hundred people now work on ADR full time in the federal government, and agency ADR programs are funded by more than $36 million in dedicated budgets.[5] The government's total commitment to ADR is even higher than these figures. Many agencies operate programs that are funded from other budgetary sources and staffed by employees who have part-time ADR responsibilities in addition to other duties.[6]

Benefits of ADR

The government and private parties have found many benefits from the use of ADR. Among them are time savings, money savings, greater predictability and self-determination, greater creativity, improved relationships, and increased satisfaction.

Time Savings

One of the greatest problems with traditional federal government dispute resolution is delay, much of it caused by an explosion of complaint filings. In U.S. district courts nationwide, annual filings of new cases have increased from about 35,000 to more than 250,000 over the past sixty years—that is, by a factor of seven times—while U.S. population during this period only doubled. At the appellate level, annual case filings grew from 2,800 to more than 57,000 over the past fifty years, a twenty-fold increase.[7]

This huge growth in litigation has had a major impact on the way the government operates, because the United States and its agencies are parties in nearly one-third of all federal district court civil cases.[8] The government simply does not have the resources to take all of these cases to trial. Indeed, less than 2 percent of federal lawsuits where the government is a party go to trial.[9] Given this reality, "alternative" dispute resolution in the government is actually trial adjudication, because trials are so rare.

The situation is similar in the administrative arena. Federal administrative equal employment opportunity (EEO) complaints rose by more than 50 percent over a recent eight-year period.[10] Over about the past ten years, agency EEO case backlogs have doubled, hearing backlogs at the EEOC have tripled, and appellate backlogs have increased sevenfold.[11]

ADR reduces these delays by sidestepping the adjudicative process and its backlogs. For example, in workplace cases involving the Office of Special Counsel, ADR resolved complaints in an average of 115 days, while the traditional adjudicatory process required an average of 465 days.[12] In disputes with the Federal Aviation Administration, parties using ADR resolved bid protests in an average of 25 days, while those seeking a final agency decision typically waited 61 days.[13] In federal court civil cases (mostly torts and employment discrimination actions), Justice Department attorneys estimated time savings averaging six months per case where ADR was used.[14] At the Department of the Air Force, the amount of time required to process an Armed Services Board of Contract Appeals contract case dropped by 50 percent after the agency began using an ADR program.[15]

ADR processes require less time from participants than litigation, which demands many hours for preparation and adversarial proceedings. For example, Justice Department lawyers estimated that using ADR saved 89 hours of staff and attorney time on average in each case.[16] Similarly, at the administrative level, the Office of Special Counsel found that the average workplace case using ADR required 24 hours of agency staff time; in contrast, the average case that did not use ADR required 260 hours.[17]

Money Savings

ADR also saves money for parties involved in federal government disputes. First, the time savings already described directly correlate with money savings. When private parties and government officials resolve disputes more quickly, they can spend the time they save on other important matters. Quicker settlements can result in lower attorney fees for private parties. When more cases settle, the government saves money as well because fewer courtrooms, judges, administrative hearing officers, docket clerks, and the like are required.

Adjudication is expensive. Estimates of the administrative costs for processing an EEO case range from $5,000 for an informal dispute to up to $77,000 for a formal dispute that goes all the way through to an appeal.[18] Federal employees contact an EEO counselor about fifty thousand times a year, so these expenses are substantial.[19] In many types of litigation, both the government and private parties must pay for deposition transcripts, expert witness consultations, expert testimony, travel costs, and other expenses.

Use of ADR can reduce these costs by resolving matters without the need for adjudication. Justice Department attorneys estimated that ADR saved an average of $10,700 in litigation expenses in each case.[20] The Office of Special Counsel estimated an average cost of $1,000 to process a case where ADR is used, compared with an average cost of $10,500 for a case that does not go to ADR.[21] The U.S. Air

Force examined travel and staff costs for base engineers, inspectors, contracting officers, pricers, auditors, and experts, and determined that ADR saved $40,000 per case for contract cases involving less than $1 million and $250,000 for cases over $1 million.[22]

Greater Predictability and Self-Determination

ADR benefits parties because it allows them to decide how to resolve their dispute. The only way a case will settle in a voluntary ADR process is if both parties agree to an outcome they created themselves. In contrast, parties relinquish this control whenever they turn their case over to a judge or jury. Once a court process begins, the results are unpredictable.

Adjudication can be surprisingly uncertain. In one study of civil cases, judges who had presided over jury trials were asked whether they would have ruled the same way the jury did. These judges had heard the same witnesses the jury had, seen the same evidence, and listened to the same arguments from counsel. Nonetheless, the judges disagreed with the jury verdicts in half of the cases.[23] One possible reason for this unpredictability, revealed in the study, is that jurors appear not always to understand the law. For example, they were asked at the end of trial what the burden of proof was for the civil plaintiff. These jurors had listened to lawyers for both sides discuss the burden of proof, and they had listened to the judge's instructions that the burden in civil cases requires the plaintiffs to tip the scales of evidence only slightly in their favor. Nonetheless, 38 percent of these jurors stated that the plaintiffs' burden was to prove their case beyond a reasonable doubt.[24]

Many individuals who have important government cases do not want to hand over control of their dispute to such unpredictable outside parties. ADR gives them the opportunity to resolve their conflict on terms they choose for themselves.

Greater Creativity

Courts are limited in the relief they can award. In many disputes, a court can offer a party only money. When plaintiffs can get only money from a case, they simply ask for as much as possible, and more creative options are not explored. In contrast, the parties in

ADR are not constrained by the need to put a monetary value on every situation, so they have the freedom to fashion their own solutions. Furthermore, they understand their needs better than anyone else, and they know what would satisfy them best. They are free to develop options that may be worth much more to one party than they cost the other to provide. Sometimes they even create solutions that make both parties better off.

Improved Relationships

Litigation destroys relationships. The litigation process forces people to attack each other's positions and prove that they are right and the other side is wrong. It is no wonder that almost all parties leave trials with negative feelings toward each other.

In many government cases, this result is particularly harmful. For example, because more people work for the government by far than any other employer in the country, there are a large number of government workplace disputes. Parties to these disputes often must continue to work together while their complaints are processed, a situation that creates awkwardness and tension that can make the workplace very uncomfortable. Many times, others in the office are affected as well. People often choose up sides in a dispute, and entire workplaces can be infected by a single conflict.

ADR allows parties to preserve their relationships by working together to resolve their disputes. The process fosters a collaborative atmosphere because the goal is agreement, not victory or defeat. Many times, parties find that participation in ADR is the start of a significant improvement in their relationship.[25]

Research has shown long-lasting relationship improvements as a result of ADR. At the U.S. Postal Service, for example, ADR appears to have helped employees and managers understand each other better. In the first full year after ADR was introduced at the agency, the number of new formal workplace complaints dropped by 24 percent from the previous year.[26] Complaints continued to drop during the following year by an additional 20 percent.[27] The agency believes this decline is due to increased communication between employees and supervisors as a result of ADR. Similarly, during a three-year period at the U.S. Air Force, the number of EEO complaints that were mediated increased by 36 percent, and the number of total complaints dropped by 39 percent.[28]

Increased Satisfaction

Parties find ADR to be a more satisfying process than litigation, which silences the parties with rigid processes that require their attorneys to take the lead. ADR, in contrast, gives the parties a voice in resolving their own disputes. Litigation forces parties into combat with each other, while ADR allows them to work collaboratively. Not surprisingly, it is the dispute resolution method parties prefer.

For example, the U.S. Postal Service has conducted satisfaction studies of tens of thousands of ADR participants. Close to 90 percent of these parties reported that they were highly satisfied or satisfied with their experience in ADR.[29] Both employees and managers were equally satisfied.[30] In contrast, parties who participated in adjudication in comparable cases reported satisfaction levels of about 45 percent.[31] Similarly, the EEOC found that more than 90 percent of parties who used ADR said they would do so again.[32]

Examples of Successful ADR

Several examples will show the wide range of government cases where ADR has been successful. One of the most important cases in which ADR was used is the Microsoft litigation. The Justice Department and a number of states sued the software maker in 1998 for alleged violations of antitrust laws. This case demanded enormous resources from all sides. A dozen Justice Department attorneys worked on the case full time, joined by another dozen who worked on the matter part time. Microsoft was represented by as many lawyers or more. Many lawyers from state attorney generals' offices also participated. All sides litigated the case through a trial, an unsuccessful attempt by a judge to settle the matter, and an appeal to the appellate court. After all of this work, the parties appeared to be little closer to reaching an agreement than when the lawsuit began three and a half years earlier.

At this point, the parties proceeded to mediation led by an experienced private mediator. All sides worked together under the guidance of the mediator to explore possible settlement options. After about two weeks, they emerged with a settlement resolving the Justice Department's claim in the case (although some states objected), which the judge approved.

Without mediation, the parties might have proceeded to yet another trial, which probably would have led to another appeal, and an appeal to the Supreme Court after that. All sides would have continued to expend tremendous resources, the country's computer industry would have continued to operate under uncertainty, and it is possible we still would not have a decision to this day.

Another example of successful ADR took place in Cincinnati after a police officer shot and killed an unarmed nineteen-year-old African American man in 2001. Following the shooting, the city erupted in violence. Protestors set fires, looted stores, and pulled motorists from their cars to assault them.[33] After police had arrested dozens of people and the fire department had made more than fifty runs, the mayor instituted a dusk-to-dawn curfew and called in more than one hundred Ohio State Highway Patrol officers wearing riot gear. Community groups filed a lawsuit alleging discriminatory law enforcement by the Cincinnati police department, and the federal government began an investigation of a possible pattern or practice of civil rights violations.

All sides were concerned that a court battle would not solve these problems. No matter which side prevailed, anger and unrest in Cincinnati would likely continue. Instead, the parties decided to turn to mediation to foster increased communication among the people in the city. The mediator met with representatives of the police, civil rights groups, and other community members many times over a period of months. The parties discussed what had happened and how they wanted to move forward. At the end of the process, they agreed to a settlement designed to help reach the goals everyone shared: improving the quality of police services and rebuilding trust among all the members of the community. Although these problems are not easy to solve, most people agree that ADR has been a better way to work on them than litigation would be.

The U.S. Air Force has had tremendous success with ADR in resolving government contract controversies. One dispute with Boeing had been pending for more than ten years before ADR was used. The parties had attempted to negotiate a settlement on their own during this time but were unable to do so. The claim involved $785 million, and the interest charges also grew by thousands of dollars every day the dispute continued. ADR was successful in settling the case.[34] The air force also used ADR to settle a contract claim against the Northrop Grumman Corporation involving $195 million.[35] Continuing to litigate either of these matters would have been extremely expensive for all parties and would have had unpredictable results. Litigation also could have damaged the government's relationship with some of its most important military suppliers. Following the air force's success with ADR in these matters, the secretary of the air force issued an order creating an official policy to use ADR "to the maximum extent practicable."[36]

ADR is successful in lower-profile matters as well. For example, ADR helped resolve a suit filed by the family of a veteran who had died during surgery at a government hospital. A court would have been able to award only money, but the family members were not motivated solely, or even primarily, by money. During mediation, the parties arrived at a unique agreement: the government purchased a tree and a brass plaque to honor the veteran who had died. The tree was planted on the hospital grounds as a memorial in a ceremony attended by the family, the lawyer for the government, and the hospital director. The monetary portion of the claim was then settled for a relatively modest amount.

The plaintiffs were pleased with the settlement that they and the government had created together. More than just money, they were seeking closure to the situation, as well as an acknowledgment from the hospital of what had happened to their father. Furthermore, every time the hospital director and other doctors walk by this tree, they are reminded of the importance of being careful in what they do, which may reduce the likelihood of a similar tragic event.

Barriers to Federal ADR

There are unique considerations in the federal government that can make ADR use more difficult. First, some government cases involve principles that are not subject to compromise. While private entities are free to settle disputes in whatever manner they choose, the government does not always have that luxury. When enforcing the law, the government cannot concede certain principles even when that would make a matter easier to resolve.[37]

Similarly, because the government is a public entity, it has a special duty to ensure that it makes decisions uniformly. This can make it more difficult to settle disputes on a case-by-case basis using ADR. While private parties can resolve complaints in different ways depending on the circumstances, the government has a responsibility to be consistent, and this can limit its flexibility in ADR processes.

Because the government is involved in so many disputes, it cannot afford to settle some claims the way private entities can. For example, private companies often pay small amounts of money to settle nuisance lawsuits that have little or no merit. The government has limited ability to do this, because it might be faced with thousands of copycat lawsuits were it to adopt a policy of making payments for frivolous claims.

The size and hierarchical structure of the government can make it difficult for officials with settlement authority to participate in ADR. Because agency officials with full settlement authority often must supervise hundreds of cases, they typically cannot participate in every ADR session. This can be a disadvantage for the government, because ADR is more effective when the people negotiating have the power to reach a final agreement. Fortunately, mechanisms exist to overcome this barrier, as discussed in Chapter Five of this book.

There also can be a conflict between the public's right to know about the activities of its government and the importance of confidentiality in ADR. As a general matter, citizens have an interest in understanding how the government transacts business, including how it settles cases. However, the ADR process is more effective when both sides can speak candidly about their goals for settlement, without having to be concerned that what they say will become public. When ADR involves private parties, they almost always agree to complete confidentiality. When the government is involved, however, these competing interests can require compromises. (Confidentiality is discussed in detail in Chapter Eight.)

While these barriers can make ADR use more difficult when the government is involved, they usually do not present insurmountable problems. The advantages of ADR have led parties to find ways to work around these issues.

Federal ADR Laws and Regulations

Congressional statutes, presidential orders, and agency regulations have helped increase the use of ADR in the government as well as guide its development. The origins of federal ADR can be traced to the late nineteenth century. The use of ADR has expanded considerably since then, with the greatest changes starting around 1990.

Historical Background

Mediation by respected community leaders and elders has been used in societies throughout history and existed in the United States among immigrant and religious groups as early as colonial New England.[38] Within the federal government, ADR began in the late nineteenth century. The Act of 1888 created the first federal ADR program: voluntary boards of arbitration that resolved controversies between railroads and their unions to avoid disrupting transportation.[39] Ten years later, Congress passed the Erdman Act, providing for mediation for these disputes.[40]

The first federal mediation agencies began in the early twentieth century. The Newlands Act in 1913 established the Board of Mediation and Conciliation to handle railroad labor disputes.[41] (This is the predecessor agency to the current National Mediation Board.[42]) That same year, Congress created the U.S. Conciliation Service as part of the new Department of Labor to offer mediation and conciliation in labor disputes.[43] (This agency now exists as the Federal Mediation and Conciliation Service.[44])

The next phase of government ADR involved its application to disputes beyond the labor area. The Federal Arbitration Act, passed in 1925, declared a national policy favoring arbitration, establishing this ADR process in the commercial arena.[45] In 1937, the Federal Rules of Civil Procedure authorized judges to conduct settlement conferences in all federal civil lawsuits.[46] The Administrative Procedure Act in 1946 created agency administrative processes that can resolve certain cases without the need for federal court litigation.[47] The Civil Rights Act of 1964 created the Community Relations Service of the Justice Department to help facilitate the resolution of community conflicts caused by differences in race, color, and national origin.[48]

The Pound Conference held in 1976 had an important effect on the development of ADR in the government. At this meeting of 250 judges, lawyers, court administrators, law professors, and others, Harvard Law School professor Frank Sander described a vision of a courthouse as a "Dispute Resolution Center."[49] In this image of a multidoor courthouse, a screening clerk would channel litigants in one of six directions, comprising "a diverse panoply of dispute resolution processes."[50] Sander issued a call to "reserve the courts for those activities for which they are best suited and to avoid swamping and paralyzing them with cases that do not require their unique abilities."[51]

As a result of the Pound Conference, Attorney General Griffin Bell commented, "Traditional procedures of the courts are generally too slow and costly to be useful in resolving relatively minor disputes. . . . The adversary process is not always the best mechanism for resolving such disputes."[52] Putting these ideas into action, Bell funded the first neighborhood justice centers to provide for ADR on the community level.[53]

At around the same time, Congress encouraged federal agencies to use mediation, conciliation, and arbitration to resolve federal employee workplace disputes by passing the Civil Service Reform Act of 1978.[54] Two years later, the Dispute Resolution Act of 1980 encouraged state and local government to experiment with ADR (although it provided no money for this purpose).[55] By this point, ADR was being used to resolve a wide range of disputes at federal agencies from the Army Corps of Engineers to the Federal Deposit Insurance Corporation.

Recent Congressional Legislation

ADR in the federal government took a major step forward starting in the 1990s. The Civil Justice Reform Act of 1990 called for the judicial branch to create plans to reduce cost and delay in civil litigation, explicitly mentioning ADR as a case management principle.[56] In recommending the legislation, the Senate Judiciary Committee commented, "The last 15 years have witnessed the burgeoning use of dispute resolution techniques other than formal adjudication by courts. . . . While the data is not yet complete, studies of various ADR programs have shown generally favorable results. . . . As the

Federal Courts Study Committee concluded, "Experience to date provides solid justification for allowing individual federal courts to institute ADR techniques in ways that best suit the preferences of bench, bar and interested public."[57]

The Administrative Dispute Resolution Act (see Appendix A, the amended version of this act), also passed in 1990, was watershed legislation for ADR programs in the federal executive branch.[58] The introductory language for this act shows Congress believed the time had come for the government to embrace ADR:

> Administrative proceedings have become increasingly formal, costly, and lengthy resulting in unnecessary expenditures of time and in a decreased likelihood of achieving consensual resolution of disputes; . . . alternative means of dispute resolution have been used in the private sector for many years and, in appropriate circumstances, have yielded decisions that are faster, less expensive, and less contentious; . . . such alternative means can lead to more creative, efficient, and sensible outcomes; . . . Federal agencies may not only receive the benefit of techniques that were developed in the private sector, but may also take the lead in the further development and refinement of such techniques; and . . . the availability of a wide range of dispute resolution procedures, and an increased understanding of the most effective use of such procedures, will enhance the operation of the Government and better serve the public.[59]

This act has a number of key provisions. First, it requires each agency to adopt an ADR policy for its formal and informal adjudications, rulemakings, enforcement actions, permit decisions, contract administration, litigation, and other actions.[60] This language is comprehensive, covering much of what agencies do.

Second, each agency must designate a senior official to be its dispute resolution specialist, with responsibility to implement the act and the agency's ADR policy.[61] Some agencies have appointed senior career officials to serve in this function, and others have chosen presidentially appointed, Senate-confirmed political officials.

Third, each agency is required to provide regular training on the practice of negotiation, mediation, arbitration, and related techniques.[62] The agency dispute resolution specialist is charged with periodically recommending to the agency head which employees would benefit from this training.[63]

Fourth, each agency must review each of its contracts, grants, and related agreements and consider amending them to authorize and encourage the use of ADR.[64] This review process is designed to cover the full range of the agency's contractual activities with the public.

The act did have several limitations. Although it authorized arbitration, the government was permitted to withdraw from any arbitration award within thirty days.[65] In this sense, government binding arbitration was binding only on private parties, who were understandably reluctant to use it. Furthermore, the law provided no exception to the Freedom of Information Act, which allows public access to government documents.[66] This limited the confidentiality of the process. Finally, Congress made the law an experiment, setting it to expire after five years.

In 1996, Congress reenacted the law and removed these restrictions.[67] The government can no longer back out of an arbitration award.[68] There is now an exemption from the Freedom of Information Act that generally provides for confidentiality of ADR documents exchanged between a party and a neutral.[69] Finally, the law is now permanent, with no expiration date.

Congress passed legislation requiring the federal courts to implement ADR programs two years later. The introduction to the Alternative Dispute Resolution Act of 1998 (see Appendix C) notes how ADR can be valuable in the court setting: "[ADR] has the potential to provide a variety of benefits, including greater satisfaction of the parties, innovative methods of resolving disputes, and greater efficiency in achieving settlements; . . . [ADR] may have potential to reduce the large backlog of cases now pending in some Federal courts throughout the United States, thereby allowing the courts to process their remaining cases more efficiently."[70]

This act requires each district court to "devise and implement its own alternative dispute resolution program," "encourage and promote the use of alternative dispute resolution in its district," "require that litigants in all civil cases consider the use of an alternative dispute resolution process at an appropriate stage in the litigation," and "provide litigants in all civil cases with at least one alternative dispute resolution process."[71] Courts can require that parties participate in mediation and early neutral evaluation (although they cannot order parties to use arbitration). Congress has not allocated additional funds to the courts to implement this act, however.

Recent Executive Branch Orders

Several presidents have issued orders requiring the federal government to increase its use of ADR. In 1991, President George H. W. Bush promulgated an executive order calling for training of government attorneys in ADR, noting that ADR can "contribute to the prompt, fair, and efficient resolution of claims."[72] However, this order included a caveat: "Whenever feasible, claims should be resolved through informal discussions, negotiations, and settlements rather than through utilization of any formal or structured Alternative Dispute Resolution (ADR) process."[73]

President Bill Clinton removed this caveat and endorsed ADR even more strongly in a 1996 executive order: "Where the benefits of Alternative Dispute Resolution ('ADR') may be derived, and after consultation with the agency referring the matter, litigation counsel should suggest the use of an appropriate ADR technique to the parties."[74]

In 1998, President Clinton issued a presidential memorandum (see Appendix D) stating, "As part of an effort to make the Federal Government operate in a more efficient and effective manner, and to encourage, where possible, consensual resolution of disputes and issues in controversy involving the United States, including the prevention and avoidance of disputes, I have determined that each Federal agency must take steps to . . . promote greater use of mediation, arbitration, early neutral evaluation, agency ombuds, and other alternative dispute resolution techniques."[75]

This order created the Interagency ADR Working Group and appointed the attorney general to act as its chair. The working group is ordered to "facilitate, encourage, and provide coordination for agencies in such areas as: 1. development of programs that employ alternative means of dispute resolution, 2. training of agency personnel to recognize when and how to use alternative means of dispute resolution, 3. development of procedures that permit agencies to obtain the services of neutrals on an expedited basis, and 4. recordkeeping to ascertain the benefits of alternative means of dispute resolution."[76]

This working group began on September 14, 1998, with a meeting hosted by the attorney general and the deputy director for management at the Office of Management and Budget. More than one hundred high-level representatives from nearly sixty federal agencies attended the meeting. Since that time, the group has hosted training sessions, meetings, and colloquia on all aspects of ADR. The group has produced guidance documents in use throughout the federal government that are available on the following Web site: www.adr.gov. A steering committee for the group meets monthly and is composed of ADR leaders from several dozen agencies. (In 2000, the attorney general presented the president with a report describing the activities of the working group. See Appendix F.)

At the Justice Department, the attorney general created the Office of Dispute Resolution to coordinate the use of ADR (see Appendix B).[77] The order establishing the office states, "The purpose of this order is to promote the broader use of alternative dispute resolution (ADR) in appropriate cases to improve access to justice for all citizens and to lead to more effective resolution of disputes involving the government." The office develops ADR policies, and it provides assistance to government attorneys in their use of ADR.

All Justice Department civil litigating divisions and the Executive Office for United States Attorneys have published statements describing their policy for the use of ADR, including descriptions of the cases where it is most and least appropriate.[78] The attorney general wrote in the introduction to this guidance, "Our commitment to make greater use of ADR is long overdue. Clearly, our federal court system is in overload. Delays are all too common, depriving the public of swift, efficient, and just resolution of disputes. The Department of Justice is the biggest user of the federal courts and the nation's most prolific litigator. Therefore, it is incumbent upon those Department attorneys who handle civil litigation from Washington and throughout the country to consider alternatives to litigation. . . . If we are successful, the outcome will benefit litigants by producing better and quicker results, and will benefit the entire justice system by preserving the scarce resources of the courts for the disputes that only courts can decide."[79]

Conclusion

One of the reasons ADR has been so successful in the U.S. government is that it is consistent with the values of the country. One example of this is provided by the Seal of the President of the United States. The seal depicts an eagle grasping an olive branch (symbolizing peace) in its right talons and arrows (symbolizing war) in its left talons. When the seal was created, the eagle's head turned toward its left, facing the arrows of war. After World War II, President Harry Truman issued an executive order requiring that the eagle's head be turned to face the olive branch, and it has remained that way ever since.[80] True to this symbol, the United States seeks to settle disputes with its citizens in the most harmonious ways possible, and ADR is playing an increasingly vital role in fulfilling this vision.

Chapter Two

Selecting Cases and Processes for Federal ADR

The first step in using ADR with the federal government is to select appropriate disputes for these processes. ADR is effective in many government disputes, but it works better in some cases than in others. Next, parties must decide which types of ADR to use. While the most common form of ADR in the government is mediation, there are a number of other processes available that can be effective in certain cases.

Case Selection

A great many cases involving the federal government are appropriate for ADR. Some are particularly good candidates for these methods. Others are appropriate for ADR, although they may not appear to be at first. Finally, ADR may not be the best choice under certain circumstances.

Good Cases for ADR

ADR is an especially good option for federal government cases in the following ten types of situations:[1]

1. *Unassisted negotiation is not working.* Cases where traditional negotiation has broken down are good choices for ADR. There are many reasons settlement discussions fail, and sometimes there is little the parties can do about this on their own. Occasionally nei-

ther the government nor the private sector party can overcome the inherent obstacles that hinder unassisted negotiation. If conventional attempts to pursue settlement have become ineffective, ADR is worth considering.

2. *Litigation would be expensive.* Litigation is almost always expensive. It makes no sense to proceed in every case with extensive investigation, followed by motions practice, leading to lengthy trials, and then appeals of the results of those trials. Sometimes the expected cost of litigating a case is more than the total amount of money in dispute. In this situation, an efficient and expedited settlement process is simply a good business decision. In other cases, litigation fees may be less than the amount of damages but would still be substantial. Settlement is often appropriate in these matters as well. ADR is most often less expensive than litigation.

It is worth noting that some in the private sector believe that saving money in transaction costs may not be a paramount concern for lawyers in government cases. These parties think that if government lawyers resolve cases, their supervisors simply will assign them more cases to keep their dockets full. However, conscientious government lawyers see their job as representing the taxpayer and look to reduce costs wherever possible.

3. *Litigation would be time-consuming.* Litigation is almost always time-consuming. In many cases, the administrative adjudication process can take more than a year. In some federal district courts, this is followed by several more years of delay before trial can even begin. ADR is generally quicker than litigation, especially when it is used early in the life of a case.

Saving time can have profound benefits for parties. The longer a conflict continues, the more it damages the parties involved and drives them further apart. Cases that could have been settled relatively easily when they began can be impossible to resolve after several years of litigation have taken their toll. Some cases fail to settle because attorney fees for private counsel have become so great that the amount of the settlement that would remain for the private client is significantly reduced. Lengthy litigation also diverts private parties and government personnel away from their day-to-day duties. Litigation forces all participants to spend valuable time and energy fighting with one another rather than working on more productive matters.

4. *Preserving the relationships of the parties would be worthwhile.* Adversarial litigation almost always harms the relationships of the people involved. Where the parties to a dispute must continue to do business with each other in the future, this damage is particularly acute. In these cases, litigation forces people whose job requires working with one another to engage in combat instead.

In the government, workplace and contracts disputes are prime examples of cases where parties often have long-term relationships that are more important than any single conflict. The fallout from a protracted trial can be much more significant than the size of the monetary judgment. Furthermore, a controversy may not disappear just because one side has won and the other has lost. Even when the government or the private party wins a case, it can find that victory has come too late and at too high a price. ADR is well worth considering in these types of conflicts.

5. *Creativity would be valuable.* In some cases, particularly where more than money is involved, creativity can play an important part in resolving a case. ADR is usually a much more creative process than a trial. Compared with judges and juries in litigation, who have very limited discretion in what they can award in a case, the parties are free to agree to almost anything in ADR. The ADR process therefore fosters a creative atmosphere, with parties working together with a neutral to fashion an agreeable remedy.

Even when a case appears to be only about money, ADR often can still be of assistance. Parties can agree to structured settlements where they pay money over time. Contingent arrangements also are possible, with payments depending on what happens in the future. Many times ADR also uncovers nonmonetary interests of which the parties were unaware at the beginning.

Furthermore, adjudication is by design limited to the specific allegations described in a claim, yet conflict between parties often involves more complex issues. These other concerns can be very important, but parties may be unwilling or unable to raise them in a rigid legal forum. In ADR, parties are free to discuss whatever matters they like and to fashion broad remedies to address their situation.

6. *One or more parties have an unrealistic valuation of the case.* Many cases do not settle because parties are overly optimistic about what their case is worth. There are many reasons for this.[2] Parties have

easier access to information that supports their position than to evidence in possession of their opponents. Furthermore, both clients and lawyers frequently overestimate the strength of their arguments and their abilities in litigation. These human tendencies make cases much more difficult to settle.

A related reason that parties have difficulty with unassisted negotiation is a phenomenon known as *reactive devaluation*.[3] Simply put, people react to whatever the other side says by devaluing it. Thus, even if one side makes a forceful argument, the other side may not give it the credit it deserves. This psychological effect has been demonstrated in numerous experiments, and it plays a powerful role in blocking otherwise reasonable settlements in all kinds of litigation.

The advantage of bringing in a neutral is that the parties tend not to devalue what the neutral says. The same arguments presented by a neutral third party can be much more persuasive than when they come from the other side. Thus, a neutral is often effective in getting unrealistic parties to recognize that they would be wise to settle rather than cling to their inflated hopes of victory in litigation.

7. *Emotional obstacles are hindering settlement.* Cases can be blocked from settling because parties have an emotional investment in them. Sometimes parties cannot let go of a claim until they have the opportunity to express their positions, vent their emotions, and feel heard. Traditional negotiation stifles these needs by silencing the parties. Lawyers run the process nearly entirely on their own, while the clients rarely speak and almost never meet face-to-face.

ADR can overcome these barriers by bringing the parties into the process. Parties report they feel that they had their "day in court" with ADR, where they can speak openly to the other side and to a neutral third party. Indeed, skilled lawyers sometimes seek out ADR in order to hear directly from the opposing client, in the presence of counsel, to learn what emotional issues may be driving the negotiation. When the parties understand each other better, including the emotional components of a dispute, they are much better equipped to settle the matter.

8. *Communication has broken down.* Many negotiations fail because the parties stop communicating with one another. Sometimes personality conflicts cause the problem, and other times the parties

simply reach an impasse and do not know what to do next. The usual response is to cease attempts to reach a settlement and instead to redouble litigation efforts.

A particular problem with communication in unassisted negotiation is called the *negotiator's dilemma*.[4] This phenomenon exists because negotiators' interest in creating value conflicts with their interest in claiming it. Creating value requires parties to be open and candid with each other in order to reach cooperative and inventive solutions. However, if parties do disclose their interests in hopes the other side will reciprocate, their opponents might use this information to take advantage of them instead. Thus, many negotiators protect themselves by delivering offers and responses in a cagey and even deceptive manner. This does little to foster settlement.

ADR can help in these situations because introducing a third party offers another avenue for communication.[5] Parties who are reluctant to speak to each other directly can be more willing to talk privately to a neutral person. Through conversations with both sides, the neutral can learn information that suggests a possible settlement the parties would never have found on their own. Also, the simple process of having everyone sit down together in ADR to discuss a resolution of the dispute can in itself improve communication and be a powerful engine for settlement.

9. *The case is complex, with multiple issues or parties.* Complex cases can be especially difficult for parties to resolve on their own. It can be an administrative nightmare even to coordinate the participants in a multiparty case. After that, it is a substantial challenge to organize the issues in complicated litigation and to agree on what topics to discuss first.

Neutral third parties can take a leadership role in managing the pursuit of settlement in these cases. Without a neutral, parties often cannot agree on the agenda for discussions or even where they should take place. Through ADR, parties can give up their need to control these issues and focus instead on achieving a resolution.

10. *One or more parties would like a confidential resolution.* In certain cases, the government, the private party, or both may want a case to go away quietly. Although the government generally conducts its business in the public eye, occasionally policy reasons suggest that a decision be made with as little fanfare as possible. Similarly, private parties sometimes wish to resolve a matter without publicity. The gov-

ernment generally will not agree to keep a settlement completely confidential,[6] but ADR is a much more private proceeding than a full-blown federal trial.

Similarly, parties sometimes want to avoid going to court because they do not want to risk a formal decision by a judge that will become precedent for future cases. A decision reached in ADR does not have formal precedential value, and it is not printed in federal case reporters. This can be an advantage for either the government or the private party in certain situations.

Questions About Whether Cases Are Appropriate for ADR

A number of questions exist about whether certain cases involving the federal government are appropriate for ADR. The following are situations where ADR has worked well, even though it may have been unclear at first whether this would be the case:

1. *Can the government use ADR even though the principles involved in a federal case should not be compromised?* Some people argue that disputes involving the government are inappropriate for ADR because the issues are too important to settle. This claim is that the government should not yield on any point where federal law is involved, because federal law is sacrosanct. Some question how the government could ever compromise on issues as important as civil rights, antitrust law, or even the amount of money a citizen should receive in a tort claim. Indeed, it is true that there are some cases where the government cannot compromise for those reasons.

However, this argument ignores the realities of federal government practice. The Justice Department alone litigates close to 100,000 civil cases in the federal courts every year, and other federal agencies handle even more cases administratively. The government is not equipped to take each of these cases all the way through a court verdict, and the costs of doing so would be prohibitive.

Nor would litigating every case all the way to the end be a wise idea even if it were possible. It would not be good policy to require that the government make a single settlement offer at the beginning of the case and then go to trial rather than ever accept any compromise. Government litigators often learn things from private parties during negotiations that cause them to adjust their initial valuations of a case. The give-and-take of the negotiation process is often valuable for both sides, and it should be encouraged rather than eliminated.

2. *Can the government use ADR when settlement of cases might encourage frivolous litigation?* Some argue that the government should not use ADR in certain cases because paying money to a plaintiff would encourage many more plaintiffs to file copycat litigation to get money. Government attorneys often make this point when they resist using ADR.

This is not a trivial argument. Indeed, the federal government is unique in the country in that more people file claims against it than against any other entity. It is true that the government should not reward people who file meritless complaints by paying them settlement money. It is also true that if the government did so, many more people would file such claims.

Nevertheless, it is a simple reality that the government settles most claims at some point. The fraction of complaints filed by citizens that are truly baseless is small. At the Justice Department, less than 2 percent of claims go all the way through a trial. Some claims can be disposed of through pretrial motions. If a case survives these motions, it usually has some merit, and the government usually pays some amount of money to settle it eventually. If the parties are amenable to settling a case, there is no reason not to use ADR at that time.

Furthermore, cases that border on the frivolous can be especially appropriate for evaluative ADR processes. Often parties who are bringing these cases will not listen to government attorneys who tell them outside of ADR that their cases are meritless. They understandably do not trust the opinions of people who are paid to oppose them in litigation. With ADR, in contrast, they work with a neutral professional who has no reason to favor one side or the other. If a neutral tells them their case is baseless, they have to take this opinion more seriously, and it may persuade them to settle. In this situation, a neutral often can make far more progress with the private party than a government attorney can.

3. *Can the government use ADR when it needs continuing court jurisdiction to monitor the parties after the settlement?* Many federal cases involve law enforcement issues where the government requires the defendant to change its actions as a condition of settlement. It is

important to have the power of a court to ensure these changes take place as agreed. However, ADR is appropriate in these cases as long as the parties bring their settlement to a judge for entry as an order. If a case has been filed, an administrative judge or a federal district court judge can review the settlement and sign it if appropriate. Once this is done, it becomes an enforceable order with the same effect as if it were the result of adjudication. (Without a judge's order, a purely private contract is more difficult to enforce. In this case, the government would have to go to court and bring a new lawsuit based on breach of contract, a more time-consuming process than moving to enforce an existing court order.) The parties in government ADR can also create remedies that involve court-sponsored officials called special masters who oversee future compliance in certain cases.

Cases That Are Not Appropriate for ADR

Most cases involving the federal government are good candidates for ADR, but some are not.[7] Of the following eight types of cases where ADR may not be an appropriate choice, the first four involve considerations that are specific to the government, and the last four have general application:

1. *The government needs a precedent.* Sometimes the federal government must litigate a case to judgment in order to obtain a formal precedent. The government is unique in that it sometimes faces hundreds or even thousands of cases that all raise similar legal issues. Under these circumstances, the government may choose to take one of these cases all the way through trial in order to obtain an official judicial decision that can serve as precedent for all the others. If necessary, the government may seek an appeal as well. While this process is pending, it may be unwilling to engage in ADR.

For example, when Congress changes a tax law, the Internal Revenue Service may identify thousands of possible cases involving the interpretation of the new law. It does not make sense for the government to negotiate individually with all of these taxpayers at the same time. Rather, the government will litigate until it receives a formal court ruling, which will then control the outcome of all the other cases. ADR may be inappropriate under these circumstances.

2. *An inflexible government policy requires a certain result.* In certain cases, the government has an absolute, fixed rule that governs its actions. The government has a duty to treat everyone consistently, and it sometimes issues rules to ensure that this takes place. In these situations, when the government has no discretion to negotiate, it must adhere to its legal position. ADR has little value when negotiation is impossible. Disputes involving immigration laws fall into this category.

This situation does not occur as often as might be expected, however. The government must treat similarly situated people the same way, but most of the time people are not in exactly the same situation. Government employees have at least some discretion to negotiate in most cases. As long as there is some possibility of compromise, ADR can be worthwhile.

3. *The government requires public proceedings for deterrence purposes.* Part of the government's law enforcement responsibility is to prevent future violations from occurring. Thus, under certain circumstances, it may determine that a public trial, with on-the-record testimony and a public decision, is appropriate. ADR is by its nature a more private proceeding, and nonparties are usually not invited to participate. Thus, ADR may not be appropriate when deterrence is necessary.

4. *The government is pursuing a criminal investigation involving the same matter.* In some cases (for example, certain fraud and environmental matters), the government may initiate both civil and criminal investigations at the same time. In this situation, government must proceed carefully to ensure that information gathered through the parallel investigations is treated appropriately.[8] Sometimes the criminal matter must proceed through sentencing before the government will consider settling the civil case.[9] ADR may be inappropriate in these matters until the criminal case is resolved.

5. *The case is likely to settle easily without ADR.* If unassisted negotiations are going smoothly, there is no reason for parties to pursue ADR. Parties can settle many cases efficiently and effectively on their own. ADR does require some time and money, and using it unnecessarily serves no purpose.

6. *Adjudication will be quick and inexpensive.* Taking a case all the way through a trial or administrative hearing is rarely quick and al-

most never inexpensive. By its nature, litigation is a thorough and time-consuming process. However, some courts are more efficient than others.[10] In certain cases, a party may decide that waiting for adjudication is worthwhile.

It also is possible in some cases to achieve a quick and inexpensive result through the use of legal techniques. Courts and administrative tribunals have options for parties to seek dismissal of a claim by establishing that the other side will be unable to prove its case. If a party has grounds to file such a motion, it may choose to pursue this route rather than use ADR. If the motion fails, the party may use ADR at that time.

7. *A party does not have enough information to assess the case's value.* There is no point in pursuing ADR unless both parties have a reasonable idea what their case is worth. The process requires that parties are able to bargain in an informed manner about a proper settlement. If more time is necessary for parties to conduct adequate investigation, they should wait until they have done so before beginning ADR.

Parties should develop a case long enough to assess its value, but not so long that they spend more time and money than necessary. Indeed, one of the advantages of ADR is that it can help settle cases before parties invest the time and money necessary to take a case all the way through trial. The proper balance on this issue will vary from case to case. In some matters, parties have employed a two-step ADR process: ADR is used first to facilitate conducting the core investigation needed for settlement and then to aid in the actual settlement talks.

8. *A party is proposing ADR in bad faith.* Sometimes parties seek to use ADR to gain a tactical advantage rather than pursue the settlement of a case. Some parties may use ADR to delay the matter, which may be of benefit to them for various reasons. Other parties may use the process to gain "free discovery" or insight into the other side's case. In these situations, the party is using ADR illegitimately because it has no intention of settling the case.

It is not always easy to determine a party's motivation for using ADR. Sometimes one side may appear to desire ADR in good faith but shows no desire to settle the case once the process begins. Other times, the opposite is the case. Fortunately, the intentions of both parties generally become clear early in the ADR process. If ADR is not advancing settlement interests, either side is free to stop it immediately and return to litigation.

If a party is suspicious of the other side's motivation, it can take protective steps. For example, when a party questions whether the other side is seeking to delay matters, it can refuse to grant a stay of litigation during the ADR. This way, litigation proceeds apace, and no time is lost because of ADR. If a party fears the other side may be seeking free discovery, it can avoid revealing unnecessary information during the ADR. Because the process is voluntary at every stage, parties can generally protect themselves from negative results. It also can be effective to discuss these concerns with neutrals, who are experienced in handling such issues in ADR.

Persuading the Other Side to Use ADR

Just because one side has determined that a case is appropriate for ADR does not mean the other side will always agree. There are a number of ways to encourage the use of ADR and overcome common resistance to it.

The Advantages of ADR

It is helpful to emphasize the advantages of ADR, particularly if the other side has limited experience with it. One place to start is to stress how it is a voluntary process, and either side is free to withdraw at any time. Thus, there is little risk: a party who is dissatisfied with what is going on may simply leave. A common misconception is that ADR requires turning over the case to a private judge, who will make a ruling that binds the parties. Even some experienced litigators are confused on this point. In fact, the parties will be bound only if they agree in advance to binding arbitration, which is a process the government uses only rarely. Far more common is mediation, where both sides are free to withdraw without penalty whenever they want. Indeed, parties can be told that they have much more control over the result of an ADR process than of a trial. The true time a party loses control is when its lawyer enters a courtroom and says, "May it please the court," the traditional beginning of a presentation to a judge or jury who will decide the case.

Parties may be more willing to use ADR when they learn how it can save time and money. If the case involves an agency that has published reports on how ADR resolves cases more quickly and cheaply, this information can be persuasive to a party deciding whether to use it. Most agencies report that they settle at least two-thirds of the cases that go to ADR, and some have settlement rates approaching 90 percent. A rapid settlement to which both sides agree is almost always beneficial for everyone involved.

Some parties may appreciate the greater degree of confidentiality provided by ADR. If a party would like a case to be handled more privately, ADR is a good choice. A federal court trial is rarely a quiet process.

Parties may appreciate learning that ADR often provides benefits even if the case does not settle. Many parties have reported improved relationships after ADR, and the process frequently narrows any issues remaining for trial.

Finally, parties sometimes agree to ADR if they are given the opportunity to choose the neutral themselves. Reluctant parties can feel more comfortable with the process when they handpick the person who will lead it. Parties who are eager to use ADR may be willing to make this concession to the other side. Good neutrals will not be biased in favor of either side, so one side should not be at a disadvantage in the process just because the other side chose the neutral. Indeed, letting the other side pick the neutral can have advantages down the line. Neutrals often engage in reality testing, challenging parties' legal claims to persuade them to settle. When parties personally select the neutral who is challenging them, they have to take these comments more seriously.

Resistance to ADR from Some Private Sector Attorneys

After Attorney General Reno addressed a group of lawyers encouraging the use of ADR,[11] she received an irate call from an attorney who commented, "Don't you realize that if you increase the use of ADR, you will be taking money away from lawyers?" On another occasion, a lawyer told her he believed he should be entitled to a premium in addition to his regular fee if he resolved a case through ADR, because he would make less profit on a matter that settled quickly. These are not isolated reactions. Litigation departments are often major profit centers for law firms. Indeed, it has been said that for a private sector litigator, "ADR" stands for "Alarming Drop in Revenue."[12]

Resistance from private sector lawyers is not limited to the United States. In Abuja, the capital city of Nigeria, a judge spoke to a group of litigators and suggested they use ADR. The judge added that if they settle a case quickly with ADR, their clients will pay their fee "without rancor." A litigator raised his hand and replied, "Yes, but they will pay less!"[13]

Fortunately, good lawyers are recognizing that they benefit from getting ahead of the ADR curve. As clients learn about the advantages ADR can provide, they are requesting it more and more. Lawyers who are effective advocates in an ADR setting can use this skill to gain business. Parties are often more satisfied with the result of ADR processes than traditional litigation, and this makes them more likely to rehire the attorneys who represented them in ADR.

Resistance to ADR from Some Government Attorneys

Some government attorneys resist ADR as well. Government attorneys who have been practicing for a long time sometimes believe they know how to settle their cases and do not need the assistance of a third party. Their attitude is that if they cannot resolve the matter, no one can. Younger attorneys sometimes resist the process because they prefer to go to trial. Some recent law school graduates come to the government in order to gain trial experience, which they cannot get if a case settles.

The growth of ADR in the government is helping to overcome this resistance. Senior attorneys are realizing that ADR is not just a passing fad. They also are recognizing, with experience, that it can be an effective tool in certain cases, assisting parties in settling matters they could not resolve on their own. Younger attorneys also are realizing the importance of developing their skill in advocating in ADR. As ADR spreads throughout the legal community, experience in this area can be as relevant as in trial advocacy.

Federal Government ADR Policies

Both the private sector and the government can benefit from the federal guidelines favoring ADR use. If a private party is having difficulty convincing the government to use ADR, it can refer to a number of policies that direct the government to do so. The Civil Justice Reform Act of 1990 recommends ADR as a case management tool.[14] The Administrative Dispute Resolution Act of 1996 states that ADR will "enhance the operation of the Government and better serve the public."[15] The Alternative Dispute Resolution Act of 1998 requires every federal district court to "encourage and promote the use of alternative dispute resolution in its district."[16] Finally, a presidential executive order states quite directly, "Litigation counsel shall make reasonable attempts to resolve a dispute expeditiously and properly before proceeding to trial. . . . Where the benefits of Alternative Dispute Resolution ('ADR') may be derived, and after consultation with the agency referring the matter, litigation counsel should suggest the use of an appropriate ADR technique to the parties. . . ."[17] Every federal agency now has an official ADR policy, which can often be found on its Web site or by contacting its ADR or general counsel's office.[18] These policies generally state that the agency favors the use of ADR in appropriate cases. Reluctant government counsel may be persuaded to try ADR when they realize this is official policy.

Government attorneys can use these policies to their advantage as well. Some government attorneys may be concerned that offering ADR might make them look weak. Although ADR is quite common, some attorneys still have the perception that suggesting it might make them appear unusually eager to settle their case. To counter this impression, government attorneys can say they are offering ADR because official policies require them to consider this approach.[19]

Conflict Assessments

If parties are not ready to agree to use ADR, they may be interested in obtaining a conflict assessment instead. This is a process where a neutral meets with the parties and provides guidance on what processes they may use to resolve the dispute. The neutral will examine the dispute in detail, along with the parties' interest in ADR and reservations about the process. At the end of the assessment, the neutral will provide the parties with a recommendation on what issues they could address, what ADR processes they might consider, and the appropriate timetable under the circumstances.

Process Selection

Many different types of ADR processes are available in federal government cases. This section begins with a background description of the spectrum of options and then discusses the forms of ADR used most commonly in the government: mediation, early neutral evaluation, minitrial, summary jury trial, and arbitration. (Ombuds offices, which are used mainly in government workplace cases, are covered in Chapter Six.)

Background

Parties in a conflict can respond in a variety of ways. At the least intrusive end of the spectrum, they can avoid the problem and hope it will go away on its own. Avoidance may be appropriate when parties believe the risks of addressing the situation are greater than the likely benefits from doing so. The next step in the spectrum is simple negotiation. Parties can attempt to resolve the problem among themselves. Many disputes are handled in this way. If this does not work, parties can move to assisted negotiation. This is where ADR comes in. A neutral individual may be able to help parties handle their dispute. The fourth stage of the progression is adjudication. At this point, the parties decide they are unable to resolve the dispute voluntarily and pursue a formal process such as a trial. The end of the spectrum, when even adjudication breaks down, is violence. Fortunately, few disputes reach this stage.

Because adjudication is the major non-ADR process available to parties who cannot resolve legal differences on their own, it is worth comparing it with ADR. A fundamental difference between the processes is control over the result: a third party determines the outcome of adjudication, whereas the parties decide what happens to them in most forms of ADR.[20] The processes also have different levels of formality. Adjudication takes place in a formal environment where rules constrain what can be said and when. ADR is more flexible, allowing parties considerable freedom to express themselves. Privacy is another difference. Adjudication takes place on the record in a public forum. ADR occurs more privately, with a greater degree of confidentiality. The processes also have different focuses. Adjudication concentrates on the facts and the legal rights of the parties in determining the outcome. ADR looks to the interests of the parties and what they want in order to settle their dispute. Similarly, adjudication emphasizes the past, looking to what happened between the parties when the conflict began. ADR focuses on the future, to discover what the parties want the resolution of their conflict to look like. Finally, the result of adjudication is win-lose, with one party defeating the other. The goal of ADR is win-win, and even when this is not possible, both sides usually are better off with an ADR settlement than they would have been at the end of a long, expensive court battle.

Once parties have decided to use ADR, they can choose from a multitude of processes. Each of the various ADR processes has different strengths and weaknesses.[21] The most common types of ADR in the federal government are mediation, early neutral evaluation, minitrial, summary jury trial, and arbitration. This list is in order of increasing levels of formality and amount of influence given to a third party. At the same time, it is in decreasing order in terms of the likelihood that the process will improve the relationship between the parties.

Mediation

By far, the most common type of ADR used in the federal government is mediation, accounting for probably 95 percent of the ADR processes in which the government participates. In mediation, a trained neutral individual assists the parties in reaching a voluntary agreement. Many mediators talk with the parties individually before the mediation begins to learn about the dispute. The mediation process then usually starts with all parties in the same room, where they give brief summaries of their positions and discuss what they want to happen in the future. Often the neutral will then talk to each side individually, engaging in "shuttle diplomacy" (named after the practice of diplomats who shuttle between various rooms containing representatives of different countries involved in a conflict). Some neutrals alternate between shuttle diplomacy and joint sessions with all parties in the room together. Others conduct the entire mediation in joint sessions. If the parties reach an agreement, they usually sign a document to that effect at the mediation. If they do not settle the case, the mediation concludes, and they are free to pursue adjudication if they wish.

Good mediators can assist the parties in a number of ways. They are skilled at improving communication among parties. Often parties participate in mediation because communication has broken down, and mediators will be able to help restore it. Mediators are good at clarifying the interests that underlie the parties' positions. They can add insight into what is important beneath the facades of parties' claims, allowing them to realize what both sides really need in order to settle the case. Mediators will probe the strengths and weaknesses of both sides' cases, helping them to understand the true value of their claims. Mediators will focus the parties' attention on what will happen if they do not settle. Examining the consequences of failing to settle gives the parties a valuable perspective on how to handle the negotiation. Mediators are often very creative people. They can develop options for settlement that parties may not have considered on their own. Finally, mediators are skilled at overcoming impasses. Many times a negotiation will get stuck for one reason or another, and good mediators have techniques that assist parties in getting around these barriers.

It is useful to analogize mediators who help parties settle cases to Sherpas who help parties climb mountains.[22] Sherpas are expert route finders, just as mediators know how to navigate the parties through a dispute. Sherpas are skilled at getting around barriers, and mediators can assist the parties in overcoming obstacles to settlement. Sherpas will carry the load for their climbers, while mediators take part of the burden off parties in resolving a dispute. Finally, Sherpas will not make climbers hike any farther than they want to, nor will mediators force a settlement on parties who do not want one.

Mediation has many advantages as an ADR process in federal cases.[23] Because it is the most common form of ADR used in the government, parties are more familiar with it. Both government and private sector practitioners are likely to know what is involved in mediation and how they can use it effectively. There are also many mediators available for hire. Locating a skilled mediator who has experience with government cases is usually not difficult. Because mediation is a voluntary process, there is little risk for either side. If a party does not like the way the process is proceeding, it can stop participating. Mediation is often effective in saving both time and money for parties. Settling a case through mediation is almost always quicker and cheaper than litigating it. Because parties work together in fashioning their own settlement of the dispute, the process tends to improve their relationship. Parties also report higher satisfaction rates in mediation than litigation, indicating they prefer it as a method of dispute resolution. Finally, perhaps because of this increased satisfaction, mediated agreements generally have higher compliance rates than litigated judgments. Parties are more likely to follow through on their commitments and less likely to require future litigation if they settle their case through mediation.

There are some disadvantages to mediation. It takes some time and usually costs money. This investment is likely to save time and money eventually, but an initial expenditure must be made up front. If the case does not ultimately settle, this investment may be lost. Furthermore, parties who participate in mediation may end up disclosing some of their litigation strategy. Mediators encourage parties to discuss their case in front of the other side, and this can tip their hand for trial if the case does not settle. Of course, parties do retain control and can always decline to share information about their case if they wish. One of the strengths of mediation, that parties decide for themselves whether to settle, is also a disadvantage: a mediator has no power to force a result. If the parties want to ensure that the case reaches a final resolution, mediation may not be the best choice. Furthermore, if parties want a court precedent, mediation will not give them one.

Mediation can take place in several different forms. Most commonly, a single mediator handles the case, but parties sometimes hire two comediators. This can be appropriate in certain situations, such as when it is valuable to have mediators with different areas of substantive expertise. Mediation usually takes place in person, but sometimes the telephone is used. Telephonic mediation can be considerably cheaper and more convenient; however, the process is much less personal and often less effective as a result. Taking the technological route even further, some parties have experimented with mediation over the Internet. This can be cheaper still, and it allows the parties to participate by sending messages whenever they wish. In certain circumstances, such as simple cases with relatively little money at stake, these approaches can be fine. For more important matters, most parties find there is no substitute for face-to-face interaction.

Early Neutral Evaluation

In early neutral evaluation (ENE), parties give summaries of their case to a neutral early in the litigation, and the neutral then provides them with a nonbinding evaluation of the case. This form of ADR began as an experiment in the federal court in the Northern District of California in 1985.[24] It has since spread to other courts and administrative tribunals. The process begins with the parties providing written submissions to the evaluator in advance. Then the parties meet in person, and each makes a statement to the neutral that can be as short as fifteen to thirty minutes. The presentations generally do not involve witnesses or formal evidence. The evaluator then gives an estimate of the likely result of the case. The estimate can include the odds of each side prevailing and a range of likely awards. The evaluator also may give an appraisal of the cost of case investigation, pretrial proceedings, and trial, should the parties choose to take that route. At this point, the parties are free to leave the ENE and consider how to proceed. As another option, they may be able to continue to work with the evaluator, who can assist them with settlement in the role of a mediator.

The goal of ENE is for parties to settle their case intelligently after receiving an unbiased opinion of the likely outcome of the litigation, before they have spent the time and money that litigation requires. This process can be especially valuable if one of the parties starts with an unrealistic view of the value of its case. Sometimes plaintiffs have a mistaken belief they will recover millions of dollars from a small claim, and other times defendants are overly optimistic about their chances of escaping liability completely. Such parties may be unlikely to believe opponents who tell them they are being unrealistic yet more inclined to credit the opinion of a neutral third party.

In this regard, the quality of the evaluator is of paramount importance. The neutral must have the respect of the parties in order for them to credit the legitimacy of the evaluation. If the case involves a technical subject matter, the neutral should have expertise in this area. In all types of cases, it is helpful if the neutral has stature and commands deference from the parties. If the parties do not believe that the neutral understands their case or has accurate knowledge of what a judge or jury will do, they will not trust the evaluation, and the ENE will have little value.

When ENE takes place in agency proceedings, the evaluation is confidential pursuant to the Administrative Dispute Resolution Act.[25] Thus, parties can be assured that an evaluation in favor of their opponents cannot be used against them later. In federal court, the parties can provide for confidentiality of the neutral's opinion contractually in their ADR agreement.

ENE is different from mediation in that it is a rights-based process. In other words, the evaluator's participation focuses on the legal rights of the parties given the facts of the case. The goal is to promote settlement by predicting for parties what the judicial outcome would be. In contrast, a mediator emphasizes the parties' personal interests and settlement objectives. The goal of mediation is to assist parties in reaching an agreement that satisfies their goals. Both processes may incorporate elements of all of these ideas, but their emphases are different.

The process has some disadvantages. For one, it requires parties to disclose their trial strategies to the other side in advance. Parties sometimes see this as compromising their litigation strategy, even though both sides will have to make disclosures during the course of ENE. Furthermore, because ENE focuses on adversary presentations of party positions rather than a collaborative search for a mutually agreeable settlement, it does not tend to promote improvement in the relationships between the parties as much as mediation does. Parties often leave ENE with feelings similar to those at the end of a trial, where one side won and the other side lost. The more collaborative approach of mediation often is more successful at mending relationships. This may or may not be important to the parties, depending on whether they are likely to deal with each other in the future.

Minitrial

As its name implies, a minitrial is a shortened version of a trial. Instead of using a jury composed of private citizens, the minitrial format involves having high-level decision makers from each side listen to the presentation of the case. They are assisted by a neutral third party, who oversees the process. This process has been unusual in the government, but parties have used it successfully in some cases, particularly contract disputes.

Before beginning a minitrial, the parties agree to a limited information-sharing process called discovery. They want to ensure they have enough knowledge to evaluate their case intelligently, but they also want to save the expenses of full-blown litigation. For example, parties may agree to limit their preliminary discovery to sixty days. Similarly, they may limit their depositions (on-the-record interviews of key witnesses) to two hours apiece (with the agreement that they may be retaken in greater depth if the case does not settle). Each side may agree to a certain number of written questions known as interrogatories, again with the provision that these may be supplemented after the minitrial if necessary.

At the minitrial itself, parties present their case. The formal rules of evidence do not apply. Parties may make oral statements, provide documentary evidence, and call witnesses, including experts. Parties agree to limit their presentations to a set amount of time, and the entire proceeding typically takes from one to four days.

The "jury" is composed of one representative from each side, in addition to the neutral. The party representatives should be high-level officials with the authority to settle the case. It is best if they did not have personal involvement in the events that led to the dispute, to ensure a dispassionate perspective. The neutral oversees the procedural aspects of the minitrial.

Once the minitrial is complete, the party representatives begin negotiating the case. The neutral usually does not participate in the negotiation at this stage, to give the parties an opportunity to work out a settlement on their own if possible. The goal of the minitrial is to give the party representatives a greater understanding of the case, to enable them to reach a sound business decision on how to resolve it. If they wish, parties can invite the neutral to assist them at some point. The neutral can function as an early neutral evaluator, giving an appraisal of the case, or as a mediator, assisting the parties in resolving the matter on their own.

It is important for parties to draft their minitrial agreements carefully before beginning this process. There are many procedural details that should be established in advance. Parties should determine what case investigation they will permit and under what timetable, for example. They may set forth specific rules governing presentations at the minitrial, including time limits for witness examinations and arguments from counsel. Typically the parties agree that the process is confidential, and witness statements may not be used against them at a future trial.

Minitrial procedures have disadvantages. It is not a simple or inexpensive form of ADR: both parties and their lawyers must prepare for an adversarial proceeding and then participate over several days. Like ENE, it does not tend to foster improved relationships between parties because it emphasizes combat instead of cooperation. A minitrial requires parties to tip their hands about their trial strategies to an even greater extent than ENE. Finally, it can be difficult for senior officials with settlement authority to find the time to participate in a multiple-day process.

However, minitrial has been effective in some cases. The participation of high-level decision makers from each side is of central importance. The fact that these individuals are participating in a minitrial process can establish momentum that encourages settlement. Furthermore, many times these individuals have little exposure to the other side's evidence until they hear it at the minitrial. The minitrial process gives them this information early enough for them to have sufficient time to construct a creative settlement before the trial itself.

Summary Jury Trial

A summary jury trial is a shortened hearing that takes place before a jury, with a judge, in an actual courtroom. Federal judge Thomas Lambros created the process about twenty-five years ago to handle a number of asbestos cases on his docket that previously had seemed unsettleable.[26] The theory behind the process is that parties who see how an actual jury reacts to the case will be better able to determine how it should be settled. The summary jury trial has been unusual in the federal government, but it can be a good choice in certain types of cases.

In order for the process to be as authentic as possible, jurors come from the regular jury pool in the court. As in a normal trial, parties can interview prospective jurors, and they sometimes receive the right to remove jurors to whom they object. Often the jurors do not learn that their verdict is only advisory until the end of the process, to ensure they deliberate as they would in an actual trial.

In limited cases, the process takes place before a judge instead of a jury, in which case it is called a *summary bench trial*. This process is essentially ENE conducted by a judge. It is important to ensure that judges who conduct summary bench trials do not preside over the actual trials if the cases do not settle. In this way, parties receive a full and fair opportunity to try their case before a judge who is not predisposed one way or the other based on a prior proceeding.

During the trial, parties make opening and closing statements and present summaries of witness testimony. Witnesses do not usually appear in person, though sometimes parties show videotaped testimony, particularly of expert witnesses. Parties are limited to evidence that would be admissible at trial, and they discuss evidentiary issues in advance with the judge to avoid disputes in front of the jury.

The focus of the process is for the parties to learn how a jury reacts to the case. Therefore, in some courts, parties can watch the jurors deliberate on closed circuit television. In almost all cases, the parties can question the jurors after they deliver the verdict in order to understand how they reacted to the evidence.

The process has some disadvantages. It can be used only late in the process, when the case is ready for trial. This means that most of the expense of discovery and pretrial litigation that ADR seeks to avoid already will have been incurred. Furthermore, the summary jury trial is itself an expensive process. Although it is shorter than a full trial, it still may take from a day to two weeks. Attorneys and clients must spend considerable time preparing for the hearing as well. Because courts must expend significant resources managing summary jury trials, they may offer the process only in larger cases, where it is clear that full trials would cost even more. Finally, parties must be prepared to tip their hand almost completely in disclosing their trial strategies.

Nonetheless, the summary jury trial can be appropriate in certain cases. It can be worthwhile for very large cases that would be expensive to try. For example, toxic tort cases such as those that led Judge Lambros to create the process can take months to go through a trial, not to mention the subsequent appeal. The process also works well when the case is not settling because the parties have vastly different perceptions of how a jury will value it. A summary jury trial, with an actual jury, can answer this question and facilitate settlement. Finally, this process can be valuable when a party wants a "day in court." Sometimes clients are unwilling to settle until they have had an opportunity to present their case and seek vindication from an official body. A summary jury trial provides this opportunity.

Arbitration

Arbitration is the ADR process closest to adjudication. In format and result, this process is most similar to a trial. Parties make formal presentations to an arbitrator, including opening statements, live witness testimony, physical evidence, and closing arguments. Unlike a minitrial or summary jury trial, where the parties remain free at the end to decide how they want to proceed, an arbitration concludes with a decision from the arbitrator. Although arbitration has been relatively unusual in the federal government, its use is growing.

Arbitration is the only ADR process that is generally binding on the parties, and this can be a source of confusion for inexperienced participants. In binding arbitration, the parties surrender control over the outcome of cases to arbitrators and agree to be bound by their decisions. Only limited grounds are available for appeal (such as fraud). Sometimes parties mistakenly believe that other forms of ADR, such as mediation, are also binding on the parties. However, all the other types of ADR merely assist the parties in reaching a settlement and leave the ultimate decision up to them. (There is a form of arbitration known as nonbinding arbitration, where the parties are free to disregard the decision. That process is analogous to ENE.[27] This section focuses on binding arbitration.)

Until relatively recently, the federal government generally was prohibited from participating in arbitration. The comptroller general took the position that absent specific authorization, there was no general legal authority permitting the government to cede control over the outcome of a case to a private party. The theory was that only duly appointed officials, such as federal judges or high-level agency executives, could make a decision in cases affecting the rights of the executive branch. Congress responded in 1990 when it passed the Administrative Dispute Resolution Act (ADRA), which explicitly authorized arbitration for federal agencies.[28]

The ADRA sets forth a number of rules that ensure administrative arbitration with the federal government is completely voluntary. The process can be used only when all parties consent to it.[29] Parties must sign a written agreement before the arbitration can proceed.[30] The government cannot require parties to agree to arbitration as a condition of entering into a contract or obtaining a benefit.[31]

Unless an agency has independent statutory authorization, it may not use arbitration until it issues official guidance on its arbitration program in consultation with the Department of Justice.[32] The guidance should describe the types of cases where the agency will use arbitration and the procedures that the agency will follow.[33] Parties who have questions about what arbitration will entail can consult the guidance issued by the agency involved.[34]

Two provisions pertaining to the government are particularly important. First, the arbitration agreement must contain an explicit cap setting forth the maximum amount of damages that the arbitrator may award.[35] Second, an official in the government who is authorized to settle the case must agree to the arbitration in advance.[36] These safeguards prevent a private arbitrator from having unbridled discretion to issue a decision that the government effectively will be unable to appeal. By requiring prior approval and placing an upper limit on the arbitrator's authority, the ADRA ensures that the government's interest is protected even when it surrenders a decision to a private party.

Other rules govern the process of arbitration itself. The arbitrator has the authority to administer oaths and affirmations and to compel the attendance of witnesses and the production of evidence, to the extent the agency involved is authorized by law to do so.[37] When reaching a decision, the arbitrator must interpret and apply relevant statutory and regulatory requirements, legal precedents, and policy directives.[38] It is a good idea for parties to explicitly set forth the applicable laws in the arbitration agreement to ensure there is no confusion on this point. When issuing a decision, the arbitrator must provide a brief, informal discussion of the factual and legal basis for the award.[39] The arbitrator's decision does not constitute precedent for a future unrelated proceeding.[40]

Arbitrators' decisions are subject to only very limited review. Federal courts can vacate awards for corruption, fraud, or other misconduct by a party or arbitrator.[41] Courts can modify awards if there was an obvious important mistake or if the arbitrators exceeded their powers.[42] However, no general review of the facts or law underlying arbitral decisions is available. Thus, parties need to be sure they are willing to forgo appellate relief before they enter into arbitration.

In addition to the general endorsement of federal arbitration given by the ADRA, certain agencies have specific statutory authorization to conduct arbitrations. For example, the Internal Revenue Service (IRS) offers the process to resolve certain tax disputes, pursuant to the IRS Restructuring and Reform Act of 1998.[43] The Environmental Protection Agency arbitrates cost recovery claims of $500,000 or less under the Comprehensive Environmental Response, Compensation, and Liability Act.[44] Many federal collective bargaining agreements provide for arbitration of employee grievances pursuant to the Civil Service Reform Act of 1978 and presidential order.[45]

When a case reaches federal court, the government will still consider arbitration under appropriate circumstances. Although not bound by the ADRA for matters in litigation, the Department of Justice generally follows the same requirements described above to ensure that arbitration awards are not unbounded. A government official with authority to settle the case must approve the arbitration in advance. The Justice Department has used arbitration only rarely, but it has been useful in specialized cases.

Several different types of arbitration have been used in government cases. The first, which is common in the private sector, is party arbitration. In this process, each party selects an arbitrator, and these two arbitrators jointly select a third. The arbitrators chosen by the parties sometimes are permitted to be predisposed in favor of the party that selected them. Using three arbitrators has been thought to be appropriate in complicated cases where a combination of substantive backgrounds is helpful for the arbitration panel. It also can be valuable to have three people participating instead of just one, to bring more perspectives to the decision. However, this approach triples the arbitration fees that parties must pay.

Furthermore, coordinating the schedules of the parties with three arbitrators instead of one can be considerably more difficult. Parties have found that a single arbitrator is sufficient in most government cases.

Administered arbitration is another option. With this approach, the parties delegate administrative duties to an outside organization. This organization manages the process, sets the procedural rules, schedules the arbitration, and handles other ministerial details. The outside group can even take charge of selecting the arbitrator, though in government cases, this can happen only if both sides explicitly agree to delegate this process.[46] Parties also should ensure that the organization's standard arbitration agreement takes into account special considerations involving the government. For example, some standard agreements require parties to post money in escrow before participating in arbitration, which violates government policy. Others provide that the result of the arbitration will remain confidential, which also violates government rules in most cases.[47] Some require that an individual with full settlement authority be present, which is not always possible with the government. Because the government has been using administered arbitration more frequently, provider organizations have begun to adapt their standard agreements in government cases to take these considerations into account.

Another format the government has used is called *baseball arbitration,* in reference to the method used to resolve Major League Baseball player salary disputes. In baseball arbitration, both sides negotiate until they each reach their last and best offer. The arbitrator then must choose one side's number or the other (no compromise is permitted). In a variation known as *night baseball,* the arbitrator does not know the numbers put forth by each party: the arbitrator reaches a decision, each party's offer is opened, and the offer that is closer to the arbitrator's decision becomes the final result in the case. Baseball arbitration creates incentives for parties to make reasonable offers (in hopes that their bid will be chosen as the final result). The goal of this approach is for parties to make offers close enough to each other that they can settle the case themselves, without having to resort to the arbitration.

Arbitration has a number of disadvantages as an ADR process in government cases.[48] It has many of the downsides of a trial, and the parties must pay the arbitrator's fee. Like trial, it can be relatively formal, rigid, and adversarial, characteristics that make it unlikely to improve the relationships between the parties or lead to creative settlements. There is also a common belief that some arbitrators "split the baby," issuing compromise decisions rather than following the law precisely. This can be particularly disadvantageous to the government. Many statutes and legal doctrines give special treatment to the government, because it a unique party.[49] Federal judges become familiar with these provisions and must follow them or be reversed by an appellate court. Arbitrators may be less familiar with these defenses and less inclined to follow them. Arbitrator decisions cannot be appealed except in very limited circumstances. Giving up the right to appeal is a particularly significant concession for the government, because it wins a far higher percentage of its appeals than private parties do.

Nonetheless, arbitration can be a useful method in certain circumstances. Perhaps its most significant advantage is that it can be quick: parties do not need to wait until a judge is available to hear the case, which can take several years in some jurisdictions. Arbitrators must be paid (unlike judges and juries, who are free), but arbitration can still be a cheaper process than a court trial if it leads to a prompter resolution of the case. It can help parties avoid the costs of preparing for and conducting a lengthier trial. Arbitration is particularly appropriate when the costs of fully litigating a matter exceed the amount of damages at stake. In this case, the speed of the process can be more important than the decision itself. Another advantage of arbitration is that the parties can have control over the selection of the decision maker and the procedures used in the hearing. In litigation, parties must follow the instructions of the court. Finally, arbitration tends to be a more confidential process than trial. Parties generally are free to disclose what happens in arbitration, but it is nonetheless a more private proceeding because the press and public are usually not present.[50]

Hybrid Processes

In a few cases, parties seek to combine arbitration with mediation. Mediation-arbitration, or *med-arb,* is a hybrid process that encompasses both types of ADR. First, the parties work with a mediator to resolve their dispute. They settle as many of their issues voluntarily as they can and then turn over whatever issues remain to an arbitrator, who makes a final decision. The parties hope to gain the collaborative advantages of mediation as well as the finality of arbitration.

This process does not always work smoothly. If the parties use the same neutral for both mediation and arbitration, they may feel reluctant to speak candidly during the mediation, because the neutral may use information against them in reaching an arbitration decision later. If the parties use different neutrals for mediation and arbitration, they must spend additional time and money presenting their case twice to both people.

A final option is arb-med. In this process, the parties present their case first to an arbitrator, who writes a decision and then seals it without showing it to them. Next, the parties negotiate either on their own or with a mediator. The parties know that the arbitrator has written a decision that will become final if they fail to reach a voluntary agreement on their own. Bargaining in the shadow of this decision may increase their motivation to settle on their own terms rather than take their chances on what the arbitrator has decided. Using the same neutral as both the arbitrator and the mediator saves costs, but it can be problematic because the neutral will know the decision in advance, which can compromise impartiality.

Chapter Three

Selecting and Hiring
Neutrals for Federal ADR

There are a number of factors to consider when choosing a neutral for federal government ADR. Neutrals come from different sources, and they have varying qualifications. Certain procedural concerns also come into play for selecting and hiring a neutral when the government is involved. The following chapter covers these topics.

Sources of Neutrals

The major sources of neutrals for federal government cases are private sector neutrals, government neutrals, and court-connected neutrals. Each source has advantages and disadvantages.

Private Sector Neutrals

Private neutrals handle many government cases. As a general matter, they have more experience and training in ADR than neutrals from other sources. One downside of private neutrals is that they are usually more expensive than other types of neutrals.

Solo or Small Firm Practitioners
Most private neutrals work on their own or in small firms. They often do ADR full time, making them among the most experienced practitioners in the field. They come from a wide variety of backgrounds, enabling parties to choose exactly the kind of neutral they

want for a specific case. Private neutrals vary in skill and effectiveness. (A detailed discussion of criteria to use when selecting a neutral follows later in this chapter.)

Neutrals from Provider Organizations

A number of private companies assist parties in locating neutrals. Many of them have large rosters of neutrals whom they prescreen based on such factors as training and experience. These organizations can assist parties who have been unable to agree on a neutral on their own. This assistance can help parties resolve preliminary disputes over whom they should select to resolve the main dispute. Provider organizations offer scheduling assistance and even conference facilities for the ADR sessions. Some require their members to follow ethical guidelines and have a process by which dissatisfied parties can raise complaints and obtain redress.

It is important to choose a provider organization carefully. They have wide differences in philosophy and quality, and not all members of the same organization have comparable abilities. With larger groups, it can be difficult to maintain quality control. When working with any of these organizations, it is important to double-check the background of a neutral and not to rely solely on the recommendation of the provider. Private provider organizations also typically charge a substantial fee for their services, which can consist of several components. First, the parties may pay administrative charges to the organization. Second, neutrals may pay the organization a percentage of their fee. This percentage is sometimes as high as 50 percent of the fee, and neutrals often pass it on to the parties by increasing their rates.

Government Neutrals

Federal employees serve as neutrals in many government cases. The Administrative Dispute Resolution Act (ADRA) specifically authorizes government employees to serve as neutrals in government cases as long as all parties consent.[1] The most obvious advantage of using government neutrals is that they do not usually require an additional expenditure of money for either the government or private parties. Some of these neutrals are very good at what they do. However, frequently government neutrals have full-time jobs in a different field and often have less training and experience than private neutrals. Also, they may not have as much time available to spend on a matter as a private neutral would.

Collateral Duty Government Employees

Many government neutrals serve on collateral duty, meaning they maintain their regular work responsibilities and serve as a neutral on a volunteer basis when they have time available. If an agency has no budget to allow the hiring of a neutral, a collateral duty neutral may be the only option. These neutrals usually handle workplace disputes, but some agencies use them for other matters as well. One advantage of these neutrals is that they are personally familiar with the issues involved in government cases because they work in the government. They understand the culture of the public sector, which can make them especially helpful to the parties. This is one reason that collateral duty neutrals are frequently used to handle internal government workplace complaints. The employee's supervisor must approve the collateral duty assignment in advance and may place restrictions on the amount of time the neutral can spend on the case. If government neutrals work to resolve cases in their own agency, parties must ensure the neutrals have no connection to anyone involved in the case that could affect their impartiality.

Shared Neutrals Programs

In order to avoid the potential bias that neutrals may have if they work on a matter involving their own agency, it is common for neutrals to work on cases involving different agencies. Without this procedure, some parties might be concerned that a neutral in the agency where the claim arose might have allegiances to fellow employees in the agency or to agency management (on the assumption that pleasing management might improve the neutral's career standing within the agency). To get around this problem, the ADRA specifically provides for agencies to swap neutrals in this way.[2]

For disputes around the country, many local federal executive boards (FEBs) have shared neutrals programs. The FEBs were created in 1961 to coordinate the administrative work of federal agencies outside the Washington, D.C., area. The Office of Personnel Management manages the twenty-eight FEBs nationwide, and more than twenty of them have active shared neutrals programs. Through these programs, agencies can exchange neutrals with each other to mediate cases.

An organization that exists to facilitate the cooperation of agencies in making neutrals available to other agencies in Washington, D.C., is the Sharing Neutrals Program.[3] This program, which began in 1994 and is run from the Department of Health and Human Services' Departmental Appeals Board, works much like a cooperative: each agency provides neutrals for other agencies' cases and borrows neutrals from other agencies for its own cases. It currently covers only workplace disputes. The program requires that all participating neutrals have a minimum level of training and experience. It further ensures quality by mandating that all new neutrals participate in at least three comediations with an experienced neutral. Only after receiving successful evaluations from these comediations will a neutral be qualified to mediate cases alone. More than two hundred federal employees currently serve as neutrals in the program, which involves more than forty federal agencies.

Federal Agencies That Provide Neutral Services

Several federal agencies have full-time professional neutrals that work to resolve disputes. The Equal Employment Opportunity Commission (EEOC) has a staff of trained mediators who assist federal agencies and employees with disputes involving allegations of workplace discrimination. The EEOC also contracts with professional private mediators to mediate charges filed with the agency, and some EEOC offices use volunteer mediators as well. All mediators are trained and experienced in mediation techniques and the laws enforced by the EEOC. The mediation and investigation functions of the agency are separated, so parties do not need to be concerned that what they say in mediation will affect the outcome of their case if it does not settle. The EEOC does not charge parties for mediation services.

The Federal Mediation and Conciliation Service (FMCS) was created in 1947 to promote sound and stable labor-management relations. The primary function of FMCS neutrals is to mediate disputes between employers and unions in the private sector, but they work on some public sector matters as well. FMCS neutrals assist with the negotiation of collective bargaining agreements, and the agency is charged with minimizing the effects of strikes and lock-outs on the free flow of commerce. Congress later expanded the agency's jurisdiction to offer ADR services on a broader basis with a mission to improve economic development, job security, and organizational effectiveness.

An agency that wishes to use an FMCS neutral enters into an agreement to reimburse FMCS for the cost of the neutral (salary, benefits, travel cost, per diem allowance, and an agency overhead charge). FMCS also maintains a roster of private mediators and arbitrators from which agencies can choose neutrals. The rosters are searchable by geographical location, professional affiliation, occupation, experience in particular industries, and other criteria.

The National Mediation Board was created in 1934 to assist with labor-management negotiations in the railroad and, later, airline industries. The board works to resolve disputes involving collective bargaining agreements, effectuate employee rights of self-organization where a representation dispute exists, and settle disputes over the interpretation or application of existing agreements. The board provides both mediation and arbitration services for disputes in these areas.

The U.S. Institute for Environmental Conflict Resolution, created in 1998, exists to assist parties in resolving conflicts with federal agencies concerning the environment, natural resources, or public lands around the country. Any citizen, organization, or federal agency involved in such a conflict can call on the institute for assistance. The institute may work with the parties directly or subcontract the project to a qualified private practitioner. It also maintains a roster from which parties can select private neutrals based on their needs and preferences, and it can assist agencies with program design issues.

The Community Relations Service is dedicated to preventing and resolving racial and ethnic tensions, incidents, and civil disorders. Created by the Civil Rights Act of 1964, it is a component of the Department of Justice.[4] Its neutrals work with state and local governments, private organizations, and community groups to resolve conflict. The organization also assists communities in developing dispute resolution mechanisms, conducting training, and taking other proactive measures to prevent or reduce racial and ethnic tension.

Court-Connected Neutrals

Once federal government cases are in litigation, courts often provide neutrals. Sometimes these neutrals are sitting judicial officers, sometimes staff professionals, and other times volunteers selected by the court.

Magistrate Judges

Almost all federal courts authorize or direct their magistrate judges to serve as ADR neutrals for pending cases. Some magistrates make excellent neutrals, and in certain districts, settling cases is one of their major functions. The settlement services that magistrates provide are always free to the parties, which can save thousands of dollars in fees for both sides. Using a magistrate is administratively easy: the court takes care of scheduling, notifying the parties, and providing conference space. A major advantage of magistrates in certain types of cases is the official imprimatur that they bring to an ADR process. Some parties are reassured and impressed by judicial officers, and this can make them more effective neutrals. Parties may take their case evaluations and recommendations more seriously. Finally, the government sometimes prefers to have a magistrate conduct ADR in cases involving a party who is not represented by a lawyer. Some unrepresented parties have later raised challenges to settlements on the grounds that the government misrepresented terms or otherwise acted improperly. Having a magistrate oversee the settlement process protects government counsel from these types of challenges.

At the same time, some magistrates are less effective as neutrals. Some have only limited experience with ADR and are not skilled at the process. Parties have reported that certain magistrates are more evaluative than other types of neutrals, and parties have reported feeling pressured by them. Most magistrates tend to take a more formal approach to ADR than other neutrals, which can sometimes inhibit creativity and frustrate the process. For example, at a training session for magistrate judges several years ago on how to mediate, the instructor suggested it can be useful to build collegiality by having participants address each other by their first names. One judge responded with a harumph, adding, "If people want to call me by my first name, they can call me, 'Your.'"

Another concern is that magistrates frequently have busy dockets and thus only limited time to spend on individual cases. Private neutrals, who are paid by the hour, generally spend as long as necessary with parties to settle a case; magistrates do not have that luxury. Sometimes parties devote several hours to ADR with a magistrate, begin to make progress, and then find the magistrate must end the process to attend to other matters.

A tension can exist when a presiding judicial officer serves as a neutral on a case. Parties may feel constrained in what they say in ADR, because they know that if the case does not settle, the magistrate may rule on discovery matters or motions in the case in the future. Parties also may be concerned that the magistrate may speak about what happens in ADR to the district judge. Although court rules sometimes prohibit this, parties may not be completely sure what might be said behind closed doors. When parties cannot be fully candid with each other or with the neutral, ADR is less effective.

The government can be particularly constrained when participating in ADR before a magistrate. Government attorneys frequently must appear before the same magistrates over and over on different cases. The long-term nature of this relationship can make government lawyers reluctant to say certain things to magistrates out of concern that a damaging admission might reflect badly on them for future cases. Government lawyers also may feel pressure to answer difficult questions from magistrates, again because of their relationship, when they would find it easier to refuse to do so with other neutrals.

All of these concerns are not meant to dissuade parties from using magistrate judges in every case. Some are fine neutrals, and their advantages of cost and convenience are substantial. However, parties should be aware of all of the implications of using a magistrate before doing so.

District Judges

Although magistrate judges handle the bulk of judicial ADR, district judges do serve as neutrals in certain cases. Most commonly, judges who serve as neutrals will not preside over the trial if the case does not settle. Some courts use a "buddy judge" system, where judges swap cases with each other for ADR purposes. If the cases do not settle, they return to the original judge for trial. In other courts, senior judges who have a reduced caseload mediate cases for other judges. In a number of ways, ADR with district judges is similar to ADR with magistrates. Some are talented at ADR, and others are not. The same procedural advantages exist, along with the same limits on parties' freedom to speak candidly.

More troublesome is the practice in a few jurisdictions where the judge who leads the ADR process is the same person who will preside over the trial of a case if it does not settle. This approach can produce extremely uncomfortable situations for parties who know that anything they say in ADR may, deliberately or not, be used against them later by the judge who will make rulings in the case. This is especially problematic if the case is a bench trial, where the judge controls the outcome of the proceedings. Because presiding judges may make a broad recommendation that parties settle a case, there are serious disadvantages to their participation in settlement negotiations in any substantive manner.[5]

Professional Staff Neutrals

Some court programs, particularly at the appellate level, hire professional neutrals to serve on their staff. These neutrals are usually talented, and often they are chosen from large numbers of applicants for each position. Because a substantial portion of a federal court docket is composed of government cases, they are usually experienced in handling these matters. Some of these professionals work solely on resolving disputes, and others also run court-sponsored programs.

Court-Sponsored Private Neutrals

In a court-sponsored ADR program, individuals in the local community serve as neutrals for pending cases. These programs vary widely. Some are very selective and choose only neutrals with considerable training and experience. Others take everyone or nearly everyone who applies. Some programs provide extensive training of their own. Certain courts protect the process and the neutrals with explicit local rules providing for confidentiality and neutral immunity. In many cases, court-connected volunteer mediators are free to the parties, with mediators providing their services without compensation. Other court policies require parties to pay neutrals for their time (sometimes after a certain number of hours are provided for free).

Quality is variable among volunteer neutrals, who come from a wide variety of backgrounds and have differing abilities. Many are current or retired attorney litigators. A litigation background can give valuable perspective on a case, but it does not necessarily make someone an effective neutral. It is worth checking out a volunteer neutral (as described in the next section) before agreeing to this process. Most judges will permit parties to decline to use a volunteer if they provide a legitimate reason, and judges will almost always allow parties to substitute a neutral of their own joint choice if they wish.

Criteria for Selecting Neutrals

ADR is still largely an unregulated industry. In most places, anyone can serve as a neutral. Even when someone claims to be a "certified" neutral, certification can mean many different things, depending on who provided it. Parties should therefore exercise care when selecting a neutral.

Experience

A primary consideration in selecting neutrals is the amount and type of experience they have. Neutrals tend to improve with experience, and as a general matter, more experienced neutrals are more effective. Participating in many ADR sessions and working with many parties gives neutrals a greater understanding of the process and more ideas on how to be of assistance. Experience can be an indirect indicator of skill, because bad neutrals tend not to be hired very often. Neutrals who have a long history in the field are more likely to have been helpful to parties in the past, which has led them to be rehired (although this is not always an accurate predictor).

Case Experience

Parties should ask prospective neutrals how many cases they have handled in their career. Because cases can vary considerably, parties also should ask for details about the cases and how many hours were involved. Case hours can include both preparation time, where the neutral worked on preliminary matters, and contact time, where the neutral was actually in session with the parties. If the case involves more than two parties, they may wish to ask if the neutral has experience with multiparty cases. The dollar amounts involved in previous cases may be relevant. Experience with the type of ADR being considered (for example, mediation, early neutral evaluation, or arbitration) is important.

Government Experience

Because cases involving the government can be different from other types of cases, it can be useful to select neutrals who have experience in these matters. It also can be helpful if neutrals have worked as a federal employee. This background can give them a personal understanding of the unique culture and context involved with government cases. Neutrals with experience in settling government cases also can assist a private party in understanding some of the federal government's unique settlement approval processes.

Some parties believe a neutral who previously worked with the government may be more sympathetic to the government's position. Some former government employees tend to be predisposed against it. Most will not be biased either one way or the other, but parties may wish to inquire about this issue beforehand.

Litigation Experience

Lawyer neutrals with a litigation background may be helpful in certain matters because they know what judges and juries are likely to do should the cases go to trial. This experience is particularly helpful when the parties want the neutral to provide a prediction of the likely outcome of the case if it does not settle. When parties do not want such a prediction and prefer a more facilitative approach, litigation experience is less relevant.

Before hiring litigator neutrals, parties also should examine whether they have worked primarily on the plaintiff or defendant side. Litigators who have spent their career representing one side or the other may be inclined to view disputes in the light of this experience. Fortunately, most are able to remain impartial, but parties should investigate this issue beforehand by talking with others who have used the neutrals.

Judicial Experience

Some former judges are skilled neutrals, but this is not always the case. Some former judges take a judicial approach to ADR even when they are not hired to serve as a judge. It has been said that some former judges "still have the robe on" when serving as neutrals. The formal, rigid approach judges usually bring from their years in the courtroom can stifle the creativity and collaborative atmosphere that can make ADR most effective. Because they are accustomed to the power a judge possesses, some former judges have a tendency to pressure parties to settle. Experience has shown that the "arm-twisting" style of ADR, where neutrals coerce parties to change their positions, is more common among former judges than other types of neutrals. Finally, the court from which a judge comes can make a difference. Former state judges may have little experience with federal issues and defenses. Judges from jurisdictions with unusually generous or skeptical juries may value cases above or below what they are worth in a different location.

Some good judges do not make the transition to become good neutrals; others can be highly effective, particularly in certain types of cases. The skills of a neutral are different from those of a judge, and they can take time to learn. Thus, it is generally a good idea to choose one who has been serving as an ADR neutral for a while.

When chosen carefully, former judges can have a number of advantages as neutrals in government cases. They usually have experience with government matters because almost all judges encounter government cases while on the bench. This can give them a greater understanding of the procedures and restrictions that come into play when the government is involved in a case. The imprimatur of a prior judgeship can also be useful in some cases. Parties tend to give greater respect to the opinion of a former judge, which can make a neutral with this background more persuasive. This factor is particularly important when the parties want a neutral who will give them an opinion on the merits of the case (and it is less important if they want to decide the value of the case themselves).

Training

Courts, ADR provider organizations, and private individuals all offer training programs. Program quality varies widely, depending on factors such as the experience of the trainers and the comprehensiveness of the sessions. One typical approach is a forty-hour curriculum, where students hear lectures, watch demonstrations, receive written materials, and participate in a series of role-play exercises. In the role plays, students alternate between playing the part of a disputant and serving as mediator. Role-play mediation exercises can be reasonably effective because participants tend to take them seriously and provide as authentic an experience for each other as possible.

There is some controversy about whether neutrals with legal training are more or less effective than neutrals from other professions. In certain cases, attorney neutrals can be at an advantage. They have a background in identifying legal issues, interpreting statutes, and applying legal principles to factual situations. Lawyers are accustomed to dealing with people who have legal disputes and thus may be more familiar with the needs and concerns of parties in ADR.

Nonetheless, in some ways, a legal background may not coincide with the qualities necessary to be a good neutral. Lawyers are educated to focus on the legal issues that will decide a case in court, and these issues may or may not be important to the parties in deciding how to resolve the dispute on their own. Lawyers who concentrate too quickly on case precedent and similar issues may diminish the chances for settlement when parties believe other factors are more significant to them. Often emotions are vital in settling a matter, and lawyers have little or no training in this area.

No hard-and-fast generalizations hold true about all lawyer mediators. Some are outstanding, and others are ineffective. The nature of the case is important as well. Some lawyers are good choices for some types of cases but not others. For example, legal training may be more valuable for an early neutral evaluation in a federal court case than for a facilitative mediation in an administrative workplace dispute. Training in the law may be valuable for a complex legal matter but irrelevant for a workplace dispute where the personalities of the parties are more important than the legal issues. Parties should consider all of these factors when deciding whether to hire a lawyer as a mediator.

Subject Matter Expertise

Parties sometimes believe they should hire a neutral with expertise in the subject matter of the dispute. However, as a general matter, skill as a neutral is a more important factor. In most cases, good neutrals can learn whatever information they need from the parties. In contrast, a neutral who has expertise in the subject matter of the dispute but is ineffective at ADR will be of little help to anyone. Indeed, considerable background in the field can make a neutral more likely to be predisposed in favor of one side or the other.

In certain limited circumstances, it can make sense to look for subject matter expertise. This is most appropriate in a highly technical matter, especially where the parties want the neutral to give an expert evaluation of the merits of a claim. Under these circumstances, a neutral without such a background could not provide what the parties need. In other cases, parties may want assistance from the neutral in fashioning potential remedies in the case. Here, too, knowledge of the subject matter could be beneficial by enabling the neutral to create solutions that are more likely to be acceptable to the parties. Highly complicated regulatory matters, such as some environmental cases, may require subject matter expertise because the neutral must be able to understand the vocabulary used by the parties.

Style

Neutrals have different styles, and this can be an important factor in choosing among them. Some styles work better than others for different types of cases and parties. If parties believe a particular style will work best in their case, they should be aware of this when selecting a neutral. Parties can ask prospective neutrals about their approach and should feel free to request a particular style. If the neutral is not comfortable using this style or the parties are not confident the neutral will be able to be effective with that approach, they should choose someone else. The three main styles in the field are known as evaluative, facilitative, and transformative.

Evaluative Neutrals

Evaluative neutrals, as the name implies, focus on evaluating the case for the parties. In this respect, they function something like advisory judges. They listen to arguments from both sides, consider the merits of the case, and then advise the parties what they believe is likely to happen if settlement fails. In addition to providing an evaluation, these neutrals generally take a more active role in other aspects of the ADR process. They direct the sessions rather than allowing the parties to lead the process.

Evaluative neutrals are good for parties who want a neutral to tell them what to do. Sometimes parties are stuck: their widely diverging valuations of their cases prevent them from reaching agreement. A neutral who provides an evaluation can sometimes overcome this problem. Other cases benefit from a neutral who takes an active role in shaping the proceedings. If parties have been unable to settle a case on their own, they may want a neutral who will control the direction of the ADR process.

Evaluative neutrals are not a good choice in other situations, however. When emotional barriers are preventing parties from settling, an evaluative neutral may be of little assistance. Furthermore, some parties resist being told what to do and want to retain more control over the ADR process. Even though parties are free to disregard the evaluation a neutral provides (unless they have chosen binding arbitration), the evaluation often has a profound effect on future negotiations. If the evaluation favors one side's initial position, that party may become reluctant to compromise. The other party sometimes responds by claiming that the evaluation was flawed or biased and refuses to credit it. If this happens, the evaluation will be of no benefit in overcoming the impasse.

Facilitative Neutrals

Facilitative neutrals take the opposite approach. They see their role as assisting the parties in resolving the dispute rather than telling them how to do so. They will let the parties take the lead in choosing the direction of the process. Facilitative neutrals do not believe their job is to provide an evaluation of the merits of the case for the parties. They will not give an evaluation unless asked, and some will resist providing one even if the parties request it.

Facilitative neutrals are good choices for parties who want a neutral who will play a less intrusive role in settling their dispute. They would like the neutral to work with them and perhaps pace them at times, but they do not want to relinquish control. Similarly, parties will prefer a facilitative neutral if they do not want to risk hiring an evaluative neutral who might give a negative evaluation of their case.

Parties may not want to hire a purely facilitative neutral if they need someone to be more active in helping them settle their case. If parties have been completely ineffective in resolving the case on their own, they may want a neutral to take a greater lead in focusing them on a settlement.

Transformative Neutrals

Another style that has gained attention in recent years is the transformative approach.[6] The idea behind this style is for a neutral to assist parties in a process that will transform their relationship. The twin goals of the process are to achieve empowerment and recognition. Through listening and fully understanding one another, parties will recognize each other's situation for the first time, leading to the empowerment of both.

Neutrals who follow this approach tend to believe that parties should lead the process whenever possible, to learn from each other rather than from the neutral. For this reason, most transformative mediations take place in joint session, with all parties together in the same room, rather than in separate sessions. Transformative neutrals take a more hands-off approach, similar to that of a facilitative neutral, rather than directing parties in the style of an evaluative neutral.

This style is gaining favor particularly in the workplace arena. In workplace disputes, parties often must continue to work with one another after the matter is resolved, so transforming their relationship is especially valuable. In the federal government, the highly regarded ADR program at the U.S. Postal Service uses the transformative approach exclusively.

Transformative ADR is used less frequently in disputes where the parties will not have a continuing relationship once the process is over. It is unusual in Justice Department litigation, for example. Parties in a one-time civil enforcement case or business dispute do not wish to spend so much time on the relationship aspects of the case.

Hybrid Styles

Many cases call for a combination of these approaches rather than any one of them alone. For example, many neutrals begin the ADR process with a facilitative approach and continue with this as long as possible. If facilitation stops being effective and the parties reach an impasse, the neutral may switch to a more evaluative style to see if that works. It is helpful if a neutral can adopt multiple styles to fit the needs of the parties and the case.

Credibility

ADR works better if parties respect the neutral. Parties are more likely to value the suggestions and opinions of someone they hold in high regard. If they do not respect the neutral, they may resist the neutral's attempts to guide them, and the process can fall apart.

Neutrals can have many different qualities that will gain the respect of the parties. Some parties value a long history of experience in the field, while others might admire a neutral with a distinguished educational background. In certain types of cases, a neutral with subject matter expertise may have greater credibility.

Some parties choose neutrals because they are famous, even when this fame comes from a field other than ADR. Celebrity neutrals (like former members of Congress, agency directors, or eminent professors) can be effective in some cases, much as former judges can, because parties tend to defer to them. These neutrals also can be appropriate in matters where a settlement will receive scrutiny from outside parties. The fact that a highly regarded individual presided over an ADR process can lead other people to view the outcome as more legitimate. This can be particularly valuable in a high-profile case involving the government that is likely to be examined by Congress or the press.

Sometimes the reputations of celebrity neutrals are more impressive than their abilities. Having served in a national office does not necessarily make someone talented at ADR. The skills involved in ADR are unique, and neutrals who bank on their fame may have limited success working with parties once the effect of their reputation wears off. While some of these people are effective neutrals, experience has shown that parties are usually better advised to hire an experienced neutral rather than a person who has attained fame in another profession. Celebrity neutrals are also notoriously expensive.

Bias

Before hiring neutrals, parties should ensure that the neutrals are free from unacceptable bias.[7] In order for the process to work well, neutrals must not favor one side or the other in the performance of their duties. Appearance of impartiality also can be important to parties in the process. For example, if someone worked for twenty years representing only plaintiffs in medical malpractice cases prior to becoming a neutral, a defendant in such a case might not fully trust the person. Even if the neutral were able to act in a totally unbiased manner during ADR, a defendant might always be concerned about bias, and this uneasiness could compromise the neutral's effectiveness.

Bias could exist regarding parties as well as issues. Neutrals who are personal friends with parties sometimes recuse themselves from cases involving those parties to avoid this problem. If a neutral receives an inordinate amount of business from one particular party, there may be a concern that the neutral could feel beholden to that party. Because of this fear, some private parties are reluctant to participate in ADR with a neutral who works frequently with the government.

Nevertheless, prior experience with parties or counsel should not automatically disqualify a neutral. Many of the best neutrals handle so many cases that clients and lawyers may end up working with them on more than one matter. This need not present a problem in every case, as long as participants disclose such prior contacts before finalizing the selection of a neutral.

Location

It can be an advantage for a neutral to be located in the same city as the parties. Certainly this makes scheduling easier because the neutral need not spend time traveling. If parties do not complete a settlement during the initial meeting, follow-up meetings are much simpler to schedule with a local neutral. They can be planned on shorter notice, without the neutral's having to block off several days for travel time. Parties also avoid having to pay travel expenses.

In certain types of cases, a neutral with local knowledge can be more helpful to the parties. Neutrals who live in the city where the dispute arose may understand the context of the situation and the needs of the parties better than someone from out of town. They also may add credibility in persuading others in the community that a proposed settlement is legitimate.

Fees

Neutrals' fees vary, and this is a relevant consideration in many disputes. There may be some correlation between the fees that neutrals charge and their quality, but it does not hold true consistently. Many times, parties can settle a dispute without requiring the services of the most distinguished (and expensive) neutral in the country. In other cases involving the government, particularly high-profile ones, parties will want to ensure they find the best neutral possible, regardless of the fee.

Parties should remember that even though ADR requires an initial outlay of money, it is generally a cost-saving process in the long run. In a typical mediation, for example, each side ends up paying the neutral an hourly fee that is roughly equal to what they would pay for a court reporter. Thus, if ADR allows the parties to avoid even a single deposition of equivalent length, it has paid for itself.

In all cases involving the government, parties should ask if neutrals offer a government rate. Many do, and this can result in substantial savings. Even if neutrals do not have an explicit government rate, they often can be persuaded to reduce their fee when the government is involved. Many neutrals like to work on government cases, which can be more interesting than the run-of-the-mill construction or insurance disputes they may usually handle. Government cases can have high public visibility, which aids neutrals in marketing themselves for future cases. Some neutrals also see working with the government as a form of public service, thereby justifying a lower rate. Occasionally neutrals offer a reduced rate to the government party while charging the private party to the dispute their full fee, but more frequently they lower their rate for both sides.

Fees can be structured in different ways. In most matters, neutrals are paid by the hour (or the day), but in a few situations, they are paid by the case.[8] Determining which is a better value involves estimating how many hours will be required to settle the dispute. Parties also should be aware that different fee structures give neutrals different incentives in how they handle a case. Neutrals paid by the hour may be more thorough in preparing and developing every aspect of the case because their fees rise the longer they work. Neutrals paid by the case may proceed more quickly, so that they can move on to another case. Some parties also have raised concerns that a neutral paid by the case may give up and declare impasse more quickly, while a neutral paid by the hour would continue to work to resolve the matter. The flip side is that a neutral paid by the hour might be inclined to continue an ADR process longer than is in the interests of the parties. Good neutrals work to resist these incentives and do what they believe is best in each case regardless of the effect on their fee.

Fees for travel time are another consideration if ADR takes place in a different city from where the neutral is located. Some neutrals charge their full hourly rate for travel, on the theory that they cannot serve as a neutral on another matter while they are en route. Others reduce their fee, typically by half, while traveling. Some charge parties only if they work on preparing for the ADR while they are traveling.

Because negotiation is a fluid and unpredictable process, cancellation fees can be important. Neutrals have different policies on what they charge if the parties settle the case on their own before a scheduled ADR process takes place. If a multiple-day process was planned, some charge parties for all of the days and others for just the first. Neutrals also have different policies depending on how much notice the parties provide. One policy is that parties giving seventy-two hours' notice pay no cancellation fee, twenty-four hours' notice results in a 25 percent fee, and no notice results in the full charge. The idea behind this approach is that with sufficient notice, neutrals can schedule other ADR sessions to replace the one that was canceled. Another option for government agencies with many cases is to see if the neutral will agree to substitute a different matter for the one that was canceled.

Availability

Parties should always look at how much time neutrals have available to handle a case. Some of the best neutrals are booked far in advance. If a case is not on a tight time frame, this is not a problem, but if parties require immediate attention, they may be more limited in whom they can hire.

Some neutrals work in a group practice with associates. If parties want a specific neutral, they should ensure this neutral will handle the case personally rather than refer the matter to a colleague.

References

Another factor in selecting neutrals is checking their references. Most neutrals are willing to supply a list of clients with whom they have worked before, and parties can learn valuable information from these references. It also can be worthwhile to locate someone who has used the neutral but is not listed on the reference list. This protects against a situation where a neutral cherry-picks references who are not representative of their general work.

Government employees can contact their agency dispute resolution specialist or ADR program officer to learn more about specific neutrals. The Office of Dispute Resolution at the Justice Department is another resource for researching neutrals.

Interviewing Neutrals

There are a number of considerations in interviewing prospective neutrals. Some parties believe that neither side should talk to a neutral separately before the process begins. This belief is based on a perception that a party may try to curry favor with a neutral to gain an advantage. This concern may be largely unwarranted because a neutral will generally have lengthy conversations with each side privately during the ADR process itself. Nonetheless, some parties prefer to conduct all selection interviews jointly.

Joint interviews of candidates are most effective when the parties work collaboratively to identify the best neutral rather than attempt to persuade each other that their preferences are superior. Cooperation in this regard can help build a positive atmosphere that leads to more productive negotiations once the ADR process begins.

Most questions that parties ask neutrals focus on the criteria already described (training, experience, subject matter expertise, style, credibility, bias, fee, and availability). One general way to approach these topics is to ask neutrals how their background and experience have prepared them to assist with this dispute. Parties also can ask neutrals to describe how they handled a relevant prior case to get a sense of their approach to ADR. It can be revealing to ask neutrals why they are interested in working on this particular matter. Parties also should ask neutrals why they believe they are the best choice to resolve this dispute. Parties may want to ask about subject matter expertise if that is important in the matter. Questions about potential bias should be asked when necessary but should be handled delicately.

Parties should ensure they elicit enough information so that they will be comfortable with an individual's neutrality. At the same time, they want to avoid coming on so strongly that they alienate the person before the case even begins. This interview is also an appropriate time to discuss neutrals' availability to work on a case promptly as well as their fee. It can be effective to conclude by asking neutrals if they have any questions for the parties, which sometimes leads to useful exchanges.

Procedures for Hiring Neutrals

All parties must agree on the neutral to be selected, and reaching a consensus is not always an easy process. Parties are fortunate if their preferences coincide. More commonly, they need to consider what procedure to use to select a neutral.

Selection from Lists

One approach to neutral selection is for each side in a dispute to list the neutrals it would like. Parties then exchange the lists. If any names appear on both lists, parties can usually agree on a neutral to handle the case. Even if there are no overlaps, one party sometimes finds someone on the other side's list with whom they are satisfied.

If this fails, a follow-up method is to create a master list with the names of all the neutrals on each party's list. Each party then ranks the neutrals in numerical order according to their preference. The rankings are then averaged, and the neutral with the best overall average is selected.

Sometimes parties use a procedure to select from joint lists that is analogous to jury selection. Using a master list with all names, each side takes turns striking neutrals to whom they object. Parties can strike a neutral for cause when they provide a legitimate, independent reason that the neutral is unacceptable, such as a conflict of interest or a credible concern over bias. Parties also are given a certain number of peremptory strikes, with which they can eliminate neutrals without specifying a reason. At the end of this process, parties still must find a way to choose from whomever is left, but these individuals will tend to be more acceptable to both sides. The final selection can be made randomly or through a consensus process.

Selection by an Outside Party

Parties who are unable to agree on a neutral can turn the selection process over to an outside party. This is essentially using an ADR process to choose a neutral for the actual ADR process. Thus, even if parties cannot agree on their neutral, they may be able to agree on who should decide for them.

Many ADR provider organizations are willing to assist parties in this regard. The parties can decide to hire one of these companies to select a neutral based on criteria they provide. If both sides are careful and thorough in specifying their requirements, they are more likely to be satisfied with the result. Before entrusting an ADR provider organization with this process, it is important to ensure that they have a large enough roster of neutrals to ensure that at least one will meet the needs of the parties.

Another option if a case is in litigation is to ask the court to select a neutral. If the court has an ADR program with private neutrals, it can select one with a background appropriate for the case. The court also may offer the services of a magistrate judge to conduct a settlement conference. In most districts, a magistrate judge is assigned at the time a case is filed, and this judge will be the most likely choice to handle the ADR.

The major disadvantage to turning the decision over to another entity is that the parties relinquish control over the selection and may have little recourse if they do not like who is chosen. Parties who are concerned about this should ensure that they provide careful direction about their needs to the decision maker beforehand.

Hiring More Than One Neutral

When parties are unable to agree on a single neutral, they sometimes hire more than one. *Comediation* is a process where two mediators work together. *Party arbitration* involves three arbitrators: one selected by each party and the third selected jointly by the first two.[9]

There are a number of advantages to using more than one neutral on a matter. Hiring multiple neutrals allows parties to combine the advantages of several individuals. One neutral might have expertise in the specific subject matter of a dispute, for example, and the other may have more experience in leading ADR. One may have a legal background and the other greater knowledge of the business aspects of a dispute. In some cases, demographic considerations may come into play. In a discrimination case, for example, parties sometimes hire neutrals with different racial or gender backgrounds to alleviate concerns about bias. It can be valuable to have multiple neutrals participating in a case because one may see or hear something important that another might overlook. Finally, additional neutrals can be helpful with large, complex matters. They can assist each other with the complicated logistical considerations involved in such cases. It is even possible to conduct ADR on multiple tracks, with different neutrals meeting with parties at different times, when a case is quite large and needs to be resolved quickly. This approach requires that the neutrals coordinate carefully with one another.

The biggest disadvantage to using more than one neutral is cost. Each additional neutral multiplies the expense of the ADR process. Also, scheduling can be more difficult when additional neutrals are involved, and it can be cumbersome to have more than one neutral involved in a dispute. Some neutrals prefer to work alone to avoid questions about who will take the lead in an ADR process. Before hiring more than one neutral, parties should ensure they will work together constructively.

Strategy Considerations

Parties who want to ensure that they end up with a neutral they prefer should pay careful attention to the selection process. They should assert their interests vigorously, but also should ensure they do not alienate the other side, which could harm the relationship and thus jeopardize the likelihood of settlement. Sometimes the neutral selection process devolves into a situation where the last neutral left standing, after everyone else has been eliminated, gets the job. In this case, the process sometimes favors parties who are more persistent in seeking their choice.

Parties should recognize that they usually need not fear using quality neutrals just because they were recommended by the other side. Skilled professional neutrals know that any appearance of bias will render them ineffective in settling the current case and damage their reputation for future cases. They are scrupulous in maintaining their neutrality because they know this is their stock in trade.

Indeed, there can be advantages to using neutrals initially chosen by the other side as long as they are qualified. Neutrals often talk to both sides about the weaknesses of their cases, a process called *reality testing*. If one party recommended a particular neutral, that party will have to take this reality testing more seriously. It cannot be dismissed as the product of the fact that a neutral was chosen by their opponents. Furthermore, conceding to the other side's choice of neutral may build goodwill and strengthen their commitment to the process, an invaluable effect.

Ultimately, the best strategy may be for parties to start by determining carefully what their interests are in selecting a neutral. During the selection process, they should seek to attain those interests yet also keep an open mind. Sometimes parties learn things during the process that cause them to change their minds about their initial priorities. Remaining flexible allows parties to take advantage of opportunities that may present themselves, even if they were initially unexpected.

Fee Arrangements

Once parties have agreed on a neutral, they must decide how to split the fee. Typically each side pays half of the fee.[10] However, fee arrangements can get more complicated if there are multiple parties involved. For example, if the government litigates as coplaintiff alongside a private party in a suit against a single defendant, do the government and the private party each split the plaintiff's half of the fee, leaving the defendant to pay the other half, or do all three parties pay one-third? No hard-and-fast rule applies to this situation, leaving it open to negotiation. Parties may not wish to disclose fee-splitting arrangements to the neutral, to avoid concerns that the neutral may be influenced by them.

Private parties often do not have to pay for ADR in one type of case: internal workplace disputes. When employees file workplace complaints against the agencies that employ them, the agencies pay the cost of the administrative ADR process. These programs are considered part of the services that agencies offer to their employees. If administrative processes are unsuccessful and the case gets to federal court, the employees will have to pay their share of any subsequent ADR fees.

Agencies have different arrangements for funding ADR processes. Some pay neutral fees out of the budgets of the general counsel's office and others out of various program budgets. Parties should identify an ADR funding source at the outset of the process and ensure they follow any necessary procedures in this regard.

The Department of Justice has a fund of approximately $1 million each year to pay for ADR. This fund is available whenever the Justice Department represents the United States in a claim that has been filed in federal court. It also can be used to resolve a matter that will be filed in federal court imminently. U.S. Attorneys' Offices, which handle local litigation in all fifty states, can access this fund directly at a level sufficient to pay for most cases. For more complicated cases involving higher fees (as well as all cases handled from the Justice Department headquarters in Washington, D.C.), the department's Office of Dispute Resolution must approve the funding.

When the government has located funding, it must follow appropriate procurement practices. Fortunately, Congress has simplified these procedures for ADR to encourage parties to use it. ADR is exempt from normal government contracting rules requiring open competition and public notice of contracts.[11] Agency administrative offices can use mechanisms known as blanket purchase agreements or task orders to procure neutrals. If the agency uses a neutral who is on a government-wide supply schedule created by the General Services Administration, the contract terms themselves are already prenegotiated.

Private parties cannot give money to a federal agency to pay a neutral through a government contract. Therefore, most ADR agreements specify that the government will pay its share through its contracting mechanism and the private parties will pay their share directly to the neutral.

ADR Agreements

The final stage in this process is for parties to enter into a formal contractual agreement with the neutral. All parties and the neutral should sign the ADR agreement, making it enforceable as a contract.

The introductory section of the contract should include a description of the parties and the neutral, as well as set forth the scope of issues to be addressed. Parties can define the dispute broadly or narrowly, or leave the scope to be determined as the process moves forward. The agreement should describe the ADR method to be used, including whether the process will be binding or nonbinding. The neutral fee should be specified, along with procedures for dividing it among the parties.

The contract should address timing issues. Neutrals should be given a set amount of time to prepare. The ADR schedule should then be set forth, especially for the initial sessions. If the process may be lengthy, parties may want to set a deadline at which point ADR will cease if a settlement is not reached. This can hold participants' feet to the fire, rather than allowing the process to continue indefinitely.

Litigation procedural issues also can be covered. The parties can set forth what information they will exchange before the ADR begins and what process they will use in this regard. If the case has not been filed yet and the statute of limitations is approaching, parties may wish to execute an agreement to suspend the statute during the ADR process. If the case has already been filed, parties may wish to agree to stay further litigation proceedings while ADR takes place. (If court deadlines have been set, parties may need to file a joint motion with the judge to extend them.)

In federal administrative cases, it is appropriate to invoke the ADRA explicitly.[12] Even though the ADRA will apply automatically to administrative cases, mentioning this in the agreement will ensure that all parties have notice of it. In federal court cases, parties can describe the rules that apply in the district where the case was filed. This can help avoid confusion later.

Parties should set forth the confidentiality provisions that apply to the ADR (described in detail in Chapter Eight). In administrative cases, the ADRA includes detailed confidentiality rules that will govern the proceedings.[13] Parties may wish to supplement these proceedings (parties commonly agree not to disclose what happens in ADR to any outside parties). In federal litigation, parties should describe the confidentiality rules that apply in the jurisdiction where the case takes place, along with any additions to which the parties agree. A common provision is that statements and materials created for ADR are confidential, but evidence that is otherwise discoverable does not become confidential merely because it is used in ADR. Parties also usually agree not to subpoena the neutral to testify about anything that is said or done in ADR.

The final portion of the contract should describe what the result of the process will be. Generally, parties agree that if they reach a settlement, they will reduce it to writing, sign it, and thus make it binding on all participants. If they do not reach a settlement, they will proceed with the dispute, and no one will be bound by anything said or done during ADR.

| **Preparing for Federal ADR**

Careful preparation for ADR is essential. Much important work takes place before the ADR process even begins. Parties must decide such matters as when to conduct the ADR, how to write their pre-ADR statements, who should attend the sessions, and what to discuss with the neutral in advance. Both attorneys and clients will find that time spent in preparation for ADR pays significant dividends. The process sometimes moves quickly once it begins, so participants need to understand their goals before they start. In this chapter, "ADR" refers primarily to mediation, which is used most commonly in the government, but other processes will be identified by name when appropriate.

Deciding When to Conduct ADR

Disputes often are easier to settle earlier rather than later. When a conflict is fresh, parties often are more willing to compromise and put the matter behind them. The longer a dispute persists, the more it tends to corrode the relationships of the people involved. Both sides become hardened in their positions. If the parties continue to have contact with each other, their negative feelings may create further disputes. Although there are exceptions, it is often best to use ADR to nip conflict in the bud.

Research by the Department of Justice and Indiana University has shown that using ADR earlier in the life of a case tends to resolve a case more quickly than using ADR later. This study considered hundreds of cases where Department of Justice attorneys used ADR (principally mediation) in pending civil cases around the country. It measured each case's time to disposition by comparing the date it was filed with the date it was resolved (whether by set-tlement, motion, or trial). Time to disposition for cases where ADR was used earlier was significantly shorter than time to disposition where ADR was used later.[1]

Administrative Stage or Federal Court Stage

Most cases involving the federal government begin with an admin-istrative process at an agency, and this is often a good place to start with ADR. At the agency level, the case is new, parties are not as set in their positions, attorney fees are relatively small or nonexistent, and the relationship between the parties has not had as long to dete-riorate. If a case is not resolved at this stage, it typically proceeds to federal court, where the government is represented by an attorney from the Department of Justice. At this point, settlement may be more difficult. Federal court litigation is generally more formal than administrative proceedings, and this can increase the tension between the parties.

Parties have found workplace cases much easier to settle at the administrative level than the federal court level. Agencies report high levels of success with ADR in administrative workplace cases. At the U.S. Postal Service, more than 80 percent of the workplace cases where the parties use ADR are resolved.[2] The comparable fig-ure for the U.S. Air Force exceeds 70 percent.[3] In contrast, the res-olution rate for workplace cases where ADR is used in federal court litigation is only about 50 percent.[4] This difference in effectiveness is likely due in part to the increased difficulty in settling cases later in the process.[5]

ADR can still work well at the federal court level, however. There are a number of reasons that certain cases can be difficult to resolve at the administrative stage. For example, agencies lack authority to pay above a certain amount of money to resolve some cases without approval from the Department of Justice. Under those circumstances, an agency will sometimes deny a claim for a higher amount, and the case will proceed to federal court without an opportunity for settle-ment. In other matters, the parties do not have sufficient informa-tion available to evaluate the worth of their case until it has been developed through the agency investigative process. Even in cases where ADR was used without success at the administrative stage, it can sometimes help settle the case when attempted again in federal court. The overall effectiveness of ADR in settling government cases in federal court litigation is 63 percent.[6]

Before or After Discovery

One of the advantages of ADR is that it can help resolve cases quickly. If parties can settle their case prior to conducting extensive discovery, they can save considerable time and money. Discovery expenses are frequently the largest component of litigation costs. Discovery also can cause considerable disruption to parties because they must spend time speaking with lawyers, responding to interrogatories, and testifying in depositions.

Some cases require discovery before they are appropriate for ADR. Parties may need to know specific details about their case in order to value it intelligently for settlement purposes. Without this understanding, they would have to rely on guesswork in determining their best negotiating position in ADR, and they might overvalue or undervalue their case. Using ADR too early in a complex case can be risky.

One approach to resolving this tension is to follow the 80–20 rule: 80 percent of the relevant information that parties learn from discovery often comes from the first 20 percent of the money they spend. Tracking down the last, difficult-to-obtain data is the most expensive part of discovery. Often, the final portion of discovery is not significantly different from the bulk that came first and thus is of limited value anyway. If parties conduct initial core discovery, they may find all they need to know in order to resolve the case appropriately.

Following this approach, parties can agree to take abbreviated depositions of the key witnesses and then proceed to ADR. If necessary, they also may serve certain essential interrogatories and requests for production of vital documents. Often this will give them everything they need to determine their negotiation position with reasonable accuracy. They may not know with absolute certainty whether they are missing something, but the benefit from taking this slight risk may be saving months of litigation and thousands of dollars of expenses. If the case does not settle, the parties agree that they remain free to take more extensive discovery at that point, including more in-depth depositions of parties they have already deposed in a limited fashion.

Even if ADR does not settle the case, it often has value in showing parties whether further discovery is necessary and, if so, what discovery will be most important. Parties may learn during an ADR session what issues are preventing them from resolving the case, for example, and then can decide how best to proceed. In one case, uncertainty about the testimony of one witness, a company vice president, was preventing the parties from settling. The mediator called the vice president and scheduled a one-hour deposition for the following morning at 7:30 A.M. The parties took the deposition, returned to mediation, and settled the case by 10:00 A.M.[7]

Attorney Fees

When a dispute has entered a legal forum, attorney fees are another reason that ADR is often better used sooner rather than later. With both sides paying lawyers, the cost of a dispute can rise rapidly. In some cases, a defendant will amass legal bills at the end of a case that are higher than the amount they could have paid to resolve the entire matter at the outset. Plaintiffs sometimes find that their recovery from a case is less than the amount of money they have spent bringing it. The earlier a party settles a case, the more money it saves on fees.

Parties should consider their opponent's perspective on attorney fees. Many times, plaintiffs want their attorney fees paid as part of a settlement. In these cases, defendants who wait to settle must often pay a much higher amount than they would have had to pay at the beginning of the dispute, just to cover the increased attorney fees for the plaintiff. Plaintiffs also are well advised to settle earlier. If they wait until defendants have spent considerable sums on lawyers, they may find that these defendants develop momentum toward trial that can be difficult to overcome.

Analyzing a Case for ADR

Preparing for ADR requires parties and their attorneys to analyze their case thoroughly for settlement purposes. Parties should start by determining what their interests are in resolving the matter.[8] How important is money in the dispute? Are timing considerations relevant? Might less money right away be as valuable as more money later? What are the parties' orientations toward risk? Would a certain gain of a smaller amount of money be preferable to an uncertain opportunity to gain a larger amount? What nonmonetary interests exist? Are injunctive provisions more important than money? How important is it to preserve good relations between the parties after the dispute is over? Are government parties focused on setting a fair precedent? Is it important for private parties to protect their reputation? This list just begins to cover the myriad of interests parties can have in federal disputes. Parties should ensure they understand exactly what they want from a claim.

It also is vital for parties to work to understand what the other side wants from the claim. Learning the other side's interests can be just as important for parties as understanding their own. A dispute can be resolved voluntarily only when both sides believe settlement is to their advantage. Parties thus should spend time putting themselves in the other side's shoes. What do they want from the matter? How important is money to them? Are nonmonetary options possible? What rank order are they likely to use for their various goals?

Once parties have determined both sides' underlying interests, they should focus on developing options for resolving the dispute. The options with the highest likelihood of success will be those that satisfy both sides' most important interests. Creativity is valuable in this part of the process. Parties should consider all possible solutions for resolving the matter. Settlements sometimes come from unexpected directions, so parties should remain open-minded. The more broad-ranging and inventive participants can be in generating options, the more likely they are to resolve the dispute.

It is also useful to consider objective criteria that could be used in evaluating settlement options. Legitimate standards are powerful tools in negotiation, and they can help parties reach an outcome that both sides perceive as fair. Examples of criteria include fair market value, recent court awards in comparable cases, and past dealings between the parties. Using such benchmarks in an ADR session can be effective when opposing parties employ positional or bullying tactics. Criteria support the legitimacy of a party's offer and allow questions about why the other side's low-ball position is fair.

Parties also should examine their alternatives to settling the dispute. Fisher, Ury, and Patton use the term BATNA, derived from the initials of Best Alternative to a Negotiated Agreement.[9] Using this analysis, parties should consider what their best option will be if they fail to settle the case in ADR. With this information, they can compare any settlement offer they receive from the other side with their BATNA. If it is better than their BATNA, they should accept it (or see if they can negotiate an even better deal); otherwise, they should reject it. Parties also should search for ways to improve their alternatives to negotiation, as this will improve their bargaining power. They should estimate the other side's BATNA as well, which can suggest appropriate negotiation strategies.

Both sides should examine the transactional costs they will incur if they do not settle in ADR. Litigating a dispute is almost always expensive and time-consuming for all parties, and sometimes the costs exceed the amount in dispute. Private parties must pay attorney fees and spend time away from their other responsibilities to pursue a case. Although government agencies generally do not have to pay attorney fees for each case on a direct basis, the government still faces considerable costs in litigation. During the time that agency lawyers and Justice Department lawyers work on one matter, their attention is diverted from other matters they could handle, and this is a cost to the government. In addition, expenses such as deposition fees, travel expenses, and expert witness costs can be substantial. Government program officials also may be required to participate in many cases, taking them away from their other responsibilities. Damage to morale and important relationships can occur while the case is processed and should be considered. Both private and public parties should weigh all of these costs when they decide how to make and respond to offers in ADR.

Parties need to ensure they are well versed in the facts and law applying to their case. They should review all discovery materials and other investigatory information to ensure they understand everything relevant in the case. They should evaluate objectively the strengths and weaknesses of their case. It also is important for parties to review the laws that apply to the matter, including statutes, regulations, and relevant court precedents.

The rules that will apply to the ADR process itself should be considered. If the ADR takes place before an agency, the Administrative Dispute Resolution Act (ADRA) will generally govern the proceeding. Agency ADR program documents may provide additional guidance on the process. If the matter is in federal court, local court rules should be considered, as well as any special policies issued by court ADR programs.

Parties should work to understand why their case has not yet settled. This information can give them insight into how to proceed in ADR. For example, if the government believes a case is not settling because the private plaintiff has unreasonable expectations of a high jury verdict in trial, the government can request an evaluative mediator who will give the plaintiff an objective assessment of the case. If a private party believes an agency case is not settling because the agency attorney is not communicating well with the Department of Justice attorney handling litigation of the case, the private party can request that both attend the ADR session to improve communication. If the case is not settling because of a personality clash between the parties, they can ask that the neutral conduct the ADR in private sessions with each side, to avoid exacerbating conflict.

Risk analysis can assist parties in their preparation. This involves identifying the possible outcomes of the matter and assigning probabilities to each outcome. Parties can then use these probabilities to calculate the overall worth of the case. For a simple example, if a party believes it has a 50 percent chance of winning at trial and winning would result in a $100,000 verdict, the expected value of the case before trial is $50,000. If the party believes its likelihood of winning is 75 percent, its expected value is $75,000. Computers are useful for complicated calculations and to consider related factors such as attorney fees, appeal costs, the time value of money, and risk profiles. By using a mathematical approach to evaluate the various possible outcomes, parties can value their case more objectively. If they find their subjective, gut feeling of the worth of the case differs significantly from the prediction made by the computer, they should work to understand the discrepancy.

Preparing a Pre-ADR Statement

Many neutrals ask the parties to submit a written statement about the dispute in advance of the first ADR session. Neutrals review these statements to learn the background of the case before they meet with the parties. These statements are usually the parties' first opportunity to educate the neutral on the merits of their positions.

Parties should spend the time necessary to prepare an effective statement. Some parties do not take this process seriously, and they file bare-bones, perfunctory statements. They may fear that anything they say could be used against them, or they may prefer to argue in person once they arrive at the ADR session. However, it is wiser to view the statement as an opportunity rather than a burden. Parties who can persuade neutrals that their position is stronger have a substantial advantage in the process. Clearly, if neutrals have decision-making authority, as is the case in binding arbitration, persuading them is essential. Even if neutrals serve in an advisory capacity, as in mediation, it is valuable for parties to have neutrals understand their position well. Neutrals often ask parties probing questions about the merits of their case in an attempt to assist them in understanding the consequences of impasse. Evaluative mediators will go further by providing their assessment of the worth of the case and attempting to persuade parties to accept it. Parties who provide neutrals with arguments to use against the other side in these efforts will be at an advantage.

Neutrals have different preferences in the format and content of statements, so parties should ensure they understand what the neutral wants from the statement. If the ADR is taking place as part of a formal program in a court or agency, the program may have rules on how to prepare the statements. Parties should generally follow the requested format of the neutral or program. If a party has a strong preference for a different format, it can present its reasons to the other side and to the neutral in an attempt to negotiate a change.

Generally, a statement begins by summarizing the case. Parties can set forth the facts of the dispute as they see them. It is useful to explain where the opposing party has a different view of key facts. Parties then move to a discussion of the law. Again, it is useful to highlight for the neutral where the opposing side differs on its interpretation of the law. In a case where damages are significant, it can be worthwhile to provide a separate discussion of this topic.

Statements also should cover procedural issues. If a case is in litigation, parties should tell the neutral about what discovery has taken place and what is contemplated for the future. The neutral should be told if there are any pending motions and if any are planned. The neutral should know all relevant upcoming dates, such as the discovery cutoff date, the pretrial conference date, and the trial date.

Neutrals benefit from knowing about any prior settlement discussions between the parties. Statements can include a summary of previous settlement offers and counteroffers. This will enable the neutral to anticipate the likely future behavior of the parties in negotiation.

Parties should provide neutrals with any important exhibits. It can be very helpful for a neutral to be able to review a key contract or other document in advance of the ADR session. Neutrals also may wish to review the written complaint, answer, and any appropriate investigative reports. If a case is in litigation, copies of crucial discovery or motions may be valuable.

In some cases, parties exchange copies of their statements, and in other cases they provide their statements only to the neutral. The advantage of circulating statements is that all sides learn each other's positions in advance. This is the standard approach in arbitration. The benefit of writing for the neutral's eyes only is that parties can speak more candidly about their positions, a common procedure in mediation. If a party feels strongly that the statement should be either private or shared, it should explain why to the neutral and the other side. Neutrals are more likely to agree to requests made jointly by both sides. It also is possible to compromise by providing one section of the statement to both parties and reserving another section of the statement for the neutral only.

It can be useful when writing a private pre-ADR statement to give a candid assessment of the reasons the case has not settled so far, along with suggestions for approaches to take during ADR to maximize the chances for settlement. (Under certain circumstances, it can be worthwhile to do this even if the statements are going to be exchanged among the parties, in which case the matter may have to be discussed more delicately.) For example, if a party believes the attorney on the other side has an unrealistic appraisal of the case and is unreasonably counseling the client to refuse a settlement offer, the neutral can be alerted to this issue in advance. The information will allow the neutral to focus on this issue during the ADR session. If a party has a creative idea that may allow the case to be settled, the party should share this information with the neutral, who may be able to use it effectively during the ADR.

Parties face strategic decisions when considering whether to reveal information to the neutral that has been kept secret from the other side. An initial question is whether the information is favorable or unfavorable. If it is favorable, disclosing it to the neutral is likely to improve the neutral's impression of the party's case, generally an advantage. If it is unfavorable, the analysis is more complicated. On one hand, a neutral who is fully apprised of the nature of the case will be in a better position to guide the parties more accurately during the settlement process. On the other hand, parties may find that neutrals use this information in an attempt to persuade them to take a weaker settlement than they otherwise would have.

Parties also should consider whether the secret information will inevitably be discovered by the other side during the course of the matter if it does not settle. If so, parties may wish to attempt to settle the matter quickly, and without disclosing the damaging information, in order to get the best settlement possible. However, if it appears that the ADR will break down without an agreement and the information surely will be discovered shortly thereafter, showing good faith by revealing it to the other side may be worthwhile. Negotiations might then proceed more productively, albeit in a posture less favorable than before the disclosure. In certain situations, ethical considerations may apply to this decision as well.

It is important for parties to note explicitly in their statements what information they want the neutral to keep confidential. Neutrals are careful about honoring confidentiality requests, but it is still worthwhile to emphasize what is to be kept private, to avoid the possibility of confusion.

Choosing Who Should Attend ADR

An important part of the preparation process is deciding whom to bring to the ADR sessions. There can be a number of choices in this regard.

As an initial matter, the parties themselves usually attend ADR sessions rather than leave the matter solely to their attorneys. The presence of the parties is important to personalize the case to the other side and to the neutral. On the plaintiff's side, the presence of the plaintiff is a powerful reminder to all participants that someone was harmed by the dispute. The attendance of the victim of discrimination in an employment case or the owner of a company that lost thousands of dollars in a contract case, for example, underscores the personal nature of the claim. Similarly, on the defendant's side, the presence of the client shows the other participants that someone will be personally affected by the settlement as well.

Parties also should attend to demonstrate to the other side that they will be persuasive witnesses before a judge or jury. Both sides will be evaluating the likely result of the case if it does not settle and goes to a hearing or trial. An important factor in this result will be the credibility of the key witnesses. Parties who can demonstrate during ADR that they will be effective witnesses can improve the settlement value of their case. (Conversely, if parties are likely to reveal that they would be poor witnesses, they should consider not attending ADR or limiting their attendance to private caucuses.)

In cases where the dispute between the parties is particularly personal, such as sexual harassment, additional factors come into play. In some especially charged disputes, parties are so upset with each other that having them meet together can be counterproductive. A session that degenerates into angry accusations usually makes settlement less likely. In this situation, the parties may wish to notify the neutral to keep strong control over the process and head off any confrontations before they start. The neutral also may be advised to conduct most or all of the ADR in separate sessions to keep the parties away from each other.

However, sometimes even in these cases, it can be beneficial for both parties to participate in ADR. In order for some parties to agree to settle a dispute, they may need to talk with each other directly, and ADR provides this opportunity. Face-to-face communication between the parties in ADR can be a far more effective engine for settlement than having their lawyers fight in court.

Some private parties wish to bring friends or family with them to ADR. For example, if a plaintiff's spouse is going to play an important role in deciding whether to accept a settlement offer, having the spouse come to the ADR may be advisable. Private parties also may wish to have a family member or close friend attend for emotional support.

The government's choice of whom to bring to ADR depends on the nature of the case. Sometimes it is useful for the government to bring an official who can explain what happened in the dispute. For example, in a contract case, the government may wish to bring the individual who made the decisions that led to the dispute. This official could explain what was done and why. It also can be worthwhile for the government to bring an official who can address possible settlement options. In a workplace case, for example, the government may bring an employee from the human resource office to advise the parties on which remedies are possible for settlement and which are prohibited by law or agency policy.

Different attorneys represent the government depending on the stage of the case. At the administrative level, the government is represented by an attorney from the agency involved in the dispute. If a case reaches federal court, a lawyer from the Department of Justice takes over the representation of the government. In federal court matters, the Department of Justice lawyer will often bring an agency lawyer as well.

Both the government and the private party may wish to bring key witnesses with them in certain cases. In arbitration, witnesses testify under oath as to what happened in the case. In mediation, witnesses can be helpful more informally to clarify critical evidence in the case. Witnesses are relatively unusual in mediation, however, because parties prefer to focus on how to resolve the dispute rather than how it arose.

Expert witnesses are sometimes useful in special cases. In technical matters, for example, the parties may wish to bring an expert to assist the neutral in understanding the nuances of the subject. If so, they should notify the other side, which may then decide to bring its own expert. Sometimes neutrals retain experts of their own, to provide a nonpartisan view.

Parties should ask the other side whom they are planning to bring to ADR. This information can give valuable clues to the other side's strategy and can help the party determine whom to bring.

A final consideration is the number of participants to bring to ADR. Parties should avoid overwhelming the process with large contingents of people. This is particularly relevant for the government, which can look as if it is overpowering a private individual. At the same time, parties should ensure that all necessary participants are present. The balance between these considerations depends on the nature of each case.

Obtaining Settlement Authority

Settlement authority can be a challenging issue for the federal government in ADR. In an ideal world, it is clearly valuable to conduct ADR with representatives of both sides who have authority to settle the dispute. Otherwise, parties must take potential settlements back to individuals who did not participate in the ADR. These non-participating parties do not have the benefit of observing the process to make credibility assessments and learn the nuances of the other side's position.

When parties must take potential settlements back to individuals who did not participate in the ADR, it also delays the process. These individuals may require changes, the changes may lead the other side to request further changes, and these must then be approved by the outside party yet again. This can take considerable time, disrupt the continuity of the process, and even prevent settlement.

Nonetheless, the government is often unable to provide someone with absolute settlement authority to participate in ADR. For example, some people define "settlement authority" as the power to agree to any settlement requested by the private party. If the private party asks for several million dollars, only a handful of officials in the United States have that authority. Thus, structural considerations frequently require the government to be represented by someone who does not have complete settlement authority.

The U.S. attorney general has the final authority to conduct and supervise litigation involving the United States.[10] The Justice Department handles close to 100,000 civil cases each year, and the attorney general clearly cannot personally attend negotiation sessions in all of them.[11] Therefore, the attorney general has delegated the authority to settle certain cases to other officials. This authority depends on the dollar value of the claim.[12] At the local level, presidentially appointed U.S. Attorneys have authority to settle most cases within their district up to $1 million. Above that figure, officials in the appropriate litigating division of the Justice Department must be consulted. For cases in the range of several million dollars and above, only the very top officials in the Justice Department, including the attorney general, may approve a settlement.

The actual attorneys who handle litigation on a day-to-day basis, assistant U.S. Attorneys and Department of Justice trial attorneys, generally do not have settlement authority on their own. They must receive approval from their supervisors before they can sign an agreement and bind the United States.[13] When nonmonetary relief is at issue, such as debarment in a contracts case or a personnel transfer in a workplace dispute, the Justice Department attorney also must obtain the concurrence of the agency involved in the case.

For cases at the administrative stage, the situation is similar. The agency head has ultimate settlement authority (in some cases, even a cabinet secretary must receive approval from the Justice Department before settling a case). The agency head may delegate authority to other officials for certain cases. However, the agency lawyers who work on most matters will need to obtain approval before they may settle a case. If the agency involved is headed by a multiperson commission, such as the Securities and Exchange Commission, Federal Trade Commission, or similar organizations, settlements are not final until the members of the commission vote on the proposed resolution.

Although this situation can be frustrating for private parties who are accustomed to participating in ADR with parties who have full settlement authority, it is a necessary part of the process of litigating with the federal government. The government has important policy reasons that require settlement decisions to be made in a uniform way. Unlike private companies, which can decide to settle claims in whatever way they wish, the government has a duty to treat all citizens fairly. An important part of ensuring fairness in handling claims by and against the government is to treat similarly situated people in a similar way. Centralizing authority in a smaller number of people helps protect these values.

Furthermore, the government responds to the will of the citizens through their elected officials, and there are relatively few political officials at each agency compared with the number of career civil servants who handle most of the daily business. These officials are charged with overseeing the government's actions, and they supervise such large numbers of cases that they cannot be directly involved with each one.

In some cases, Congress has passed statutes requiring that the public be allowed to comment on proposed government settlements before they can become final. A number of such statutes cover environmental matters.[14] In these cases, the parties in ADR can agree to a settlement in principle only, pending the result of public comment.

The Federal Rules of Civil Procedure acknowledge the special concerns of the government in this regard: "Particularly in litigation in which governmental agencies . . . are involved, there may be no one with on-the-spot settlement authority, and the most that should be expected is access to a person who would have a major role in submitting a recommendation to the body or board with ultimate decision-making authority."[15]

Congress has recognized the issue as well, noting that the Justice Department "cannot realistically send officials with full settlement authority to each settlement conference."[16]

Federal courts also have addressed this topic. The U.S. Court of Appeals for the Fifth Circuit wrote, "Obviously, high-ranking officials of cabinet agencies could never do their jobs if they could be subpoenaed [to participate in settlement talks] for every case involving their agency."[17] The court overruled a lower court that had required a government official with ultimate settlement authority to be present at all settlement conferences, stating that this order was an abuse of discretion.[18] The court held that under certain circumstances, a court could issue such an order, "but it should consider less drastic steps before doing so."[19] The court later upheld a district court order requiring the government to bring an official with settlement authority in a specific case (as opposed to the blanket policy applying to all cases in the previous example). However, the appellate court requested that the district court contemplate the alternative of ordering an official with settlement authority to "consider settlement in advance of the mediation and be fully prepared and available by telephone to discuss settlement at the time of mediation."[20]

Many federal court-sponsored ADR programs now acknowledge the limitations of the government by defining "settlement authority" more leniently. Local court rules recognize that it can be sufficient for the government to be represented by someone with significant *recommendation authority*. This means that the attorney has the ability to recommend a settlement to a supervisor, and it implies that the supervisor will often agree to the recommendation unless special circumstances exist.

Government attorneys should take steps to minimize the disruption these policies can cause. It is good practice to notify the neutral and the opposing side well in advance of ADR if it will not be possible for someone to attend with full settlement authority. This information can be a surprise to parties inexperienced in dealing with government cases. Government parties should explain the situation and ensure that private parties understand the reasons for it. If a government party waits until the ADR session is under way before addressing this issue, both the neutral and the other side may be understandably upset that the government is not following the rules that normally apply to ADR.

It also is important for government attorneys to discuss upcoming ADR sessions with appropriate supervisors in advance. In some cases, an attorney may be able to obtain delegated authority at a certain amount prior to the beginning of ADR. If that amount of money is sufficient to resolve the case, the attorney will be able to settle on the spot.

While ADR is in progress, government attorneys should maintain close contact with supervisors to keep them apprised of developments. This will enable them to make a quick and informed decision when asked to approve a settlement. Regular contact with a supervisor also will allow the attorney to represent the supervisor's interests most effectively during the ADR.

It is useful for supervisors to be available for discussions by telephone while an ADR session is taking place. This will allow a government attorney to obtain settlement approval more quickly, without having to delay the proceedings very long. Sometimes neutrals and opposing parties who object to the absence of someone with settlement authority will be satisfied when they know that a supervisor will be readily available by telephone.

In rare cases, it may be worthwhile to bring someone with settlement authority if possible. Senior Justice Department officials have personally participated in a few ADR sessions, such as defense contracting cases where many millions of dollars have been at stake. At a local level, some civil chiefs or U.S. Attorneys have participated in ADR sessions in major cases, such as medical malpractice matters with significant government exposure. In large enough cases, it can be worth the time of high-level officials to participate in the ADR process and ensure that their interests are represented directly.

These issues affect the government most dramatically, but it is worth noting that private parties also sometimes have difficulty bringing someone with settlement authority. Private corporations, for example, may not be able to obtain the participation of the general counsel at every ADR session. At other times, a high-level official may come at the beginning but be called away during later sessions. Companies may also need approval from their board of directors for a settlement. These limitations can be difficult, but parties who work together to cooperate with each other usually can work around them.

Preparing the Client

Attorneys who represent clients in ADR have the responsibility of preparing them for the process. Many private sector clients and government client agency officials have little or no experience with ADR, making preparation essential. Even when the client is familiar with ADR, preparation is valuable.

Preparing the Client Generally

A good place for attorneys to start with clients is to cover all of the points in the "Analyzing a Case for ADR" section of this chapter. They should consider their underlying interests for settlement, creative options for addressing these interests, and legitimate objective criteria to support these options. It is important to discuss what they will do if they cannot settle and to determine their best alternative to a negotiated agreement. They should conduct the same analyses from the perspective of the other side, exploring their opponents' interests, options, criteria, and alternatives. They should go over the facts and law of the case and the strengths and weaknesses of their position. This initial work is an important part of a preparation session and should be done carefully.

If a client is new to the ADR process, the attorney should explain in detail what will happen. The lawyer should tell the client in detail about the processes involved in opening statements, joint sessions, and private caucuses.

It is important to explain to inexperienced parties that neutrals do not function as judges (except in arbitration and early neutral evaluation). Parties often instinctively turn toward neutrals and treat them as if they were presiding over a trial. Clients should understand that the goal of the process is to persuade the other side to agree to a voluntary settlement, not to convince the neutral to make a particular ruling.

Attorneys should tell their clients that the ADR process, unlike a court proceeding, is voluntary. They can ask for a break at any time for any reason. Clients should feel free to request a break themselves or ask their attorney to call for one. They may want to discuss strategy, ask their attorney a question, or just get a cup of coffee, and any of these is appropriate. Neutrals sometimes talk directly to clients and ask them, rather than their lawyers, questions. If clients want to have a discussion with their lawyers before responding, they should be encouraged to request a break to do so. In most forms of ADR, parties are even free to stop the proceedings entirely if they do not like what is happening.

Clients should be told about the confidentiality rules that apply to ADR sessions (see Chapter Eight). As a general matter, anything said in ADR in private sessions with the neutral is confidential. However, parties should be aware that what they say in joint session in front of the other side may not be confidential. Under the ADRA, statements in joint session are not generally confidential in agency ADR.[21] Even in federal court ADR or in situations where the parties sign a contract providing for confidentiality, participants may not be completely protected. Freedom of Information Act requests may require the release of written documents used in ADR joint sessions. Opposing parties may file requests for admission about comments made in ADR or ask parties questions in depositions that are based on what was said in ADR. Thus, parties should be advised to be careful about what they say when the other party is in the room.

Clients also need to know that the other side will be evaluating their effectiveness as a potential witness if the matter later proceeds to trial. It is surprising how often unprepared parties make sarcastic comments or sneer when the other side is talking, thinking their reaction somehow advances their case. If they disagree with something the other side is saying, they should resist the temptation to interrupt or make disapproving gestures. Instead, they should pass a note to their attorney, who will address the matter at an appropriate time. Otherwise, clients may indicate to the other side that they could be made to look angry or inappropriately emotional at trial, which would make them less persuasive. Overall, they should maintain a calm, professional demeanor, to show that they would be compelling witnesses.

Preparing the Client for the Opening Statement

It is usually effective for clients to participate in the opening statement in ADR, and this should be planned carefully. Plaintiffs should prepare to describe how the actions of the defendant affected them personally. Defendants should be ready to explain their conduct and note how any harmful results were not their responsibility. Clients who participate in ADR can personalize their case much more effectively than those who have their lawyers do all of the talking.

Defendants should consider whether they want to offer an apology during the opening statement. (This issue is discussed in detail in Chapter Five.) Apologies can establish a positive tone from the outset. In some cases, however, parties may decide to hold the apology in reserve, offering it as a concession if necessary later in the process. Well-delivered apologies have caused plaintiffs to lower their damage demands significantly. In other cases, insincere or incomplete apologies have inflamed plaintiffs and harmed the chances for settlement. Parties should discuss these ideas thoroughly as part of their preparation.

Clients should practice what they expect to say in the opening statements. After hearing a dress rehearsal, the lawyer should offer suggestions for improvement. Both parties should be clear on which matters the client will cover and which the client will leave for the lawyer. The opening statement is the only part of the process where the parties have complete control over what they will do. Once the ADR moves beyond that point, they will have to react to what happens as they go along.

Preparing the Client for Subsequent ADR Sessions

Inexperienced clients may expect their attorneys in ADR to be aggressive advocates on their behalf, arguing combatively against the other side. This expectation comes from watching lawyers on television and in the movies arguing forcefully in open court in front of a jury. Clients need to understand that the ADR process is different, and it calls for a different style on the part of attorneys. If lawyers attack their opponents personally during ADR, as they might in court, they are likely to damage the prospects of settlement. Clients should recognize that their lawyers are behaving more cooperatively because this is required by the process. If the case goes to trial, the lawyers will become more aggressive at that point.

For their part, clients are well advised to avoid overt aggression as well. Some clients may have a natural tendency to engage in venting, where they describe with great emotion all of the injustices they have experienced. Some believe this process will have a therapeutic value, allowing them to release their pent-up hostility and become psychologically ready to settle the case. However, many times, the opposite occurs: after expressing their anger, clients find they have become even more upset.

If a client believes venting is necessary, it usually should be confined to a private session with the neutral. When done in front of the other side, venting can be counterproductive. The other side generally responds with equal anger from its own perspective, and the parties end up driving themselves further apart. If venting in front of the other side is determined to be necessary, the lawyer should notify opposing counsel in advance that it will be coming. The opposing lawyer can tell the client what to expect, which may avoid escalating the conflict.

It also is usually best to instruct clients not to react openly to any settlement offers presented by the other side. Rather, clients should wait for a break to discuss the matter with their attorneys and formulate a joint plan of response. Otherwise, inexperienced clients may tip their hand when a more effective reply could have been developed by consulting with counsel.

Clients should be told that neutrals often challenge parties on their positions in an attempt to encourage them to settle. The process where neutrals examine parties' assessments of their likelihood of prevailing is called reality testing. Experienced parties know that the neutral will do this to both sides. Inexperienced parties, however, sometimes become concerned that pointed questioning by the neutral indicates the neutral is biased against them or does not understand their case. They may react defensively, becoming angry or revealing information they had planned to keep confidential. Parties should be told to expect reality testing and that they should treat it as a normal part of ADR.

Lawyers should tell their clients that the ADR process often includes long periods of waiting while the neutral is meeting privately with the other side. Parties can use some of this time productively to plan their strategy. Often, however, there will be significant stretches of waiting time where they must remain at the site of the ADR. Parties can be advised to bring reading material, a laptop computer, or a cell phone to use this time productively.

When clients are sophisticated and experienced with ADR, they may discuss other strategies. In these situations, lawyers and clients may wish to coordinate their presentations. For example, the client may be the primary speaker on the facts and the lawyer may take the lead on the legal issues. Another negotiation strategy is for one to be more aggressive and the other to be more conciliatory. They should discuss such ideas in advance to ensure they know what they will do once ADR begins.

Discussing the Case with the Neutral Before ADR Begins

A key difference between ADR and trial is that parties in ADR often have detailed discussions with the neutral in advance. Judges are generally restricted in this regard because they have large caseloads, limited time, and strict procedural rules they must follow. In contrast, the parties usually pay the neutral in ADR, and thus they are able to play a greater role in shaping the process. These conversations can be very helpful for both the parties and the neutral.

Parties should discuss with the neutral how they would like the process to operate. There is considerable flexibility in ADR, and parties should take advantage of this characteristic. Certain types of cases are easier to settle with certain types of ADR. For example, if parties work together well and believe the process should take place entirely in joint session, they should express this to the neutral. Neutrals generally want to please the parties who have hired them, so they are usually responsive to requests like this, particularly if all parties agree. Careful preparation and advance agreement on the format for the proceedings will save time and avoid confusion.

Parties also should use these preliminary discussions to learn more about the style and preferences of the neutral. Some neutrals are more receptive to certain types of presentations, and this may become clear during the conversation. It is advantageous for parties to understand how to present their case best. Information learned during pre-ADR discussions about the background and orientation of the neutral can be helpful once the process begins.

It also can be useful for parties to speak with the neutral privately. Such ex parte contacts would be prohibited in a trial setting, because they could influence the decision maker and deny the other side the opportunity to know what was said and to respond. Similarly, ex parte contacts can be improper in trial-like ADR processes, such as binding arbitration and early neutral evaluation. However, they are common in mediation. Indeed, much of mediation itself takes place in private caucuses with the neutral, so there is less concern with having private conversations beforehand.

Parties should exercise some care before having private conversations with the neutral. If the other side is inexperienced, they may not understand that this is appropriate procedure and be taken aback when they learn what has happened. Therefore, good practice is to notify an inexperienced party before contacting the neutral. It can be helpful to encourage that party to speak with the neutral as well, because such communication by both sides in advance usually makes the process run more smoothly.

During these conversations, parties should discuss the substance of the case and the personalities of the participants. Parties may begin by briefly highlighting key points from their pre-ADR statement. After that, they should give the neutral insight into why the case has not settled. This will assist the neutral in planning how to handle the ADR. For example, government counsel may believe the private lawyer is discouraging settlement in order to earn more attorney fees. A neutral who learns about this in advance can look for it during the ADR session and take steps to address it if it exists. As another example, a private lawyer may believe the government counsel is avoiding settlement in order to obtain trial experience. The neutral may be able to address this issue as well if told about it ahead of time.

Lawyers should tell the neutral about the personalities of the clients if this is relevant to the settlement. For example, lawyers with argumentative clients may want to alert neutrals of this beforehand, so they are not caught off guard. In some cases, lawyers may believe their clients would benefit from having an opportunity to vent and express emotional upset. Lawyers can suggest that neutrals encourage this during an early private session.

Chapter Five

| **Advocacy in Federal ADR**

Advocacy in ADR is very different from advocacy in other settings. Parties experienced with trial adjudication, for example, often have difficulty making the transition to advocating effectively in ADR. Accustomed to attacking their opponents in open court, they adopt a similar aggressive style in ADR. Rather than helping to settle the case, these approaches usually backfire: the party being attacked reacts by becoming defensive and even less likely to cooperate in a resolution.

Participants should recognize that their goal in ADR is to persuade rather than to defeat. Because both sides must agree to any settlement, they need to work together to ensure everyone is satisfied. It is more effective for parties to see themselves as working side by side to solve a common problem rather than as enemy combatants.

Nevertheless, the parties are involved in a dispute and by definition have adversarial interests. Although it is useful to take a collaborative approach, parties should not lose sight of the need to protect their individual interests.

This tension makes it vital for clients and their representatives to be purposeful in ADR. Many participants arrive at an ADR session and simply react to whatever happens. It is a mistake for parties to sit passively and let the process happen to them. Instead, they should remember that a result reached in ADR is just as final as a verdict delivered by a jury. Parties should be as careful and deliberate in their actions as they would be in a trial. Proper advocacy requires that parties develop a strategy to advance their interests in ADR and then implement it. In this chapter, "ADR" refers primarily to mediation, which is used most commonly in the government, but other processes will be identified by name when appropriate.[1]

Initial Considerations

In planning how to advocate in ADR, parties should begin by considering the special dynamics that are involved in cases with the government. When private parties are plaintiffs suing the government, for example, they sometimes feel as if they are single-handedly taking on a giant, faceless bureaucracy. The litigation process with the government can be depersonalizing and frustrating.

It is a good idea for government lawyers in ADR to be sensitive to these concerns. Indeed, ADR is a uniquely useful process in this regard, because it gives parties the opportunity to discuss their issues in a face-to-face forum. Some government lawyers have been effective by working to reduce the impression that the government is ganging up on the private party. This approach can reduce the defensiveness on the other side, which can increase the chances for settlement. Lawyers who represent the government often find that treating private parties with respect in ADR pays dividends in settling the case.

Private parties should pay attention to the special concerns of government parties. Although the government certainly can bring considerable resources to bear in large cases, most government matters are litigated by a single attorney. In the typical case, they are not facing the entire United States but only one lawyer, who may have a large docket of cases to manage, with only limited resources to help manage them. Supervision may also be modest. Many private parties would be less intimidated if they knew the actual situation on the government side.

Parties must decide where they will conduct ADR. Government parties often prefer to hold ADR in federal buildings. They are often conveniently located downtown and have conference space where the parties can meet. Parties know how to get there, the facilities are free, and they are often comfortable.

Government parties sometimes suggest meeting in a federal building for tactical reasons as well. These buildings, often large and solemn, can convey the impression that the power of the whole federal government is behind the case. However, this can backfire for the government if the setting causes the plaintiff to feel defensive and less willing to cooperate. For their part, private parties should remember that the government must prove its point in court just like any other party.

Private parties sometimes suggest meeting in their offices. The government may agree to this arrangement to make the private client feel more at ease in the process. Meeting in the clients' own offices also may make it easier for them to obtain documents and exhibits if questions about the case arise during the proceedings.

A compromise arrangement is to meet in the offices of the neutral. This is territory that belongs to neither side and thus is equally comfortable for both. However, some neutrals who are sole practitioners may not have conference space available. In this case, the parties may have to pay for the cost of rented outside facilities.

Seating arrangements can be relevant. The most common arrangement is for the neutral to be at the head of the table, with parties on either side. This creates the traditional image of two opposing parties with a neutral peacemaker in the middle. To counter the impression of opposition, a few neutrals sit on one side of the table and place parties next to each other on the other side. However, this arrangement can be awkward because the parties are facing across the table at the neutral and have to turn in order to talk to each other. Some neutrals have built special three-sided tables as yet another approach to this situation.

Where the parties sit at the table is another consideration. Many lawyers prefer to sit between their client and the neutral. This way they maintain more control over the interaction, because they are closer to the neutral, where most of the interaction takes place. Some neutrals like to talk to the parties directly and may prefer to have the lawyers take the seats farthest away at the table. Parties should decide whether they want the lawyer to take the lead role. If so, they should feel free to express their preference. Because the parties are paying the neutral (in most situations), the neutral will generally cooperate with this request.

Opening Statements

ADR usually begins with opening statements from each party (after the neutral has made introductory procedural remarks). Parties have the opportunity to script and rehearse exactly what they will say and how they will say it. They should make strategic decisions about the opening statement carefully, because it often sets the tone for everything that follows.

Most neutrals believe that the opening statement can be a valuable part of the process. It gives each side an opportunity to state its case in the presence of the neutral and the other side. This can be valuable psychologically to some clients, giving them their "day in court." It also gives the neutral a chance to observe the parties interacting with each other. This can provide valuable insight into the nature of the dispute.

A few neutrals choose not to have parties make opening statements. They note that parties often criticize each other and believe this can start the process in a hostile manner. These neutrals prefer to meet with the parties privately and bring them together only if things are proceeding smoothly.

Parties may have different preferences in certain types of cases. If the two sides have an especially poor relationship with each other, opening statements may be more damaging than helpful. Parties should discuss their desires with the neutral. Neutrals generally agree to follow the parties' wishes regarding opening statements, particularly if both sides agree.

By custom, plaintiffs usually make the first opening statements. This is generally a sensible approach, because they are the parties who initiated the claim. However, if there is a special reason that the defendants should begin, the parties should discuss this with the neutral in advance.

The Substance of the Opening Statement

Parties should present their case in the opening statement, setting forth the nature of their claim and the evidence supporting it. After the opening statement, the emphasis of the process can switch to a discussion of possible settlement options rather than the facts that gave rise to the dispute. Therefore, the opening statement is the best opportunity for parties to present the reasons that they should prevail if the case goes to trial.

Clients and lawyers should determine who will speak about what topics and in what order. Typically, the lawyer will talk first, providing an introduction and setting forth the nature of the claim. Then the lawyer will turn to the client to describe what happened from a personal perspective. The length of the client's comments will depend on the client's comfort with speaking and effectiveness. Clients who are poised and well spoken may deliver the bulk of the opening statement. Clients who are more reticent or not experienced with the process may prefer to leave most of the talking to the lawyer. When the client is finished, the lawyer may make closing remarks before turning the proceedings back over to the neutral.

Having clients participate in the process can bring important benefits. Plaintiffs who describe how they were harmed by the dispute can personalize the case and show how their damages are real. Defendants can sometimes present more persuasive accounts of their actions than their lawyers, who would have to speak about matters in which they did not participate. To be sure, clients should be well prepared by their attorneys before they participate in the opening statement. With preparation, clients can change the dynamics of the process by giving compelling personal statements.

It also can be valuable for clients to participate in the opening statement because they are ultimately the parties who must decide whether to settle the claim. When they participate in ADR directly, they are more likely to buy into the process and work to resolve the dispute. One of the virtues of ADR is that it allows both plaintiffs and defendants to take an active role in resolving their problems rather than having to turn over control to their representatives.[2]

Opening statements should include a description of the interests the party wants satisfied in any settlement. Rather than focusing on positional demands ("We will not settle for a penny less than $100,000!"), parties can be more effective by setting forth their underlying interests ("We need sufficient money to ensure that the plaintiff's medical needs will be met for the future"). This approach focuses the parties on the goals that both sides ultimately want to reach rather than the positions they take as part of an adversarial horse-trading process.

Parties also should describe what they will do if the case does not settle. In doing this, some parties feel a tension between expressing their interests assertively and establishing a cooperative atmosphere to encourage settlement. Parties want to show that they are confident of their likelihood of success at trial while also indicating they would prefer to settle if possible. One way of handling this situation is to preface comments about a future trial with a statement along the following lines: "In the interest of completeness, I also should describe what we would show at trial if we cannot reach agreement today. We would prefer to settle the case if possible, so that all parties can avoid the costs and aggravation of trial. However, if necessary, we are fully prepared to litigate, and we would argue the following. . . ."

Exhibits and visual aids can be powerful in opening statements. Providing a copy of the contract at issue in the case, for example, can be much more persuasive than just describing its terms. People pay more attention to things they see as well as hear. However, parties should not bring all the evidence they would use at a trial. ADR is an alternative to litigation, so the focus is more on settling the dispute than proving which side is liable.

Apologies

Some defendants have found it effective to offer an apology during the opening statement. The goal of this approach is to encourage resolution of the complaint rather than start a fight about who should win. A defendant who apologizes can disarm the plaintiff and allow productive settlement talks to begin. Sometimes this can ultimately advance the defendant's interests more effectively than assailing the plaintiff, which can escalate the conflict.[3]

Plaintiffs frequently assume that defendants do not appreciate fully the harm done to them. They may believe this lack of understanding is the reason the defendants' settlement offers are low. By acknowledging in a genuinely empathetic manner the harm suffered by plaintiffs, defendants may garner goodwill and at the same time defeat the assumption that their position did not contemplate the full degree of plaintiffs' damages.

Apologies should be carefully worded. If a party goes too far and admits wrongdoing, the other side may believe victory is at hand and raise its settlement demands. If a party does not go far enough, delivering only a perfunctory statement, the other side may be offended at its inadequacy.

A useful approach is to offer comments that express regret but do not concede liability in the case. When considering the entire dispute, parties may find there is something they genuinely wish had happened differently. For example, some government parties have made statements to plaintiffs such as the following: "Thanks for coming this morning. I know this is stressful. I can see how hard this has been for you and your family. No one should have to go through what you have in this case." When the government does not plan to contest liability in the case, apologies can be even stronger. Some plaintiffs have appreciated apologies greatly and even have reported that they were the first kind words anyone from the government said in the dispute.

Apologies are not appropriate in every situation. Sometimes plaintiffs are so upset that they will not believe an apology in any case. Skepticism is often highest at the beginning of ADR, when the parties are suspicious of each other. In these situations, it may be advisable to avoid apologizing until the later stages of the proceedings, if at all. Also, in some cases, the plaintiff will want an apology as part of the terms of the settlement of the case. If so, it may be advisable to wait and save the apology until later for tactical reasons.

The Tone of the Opening Statement

Tone is very important in an opening statement. A good approach is to be direct but not adversarial. Parties should establish from the beginning that they want their interests met in order to settle but that they will be cooperative if possible. An opening should show that the party is friendly but firm, collaborative but not a pushover.

Many inexperienced parties come on too strongly in the opening statement. For example, some government parties have started along the following lines: "This case is about a greedy plaintiff who is seeking millions of dollars for a nonexistent injury." Some private parties have then responded, "The government's opening statement shows how it continues to be heartless and cruel." These types of openings are more appropriate for a trial, where a judge or jury will make the final decision.

In ADR, these kinds of statements usually hurt far more than they help. Parties may feel that being aggressive in the opening will show the other side that they mean business. Certainly this is the model most often shown on television and in the movies. Sometimes it can be effective against a party who is easily intimidated. Usually, however, inflammatory opening statements result in alienating people on the other side rather than persuading them. It is important for parties to remember that they need the agreement of their opponents in order to resolve the dispute. Highly aggressive opening statements are likely to hurt more than they help.

It can be effective to focus attention on the opposing client when delivering an opening statement. Ultimately, this is the person who must be persuaded to agree to any settlement. In this sense, the opposing client is closer to the role of the judge than the neutral is. Parties commonly take the approach of directing their presentations to the neutral, but this can be less effective. Even if they persuade the neutral that their position is correct, this will not lead to settlement of the case unless the other client agrees.

Focusing on the opposing client also will assist parties in adopting an appropriate tone. Parties who argue to the neutral often use a more aggressive approach, as they would when arguing to a judge or jury. Aiming the opening to the client will remind the party of whom it has to persuade.

This approach should not be taken to an extreme, however. Parties should pay attention to the other participants in the ADR as well. Neutrals are accustomed to playing a central role in ADR proceedings, particularly at the beginning, and parties should respect this by directing attention to them during the opening statement. Opposing attorneys should be addressed as well because they may become concerned if parties talk directly to their client instead of to them.

If parties have aggressive arguments to make about the case, they may wish to direct this portion of their opening statement to the neutral rather than the other side. Doing so can help avoid escalating the tensions between the parties. Another option is to refer to contentious assertions only in broad outline and to say that they will be developed further in court if necessary.

Despite parties' best intentions, opening statements sometimes break down and become hostile shouting matches. Good neutrals will recognize when this is happening and will call for a break before the meeting gets out of hand. If the neutral does not do so, the parties should feel free to request a break themselves. It can be more difficult to restore a positive atmosphere once an ADR session has started off badly. A certain amount of conflict in the opening can be fine, and it can give the neutral a clue as to the dynamics between the parties. If things become too heated, it is sometimes best to move the parties into separate sessions.

Advocacy in Separate Sessions

After the opening statement, neutrals generally meet with each side individually in separate sessions. Because so much of ADR takes place in private sessions with the neutral, advocacy during this stage of the process is very important. Parties should remember that they, not the neutral, will control how they resolve their dispute. Nevertheless, neutrals can play an important role in the process, and it is worthwhile to discuss how parties can work with them most effectively.

General Considerations

A primary goal for parties in separate sessions is to ensure that the neutral understands their interests completely and will work to find ways to meet these interests. Good neutrals know that settling a dispute requires that all parties get their most important objectives met. No one will sign a settlement agreement otherwise. Parties therefore must educate the neutrals on what they want from a settlement.

Parties should discuss their interests fully with the neutral. The more the neutral understands all of the parties' settlement needs, the easier it will be to craft proposals to meet those needs. Parties also should indicate which interests are required, which are desirable, and which are optional. Some neutrals ask for rankings of parties' interests in this regard. Others ask parties to display their interests in a pie chart, sizing each piece to show the relative importance of that interest.[4]

Once parties have expressed their interests, they should work to generate options for settling the dispute. This stage of the process requires creativity, flexibility, and patience. Parties should work with the neutral to brainstorm as many creative options as possible to resolve the matter. They should remain open-minded about the process, because solutions to problems sometimes come from unexpected places. Patience is required; this process sometimes moves slowly and haltingly.

Parties should be open with neutrals about interests and options, but they should not feel they have to disclose everything about their case. Sometimes parties believe the more cooperative nature of ADR means that they should confess the weaknesses in their position. Parties may wish to do so, but it is by no means required. They should make a conscious strategic decision about what is most advantageous for their side. For example, if parties believe damaging information about their case inevitably will come out soon anyway, they may decide to disclose it to the other side during the opening session. This can establish a cooperative atmosphere and enhance their reputation as trustworthy. If parties are unsure whether their opponents will discover the negative evidence, they may decide to disclose it in confidence to the neutral and request the neutral's advice on how to handle the situation. Finally, if parties decide there is little to be gained by disclosing the information to anyone, they may decide not to raise it during ADR. Of course, they also should ensure they follow appropriate legal and ethical standards when making these decisions.

When the neutral is meeting with the other side, parties should use this time effectively. If the neutral has given them questions to think about, they should prepare answers to those questions. If not, they should anticipate what the neutral will ask them during their next meeting and determine how they will respond. It is useful to work to stay one step ahead of the process throughout.

Parties should consider confidentiality issues. Misunderstandings, which do occur on this point, have been distressing to the parties. Neutrals have two main ways of dealing with confidentiality in private caucuses. These two approaches are very different, and parties should be certain everyone understands which one is applicable. Under the first approach, neutrals treat everything said in private caucuses as confidential and will not reveal anything without first asking permission. Even under this approach, parties are well advised to avoid confusion by underscoring with the neutral the confidentiality of any information that is especially sensitive.

With the second approach, neutrals feel free to share anything said in private caucuses with the other side unless a party specifically asks for it to be kept confidential. Good neutrals using this method still make it a practice at the end of each private caucus to ask the parties if they would like anything they have discussed to remain confidential. If neutrals do not do this, parties should do so themselves, telling the neutral what they want to remain private.

Parties should remain vigilant on this issue. Over the course of a long ADR proceeding, people sometimes forget to concentrate on these matters, which can have negative results.

Using the Neutral Effectively

The presence of the neutral in the ADR process provides parties with strategic options that do not exist in traditional negotiation. Parties can take advantage of these opportunities in a number of ways.

For example, at the start of most private caucuses, the neutral will have just completed a private caucus with the other side. The first things the neutral says after entering the room often provide useful clues as to what was discussed in the session immediately before. For example, sometimes parties expect the neutral to address a specific point as soon as they return. If the neutral instead says nothing on this point, this silence may provide information about what was said in the private caucus with the other side.[5] It may indicate, for example, that the other side reacted negatively to a certain settlement proposal. Inferences like this are not always reliable, however, so they should be verified if possible. Nonetheless, they can be useful in determining what to do next.

Reactive Devaluation

Parties can use neutrals to convey settlement proposals in a way that helps avoid resistance from the other side. Researchers use the term *reactive devaluation* to describe how parties tend to devalue offers made by the other side.[6] This term describes the phenomenon that occurs when parties hear their opponents make an offer and react by devaluing it. For example, a plaintiff who comes to ADR willing to settle a case for $50,000 may no longer be willing to do so if the defendant offers that amount in the opening session. Instead, the plaintiff is likely to respond by asking for more.

This effect was shown in an experiment conducted by the Justice Department, where a group of attorneys all received the same written factual scenario and the same proposed settlement offer.[7] The group was divided into three subgroups, and each was told the offer came from a different source. The attorneys who were told that the settlement offer came from their opponents rated it as least acceptable, those who were told it came from their own expert rated it as most acceptable, and those who were told it came from the neutral rated it in the middle. This result shows that attorneys sometimes react more to the person making an offer than to the substance of the offer itself.

If the neutral presents an offer without disclosing its source, the other side is less likely to devalue it. They may believe the offer came from the neutral or may not even pay attention to its source as long as it is not identified as coming from an opposing party. There are several ways a neutral could do this. One approach is for the neutral simply to ask, "Would you be willing to take $50,000 if the other side were to agree?" Another is to say, "If you are willing to take $50,000, I believe I can get agreement from the other side." Neither of these statements discloses that the other side has already agreed to the offer, and thus they may make it seem more acceptable.

Reality Testing

It also is useful during private caucuses for parties to persuade the neutral that their side is more likely to prevail in court. Neutrals often engage in reality testing, where they challenge the validity of both sides' positions in private caucuses in an attempt to persuade them to settle. Parties should give the neutral as much information as possible so that reality testing done with the other side will be most effective. Neutrals do not know as much about the case as the parties do, so parties should ensure they educate the neutrals fully on the weaknesses of their opponents.

Parties may even decide to hold back some arguments during their opening statement and instead provide them during private sessions to the neutral to use with the other side. This idea builds on the concept of reactive devaluation. If parties make arguments to their opponents during the opening, the opponents are likely to discredit and devalue them. If the neutral makes the same arguments, they may be taken more seriously.

In some cases, attorneys may want the neutral to conduct reality testing with their own clients. When clients have an inflated view of the worth of their case, they sometimes instruct their attorneys to ask for an unreasonable amount in settlement. Part of attorneys' jobs in these cases is to let the clients know their demands are too high. However, clients sometimes resist this information when it comes from their own attorneys. This can be a form of reactive devaluation between individuals who are on the same side of the dispute. Neutrals can sometimes be effective in bringing clients back down to earth in these cases.

Asking the Neutral for Help

Parties should take advantage of neutrals' expertise in settling cases. When they do not know what to do, parties should feel free to ask neutrals for advice. Neutrals who have handled hundreds of ADR sessions often have ideas on how to proceed most effectively. They also have the advantage of hearing from both sides in private caucuses. Although neutrals will not directly reveal what the other side said in a private session, they will have this information in mind when they make a recommendation on what to do.

It also can be effective to ask the neutral to find out specific information from the other side. Opposing parties may be more willing to respond to a request for information from the neutral. To be sure, if the information is critical, they may ask the neutral to keep their responses in confidence. However, they may decide to discuss the matter with the neutral without requiring confidentiality, in which case the neutral can report back on what was learned.

Handling an Assertive Neutral

Some neutrals can be assertive with parties in private caucuses, and parties should understand how to respond to this. A first step is to listen to the neutral carefully. The neutral may have important information for the parties to know. For example, sometimes neutrals express things emphatically when they are unable to provide complete information due to confidentiality concerns. The other side may have told them something in confidence that affects the proceedings. The neutral will not be able to disclose this information directly but may endeavor to send the message in other ways.

After they have listened carefully to an assertive neutral, parties should feel free to push back if they wish. If they disagree with the neutral, they should say so and explain why. The neutral may just be testing the parties to see how they will respond. Parties should indicate to the neutral that they feel strongly about their case. Neutrals are human beings, and sometimes they will press a party harder if the party appears weaker. A neutral's job is to assist the parties in reaching resolution, and if settlement looks easier to obtain by pushing one party, some assertive neutrals will do so.

Some neutrals prefer to speak directly to clients, minimizing the role of the attorneys. In certain cases, neutrals have even asked to speak privately with clients, with the lawyers out of the room entirely. Parties should prepare for this situation and decide how they will respond. Sometimes working with the client directly is a useful approach; the client, after all, is ultimately the party that will make the decision on whether to settle the case. Neutrals can have good instincts about how to proceed in ADR, and it can be worthwhile to trust a neutral who believes that working with the parties alone will increase the likelihood of settling the case. This is a particularly viable option if the client is sophisticated and able to respond effectively to the neutral's questions. When clients are less experienced or less confident, however, they should feel free to decline such approaches, telling the neutral they want to have their lawyers present.

Parties should not feel that they have to answer every question that aggressive neutrals ask them. They may prefer to keep some information to themselves, even if neutrals promise not to disclose it to the other side. This can be tricky for lawyers who are participating in court-sponsored ADR, particularly if ADR is conducted by judicial officers. Lawyers may find it difficult to avoid answering questions from judges, especially judges before whom they appear regularly on other cases. This can be a reason to avoid ADR conducted by judges and instead hire private neutrals. With private neutrals, parties should feel free to resist answering questions when they do not want to do so.

Parties also should call for breaks whenever they want. If caucuses start to get heated and clients want to discuss matters with their attorneys, they should do so. Taking a break can give parties a better perspective on how to proceed.

The overall point to remember here is that the neutral works for the parties, not the other way around. Sometimes parties become intimidated and believe they must do whatever the neutral wants. In contrast, experienced parties work to take an active role in determining what happens to them in ADR.

Advocacy in Joint Sessions

When parties are in joint session with the other side, they should remember that they are not in a trial where their goal is to persuade a third party to decide in their favor. Rather, they are in a collaborative process where they must obtain the agreement of the other side before settlement will be possible. Tactics in joint session therefore must be designed to motivate the other side to settle the dispute voluntarily. This is generally best accomplished by appealing to their interests.

The most straightforward way to learn about the other side's interests is to listen carefully to what they say. One way to express this point is the motto of the American Bar Association's dispute resolution section: "When we listen, people talk." Rather than dominate the conversation in an attempt to overwhelm the other side, it is often better to let them talk and to pay careful attention to what they say. Litigators may find it useful to think of a joint session more like a deposition than a cross examination. The goal of a deposition is to get the other side to speak freely, in hopes that something said will be useful at trial. Similarly, encouraging the other side to talk in a joint session can result in learning information that will be useful for settlement.

Parties should listen specifically for the interests that are driving the other side's decision on whether to settle the dispute. By learning what the other side needs, a party can determine whether there are acceptable ways to meet these interests. Parties in ADR ultimately find that the best way to get their interests met is to meet those of the other side as well.

It is effective for parties to show that they understand the other side. When participants feel heard, they usually find it easier to hear their opponents. Sometimes they will not truly listen until they feel they have been heard. Parties may find it useful to explain their understanding of what the other side wants. They need not say they agree with these demands, only that they want to comprehend them fully.

If the other side is speaking in terms of positions, it may be worthwhile to ask questions to discover the interests that underlie those positions. For example, if a plaintiff sets forth a positional demand for $100,000 in order to settle a workplace discrimination dispute, the government party should ask why the plaintiff chose this number. If the plaintiff replies that is the amount necessary to show that the government takes the complaint seriously, this can provide helpful clues for how to settle the case. The government may be able to meet this underlying interest by showing it takes the case seriously in other ways. Various options could include apologizing, helping to locate a new job for the plaintiff, or providing racial sensitivity training to others in the workplace. All of these solutions may be satisfactory to the plaintiff while allowing the government to pay less money.

Parties also should use joint sessions to learn who the key decision maker is on the other side. Private parties may notice that one particular government representative seems to be calling the shots. If so, they should address their comments to this person. Similarly, the government can find out who is the leader on the other side: the client, the attorney, or perhaps the client's spouse. This information can be useful in determining how to approach settling the case.

Body language can provide useful clues as to the other side's interests in ADR. Parties may notice that their opponents lean in during certain discussions and appear to be paying close attention, behavior that may indicate these topics are of special interest. In contrast, the other side may recoil in reaction to other points or simply appear bored and uninterested. All of these reactions can supply insights into how to proceed with the negotiation.

In addition to learning about the other side's interests, parties should ensure that they fully express their own. Although it is often effective to start by understanding the other side in order to build trust, parties also should make sure that the other side understands them. If the other side does not know what a party wants in order to settle, they will not be able to work on ways to accommodate these interests. Thus, empathy must be balanced with assertiveness.[8]

Parties should explain thoroughly what they require in order to settle the case. It can be useful to set forth the priorities of the various interests. Parties can describe what they absolutely need, what they want, and what they would like if possible. Once all interests for both sides are on the table, the parties can begin to work on developing options to meet these interests.

Joint sessions sometimes become emotionally charged. Parties to a dispute can have sharply antagonistic feelings toward each other, which can become exacerbated when they spend long stretches of time in the same room together during ADR. If parties find that the meeting is getting too heated, they should request a break. If a break may not be sufficient, parties should tell the neutral that they would like to proceed in separate sessions.

Requesting separate sessions also can be effective for tactical reasons. Sometimes in joint sessions, parties respond to offers from the other side reflexively and negatively, and this reactive devaluation can harm the chances for settlement. Parties may wish to discuss offers privately with the neutral and then let the neutral present the offers without disclosing where they came from. Parties also may wish to go into separate sessions to discuss matters privately with the neutral.

Parties in federal administrative ADR should pay careful attention to confidentiality concerns in joint sessions. Under the Administrative Dispute Resolution Act (which does not apply to federal court ADR), statements that parties make in joint sessions with all other parties present are ordinarily not confidential (see also Chapter Eight). Thus, parties need to be aware that anything they say may be revealed to outside individuals. To address this situation, parties sometimes agree to provide for confidentiality of joint sessions by signing a contract. Even this approach, however, does not provide for total confidentiality. Outside parties still can file Freedom of Information Act requests for documents used in joint sessions and ask questions in discovery about what was said. Therefore, parties should be cautious about making admissions in joint sessions.

Breaking Impasse

Negotiations in ADR, like negotiations in general, sometimes get stuck. Parties become set on demands that are far apart and do not know how to proceed. There are a number of things to do in this situation.

The first step in an impasse is for the parties to return to an exploration of their interests. Frequently, parties who reach deadlock on positional demands are able to move forward by looking beneath the demands to the interests that underlie them. For example, when parties are unable to agree on how much money should be paid in a lawsuit, they can make progress by searching for non-monetary relief that will satisfy important interests of the plaintiff. Perhaps a plaintiff has an interest in feeling vindicated and will accept an apology from the defendant in exchange for lowering the damages demand. In other cases, the plaintiff may have an interest in receiving a certain amount of money each year (perhaps for medical care) and the defendant can agree to a structured settlement that will meet this need while reducing the total cost of the settlement in present value terms. Before giving up on ADR, parties should ensure they have thoroughly developed the interests on both sides.

Changing the structure of the ADR session is another approach. If parties have been meeting in separate caucuses, bringing everyone together in a joint session can be effective. The changed dynamics of a joint session may lead to new ideas. Conversely, if ADR has been proceeding in joint sessions, it can be worthwhile to split parties into separate caucuses to see if that inspires fresh lines of thinking.

Parties who do not know how to proceed should consider asking the neutral for advice. Neutrals are paid to facilitate settlement and usually welcome such questions. Experienced neutrals have seen many impasse situations and can provide useful ideas. Also, neutrals who have been leading ADR in private caucuses have the benefit of hearing both sides' perspective on the dispute. Although they will not be able to breach confidentiality, their knowledge of interests on both sides can allow them to come up with creative solutions that the parties might not be able to reach by themselves.

Another option is to take a lengthy recess. Often problems are easier to solve after time has passed. With a fresh perspective, parties may develop solutions to disputes that had seemed intractable. It can be worthwhile to stop an ADR session and reschedule another meeting in a week or even a month in these situations.

Changing the individuals who are participating in ADR is another technique for overcoming an impasse. Bringing new representatives to the bargaining table can introduce additional perspectives to the negotiation. Different attorneys or different client representatives may come up with ideas that the original participants missed.

Risk Analysis

Risk analysis (also discussed in Chapter Four) can be a useful tool for parties who are at an impasse.[9] In risk analysis (sometimes called decision tree analysis), parties evaluate the case by examining their chances of winning. For example, if the plaintiff has a 50 percent chance of prevailing in a lawsuit seeking $100,000, the expected value of the case before trial is half of $100,000, or $50,000. Under this analysis, the plaintiff should take any settlement offer of $50,000 or more.

More complicated analyses are also possible. For example, consider a defendant who has filed a motion that would dismiss the case if successful. If the defendant believes it has a 50 percent chance of winning the motion and a 50 percent chance of winning the trial (were the motion to fail), its overall chances of winning the case are 75 percent. If the damages at trial would be $100,000, the defendant should accept any offer to pay $25,000 or less (a 75 percent discount from the $100,000 total). Computers can easily calculate complicated examples.

Risk analyses that consider attorney fees can show parties how they would benefit from settling their case. Suppose that both parties agree that the chances of the plaintiff's winning at trial are roughly 50 percent. Risk analysis predicts that the plaintiff will win, on average, $50,000, and the government defendant will pay, on average, $50,000. Assume that the plaintiff would incur attorney fees of $10,000 in order to take the case all the way through trial. While government parties do not pay attorney fees as such, a trial does represent a cost to the government: an attorney who works on a trial is unable to work on other matters during that time. Also, the government must pay expenses such as deposition charges, travel costs, and expert witness fees. Assume that the total of these costs also would be $10,000. In this case, the expected recovery from the case for the plaintiff is only $40,000 ($50,000 minus its fees), and the expected cost of the case for the government is $60,000 ($50,000 plus its fees). When confronted with these numbers, parties should recognize that any settlement more than $40,000 but less than $60,000 will make both sides better off because they will avoid the costs of trial.

Even if the parties do not agree on their exact chances of winning a trial, risk analysis can still be useful. Many times parties are overly optimistic about their settlement position, and they find when they actually look at the numbers that their case is not as strong as they thought it was. Thus, even defendants who do not agree with plaintiffs' estimate of the chances of winning the case may still be persuaded to settle. They may find that risk analysis, even using their own numbers, shows that the plaintiffs' offer is more reasonable than they thought. Also, risk analysis sometimes can be useful in closing the gap between parties' demands, even if it does not completely eliminate the difference.

Evaluations and Proposals from the Neutral

If parties have tried these methods and still are unable to agree, they may wish to ask the neutral to provide an evaluation of the case.[10] Parties should remember they are free to instruct the neutral on the standards to be used in making the evaluation. Evaluations can provide additional information to the parties that helps them reach settlement in some situations.

Requesting an evaluation can be risky, however. If parties are dissatisfied with the evaluation the neutral provides, they may wish they had never requested it. Evaluations can profoundly change the parties' negotiation posture for the rest of the case. Parties who have evaluations come out against them can find their opponents' positions harden, leaving them with no chance of obtaining the settlements they originally desired. Even if the evaluation favors a party, this may be of relatively limited benefit. The other side may discredit the evaluation by claiming the neutral is biased or uninformed.

Furthermore, once neutrals deliver evaluations, their effectiveness for subsequent ADR sessions can be hampered. Parties may no longer perceive them as independent advisers. Rather, parties tend to look at them as stakeholders who want to see their evaluations upheld. If an evaluation favors one side, the other side often feels that the neutral is biased against them. For these reasons, it is best to request an evaluation only at the end of an ADR process, when an impasse appears inevitable without it.

Despite these disadvantages, there are occasions when an evaluation is useful. Parties may want to request one when the sole issue separating them is their assessment of what a judge would do with the case. In this situation, the opinion of the neutral can serve as a guideline as to how a court may rule. If the neutral's evaluation is between the parties' original estimates, they may be able to agree to compromise on this figure. Sometimes neutrals provide compelling reasons that persuade the parties to accept their evaluations.

Evaluations from neutrals who have expertise in the subject matter of the dispute and the respect of the parties are more effective. Parties give deference to an evaluation in direct proportion to how well they believe it is an accurate prediction of how a judge or jury would rule in the case. Some parties pick former judges when they expect they will want an evaluation, and others choose neutrals who have extensive professional experience in the issues involved in the case.

Another option is for parties to ask the neutral to create a proposal to settle the case. While an evaluation is simply an estimate of the dollar value of the case, a proposal is a comprehensive settlement plan that can include nonmonetary relief. Neutrals are often creative people, and they can develop ingenious settlement ideas that the parties would not have come up with on their own.

One technique that can work well is for neutrals to deliver the proposal to each side separately and to promise not to disclose how either side reacted unless both sides agree to the proposal. Parties are sometimes reluctant to agree to a neutral's proposal because they fear their bargaining position will be harmed if they agree and the other side does not. They may fear that the neutral's proposal will be considered their own new position, while the other side will not have made any concessions. This problem is avoided if the neutral agrees not to disclose either side's reaction unless both sides agree.

When considering both evaluations and proposals, parties should pay careful attention to how the neutral seems to be reacting to the case. If the neutral appears favorable to their side, parties should be more willing to request an evaluation or proposal. Otherwise, they should resist such suggestions by the other side.

Parties should ensure that the neutral fully understands their case before giving an evaluation or proposal. Before an evaluation, they should present all the arguments supporting their case to persuade the neutral of their likelihood of success at trial. Before a proposal, they should consider whether the neutral is likely to suggest a particular settlement provision that is unacceptable to them. If so, they should make this clear immediately, because once a neutral makes a proposal, it gains momentum. Therefore, parties should cut off objectionable ideas before the neutral formally suggests them.

Working with Government Parties in ADR

In order to work with the government effectively, private parties should understand how the government handles disputes. At most agencies, the general counsel's office takes the lead in resolving legal disputes. A lawyer from that office will represent the agency in administrative proceedings, consulting as necessary with officials in the component of the agency where the dispute arose to learn about the matter and determine how to handle it.

When a case is in litigation before a federal court, the Justice Department takes over representation of the United States. For most cases, a local assistant U.S. Attorney will have first-level responsibility for a matter. For certain types of disputes, including many civil rights, environment, tax, and antitrust matters, a lawyer from the Justice Department in Washington, D.C., will represent the government. These lawyers may work on a cocounsel basis with an assistant U.S. Attorney in the region where the litigation takes place.

When the Justice Department represents a federal agency in litigation, a lawyer from that agency usually participates. The Justice Department lawyer takes the lead but consults with the agency lawyer during the case. The agency lawyer may be responsible for answering discovery requests from the private party and may participate in ADR sessions.

Monetary awards in government cases generally come from the judgment fund, a government-wide pool of money created by Congress to pay for settlements and litigated judgments in civil cases. The Justice Department oversees this fund and has the authority to determine what payments are made from it. Agency lawyers may make recommendations as to the settlement amount, but the final decision usually rests with the Justice Department lawyer.

In some cases, monetary awards come from other sources. For example, when the government settles a contract case, money may initially come from the judgment fund, but the agency may ultimately be required to reimburse the fund from its own resources. Agencies are responsible for paying any awards against them in employment discrimination cases.[11] The U.S. Postal Service pays for settlements out of its own funds. In these matters, the lawyer representing the agency can have a greater influence in determining how much money will be paid in a settlement.

Agency lawyers also will play a critical role in determining nonmonetary relief that involves the agency directly. One example is employment discrimination suits. If the plaintiff seeks a transfer to another office, a promotion, or similar relief, the agency must agree to such a remedy. Similarly, in contract suits, the agency must approve nonmonetary relief, such as debarment from future contracts.

Sometimes private parties believe a case is not settling because the government attorney is unreasonably refusing to compromise, and they wish to talk to the attorney's supervisor. When deciding how to proceed in this regard, private parties can benefit from an understanding of the hierarchical structure of the government.

Generally, the lawyer who represents the government in ADR is the attorney with primary responsibility for the matter, and this lawyer will handle most of the day-to-day aspects of the dispute. This person (sometimes called a line lawyer) reports to an intermediate supervisor (called a deputy general counsel, assistant branch director, or similar title), who may supervise about a dozen attorneys. A section chief or branch director supervises several deputies. Management above this level is handled by political appointees at most agencies. A subcabinet official, appointed by the president and confirmed by the Senate, oversees an agency division, and a cabinet secretary runs the agency. Before settling cases administratively for more than a certain amount of money, even an agency secretary must obtain the approval of the Justice Department.

At the Justice Department, assistant U.S. Attorneys report to a civil chief, who supervises all civil litigation in each local office. The civil chief is supervised by the U.S. Attorney for that region, who is presidentially appointed and Senate confirmed. The U.S. Attorney controls most litigation in the local district but works with officials in Washington on certain matters. Assistant attorneys general in Washington have nationwide jurisdiction over certain litigation in the antitrust, civil, civil rights, environmental, and tax areas. These officials report to the associate attorney general (the number three official in the Justice Department), the deputy attorney general (the number two official), and ultimately the attorney general. On the most sensitive national matters, White House staff and the president may make final decisions.

Going over the head of the line government lawyer to any of these officials can be a risky endeavor. Line lawyers may not appreciate it when private parties challenge their positions with their supervisors. This practice questions their authority and the validity of their decisions. Line lawyers usually control most of what happens in the case, so alienating them can make future dealings more difficult.

Also, supervisors do not overrule line lawyers in most cases. They recognize that the line lawyers are handling matters on a day-to-day basis and know them best. Supervisors have to oversee a large number of cases and do not want to have to become intimately involved in them. They tend to support their lawyers and avoid second-guessing them whenever possible.

Nonetheless, in some situations, private parties may wish to discuss a matter with a higher-level official. Sometimes line lawyers are junior attorneys who appear to be making mistakes through inexperience. Other times, private parties may have a personality conflict with the government counsel that is interfering with productive communication. Some issues may be so important that private parties need to press the matter with a supervisor.

Before speaking with a higher-level official, it is usually good practice to mention this plan to the line lawyer. In this way, the line lawyer, who will most likely find out about the contact in any case, is less likely to feel blind-sided. Private parties can say that they believe they need to seek review from a supervisor, briefly explain the reason, and say they wanted to make sure the line lawyer knew about it in advance. These conversations should be handled delicately and respectfully. One disadvantage of this approach is that the line lawyers may then brief their supervisors ahead of time, which may make the private parties' appeals less effective. However, supervisors will almost always discuss matters with line lawyers before making a decision, so this risk is usually worth taking.

Private parties also must decide what official to contact. Generally the first-level supervisor is the best starting point. This person will have some knowledge of the case and will be in a position to change a line lawyer's position most readily. Higher-level officials have the authority to intervene, of course, but the further up the hierarchy they are, the less likely they are to want to interfere with a lower-level decision. Indeed, some private parties who write letters to the attorney general to complain about the actions of Justice Department line lawyers would be surprised to find out that their letters are often referred to the line lawyers themselves for response. The reply letters may be sent over higher-level officials' signatures but are often drafted by the line lawyers.

There can be different considerations in high-profile, politically charged matters. In these cases, political appointees in an agency are likely to care more about the issues and to become personally involved. They may already be playing a significant role behind the scenes and may be willing to talk with private parties. Even in these cases, it can be worthwhile to include the line lawyers, or at least notify them of the contact. Otherwise, they may resent the interference, and they will be playing a significant role in the future of the case.

In some matters, private parties have contacted their U.S. senator or representative. In most cases, this is no more effective than writing to the attorney general. The legislator will respond by writing a letter to the agency, and the line lawyer at the agency will write back that the agency does not comment on active cases. Only in the most important matters would a legislator personally contact an official at an agency, and even then the legislative branch of the government has limited authority over the day-to-day operations of the executive branch. Ultimately, Congress can hold oversight hearings and affect an agency's budget, but such considerations are unlikely to come into play in the vast majority of cases.

Negotiation Tactics in ADR

Because ADR is a negotiation process, many tactical considerations are similar to those involved in general, unassisted negotiation. This section discusses these ideas and notes some special factors that come into play when the government participates in ADR.

Opening Offers

An initial question for both government and private parties in ADR is whether they should make the first settlement offer or wait for the other side to do so. Some parties believe that the plaintiff should make the opening offer, because the plaintiff is the party who filed the claim. Sometimes the plaintiff will respond that it effectively made an initial offer in the written complaint that started the dispute and that it is up to the defendant to reply to that offer. Some private parties argue that the government should open first because of its unique nature as a public party. If negotiation efforts have preceded ADR, this may affect which party makes the opening offer once ADR begins.

There are advantages and disadvantages to making the first offer. Parties who open first can set the tone for the negotiation. The initial offer can affect everything that follows through a phenomenon called *anchoring*.[12] Parties tend to anchor their expectations on the first number presented in ADR, giving it inordinate weight in further negotiations. Opening first allows a party to set the initial anchor.

Presenting an offer after hearing the other side's opening, however, allows a party to gain information before having to disclose its position. This avoids the risk of opening too high, which may offend the other side, or too low, which may concede more than was necessary. In some cases, the other side may open with a more favorable number than anticipated, which can allow a party to adjust its response accordingly. Opening second also allows a party to choose a response that establishes an advantageous midpoint between the two offers. Parties in negotiation have a tendency to split the difference between each side's opening figures.

Another factor in this decision is the relative experience of the parties. ADR participants who have dealt frequently with similar cases are less likely to be affected by anchoring, because they already have a sense of what the case is worth. Conversely, parties with limited experience are more likely to place undeserved weight on an opening offer by a party perceived to have more expertise.

The government often has an advantage in this regard. Because the government has so many cases, its attorneys are usually specialized in narrow areas. It is not unusual for an entire group of lawyers to work on enforcing a single statute, for example. These lawyers will have detailed knowledge of how similar cases have been settled and what judges and juries have decided in comparable trials. In a typical case, private parties will not have such background.

Fortunately, most government attorneys recognize they have a duty to treat private parties fairly because they are public servants. With the privilege of representing the government comes the responsibility to do so justly. However, different government lawyers place different emphasis on this. Some believe their duty to represent the government zealously means they should seek results that, while fundamentally fair, are more advantageous to the government.

Therefore, private parties should proceed carefully and not assume that every government attorney will act the same way.

The amount to offer is another consideration. Research shows that higher opening offers generally result in more money for plaintiffs at the end of ADR.[13] Conversely, defendants who open with lower amounts usually end up paying less. This phenomenon is related to anchoring; parties' opening offers set expectations for both sides at the beginning of ADR. However, if parties open so high (or low) as to lose credibility, they can harm their negotiating position when they inevitably have to make a major concession.

Parties also should pay attention to legitimate criteria for their opening offers. When they support their offers with objective standards, they tend to do better in negotiation. Such criteria include out-of-pocket expenses, verifiable future expected costs, and prior court awards for similar cases. Appealing to independent standards adds legitimacy to parties' claims. This approach is particularly appropriate in government cases, where negotiation optimally will be a search for a fair result, not a battle to see which side will dominate.

The Middle Phase of Negotiations

After both sides make their opening offers, the next tactical decisions involve how to move to a mutually acceptable settlement. This process is often something of a dance as both sides make concessions and their positions approach each other. The pattern of these concessions can involve important strategic decisions.

Some government attorneys prefer not to engage in a series of concessions at all. They believe that as representatives of the government, they should make a single, fair settlement offer and not negotiate after that. These lawyers believe there is no place for horse trading in government negotiation.

When private parties face government parties who follow this philosophy, their best option may be to work to argue that the government representatives made an incorrect evaluation of the case at the outset and should adjust it accordingly. In order for this approach to work, they may need to provide new evidence or arguments that the government did not consider when making its initial offer.

Most government parties engage in some give-and-take in negotiation because making just a single offer can be a poor negotiating strategy. Parties enter ADR with the expectation that both sides will be willing to cooperate with each other and compromise in order to reach a settlement. If the government refuses to budge, it is often perceived as not participating in the process in good faith. The dynamics of the ADR process can make it difficult to refuse to compromise at least a little. Furthermore, many parties do not believe the government when it says it cannot move. Therefore, a government party that picks an opening offer and allows no room for compromise may have great difficulty getting the other side to agree to it.

One tactical issue that parties should consider is the message they send with the pattern of their concessions. For example, consider a party that wishes to reach an agreement in ADR where it will pay $100,000 to settle a dispute. If the party opens with $50,000 and then offers $90,000 as its next move, the other side is likely to see this $40,000 jump as a signal that the party has considerably more money to offer in negotiation. If the party then presents $100,000 as its bottom line, the other side may not believe it and may push for more money.

In contrast, imagine that the party opens with $40,000 and offers $60,000 as its next move. Its next offer is $70,000, followed by $75,000. Note that each of these concessions is half as large as the one before it. This sends a signal that the party is running out of room and will not offer much more. If the next offer is $77,500, for example, the party will send the signal that its final offer will be around $80,000. With this approach, if the party ultimately agrees to pay $100,000, the other side is more likely to settle and may even feel it "won" the negotiation.[14]

This is an example of the general rule in negotiation that parties should make concessions slowly and sparingly.[15] Parties tend to devalue concessions that the other side makes quickly, thinking they must not be worth much because they were made so easily. The party that makes the first major concession may find itself at a disadvantage.

Bottom Lines in Negotiation

During ADR, discussion sometimes turns to the delicate topic of parties' bottom lines, meaning the final offers beyond which they will not move. Parties should be careful how they proceed in this area. Because this issue is complicated, many neutrals will not ask parties for their bottom lines until late in ADR, if at all. Some neutrals report that they never ask for bottom lines because they do not believe what parties tell them in any case. Neutrals also can face an awkward situation if they learn confidentially that there is room to settle between the two parties' bottom lines, as it is unclear what settlement amount is appropriate in this case.

If neutrals do ask for a bottom line, this can put the parties in a difficult position. They may not want to seem uncooperative by refusing to answer the neutrals' question. However, if they do reveal a bottom line, even in confidence, neutrals may end up pressuring them toward this number. In order to settle the case, neutrals have a tendency to push the party whose bottom line is more flexible than the other side's.

Another problem with giving a bottom line is that parties' evaluation of their settlement posture may change during the process. Parties often learn more about the case during ADR. If they commit to a bottom-line figure before they have complete information, they may put themselves at a disadvantage. If they have to change their bottom line, they may lose credibility. If they refuse to do so, they are stuck with the number they chose prematurely.

Therefore, it is often advisable not to answer questions about bottom lines directly, particularly early in an ADR session. Parties can reply that they have not settled on a definitive bottom line, pending further developments in ADR. Or they can be even more direct and respond that they do not believe disclosing their bottom line is tactically wise at this point. If they do want to give an answer, they may decide to leave themselves room to move by providing a figure with a caveat, such as, "This is the number we are looking at right now."

Parties should still consider what they will require to settle the case, however. As discussed in Chapter Four on preparation, parties should approximate their best alternative to a negotiated agreement before ADR begins and then reassess their alternatives throughout the ADR process. The thing to avoid is locking into a specific bottom line and revealing it to the neutral (or the other party) early in ADR.

At the final stages of ADR, it may become necessary for parties to disclose some information about their bottom line in order to know whether the negotiation process is worth continuing. If ADR looks as if it is about to break down, parties may wish to discuss their bottom line privately with the neutral to determine if the neutral sees a way to resolve the case. Such discussions should be conducted carefully. If a party does not exercise caution, it may find that the other side takes its bottom line as just another offer from which it is expected to negotiate in the future.

Because of the dynamics of the negotiation process, participants (and neutrals) often consider what a party refers to as its "bottom line" really to be its "almost-bottom line." Most people expect that there will be a little more movement at the very end, especially if the parties are reasonably close to an agreement. For example, if one side reveals its bottom line as $50,000 and the other side says $55,000, there will be strong pressure on both sides to settle for $52,500. If a party picked $50,000 as an absolute, walkaway number, it might find itself in an awkward position at this point. Therefore, parties may wish to leave a little room to move when discussing bottom lines.

One approach to this situation is for parties to discuss with the neutral their "public" bottom line and their "private" bottom line. The neutral is authorized to disclose the public figure to the other side, and this figure is chosen to leave a little breathing room if necessary. At the same time, the neutral also knows the party's true, private bottom line, which can be useful to determine whether settlement will eventually be possible.

Advocacy at the End of ADR

After parties have participated in ADR for a period of time, they generally will be able to recognize if settlement is possible. If it is not, they should leave open the possibility of future sessions. Many cases that initially appeared impossible to settle eventually do get resolved. Parties may even wish to set a specific time to resume ADR.

If the parties do reach agreement, they usually should formalize it in some fashion right away. If they wait until they return to their office the following day, they may find that the deal falls apart. The phenomenon of settlers' remorse can set in as parties back out of a deal to which they had previously agreed. Some parties wish to allow for this possibility and purposely provide for a one-day cooling-off period before signing the agreement. They believe that any agreement the parties do not still want after twenty-four hours is not a good one. However, when most parties reach a settlement, they want to resolve the case and move on. In this case, they should consider putting something in writing before they leave.

The simplest form of settlement in ADR is an agreement in principle. This approach involves drafting a document that includes a broad outline of the main features of the agreement. Parties may wish to bring a laptop computer to aid with this drafting. They can bring possible provisions with them on the computer and use them to draft others during the ADR process as well as to print out the final document. Both parties should sign the agreement in principle before leaving the ADR session. They can expand it into a final settlement agreement later.

Settlement provisions in some government cases must follow special rules. For example, attorney fee awards in tort claims are capped at 20 percent of the amount of an administrative settlement and 25 percent of a federal court settlement.[16] Some settlements in workplace cases, such as those that involve reemployment benefits, may need to be provided to appropriate union representatives for review. Other workplace provisions should be discussed with the Office of Personnel Management to ensure they are valid. In contracting matters, parties will need to ensure they have followed relevant provisions in the Federal Acquisition Regulation. (Chapter Six on workplace and Chapter Seven on contracting ADR discuss these issues in more depth.)

Parties also should include provisions on how to resolve any future disputes under the agreement. Such provisions often call for the use of ADR. They may require that a party claiming a breach of the agreement must use ADR in an attempt to resolve the dispute before going to court. This type of provision should describe what ADR process will be used, how the neutral will be hired, and how the cost will be paid. Parties often agree to retain the neutral who negotiated the original agreement to resolve any disputes that arise under it in the future.

Parties often find it to be a tactical advantage to volunteer to draft the final agreement themselves. This involves additional work, but it can be worthwhile. The party that drafts the actual settlement contract has initial control over the terms it includes. The other side can certainly object to language it does not like, but this is often more difficult than writing the language in the desired way in the first place. One disadvantage of being the drafter, however, is that courts traditionally interpret ambiguous language against the party that drafted the agreement.

Once both sides have signed the settlement agreement, it becomes enforceable as a contract. If one party fails to follow the agreement, the other side can file a court action for breach of contract. If a case has been filed in federal court, the parties can submit their settlement agreement to the judge for entry as a consent order. In this case, the judge will review the terms of the settlement to ensure they are proper. Judges generally give some degree of deference to agreements negotiated by the government. Once the judge signs the agreement, it becomes an order of the court. In this case, a party that claims the other side has breached the agreement may be able to obtain relief more quickly and may have more enforcement options available.

Chapter Six

ADR in Federal Workplace Cases

In the federal government, parties use ADR more in workplace cases than in any other type of dispute. There are more than 2.5 million federal civilian employees in the United States, making the government by far the largest employer in the country. In a workforce of this size, it is inevitable that many complaints will arise. People are increasingly turning to ADR to resolve these complaints.

ADR is uniquely appropriate for workplace cases because they involve personal relationships. Unlike simple commercial disputes where the parties may meet only once and never see each other again, workplace conflict by its nature involves people who work together, sometimes every day. Because of this, traditional litigation can be especially damaging to the parties in these cases. The adversarial process requires people who need to work together to fight with each other instead. Processing a dispute, which can take months or even years, can be extremely corrosive to the productivity of an office and the morale of its employees.

ADR can help rebuild relationships rather than destroy them. The ADR process requires the parties to work with each other to search for a solution to their common problems. This fosters cooperation between parties rather than locking them in a battle that drives them further apart. ADR does not work in every case, but it offers a far greater chance of preserving a workplace relationship than does litigation.

The federal government uses ADR in a broad range of workplace matters, including statutory claims, administrative grievances, negotiated grievances, and other types of disputes.

ADR Programs in Equal Employment Opportunity Cases

The most common type of workplace claim in the federal government concerns equal employment opportunity. In 2001, federal employees contacted an EEO counselor or ADR intake officer almost
fifty thousand times.[1] The parties used ADR in almost one-third of
these matters—about fifteen thousand times.[2] Federal trial courts
also handle huge numbers of workplace discrimination claims. In
2001, more than twenty thousand employment civil rights suits,
public and private, were filed in federal district courts around the
country.[3] This is almost 10 percent of the entire federal court civil
caseload.[4]

Value of ADR in EEO Disputes

ADR has been highly effective in EEO disputes. When parties used
ADR at the informal administrative stage (prior to the filing of a
formal administrative complaint), they settled the matter more
than half the time (56.1 percent).[5] At the formal administrative
stage, ADR resulted in settlement or withdrawal of the complaint
almost two-thirds of the time (64.3 percent).[6] When a matter leaves
the administrative process and gets to federal court, ADR leads to
a settlement more than half the time it is used.[7]

ADR in this area has been growing, and one of the reasons is
that the EEO caseload has increased dramatically. From 1991 to
1999, federal EEO complaints rose by more than 50 percent.[8] The
number of hearings the Equal Employment Opportunity Commission (EEOC) was asked to hold more than doubled during this
time.[9] The number of appeals requested grew by about two-thirds.[10]

The General Accounting Office attributes the rise in the number
of EEO complaints to four main factors.[11] First, the federal government has been downsizing, resulting in job losses and reassignments,
and workers have protested these changes. Second, the Civil Rights
Act of 1991 increased the monetary recovery possible in these
claims.[12] Third, the Americans with Disability Act has resulted in additional EEO claims as the public has become more aware of its existence.[13] Finally, new regulations issued in 1992 improved access to
the EEO complaint process.[14]

It can be valuable for employees to exercise their statutory EEO
rights and bring conflict out into the open, but these burgeoning

caseloads have created delays in processing claims. The average administrative EEO case takes three and a half years to process at the agency level.[15] The average federal civil trial process takes almost two years on top of that.[16] Not surprisingly, over roughly the past decade, agency EEO case backlogs have doubled, EEOC hearing backlogs have tripled, and EEOC appeal backlogs have increased by almost seven times.[17]

ADR can be extremely effective in reducing these delays. At the U.S. Air Force, for example, extensive use of ADR has allowed the agency to process its EEO complaints in an average of less than nine months, well under the government average.[18] In the U.S. Postal Service, the average mediation takes only four hours, and it settles the case more than 80 percent of the times it is used.[19] At the Justice Department, attorneys estimate that ADR saves an average of more than one hundred hours of staff time and five months of litigation delays in each federal court case where it is used.[20]

Adjudication of workplace disputes also can be expensive. Processing a simple workplace case costs the government a minimum of $5,000 in administrative expenses alone, and a more complicated case that the agency formally adjudicates can cost up to $77,000.[21] ADR is almost always much less expensive. At the Justice Department, for example, the average amount the government pays for a mediator in an employment case is only $1,007.[22] Justice Department attorneys estimate that this expenditure saves the government an average of more than $17,000 in litigation costs in each case.[23] The air force estimates that it achieves cost savings of $14,000 and labor hour savings of 276 hours per case resolved.[24]

The total cost of adjudicating a workplace dispute is much higher than these numbers indicate. A complete accounting would have to include indirect costs such as the salaries, benefits, and overhead costs of all the counselors, investigators, and lawyers who work on processing these cases. The emotional fallout from these complaints often extends beyond the parties themselves and affects others in the workplace, reducing morale and productivity. If the affected employees leave a job as a result of the dispute, the government loses experienced employees and incurs costs to locate and train replacements.

EEO complainants face considerable costs as well. They must pay their attorney fees. Most complainants find litigation stressful and emotionally upsetting. It can damage relationships that are important to them. They also face considerable costs to locate a new job if they decide to leave the government.

Studies have shown that ADR is more effective in increasing party satisfaction with the way their dispute is processed, which can help reduce the emotional costs of these complaints. At the Postal Service, participants in ADR reported they were satisfied with the process close to 90 percent of the time, compared with satisfaction rates of less than 50 percent with adjudication.[25] A study of the EEOC's private sector ADR program reports that ADR participants said they would be willing to use the process again more than 90 percent of the time.[26]

ADR can be particularly helpful in these cases because many times they are not about discrimination at all. Both the EEOC and the General Accounting Office have determined that many of these claims are unrelated to discrimination, but the only way employees can get their complaints heard is to enter the EEO process.[27] Indeed, agencies found discrimination in only 1.4 percent of claims filed, and EEOC administrative judges found it only 9 percent of the time.[28] ADR can assist parties in resolving complaints regardless of whether they involve discrimination. Some agencies have expanded their ADR programs to include non-EEO complaints as well, because it can be valuable to resolve workplace conflict no matter what its source.

A final indicator of the success of ADR in handling workplace conflict is the finding that fewer new complaints arise once an ADR program is implemented. The year after the Postal Service instituted its ADR program, for example, complaints dropped by 24 percent.[29] The following year, complaints dropped by another 20 percent.[30] The air force experienced similar drops in its workplace complaints once it began using ADR.[31] Agencies believe these drops are caused by the increased communication that ADR provides. When employees and employers talk with each other about conflicts in the workplace, they begin to understand each other better. With this improved understanding, they are able to avoid problems in the future.

The Federal EEO Process

To understand the role ADR can play in these cases, it is worthwhile to review the federal EEO process. Federal employees are protected from discrimination on the basis of race, color, religion, sex, national origin, age, or disability.[32] Individuals who believe they have been discriminated against must contact an EEO counselor at their agency within forty-five days of the alleged discriminatory incident.[33] An individual who is subject to a collective bargaining agreement that permits grieving discrimination claims may choose between the EEOC procedure and the negotiated grievance procedure but cannot pursue both.[34] This part of the process, called the counseling, precomplaint, or informal stage, is designed to see if the agency and the aggrieved person can resolve the matter without moving on to a formal complaint.

In the traditional counseling process, counselors begin by explaining the aggrieved persons' rights and responsibilities.[35] Counselors then conduct limited inquiries into the matters and determine whether they may be resolved informally. Unless the aggrieved parties waive confidentiality, counselors preserve their anonymity during this stage. Counselors may interview witnesses and review records. At an appropriate point, counselors meet with agency officials and summarize the allegations of discrimination. Counselors will attempt to reach resolutions of the matters acceptable to all sides if possible. The counseling process is limited to thirty days,[36] but aggrieved persons can agree to extensions of time for up to an additional sixty days.[37] If no agreements are reached within this time frame, counselors must hold final interviews with the aggrieved parties and describe the procedures for filing a formal complaint.[38]

If an aggrieved person decides to file a formal complaint, the individual is then termed a complainant, and the formal stage of the process begins. In some cases, the agency may dismiss the formal complaint, such as when it fails to meet applicable time limits or fails to state a claim for which relief can be granted.[39] If the agency does not dismiss the complaint, it must complete an investigation within 180 days.[40] Investigations may include letters, interrogatories, factfinding conferences, and other techniques.[41]

At the end of the investigation, the agency must provide the investigative file to the complainant, who then has thirty days to withdraw the complaint, request a final decision from the agency, or request a hearing with the EEOC.[42] If the complainant withdraws the claim, the case ends. If the complainant elects a final agency decision, the agency has sixty days to issue one.[43] If the complainant elects an EEOC decision, an EEOC administrative judge will hear the case[44] and issue a decision.[45] Under any of these procedures, a complainant may appeal a denial of the claim first to the EEOC's Office of Federal Operations,[46] then to the full EEOC,[47] and then to federal court.[48] An agency, however, may appeal only to the EEOC and may not take the case to federal court.[49]

Federal EEO ADR Programs

Pursuant to law, regulation, and policy, ADR is an integral part of the federal EEO process. The Civil Rights Act of 1991 explicitly promotes ADR use: "Where appropriate and to the extent authorized by law, the use of alternative means of dispute resolution, including settlement negotiations, conciliation, facilitation, mediation, fact finding, minitrials, and arbitration, is encouraged to resolve disputes arising under the Acts or provisions of Federal law amended by this title."[50]

EEOC regulations mandate that federal agencies work to settle complaints whenever possible, and they encourage the use of ADR:

> Agencies are encouraged to incorporate alternative dispute resolution techniques into their investigative efforts in order to promote early resolution of complaints. . . .
>
> Each agency shall make reasonable efforts to voluntarily settle complaints of discrimination as early as possible in, and throughout, the administrative processing of complaints, including the pre-complaint stage.[51]

The EEOC sets forth the extensive benefits ADR provides in these cases:

> Agencies and complainants have realized many advantages from utilizing ADR. ADR offers the parties the opportunity for an early, informal resolution of disputes in a mutually satisfactory fashion. ADR usually costs less and uses fewer resources than do traditional administrative or adjudicative processes, particularly processes that include a hearing or litigation. Early resolution of disputes through ADR can make agency resources available for mission-related programs and activities. The agency can avoid costs such as court reporters and expert witnesses. In addition, employee morale can be enhanced when agency management is viewed as open-minded and cooperative in seeking to resolve disputes through ADR.[52]

Pursuant to EEOC regulations, agencies must offer ADR programs at both the informal and formal stages of the EEO process.[53] However, they do not need to agree to ADR in every dispute and may determine whether ADR is appropriate on a case-by-case basis.[54] If the agency is willing to use ADR during the precomplaint stage of a particular case, the counselor must explain this to the aggrieved person and offer a choice between ADR and the traditional counseling process.[55] If the agency agrees to ADR at this stage, the precomplaint time period is extended to ninety days.[56] If no settlement is reached, the traditional processes come back into effect, and the counselor must hold a final interview with the aggrieved person to describe the procedures for filing a formal complaint. Similarly, at the formal stage, if no agreement is reached, the case proceeds as if ADR had never been used.

Core Principles for ADR Programs

EEOC guidelines set forth a number of core principles for agency ADR programs in this area.[57] First, ADR programs must be fair.[58] Thus, parties must be provided as much information about the process as possible and as soon as possible.[59] Parties have the right to be represented throughout the ADR proceeding.[60] If they are not represented, they have the opportunity to obtain legal or technical assistance during the proceeding.[61]

Voluntariness is another vital component of the process.[62] Parties have a voluntary choice whether they wish to participate in ADR.[63] They also retain freedom to decide whether to settle a case, and they must not face coercion, including from the neutral.[64] Voluntariness is required because parties might otherwise be dissatisfied with the result of the ADR process or even charge that the resolution was reached under duress.[65] Aggrieved persons are free to end the ADR process at any time.[66] Agency managers, however, have a duty to cooperate in ADR once their agency has determined that ADR is appropriate in a given case.[67] This is because the agency, not the management officials, is considered to be the party and the agency's participation is considered voluntary because it retains the initial flexibility in whether to accept a case for ADR.[68]

ADR proceedings must be neutral to be effective. Both perception and reality are important in this regard. Thus, agencies are urged to use neutrals from outside the organization for these cases whenever possible, to ensure the parties perceive them as truly neutral.[69] An agency that uses an employee from inside the organization must ensure that the person is neutral and impartial.[70] An agency that uses an EEO counselor as a neutral must ensure that the counselor serves only as a neutral and does not handle any other counseling functions on that particular case.[71]

Next, ADR must provide for confidentiality.[72] ADR is most effective when parties can speak freely with each other, and they are more likely to do this when they know what they say will remain private.[73] The Administrative Dispute Resolution Act provides for confidentiality in federal ADR proceedings.[74] As a general matter, what the parties tell neutrals in private remains private, but discussions with all parties together in the same room are not confidential.[75] Parties may agree by contract to a higher degree of confidentiality. (These issues are discussed in greater detail in Chapter Eight.)

Enforceability is another key part of an ADR process. EEOC regulations provide that "any settlement agreement knowingly and voluntarily agreed to by the parties, reached at any stage of the complaint process, shall be binding on both parties."[76] A complainant who believes the agency is not complying with the agreement can notify the agency's EEO director.[77] At this point, the agency must respond in writing and resolve the matter.[78] A complainant who is not satisfied with the agency's response can appeal to the EEOC, which may conduct an additional investigation.[79] If the EEOC determines the agency has not followed the agreement, it may order the agency to comply.[80]

Agency ADR programs also must be flexible.[81] Workplace complaints involve a variety of situations, and different approaches may be valuable in different cases. Agencies are urged to adapt their programs to changing circumstances that may not have been anticipated when the programs were designed.[82]

Finally, an ADR program must include appropriate training and education for agency employees and managers, as well as evaluation to determine its effectiveness. Training is required so that participants will know that ADR is available and how they can best use it. Evaluation will help an agency fine-tune its program based on feedback from participants.

EEOC Mediation Program

The EEOC has its own ADR program and offers mediation in cases it handles (both public and private). The EEOC will not use mediation where there is a need to establish policies or precedents in a case, resolution of the dispute would have a significant effect on nonparties, a full public record is important, or the agency must maintain continuing jurisdiction over the matter.[83] Nor will it mediate cases that it determines to be without merit.[84]

Once the EEOC approves a case for mediation, it offers the process to both sides.[85] If either declines, the case proceeds in the traditional fashion. If both agree, mediation proceeds. Either side may bring an attorney if desired.[86] Both sides must come with authority to settle the dispute.[87] The EEOC uses both internal staff mediators and external mediators, and all are trained in EEO law.[88]

All mediation sessions are free, and most take only one to five hours.[89] The sessions are not tape-recorded or transcribed.[90] Mediator notes and documents that the parties present during the process are destroyed when the process is complete.[91] The mediation program is insulated from the investigative and litigation branches of the agency to ensure confidentiality.[92] If the case is not settled, it goes forward as if mediation had never occurred.[93] If the case does settle, the agreement does not constitute an admission by the employer of violating the law.[94]

Using ADR to Settle Federal EEO Cases

EEO cases in the federal government have specialized features that affect the way parties should use ADR.

Selection of the ADR Process

The most common type of ADR used in federal EEO matters is mediation.[95] In the precomplaint phase, mediation was used in 96 percent of ADR matters; no other process was used in more than 2 percent.[96] The high use of mediation is appropriate because it is particularly suited for these cases, where the underlying issues often involve poor communication and the parties often wish to preserve their working relationship. (The advantages and disadvantages of various ADR processes are discussed in detail in Chapter Two.)[97] ADR techniques with a more adjudicatory nature, such as arbitration or early neutral evaluation, are less useful because those processes require the parties to argue against each other as they attempt to persuade the neutral of the strength of their positions and the weakness of their opponents' positions. Thus, they do not have as beneficial an effect on the relationship of the parties and often fail to address the underlying issues that are important to the complainant.

After a complaint has been filed, mediation is used in 74 percent of ADR matters, while settlement conferences increase in prominence, taking place 16 percent of the time.[98] At this stage of the process, mediation is still predominant, as relationships continue to be important. Cases become more serious once a formal complaint has been filed, however, and the parties sometimes wish a neutral party to act in the mode of a judge.

There are different styles of mediation available, and some tend to work better with EEO complaints than others. Parties in these cases often respond better to a facilitative approach rather than a directive one; that is, mediators assist parties with the process but do not directly tell them what to do. If a mediator directs the parties too forcefully, they may stop cooperating with the process. Similarly, if a mediator gives an evaluation of the worth of the case, a party who does not like the evaluation may withdraw. One reason that these reactions are particularly problematic in EEO cases is that preserving the relationship between the parties is often a vital consideration. Parties in these cases are usually better off when they can work together to resolve their own dispute. If they can cooperate in reaching a solution with the assistance of a mediator, this can rebuild their relationship.

The U.S. Postal Service has had success with an even more party-driven style, *transformative mediation*.[99] This approach (described further in Chapter Three) has a goal of transforming parties' relationships with each other. The process seeks to empower parties to resolve their own disputes by fostering an atmosphere where they will recognize each other's interests. Mediators who follow this approach let parties take the lead in the process, setting their own ground rules and deciding for themselves when to meet together or separately. Because parties have such a central role in determining what happens, they must work together in order for the process to succeed. The method seeks to maximize the opportunities for improving the parties' relationship, of central importance in workplace cases.

Selection of the Neutral

The source of the neutral is another relevant consideration. During the precomplaint process, parties use neutrals from private organizations (bar associations, individual volunteers, and contractors) 80 percent of the time.[100] They use in-house neutrals (from the agency itself) 15 percent of the time and neutrals from a different agency 4 percent of the time.[101] Once a complaint has been filed, parties used private neutrals 40 percent of the time, in-house neutrals 30 percent of the time, and neutrals from a different agency 27 percent of the time.[102]

Each source of neutral has its own advantages and disadvantages. (Chapter Three provides additional information on this topic.) Neutrals from private organizations have greater independence from the process, which can give them credibility with the parties. Private neutrals often work full time on ADR, giving them more experience than government employee neutrals who serve only intermittently, on a collateral duty basis. Because private neutrals are not government employees, they can have less appearance of bias, although there is a possible concern that outside neutrals may favor agency management in order to obtain repeat business.

In-house neutrals from the agency where the complaint arose can have an appearance of bias because they are employed by the agency. Even if they are from a component of the agency other than where the alleged discrimination occurred, they ultimately report to the same chain of command at the top of the agency. For this reason, employees may be concerned that they may be more inclined to favor management. At the same time, because in-house neutrals work at the agency, they have a better understanding of the specific workplace issues involved in the claim. They may have a greater appreciation for the context of the complaints than private neutrals would. Agency management might be concerned they would have more sympathy for employees for this reason.

Neutrals from another agency represent a compromise between the previous two sources of neutrals. As federal workers, they understand the nature of employment with the government. However, because they work for a different agency, they do not report to the same chain of command, reducing fears of bias. In Washington, neutrals from other agencies are available through the Sharing Neutrals Program. Outside Washington, parties can often locate neutrals through the local Federal Executive Board. (These issues are discussed in Chapter Three.)

Preparation for ADR

An initial question in preparing to use ADR is deciding when to conduct it. In EEO cases, earlier is often better. Parties are usually more amenable to resolving these disputes in their early stages. Conflict tends to erode workplace relationships the longer it exists. If parties wait until a dispute has been around for a while, they frequently find that positions on both sides have hardened. Parties in workplace cases often continue to work with each other during the processing of the complaint, and the underlying presence of the dispute almost always harms their relationship. All of these reasons make it good practice for parties in workplace cases to use ADR as early as possible.

Parties then must decide who should attend the ADR sessions. Because workplace conflict can be so highly charged, complainants may prefer not to attend sessions alone. They can bring an attorney with them if they wish. However, if a matter is in its early stages or is not too severe, a complainant may prefer not to bring a lawyer. Lawyers can be expensive, charging either an hourly rate or a percentage of the recovery. A complainant who wants support but does not want to retain a lawyer may choose to bring a union steward, family member, or friend instead.

The government also must choose whom to bring to ADR. At the administrative stage, the agency selects someone to represent it—often a lawyer. Sometimes the agency also sends an official with expertise in personnel matters if settlement of the case may involve these issues. If possible, the government should be represented by someone who has settlement authority or can get it easily during the session (this issue is discussed further in Chapter Four).

An important decision for the government is whether to bring the individual alleged to have committed the discrimination. This person is not technically a party, because EEO claims are filed against the agency as a whole. However, the presence (or absence) of this person can have a profound effect on the proceeding. Bringing the official can facilitate communication with the complainant. Sometimes the complainant will want to talk with this official directly in order to clear the air before a settlement can occur. If the official is willing to apologize in appropriate cases, this can improve the chances for resolution. In some cases, the complainant may be offended if the official does not attend personally and may see this as an indication that the official does not take the matter seriously.

In some cases, however, bringing the official does more harm than good. When the parties have lingering bad feelings for each other, putting them together in the same room can cause a confrontation that damages the chances for settlement. Often officials charged with discrimination are angered by the accusation. This anger, if expressed in ADR, can destroy the cooperation necessary for resolution.

During preparation, parties should consider how they will deal with their feelings in an emotionally charged workplace case. Some ADR sessions break down when parties became too emotional with each other. In especially volatile situations, parties may decide to limit strong expressions of emotion to private sessions with the neutral when the other party is not present. However, expressing negative feelings, or venting, sometimes can have therapeutic value. Some parties find venting in ADR to be a cathartic experience that assists them with reaching settlement. Even more significant, ADR participants sometimes report that they gain vital clues about what is important to the parties during emotional exchanges. It is important to balance these considerations in each case. In general, parties may find it valuable to learn as much as they can from emotions in ADR by asking questions and listening especially carefully when they see that the other side is reacting with strong feelings.

The roles that parties and their attorneys will take in ADR should also be considered in advance. Generally, parties participate more actively in workplace ADR than they do in other types of ADR. Attorneys often are less dominant in the process. Because parties may need to work together in the future, they often find that cooperating with each other directly in reaching a resolution, rather than relying on their attorneys, can be valuable. Even if they will be severing their working relationship, parties are often personally invested enough in the dispute that they benefit from working it out together if possible.

Interests of the Parties

Parties have many different interests in bringing EEO complaints, and it is worthwhile for both sides to focus on what issues underlie a case.[103] When parties truly understand each other's interests, they will be able to craft the best possible solutions to their disputes. In workplace matters, the goals of the parties fall into three broad categories: emotional interests, financial interests, and professional interests. The interests of complainants and agencies overlap in some of these areas, and they also have distinct concerns.

For complainants, emotional interests are usually substantial. Employees who believe they have been mistreated can have strong feelings. They may want to restore their pride and overcome their embarrassment from a situation. They often desire vindication. Saving face can be another concern.

Complainants frequently have financial goals as well. They may seek damages for emotional distress. If their salary was affected, they may look for back pay for past losses and front pay for future losses. Benefits, another interest, can be a substantial part of the compensation for a government employee. Complainants may seek payments of health and life insurance premiums, as well as contributions to their retirement plan. Annual leave and sick leave can be sought as well.

Finally, complainants have professional interests. In an immediate sense, they want to have their career restored to where it would have been had the alleged discrimination not occurred. If they were not hired, transferred, or promoted, they may want the job they sought. If they were fired, they may want their job back. If they received an appraisal or work plan with which they disagree, they may want it changed. If they sought a reasonable accommodation for a disability, they may want it made.

The professional interests of complainants also include longer-term concerns. They want to ensure their reputation is not harmed. If they are moving out of the government, they may want to ensure they will receive good references. If they are staying, they may want training and opportunities for good experience to enable them to move up in the agency in the future.

On the agency side, emotional interests also can be substantial. While the legal defendant in an EEO claim is the agency, managers who are accused of discrimination often have strong feelings about the situation. These interests can be the mirror image of what complainants experience, such as the desire to maintain pride and avoid embarrassment. They may seek to be vindicated for their decisions. They may want to save face and preserve their reputations.

Agencies' financial interests include preserving budgetary resources as much as possible. Furthermore, before they will agree to pay money, agencies want to ensure they are comfortable with the precedent such a payment would set. They need to be aware that they may face future complainants who may seek similar awards. Where benefits are concerned, agencies want to ensure they follow relevant laws that govern what can and cannot be part of an EEO settlement.

Finally, agencies have professional interests as well. Management needs to maintain discipline in the organization. Agencies must preserve their ability to control the work environment and respond to inappropriate behavior. They also want to treat everyone fairly and equally and not to give undeserved benefits to people who file complaints. Agencies want to maintain morale in the workplace, preserve relationships among employees, and minimize disruption in the office. They also want to hire, promote, and retain the most appropriate person to do each job.

Employees and agencies have some interests in common in EEO cases. Both sides prefer to spend as little time and money litigating these claims as possible. They would prefer to put the claim behind them and move on to more productive pursuits as long as they can find a satisfactory solution.

Potential Resolutions of EEO Complaints

Complainants bring different types of EEO complaints. The ten most common bases for initial federal EEO complaints are listed below, along with the percentage each issue comprises of the total number of issues (all others are less than 3 percent):[104]

Issue	Percentage of All Issues
Harassment (nonsexual)	23
Promotion or nonselection	16
Terms and conditions of employment	11
Assignment of duties	7
Termination	5
Time and attendance	5
Evaluation or appraisal	4
Reprimand	4
Suspension	3
Pay, including overtime	3

Parties who are preparing for ADR in an EEO complaint should consider what solutions, in addition to monetary payments, may be possible for the dispute. The types of remedies available depend on the nature of the complaint.[105] The following sections are not intended to imply what, if any, remedy is appropriate for a given case. Instead, they set forth options for parties to consider.

Harassment

Complaints of harassment can be settled with an agreement to provide sensitivity training to the alleged discriminatory official. Another option, when the complainant requests it, is to reassign the complainant to another position at the same grade and in the same pay plan. In some cases, an apology by the alleged discriminatory official can be helpful. Apologies can be either oral or written, and they can be worded in different ways, to cover real or perceived harm. Sometimes language can be found that is satisfactory to both sides.

Nonselection for Promotion

Complaints about nonselection for promotion can be settled with an agreement to automatically place the complainants in the next-occurring vacancy for which they are qualified. Complainants also may be granted the promotion sought, even when this requires the creation of an extra, or over-hire, position. Both solutions involve noncompetitive actions that raise legal and policy concerns, and therefore they must be cleared in advance with appropriate offices within an agency. An agency may instead agree to give a complainant priority consideration for the next vacancy, which means that the complainant's name will be forwarded to the selecting official before the names of other candidates. The complainant can be offered training and career counseling to improve opportunities for future promotion.

Reasonable Accommodation

When the complainant seeks reasonable accommodation for a disability, the agency can grant the accommodation. Accommodations can take many different forms, including purchasing special equipment and altering work schedules. The parties also may agree to a reassignment, where the complainant goes to another job within the agency where the disability is not an issue.

Performance Appraisal

When the complaint concerns a performance appraisal, the agency can agree to change the overall appraisal rating or individual elements of it. Another option is for the agency to give the complainant an out-of-cycle replacement rating. With this procedure, the complainant is given an additional amount of time to improve performance, after which a new appraisal is issued. This rating, although it is given out of the normal time cycle, then replaces the previous annual rating. The parties can agree to a revised performance plan to clarify the requirements of the position for the future. The agency also can agree to provide counseling and training to improve the complainant's performance.

Disciplinary Action

When an employee is complaining about a disciplinary action, one option is for the agency to agree to hold the penalty in abeyance. In exchange, the complainant may admit the misconduct or agree not to engage in misconduct during the abeyance period. This constitutes a conditional reprieve from the punishment rather than a removal of the discipline. Another option is to reduce the severity of the penalty, for example, from a fourteen-day suspension to a five-day suspension. The agency can agree to change a removal or termination to a voluntary resignation, which could improve the complainant's opportunities to get future jobs. The agency can agree to write a reference letter recommending the complainant, or a neutral letter, or the complainant can agree not to seek a recommendation. Another option is for the agency to rescind the disciplinary action and expunge the complainant's record.

If a disciplinary action is based on the complainant's performance, the parties can agree that the complainant will be reassigned to a different job at the same grade or at a lower level. The complainant can voluntarily request a lower grade or agree to resign. The agency can agree to extend the performance improvement period, giving the complainant a longer opportunity to upgrade job performance. The agency can provide training to improve future performance.

Legal Issues in EEO Settlements

Agencies are permitted to award complainants whatever relief a court could order if a case went to trial, in the light of the facts and recognizing the inherent uncertainty of litigation.[106] Courts have considerable discretion to fashion remedies in these cases: "The court may enjoin the respondent from engaging in such unlawful employment practice, and order such affirmative action as may be appropriate, which may include, but is not limited to, reinstatement or hiring of employees, with or without back pay . . . or any other equitable relief as the court deems appropriate."[107] The Supreme Court has interpreted this provision broadly: "to allow the most complete achievement of the objectives of Title VII that is attainable under the facts and circumstances of the specific case."[108]

Thus, agencies have broad latitude in settling EEO complaints, with some limits. Agencies can give complainants cash payments to settle matters, even without a finding of discrimination or an admission of wrongdoing.[109] Agencies also are free to offer relief different from that which a court could order, as long as they do not exceed what a court could order.[110] For example, an agency could offer to pay for outplacement services to locate a new job for a complainant, as long as this cost was no greater than the monetary relief a court could order if the case went to trial.[111] However, an agency could not agree to promote an employee to a position for which the employee does not meet necessary requirements, such as minimum time in grade.[112]

Parties should ensure that they have followed appropriate rules before agreeing to a settlement with unusual provisions.[113] For example, the Office of Personnel Management prohibits using the Retirement Fund to settle cases except under certain circumstances. Parties should discuss these types of remedies with the agency general counsel's and human relations offices, as well as other relevant federal agencies. Furthermore, when a complainant is part of a collective bargaining unit or if the settlement will affect bargaining unit employees, the parties should contact the union. Union agreement is required before any changes may be made to the collective bargaining agreement or the way it is interpreted.

ADR in Non-EEO Workplace Cases

Federal employees have substantial protections against unlawful workplace conduct in addition to discrimination, and ADR is used increasingly in these areas. Agencies offer ADR in administrative grievances and grievances under their collective bargaining agreements. In addition, agencies exist specifically to assist federal workers with workplace complaints: the Merit Systems Protection Board, the Office of Special Counsel, the Federal Labor Relations Authority, and the Federal Mediation and Conciliation Service. Some agencies also offer ADR for workplace conflict that does not fall under any of the above categories.

Administrative Grievance ADR

Many agencies encourage ADR during all phases of the administrative grievance procedure until the agency has made a final decision. Binding arbitration has long been a part of labor grievance procedures, and mediation is being used increasingly as well. Agency officials and employees may decide to turn a grievance procedure into an ADR session. Both agencies and employees often find that ADR leads to a quicker and more satisfactory solution than the grievance process.

If a grievant is a member of a collective bargaining unit, special considerations apply. Agencies should review the applicable bargaining agreement and consult with appropriate labor relations specialists to determine how to proceed. In general, the union will have an independent right to be present at formal discussions between management and bargaining unit employees concerning grievances or conditions of employment.[114] Many agencies have found it important to work closely with unions in designing and implementing mediation programs. Many unions have endorsed mediation for their members because it provides a valuable alternative to the grievance process. Union support has increased the use of mediation programs and made them more effective.

Many times, grievance procedures cover agency actions that employees also could appeal to other specialized agencies, such as the Merit Systems Protection Board. In these cases, employees generally have a choice as to which procedure to follow: filing a grievance with their employer or filing an appeal with the appropriate enforcement agency. They generally must choose one and cannot pursue both.[115]

Merit Systems Protection Board

The Merit Systems Protection Board (MSPB) is an independent agency created to ensure that the federal government follows merit systems practices. Federal employees may appeal to the board when an agency takes serious action against them, such as removing them from their job, suspending them for more than fourteen days, or reducing their pay.[116] The MSPB also has jurisdiction over discrimination allegations if they arise in connection with an action that is appealable to the board.[117] The agency hears and decides close to ten thousand cases each year.[118]

The MSPB provides ADR primarily through settlement conferences run by board judges. Sometimes the judge assigned to handle the appeal works with the parties to attempt to settle the case before rendering a decision. Other times, one judge conducts the ADR and a different judge presides over the case if it does not settle. This approach helps parties to be more candid in the ADR process because they know that a different person will hear the case if they do not reach agreement. In most cases, the judge officially enters the settlement agreement into the record, and the MSPB retains enforcement authority.[119]

The MSPB has another ADR program for appeals involving petitions for review by the full board of initial decisions. In this program,

MSPB staff attorneys select cases that appear to be most likely to settle. Staff attorneys or private neutrals lead these ADR sessions.

In order to encourage parties to use ADR prior to the filing of a formal appeal, the MSPB amended its regulations to provide for additional time for ADR processes. If an employee and an agency agree in writing to attempt to resolve their dispute through ADR, the time limit for filing the appeal is extended by an additional thirty days.[120] This gives parties more time to work on settling their dispute voluntarily before they have to file a formal appeal in order to preserve their rights.

Office of Special Counsel

The Office of Special Counsel (OSC) is an independent agency that protects federal employees from certain prohibited personnel practices, particularly reprisal for reporting improper government actions (whistle-blowing). The OSC is designed to serve as a safe channel for federal workers who wish to disclose violations of laws, gross mismanagement or waste of funds, abuse of authority, and specific dangers to the public health and safety. The OSC also enforces the Hatch Act[121] and protects the rights of federal military employees pursuant to the Uniformed Services Employment and Reemployment Rights Act.[122] It investigates violations of these laws and seeks appropriate corrective or disciplinary action.

The OSC offers a mediation program for parties involved in these cases.[123] The agency's ADR specialist selects cases that may be appropriate for mediation based on the nature and complexity of the case, the relationship of the parties, and the relief sought in the complaint. Cases are selected before they are referred to the Investigation and Prosecution Division, and if an allegation does not warrant referral to this division, it will not be mediated. If a case already has been referred for investigation and prosecution, the OSC nonetheless may offer mediation at its discretion.

The OSC's ADR specialist invites both the agency and employee to participate in these cases. If both agree, they proceed to mediation. OSC mediators are internal staff members who have training and experience in federal personnel law. Most mediations take eight hours or less, but complex cases may require additional time. If the case settles, the agreement is put into writing and is binding on both parties. Otherwise, the case is referred to the Investigation and Prosecution Division and is handled as if mediation had never taken place.

Federal Labor Relations Agency

The Federal Labor Relations Agency (FLRA) is charged with administering the federal labor-management relations program.[124] About 2 million federal employees are covered by this program, and half of them are exclusively represented in about two thousand bargaining units. The agency is governed by the Federal Service Labor-Management Relations Act,[125] which protects employee rights to form, join, and assist labor unions, as well as to refrain from such activity. FLRA responsibility includes supervising and conducting union elections, resolving issues regarding the requirement to bargain in good faith, and conducting hearings to resolve complaints of unfair labor practices. The agency also reviews arbitrator awards in grievance cases to determine if they are contrary to law, fail to draw their essence from the collective bargaining agreement, are based on a nonfact, violate public policy, deny a party a fair hearing, exceed the arbitrator's authority, show bias, or are ambiguous, incomplete or contradictory.

The FLRA offers ADR through its Collaboration and Alternative Dispute Resolution Program. ADR is available at every stage in a labor-management dispute, including investigation, prosecution, adjudication of cases, and resolution of bargaining impasses. The FLRA Office of General Counsel offers ADR to resolve unfair labor practice and representation disputes. Parties desiring assistance file a joint request, and then a regional office agent assists them with ADR prior to the filing of charges.[126] The Office of Administrative Law Judges offers an ADR program to resolve unfair labor practice complaints.[127] In this program, the chief administrative law judge assigns an attorney or a judge (other than the judge who will try the case) to conduct a settlement conference with the parties before trial. In most cases, the FLRA will stay proceedings in a matter in order to permit parties to pursue a settlement.

The Federal Services Impasse Panel, also part of the FLRA, assists agencies and exclusive employee representatives in the resolution of negotiation impasses.[128] The panel is the federal sector substitute for strikes and lockouts in the private sector. It assists parties in resolving impasses with various types of ADR, including mediation, informal conferences, and arbitration by staff and private neutrals. If the parties do not arrive at a voluntary settlement, the panel may hold hearings and take whatever action is necessary and appropriate to resolve the impasse, including issuing a decision and order that is binding on the parties.

Federal Mediation and Conciliation Service

The Federal Mediation and Conciliation Service (FMCS) is an independent agency created by the Labor-Management Relations Act[129] to assist in resolving collective bargaining disputes.[130] It handles disputes in both the public and private sectors, and its mission has expanded to provide ADR services outside the workplace arena as well.

The FMCS mediation program is staffed mainly by trained neutrals who are employees of the agency. Currently, more than two hundred mediators serve in seventy-five FMCS offices around the country. If the parties want an FMCS neutral, the agency involved must agree to reimburse FMCS for the cost of this neutral. The FMCS also has a roster of private neutrals. If an agency wants to use one of these neutrals, it must negotiate the fee with the neutral.

The FMCS also offers arbitration. The arbitration program uses approximately fifteen hundred private arbitrators whom FMCS selected based on their qualifications, including their expertise in labor relations issues and experience as a decision maker in disputes arising under collective bargaining agreements. FMCS arbitrators must agree to cease any advocacy role representing employers, labor organizations, or individuals in labor relations matters. For a nominal fee, the FMCS will provide parties a panel of arbitrators based on geographical location, professional background, experience, and other criteria the parties provide. The parties then can select the individual they want, often pursuant to a procedure set forth in the collective bargaining agreement.

Ombuds Offices

Federal agencies are increasingly offering employees another option for resolving workplace conflict: the ombuds office. The general ombuds concept has existed for a long time, but it was formalized in the early nineteenth century, when the Swedish legislature created an official public agent to investigate complaints against the government. (The term *ombuds* derives from a Swedish word meaning "agent.") In the federal government, the Administrative Dispute Resolution Act of 1996 specifically added the term *ombuds* to the examples given in the definition of ADR.[131]

Ombuds offices provide a number of services for federal employees.[132] Ombuds staff are neutral parties who answer questions, give guidance, brainstorm options, and refer people to appropriate outside resources. They may help work for the resolution of a particular problem or issue. They will work to preserve the employee's anonymity if requested, or they can act openly to broker a deal between the employee and others in the agency.

Federal agencies have found that ombuds offices can provide an invaluable additional channel for employees with workplace conflicts. Many times when employees have disputes with others in the agency, they are unwilling or unable to raise them to the level of formal complaints. An ombuds office can serve as an informal sounding board for these employees, allowing them to obtain professional counsel without having to take formal action against someone else in the agency.

Employees can seek assistance from ombuds offices in a multitude of situations. For example, they may be unsure whom in the agency they should contact with a specific problem. They may have made a request to an official who has not responded promptly. They may have a complaint about the way the agency treated them but are not sure whether the complaint is valid. They may want someone to explore their situation anonymously, so they can learn more without having to risk reprisal.

Agencies as well benefit from this approach. By providing an ombuds office to work with employees, an agency can sometimes resolve claims more informally, before they develop into more serious complaints. As they work with dozens of employees, ombuds staff can develop a comprehensive perspective on the way the agency is handling conflict. This understanding can allow them to provide valuable insights to agency decision makers. They can provide general suggestions for improvement, while preserving anonymity for specific complainants. They may issue reports aggregating information about the types of matters they have handled.

There are different types of ombuds offices. A classical ombuds office takes complaints from both the general public and individuals within the agency, formally investigates them, and issues findings. An organizational ombuds office works within the agency only, to informally resolve complaints. In the federal workplace context, organizational ombuds offices are the most common.

The federal government has established ombuds offices in different ways.[133] For example, Congress established ombuds offices at the Federal Deposit Insurance Corporation,[134] the Office of the Comptroller of the Currency,[135] the Small Business Administration,[136] and the State Department through legislation,[137] while the agencies themselves created offices at the Customs Service, Federal Bureau of Investigation, Food and Drug Administration, and Justice Department. Ombuds staff are usually agency employees, and they generally have career status to insulate them from political pressures. Frequently, they are located in agency headquarters in Washington, D.C., but they can assist employees in other parts of the country. Some agencies have ombuds staff in field offices as well.

Ombuds offices have been very effective in the federal government. The General Accounting Office has reported that they successfully resolve 60 to 70 percent of their cases.[138] The ombuds office at the National Institutes of Health achieves full or partial resolution in 65 percent of its cases, closing 60 percent of its cases within six weeks.[139]

There are three core principles for ombuds offices, and the first is neutrality.[140] Parties can be assured of fair treatment because ombuds staff are officially neutral in all matters. They serve as advocates for neither employees nor management. Instead, they may be advocates for fairness, equality, improved communication, and resolution. They conduct investigations in a neutral fashion, without a predefined goal either to vindicate the employee or to defend the agency. They seek only a just resolution of the situation.

The second core principle is independence. Ombuds offices should have autonomy and be insulated from the internal politics of the organization. To realize this goal, agencies usually set up ombuds offices to report directly to a top official, such as the agency head or deputy. Placing an ombuds office in a human relations office is problematic, because employees may not perceive it as neutral.

Agency policy generally prohibits anyone from controlling or limiting the actions of the ombuds office, reducing its budget as a result of specific actions, or firing staff except for good cause. This frees the office to act as fairly as possible, without fear of retaliation for taking unpopular positions. Conversely, ombuds offices are not given power to make management decisions or set agency policy. While this limits their authority, it augments their independence by ensuring that they are not perceived as part of the agency management team.

The final core principle is confidentiality. Parties should feel free to share concerns openly with ombuds staff because they know that ombuds offices will maintain confidentiality whenever possible. Ombuds staff keep limited records, to avoid creating written documentation that could be viewed by outside parties.

The legal bases for federal ombuds confidentiality come from federal law and agency policy. The Administrative Dispute Resolution Act (ADRA) provides general confidentiality protection for communications occurring in a dispute resolution proceeding.[141] However, it should be noted that the ADRA requires a "disagreement" between "parties."[142] Thus, if an individual merely asks an informal question, this may not be covered by the act. Agency policy may provide additional protection. When agencies set up ombuds offices, they often create an official policy establishing confidentiality for communications with staff.

Ombuds confidentiality may not be absolute. There are requirements that federal employees report information about a felony;[143] evidence of waste, fraud, abuse, and corruption;[144] and information about crimes involving government officers and employees.[145] The interplay between these provisions and the ADRA is discussed in Chapter Eight. Some agency policies provide that ombuds staff should disclose information when individuals may be a danger to themselves or others. However, ombuds staff work diligently to avoid disclosing information in a manner that would be detrimental to the individuals who sought their assistance.

Ombuds staff should discuss their confidentiality policies with individuals before beginning substantive conversations. Parties should feel free to raise questions before disclosing information about which they are concerned. Because of careful practice in this area, problems with confidentiality in federal ombuds programs have been extremely rare.

Chapter Seven

ADR in Federal Contracting Cases

In the federal government, contracting is one of the most important areas where ADR is used. The government enters into billions of dollars worth of contracts every year, and this is a major portion of the federal budget and a vital part of the entire national economy. ADR affects the disposition of more and more of this money every year. Federal regulations now make it official government policy to use ADR in contract disputes: "Agencies are encouraged to use alternative dispute resolution (ADR) procedures to the maximum extent practicable."[1]

One of the most important reasons ADR has thrived in the government contract area is that these matters involve continuing relationships. The government regularly does business with the same companies, and both sides benefit when they resolve disputes in a way that preserves good working associations. For example, maintaining harmonious relations between the Defense Department and a major supplier can be more important than the outcome of any single dispute between them. Nonetheless, each dispute must be resolved, and ADR often can do this in a way that most effectively avoids unnecessary animosity.

As an example of the success of ADR in government contracting cases, it is worthwhile to look at the experience of the Department of the Air Force. ADR has been used in more than one hundred air force contract cases in recent years, and more than 90 percent have settled. The parties have resolved some very large air force cases, including a $785 million contract claim with Boeing that had been pending for more than a decade before ADR was used. This is one of the largest contract claims ever settled using ADR. A $201 million claim with Northrop Grumman was settled with ADR as well. For both the government and the contractor, the costs and risks of taking these huge claims all the way through trial would have been enormous. Important relations between the military and some of its largest suppliers would have been strained and perhaps damaged significantly by litigation.

In addition to preserving relationships, ADR saves time in contracting cases. The amount of time required to resolve a contract matter through ADR is about half that required with adjudication. For the year 2000 alone, the air force estimates that ADR saved nearly $2 million in staff time and interest on claims. Studies by the agency have shown that ADR favors neither the government nor the private sector. Payouts in ADR claims are equivalent to the historical averages for adjudication. These results explain why it is now official air force policy to avoid litigation wherever possible in these cases and to use ADR first.

Other agencies have reported similar successes. The Federal Aviation Administration (FAA) uses ADR as its primary means of dispute resolution. The FAA initiates a discussion of ADR options at the beginning of every case. ADR has led to the settlement of more than half of all bid protest cases and almost 90 percent of all contract claims that have been filed. Settlements have been achieved in matters ranging from simple contract claims to major acquisition disputes involving multi-billion-dollar improvements to the nation's aviation system. The agency's ADR program also has been effective in settling disputes quickly. ADR has resolved bid protest cases in an average of only twenty-four days and contract disputes in an average of only sixty-five days. Participants in ADR report they were satisfied or very satisfied with the process about 90 percent of the time. The Army Corps of Engineers, which had the first federal ADR contracting program in the mid-1980s, has resolved 95 percent of the cases taken to ADR. The Corps of Engineers' use of ADR has reduced its caseload in both contract claims and appeals by 80 percent.

Contracting ADR Laws and Regulations

A strong legal foundation supports the use of ADR in government contract cases. The three major sources of law in this area are the

Administrative Dispute Resolution Act, the Contract Disputes Act, and the Federal Acquisition Regulation. Several other regulations and executive orders play an important role as well.

Administrative Dispute Resolution Act

Congress required agencies to promote the use of ADR in contract disputes with the Administrative Dispute Resolution Act (ADRA).[2] The ADRA requires agencies to "examine alternative means of resolving disputes in connection with . . . contract administration."[3] The ADRA continues, "Each agency shall review each of its standard agreements for contracts, grants, and other assistance and shall determine whether to amend any such standard agreements to authorize and encourage the use of alternative means of dispute resolution."[4] This is a broad requirement, mandating that agencies examine all of their contracts to look for ways to increase the use of ADR and to amend their standard agreements whenever appropriate to promote ADR. The ADRA also amended the Contract Disputes Act to provide explicitly for ADR for claims involving federal contracts.[5]

Contract Disputes Act

As amended by the ADRA, the Contract Disputes Act (CDA) specifically authorizes ADR in federal contract matters: "Notwithstanding any other provision of this chapter, a contractor and a contracting officer may use any alternative means of dispute resolution under subchapter IV of chapter 5 of title 5, or other mutually agreeable procedures, for resolving claims."[6] Prior to this legislation, a number of agencies already were using ADR, believing they were authorized to do so under existing law. Passage of the amendments to the CDA removed all doubt and encouraged other agencies to follow suit.

The CDA promotes ADR by creating a procedural hurdle for parties who do not wish to participate. If either the government or the contractor suggests ADR, the other party must either accept it or give the reasons for their rejection in writing.[7] This requirement promotes the use of ADR without making it mandatory. The CDA refers to the following list of appropriate reasons for the government to decline ADR: the government needs a precedential decision, significant questions of government policy are involved, consistency among individual decisions is of special importance, the matter significantly affects parties who are not present, a full public record of the proceeding is important, or the agency must maintain jurisdiction to alter the disposition of the matter if circumstances change.[8] The government is permitted to provide other explanations, and contractors are not limited in the reasons they may provide, but either side must furnish a written justification for refusing ADR in order to be excused from participating.

The CDA has encouraged agency boards of contract appeals to offer ADR programs pursuant to the provision requiring boards to "provide to the fullest extent practicable, informal, expeditious, and inexpensive resolution of disputes."[9] Although the boards were originally created to give parties a viable alternative to federal court litigation, increasing workloads and other factors have made them more and more like courts. The introduction of ADR has allowed the boards to meet their original mandate more effectively by reducing the formality, time requirements, and expense of contract dispute processing.

Federal Acquisition Regulation

The Federal Acquisition Regulation (FAR) implements the CDA's call for ADR in this field. The FAR highlights the importance of these procedures to the government in clear terms: "Agencies are encouraged to use alternative dispute resolution (ADR) procedures to the maximum extent practicable."[10] This is bold language, and it indicates that the government's official policy is to use ADR in all appropriate cases.

The regulation encourages parties to use ADR at the lowest possible level and avoid requiring the involvement of senior managers if possible. Whenever a contracting officer can resolve the case directly, the officer is mandated to do so: "The Government's policy is to try to resolve all contractual issues in controversy by mutual agreement at the contracting officer's level."[11] Experience has shown that it is often considerably easier to settle disputes without involving unnecessary levels of review.

The regulation also explicitly directs parties to consider using ADR as early in the dispute as possible, including prior to the submission of a formal claim. The definitions section of the regulation states that an "issue in controversy" where ADR should be used includes a disagreement that "may result in a claim," indicating that a formal claim is not required.[12] Another provision states even more clearly, "Reasonable efforts should be made to resolve controversies prior to the submission of a claim."[13] This regulation appropriately reflects the fact that parties often can settle disputes more effectively by addressing them earlier rather than later.

ADR also may be used to settle one portion of a claim, even if other aspects are reserved for litigation. The regulation says ADR is appropriate for "all or part of an existing claim."[14] It is not necessary for the entire case to be suitable for ADR in order for the process to be worthwhile. Many times parties benefit from using ADR to streamline a claim, resolving the issues on which they can agree. Then they can use adjudicative techniques more easily for the part of the claim that still remains.

The regulation sets forth four requirements for government contract ADR: an issue in controversy, a voluntary agreement by both sides to use ADR, an agreement on which ADR process to use, and officials participating on both sides with authority to resolve the issue.[15] These requirements are straightforward and rarely present a problem.

A contractor must follow all time limitations and procedural requirements for filing an appeal even if ADR is going to be used, because using ADR does not stop the statute of limitations from running once a contracting officer issues a final decision.[16] Nor does using ADR constitute reconsideration of the final decision.[17] Contractors must be aware of these factors and ensure they do not miss a deadline while pursuing ADR. In some cases, contractors file an appeal in order to preserve litigation rights and then proceed with ADR.

The regulation also sets forth policies on arbitration, a process that is unusual in government contracting. The government ordinarily may not require arbitration as a condition of award in a contract solicitation.[18] (The only exception to this rule is a situation where Congress specifically requires arbitration, which it has done in a handful of statutes.) The regulation does leave parties free to agree voluntarily to arbitration.[19] However, in order to use arbitration, all parties must follow specific procedures.

Federal Executive Orders and Policies

Recent presidential administrations have encouraged the use of ADR in government contract cases. In 1994, the Office of Federal Procurement Policy, which is part of the Executive Office of the President, hosted a pledge-signing ceremony where twenty-five senior agency officials formally agreed to promote the use of contract ADR. The officials promised to review all contract disputes in their agencies for use of ADR, identify and eliminate impediments for using ADR in these cases, participate on government teams to expand the use of ADR, and share their ADR experiences with each other and with the Office of Federal Procurement Policy.

In 1995, the president issued executive order 12,979 on agency procurement protests, which required agencies to establish procedures, including ADR, to resolve bid protests in ways that are inexpensive, informal, simple, and quick.[20]

In 1998, the attorney general created the Contracts and Procurement Section of the Federal Interagency ADR Working Group. This section leads programs for the executive branch on contracting ADR, provides training, and issues guidance in this field.

In 2002, the Office of Federal Procurement Policy hosted an awards ceremony at the White House to recognize leading programs involving government contracting ADR. Speakers including the general counsel of the Department of Defense and the associate attorney general praised the use of ADR in these programs.

Using ADR in Federal Contracting Cases

Contracting cases have unique features, and thus there are special considerations for using ADR in these matters.

The Contract Dispute Process

The first stage in the contract dispute process is the administrative process, which begins when a party makes a written claim under the CDA. The claim can seek payment of money, an adjustment of contract terms, an interpretation of contract terms, or other relief relating to the contract.[21] A party initiates a claim by submitting it to the contracting officer for a final decision (or, if the government is the claimant, by issuing a written decision by the contracting officer).[22] The contracting officer, who has the authority to enter into contracts on behalf of the government and administer them during their term, represents the government in these matters but also is charged with making neutral, objective determinations of the validity of claims brought under the contract.

Upon receiving a formal claim, the contracting officer reviews the pertinent facts, obtains assistance from the agency's legal and contract administration offices as appropriate, and prepares a written decision.[23] The decision must include a description of the claim, a reference to the pertinent contract terms, a statement of the factual areas of agreement and disagreement, and the supporting rationale for the decision.[24]

A party who is not satisfied with this decision may file an appeal to either an agency board of contract appeals or the U.S. Court of Federal Claims. The statute of limitations for filing an appeal starts running on the date the contractor receives the contracting officer's final decision. Appeals to a board of contract appeals must be filed within ninety days, and appeals to the Court of Federal Claims must be filed within twelve months.

Appropriate Cases for ADR

Many contract cases are appropriate for ADR. Because of the continuing relationships involved between the government and its contractors, ADR can be particularly valuable in these matters. Whenever the parties believe they could benefit from the assistance of a neutral in settling their case, they should consider ADR. Examples include cases where parties may benefit from hearing directly from the opposing side, either party would be influenced by the opinion of a neutral third party, either side has an unrealistic view of the case, the tribunal that will decide the case is disadvantageous, it is desirable to avoid adverse precedent, there is a desire for flexible relief, adjudication would be costly, and swift resolution is desirable.[25]

Cases where ADR may not be appropriate include matters in which a party desires a precedent to use for future disputes, a public record is important, the case is likely to settle quickly without assistance, or the government will never offer any settlement because it views the claim as frivolous.[26]

If the contractor's claim involves fraud or fraud is alleged, ADR may not be used. The CDA prohibits federal agencies from settling, paying, compromising, or otherwise adjusting any claim involving fraud.[27] Regulations require a contracting officer to examine situations where a contractor is unable to support any part of a claim and determine whether that inability may be attributable to fraud or misrepresentation.[28] If so, the contracting officer is required to refer the matter to the agency official charged with investigating fraud, typically the inspector general or general counsel.[29]

Bid Protest Cases

Bid protests, where parties complain of impropriety in the government contract award process, raise special issues for ADR. This is an area of contract law where formal ADR methods have been used only recently. Traditionally, practitioners saw this as a field where ADR was less likely to be effective, because there are fewer options for resolution available and because protests move quickly through the process; the General Accounting Office (GAO), which hears the majority of protests, has a hundred-day deadline for decision making. However, its use has been growing, particularly at the administrative level (settlement options are more limited once a case reaches the litigation stage). In 1995, President Clinton encouraged this trend by issuing an executive order requiring agencies to use ADR in bid protest cases where appropriate.[30]

Agencies and protestors have found they can use ADR in these cases with considerable success. The FAA, for example, settles more than half of its bid protests through ADR, typically through a combination of early neutral evaluation and facilitated negotiation. The GAO resolved more than 140 bid protest cases through ADR in a recent two-year period.

If a company believes a government agency's solicitation provisions are improper or unfair, it may file a preaward protest with the agency. In addition, once an award has been made, a company that believes denial of its bid for a contract was improper may file a postaward protest. The agency will review the protest and provide a written response granting or denying it. However, the protest does not stop the procurement process, and the agency may continue to evaluate proposals, decide to make an award, or permit performance to continue. There is no time limit for the agency to respond to the protest. ADR is possible at the agency level, and agencies have differing practices in this regard.

Another option is for the company to file a pre- or postaward protest with the GAO, a more formal process. Filing a GAO protest generally suspends the procurement proceedings at the agency. The agency must provide a formal reply to the protest in the form of an administrative report accompanied by relevant documents.

The GAO has a formal ADR program for resolving bid protests. Neutrals from the agency may act as advisers to parties at several different points: before the filing of a formal protest, immediately after filing, and after the development of a written record. All of the processes are nonbinding. Parties can participate as long as they want. If they are not satisfied with the results, they can proceed with the normal bid protest procedure at any time.

The GAO offers two processes: negotiation assistance and outcome prediction. *Negotiation assistance,* analogous to traditional mediation, is used early in the process and has a 50 percent settlement rate. This type of ADR is less effective in certain types of bid protest cases. When an outside party (other than the agency or a company that bid for the contract) is involved, the chances of success drop considerably. Also, ADR may have little likelihood of being effective in cases where the protestor has already lost a protest before the agency on the same claim. If the agency has shown it is absolutely unwilling to alter its position on a key point, this may not change during ADR.

Outcome prediction, similar to early neutral evaluation, has a 90 percent settlement rate. In the outcome prediction process, the GAO neutral offers an oral assessment of the case after reviewing the record. One of the reasons for the high settlement rate with the outcome prediction method is that the lawyer who serves as the neutral also will draft the decision if ADR does not settle the case. The GAO believes this approach saves time, which is important given the short time frame for reaching a decision. After working on the ADR, the neutral will have considerable familiarity with the case, making decision writing much easier. The GAO ensures that the parties are aware of this procedure before beginning the ADR, so they do not make any statements they do not want the GAO lawyer to hear. The decision drafted by the lawyer is subject to review by higher levels within the GAO, and thus it may be changed.

Parties generally respect the analysis of the GAO neutral in outcome prediction cases, particularly when the neutral can support the prediction with compelling reasons. Protestors often agree to withdraw a protest that has little likelihood of success (as long as delaying the matter is not in their interest). Agencies almost always agree to take corrective measures when they learn a protest is likely to be affirmed. It also is possible to reach agreement on one or more issues and maintain the protest with only the remaining issues.

Timing

ADR should be used in a contracting claims case as early as possible. Contract disputes, like most other disputes, almost always are easier to resolve when they are addressed early. Parties are less entrenched in their positions at the beginning, relationships are still on friendlier terms, and funding is more likely to be available earlier in a case (government contract funding usually expires after a period of time). If a case is not settled before it reaches the federal court litigation stage, parties may need still more time to develop the evidence before they can consider ADR. These are all important reasons that it is official government policy "to try to resolve all contractual issues in controversy by mutual agreement at the contracting officer's level"[31] and to make "reasonable efforts . . . to resolve controversies prior to the submission of a claim."[32]

In government cases, it is usually easier to settle midperformance disputes (while the contract is still in effect) than postcompletion disputes (when the contract is over). Parties that are still doing business with one another have greater incentives to resolve disagreements because they must continue to work together. Moreover, there are generally additional options available to resolve a dispute when the contract is in progress. Parties have greater flexibility to reach agreement by making adjustments because there are more issues that are still in play under the contract. Once the contract is over, fewer options exist.

The value of resolving claims during performance is particularly significant in government cases. In contracts between private parties, both sides are often interested in resolving disputes in order to facilitate their doing business in the future. In federal cases, however, the law prohibits the government from promising favorable consideration down the line in exchange for resolution of a current dispute. Nevertheless, even postcompletion government ADR has been relatively successful, because parties still want to avoid the delays and expense of adjudication.

The law permits and even encourages parties to use ADR before submission of a formal claim under the CDA. Many boards of contract appeals are willing to supply neutrals at this stage, and others will do so on request on a case-by-case basis. Boards have found that devoting resources to ADR at this point can avoid a formal claim that is more difficult and expensive to resolve later. Using ADR early can avoid the substantial costs of extensive discovery for the parties and conserve the resources of the boards as well.

Before parties can use ADR productively, however, they need to know enough about the matter to accurately assess its value. At the preclaim stage, formal discovery procedures are not officially available. Nonetheless, parties are free to undertake a voluntary information exchange, and this is often a key part of ADR preparation at this phase. Parties frequently agree to exchange certain documents and even conduct limited depositions. This can provide information necessary to make an informed decision about how to proceed without engaging in full-blown contested discovery. A skillful and experienced ADR neutral can provide valuable assistance in formulating a plan for focused fact finding and can help resolve differences in connection with the fact-finding process.

There are several caveats to the use of ADR at the preclaim stage. One disadvantage of ADR at this point is that parties cannot obtain formal subpoenas to compel information from each other or from third parties because litigation has not officially commenced. Contractors also should ensure that their participation in ADR does not lead them to miss any statutes of limitations for filing claims. An agreement between the parties to do preclaim discovery should specify that it does not limit their ability to conduct formal discovery if the case does not settle. It also is important to remember that even if the case does settle at the preclaim stage, it still must be appropriately documented and justified.

Parties also can use ADR after a claim has been filed but before the contracting officer issues a final decision. Upon agreement of the parties, the contracting officer can suspend issuance of the decision pending ADR. This is an unusual procedure, however, and ADR is more typical at the postappeal stage.

In practice, the most common time when ADR occurs in federal contract cases is following the final decision of the contracting officer. The Court of Federal Claims and the boards of contract appeals all have ADR programs to handle cases at this stage. These forums generally will agree to suspend litigation deadlines to enable parties to pursue ADR. This can be helpful to allow parties to focus their energies on settlement without the press of discovery and other pretrial procedures.

It is vital to remember that ADR at this stage does not toll the statute of limitations. The regulation states, "When ADR procedures are used subsequent to the issuance of a contracting officer's final decision, their use does not alter any of the time limitations or procedural requirements for filing an appeal of the contracting officer's final decision and does not constitute a reconsideration of the final decision."[33] This rule applies for appeals to a board of contract appeals and to the Court of Federal Claims. Thus, contractors should ensure they file a protective appeal before the applicable statute of limitations expires. Because of this, government attorneys should not be dissuaded from using ADR just because a contractor files an appeal. Filing an appeal does not necessarily signal a lack of interest in settlement by the contractor, who may have filed merely to preserve legal rights.

Agencies may wish to have litigation staff conduct an ADR review of all proposed contracting officer final decisions above a certain dollar amount prior to their release. Agency lawyers can examine the decisions for issues in controversy that may be appropriate for ADR. If the agency believes ADR may be useful, officials can offer it at the same time they issue the decision.[34]

Choosing an ADR Process and a Neutral in Contract Cases

Because government contract cases are a specialized field of ADR, the considerations in selecting a process and a neutral in this area are different from those used in other arenas. In these cases, parties often seek a neutral with experience and stature in the contract area. Federal contract law is a technical field, and a knowledge of its intricacies can be helpful in assisting parties in reaching a settlement.

With cases that are not particularly complicated, parties have had success with neutrals who did not have contracting expertise. Good neutrals can rely on the parties to give them whatever technical background they need.

A neutral with a good reputation and authority in the field can be helpful in persuading the parties to settle. Stature on the part of the neutral can be important to justify a settlement to senior agency management officials who did not participate in the ADR process and important outside parties. Contracting cases can attract attention from outside entities such as the press, inspectors general, the GAO, and Congress. If a highly regarded neutral participated in the shaping of the settlement, this can help protect it from later challenge for being biased in favor of one side or the other.

Settlement Judges

The most common ADR procedure in federal contract ADR cases involves the use of settlement judges, an especially appropriate choice for contract cases because of their substantive expertise and stature. This can make the parties take the process and the recommendations of the neutral more seriously. Settlement judges who are currently sitting on a board of contract appeals have the added advantage of being free to both parties.[35] The process can take place in the board's offices, lending gravity to the proceedings. Many board judges also are willing to travel to another location for the convenience of the parties. Board judges often are sophisticated neutrals who are effective in leading ADR processes.

Parties who wish to use a settlement judge should make a request to the chair of the board of contract appeals where the case is pending, who will assign a judge to conduct the ADR. Parties typically sign a joint request letter, or one party can write and indicate that the other party agrees. If a judge has already been selected to preside over the case, this judge should be sent a copy of the request letter.

Settlement judges are available for contract claims at both the preappeal and postappeal stages, and from some boards for bid protest cases as well. At the preappeal stage, the board may wish to talk with the parties to ensure that the proposed ADR proceeding is an appropriate use of the board's resources. In this case, parties should be prepared to discuss why they have been unable to resolve the case on their own and how the board will be able to assist them in this matter. In a few cases that did not settle, the settlement judge has become the presiding judge (with the agreement of all parties) in the interest of saving time.

Board procedures provide for confidentiality, and the settlement judge will not participate in the adjudication of the case if it does not settle (unless all parties agree). Furthermore, if there is no settlement, board rules preclude the settlement judge from discussing the substance of the discussions with the judge who presides over the case.[36]

Settlement judges tend to be evaluative mediators, focusing the parties' attention on the strengths and weaknesses of their cases. This can be an advantage for parties who want an objective assessment of their likelihood of success. Other parties may want a more facilitative approach, where the participants have a greater role in leading the process. Parties who want a less directive neutral may wish to choose another process. Parties also are free to discuss their preferences for the style and format of the discussions with the judge. Some judges are more flexible in this regard than others.

Board judges generally take this process very seriously and can be of considerable help to the parties in reaching a settlement. At the Armed Services Board of Contract Appeals (ASBCA), for example, the settlement rate over recent years is approximately 95 percent.[37] This success has led to considerable growth in the program, and the ASBCA has handled almost a thousand matters since 1987. The ASBCA now sends documents to parties encouraging ADR use along with docketing notices at the beginning of the process (when parties are deciding how to proceed with their appeals) and again after the board receives the complaint and answer.

The boards provide another option for parties who want to use a settlement judge but do not want a judge from the board that will decide the case if it does not settle. Under the BCA-ADR Sharing Arrangement, parties can contact the chair of the board that would normally adjudicate the case and request that a settlement judge be appointed from another board. Some board chairs may be willing to entertain a request for a specific judge. Although board rules provide for confidentiality for statements that parties make in mediation, some parties nonetheless feel more comfortable discussing their case with a judge from a different board. If parties appear regularly before a particular board, for example, they may feel pressure to defer to a judge who is serving as a mediator. Although judges will not rule on the case being mediated, they will rule on other litigated cases involving the party in the future. Some parties prefer to avoid the tensions this situation can create. Every federal board participates in the sharing program except the board of the General Services Administration. This board will provide neutral services for contract cases involving other agencies, but they require a reasonable reimbursement of their costs. Parties can determine how to split this modest expense.[38]

Summary Trial with Binding Decision

Although the settlement judge process is generally nonbinding, the boards of contract appeal provide a binding process as well, which is called a *summary trial with binding decision*. This approach also has been popular in some boards of contract appeal, with the ASBCA handling 45 percent of its ADR matters this way.[39] With this process, each party presents its case to a single board judge or a panel in an expedited proceeding. Parties often agree to limit documentary evidence, the number of witnesses, and the length of oral presentations. Many of these processes take only one day, and evidentiary rules are relaxed. In order to use the process, parties waive their right to appeal the decision (other than for fraud). The judge's decision has no precedential value.

Parties often choose this process when a quick decision is necessary or the costs of litigating a claim through the traditional process would exceed the amount of money in dispute. There is no charge to either party. However, parties typically have no control over which judge is chosen to make the decision.

Private Arbitration

If parties want a binding process where they can choose their own neutral, regulations permit them to use private arbitration. However, this process is rare in federal contract cases because of significant procedural hurdles. First, pursuant to the ADRA, the parties must sign an agreement to arbitrate that sets forth a maximum award that may be issued by the arbitrator.[40] An agency official with settlement authority at this level must approve the process before arbitration begins. The agreement also may contain other conditions limiting the range of possible outcomes.[41] Furthermore, the agency must issue arbitration guidance developed in consultation with the attorney general.[42] As of 2003, the only agencies to have done so are the Federal Deposit Insurance Corporation, the Federal Aviation Administration, and the Federal Motor Carrier Safety Administration.[43]

Minitrial

Minitrials are used relatively infrequently, but they are more common in federal contract cases than in other types of disputes (they are discussed further in Chapter Two). In this process, senior representatives from the contractor and the government agency sit as a type of jury and hear a shortened version of a trial in the case. Typically, the representatives are high-level officials who were not directly involved in the dispute and have authority to settle the matter. A neutral supervises the process and becomes a mediator once the presentations are completed. Some boards of contract appeal provide a neutral for a minitrial.

Parties use this process because it is quicker than formal adjudication. It is most common in high-dollar or high-visibility cases, where senior officials from both parties are willing to devote the time necessary to participate personally in the process. Often the mere presence of these individuals is a powerful engine for settlement, as they become invested in the process and focus their energies on resolving the dispute.

Dispute Review Boards

Another process that is used in the contracting context, particularly in construction cases, is the dispute review board. At the outset of the contract and before any disputes have arisen, parties select members of a board to assist with the resolution of any future conflicts. Members have no connection with either the government or the contractor. As disputes develop during the performance of the contract, the board gives neutral, nonbinding assessments to the parties. By keeping in close contact with all sides, these boards can help forestall future problems and minimize conflicts that do develop. This process can be costly and is thus typically used only with larger contracts. For the board to be effective, it is helpful to choose members who command respect from the parties.

Private Mediation

Finally, parties are free to engage in private mediation. One advantage of this process is that a private mediator generally can spend as much time on a case as necessary. Although board judges can be generous in the time they devote to settlement, they have other responsibilities that can limit their availability. Furthermore, using a private mediator allows the parties to choose whomever they want.[44] One disadvantage is that private mediators cost money.

In contracting cases, parties often hire an individual with contracting experience, though this is not required. Former judges and practitioners in this area of the law are common sources of neutrals. They may serve as fact finders, giving nonbinding assessments of the factual bases of a claim. Subject matter expertise is particularly important in this type of ADR, where the neutral will provide outcome prediction. Private individuals also may serve as traditional mediators, assisting the parties in the resolution of their dispute. With this approach, experience and talent at facilitative mediation may be more important than extensive knowledge of the technical aspects of federal contract law.

ADR in the Court of Federal Claims

The Court of Federal Claims calls for parties to consider ADR as part of its case management procedure. Court rules require parties to have an early meeting of counsel to discuss, among other things, settlement of the action and the use of ADR.[45] Following this meeting, the rules require parties to file a joint preliminary status report, which must include a discussion of whether they contemplate using ADR.[46] It is worth noting that in cases before the Court of Federal Claims, the government will be represented by an attorney from the Department of Justice, with the participation of agency counsel. Court rules require the parties to submit a joint request for ADR to the judge presiding over the case, who makes the final decision on whether to approve it.[47]

The first option under the court's ADR program is for the case to be assigned to another Court of Federal Claims judge to act as a settlement judge. This method is similar to settlement judge programs in the boards of contract appeals, and Court of Federal Claims settlement judges tend to have the same advantages and disadvantages as board of contract appeals judges.

A second option is for the parties to request a minitrial. In a minitrial, parties present an abbreviated presentation of their case, after which the presiding neutral may render an advisory opinion or assist the parties in their discussions to resolve the dispute.

A third option is for the parties to request a private neutral to conduct mediation. This program is similar to traditional third-party mediation. Parties may choose their own neutral or select from a limited panel of experienced attorneys trained to handle ADR and selected by the court for this program.

Finally, under an ADR pilot program begun in 2001, all contract claims cases assigned to several judges will be assigned simultaneously to another judge to offer an early neutral evaluation. The pilot will compare the results of these cases with the results of cases that do not undergo early neutral evaluation, to determine if the program serves the interests of the court and the parties.

Preparation for Contract ADR

Contract cases are unusual in that they often involve a large number of interested parties, and an initial step in preparing for ADR is determining who should be at the table. In addition to the contractor and the government, other involved parties may include lenders, insurance companies, sureties, architects, engineers, and subcontractors. Including too many parties in an ADR process can create confusion and lack of efficiency. However, if any of these parties will have substantial power over whether an agreement can be reached and whether it can be put into effect once it is reached, they ordinarily should be present at the negotiating table.

Individuals who participated in the day-to-day administration of the contract in a claims case (or who prepared or evaluated the submissions in a bid protest case) sometimes have a less objective understanding of the matter. They may feel a need to rationalize and defend their earlier decisions in the case. Although it can be valuable for them to participate in the process because of their knowledge of the facts of the claim, lead representation is often better handled by an independent individual.

Audits are another important consideration. In many cases, it is necessary for the government to request an audit of contractor claims and equitable adjustment proposals. It can be valuable to give the contractor a copy of the audit report prior to engaging in ADR, so the contractor has an opportunity to provide additional information to satisfy the auditor's concerns. This can result in time savings for all parties. If questions persist, the government may wish to bring the auditor to the ADR process. Auditors also can contribute to the success of an ADR process because they have specialized expertise that can be invaluable in justifying a settlement financially. Contract claims based on audit exceptions, for example, can involve issues that are difficult to understand fully without specialized technical knowledge. In some cases, where the only issue is entitlement, an audit is not required, and the parties may prefer not to pay for one.

Parties should examine interest costs carefully in preparation for ADR. Interest often is a substantial part of a monetary claim in a contract case. The CDA and its implementing regulation provide that the government shall pay interest on a contractor's claim starting on the date the claim is received, at rates set by the treasury secretary.[48] The interest rate changes semiannually, on January 1 and July 1 of each year. Interest computations can be complicated, so parties should ensure they have calculated the total cost correctly. To avoid later confusion, it is best to specify the exact amount of interest in a settlement rather than state, "such interest as is due." Parties can agree to suspend the accumulation of interest during an ADR process.

Claims under the Equal Access to Justice Act are another issue in contract cases.[49] If a contractor is deemed a prevailing party in its claim, it may recover attorneys' fees and litigation costs if the government's defense is determined not to have been "substantially justified."[50] Similarly, in bid protest cases, a contractor can sometimes recover the costs of the protest and attorney fees. Under the Competition in Contracting Act of 1984, these costs may be available when the agency violated a procurement statute or regulation.[51] If these claims are at issue, parties will want to resolve them during the ADR process.

The source of funds to pay for a settlement should be of paramount concern to both parties. When a federal agency receives an appropriation for a government contract, monies are available only under certain circumstances and for specific, limited times. Congress has passed laws in this area to ensure that the executive branch is answerable to the legislature in the expenditure of federal funds.

During the what is referred to as the current phase of an appropriation, an agency may obligate funds on a contract. This phase lasts one year for operation and maintenance funds, two years for research and development funds, and three years for procurement funds. After this period is over, the funds are classified as expired.

During the expired phase of an appropriation, an agency may use funds to make payments only on the obligations incurred during the current phase. Money is available for liquidation and adjustment of previous obligations only, and an agency cannot incur new obligations. Within-scope changes and price adjustments, such as cost overruns and rate adjustments, are permitted. ADR during this phase can be more difficult, because there are tighter restrictions on the use of money. A higher level of scrutiny is involved in an agency's use of expired funds. Many agencies require an internal review process before permitting access to expired funds in a contract case. The expired phase of an appropriation lasts five years from the date the current phase ends.

In the final phase of an appropriation, the funds are considered canceled. At this point, the funds are completely unavailable to the agency for any purpose, including incurring new obligations or making payments on a previous obligation. An agency that wants to make payments on a contract at this point must find another funding source from a current appropriation. Even these payments can be subject to congressional approval. Thus, it is especially difficult to use ADR at the canceled phase. On rare occasions, an agency can obtain a supplemental appropriation at this point, but generally this is limited to exceptional circumstances and high-dollar matters.

Under certain circumstances, the government may pay for the settlement with the *judgment fund,* a government-wide pool of money available to satisfy claims. This fund is available where the settlement amount is entered as a judgment by a board of contract appeals or court pursuant to the parties' stipulation. This method is sometimes referred to as obtaining a *consent judgment* or *stipulated entry of judgment.* Parties can obtain this approval most easily by conducting the ADR under the auspices of a board or court, but they also may use this procedure for settlements they reach privately. The advantage of using this process is that judgment fund money is available immediately, reducing the delay that sometimes is required for approvals to obtain the money from agency funds. Saving time cuts down on interest payments for the government and allows the contractor to receive the money more quickly. A disadvantage of this method is that the agency must reimburse the judgment fund within two years, and it must do so using current-year funds. Thus, if expired funds are available under the contract to pay for the settlement, the government may wish to use them rather than tap into the judgment fund (which may not be reimbursed with expired funds).

Before engaging in ADR, parties should sign a written agreement covering the issues they will discuss and the procedures they will follow. In processes where the parties will make formal presentations (such as minitrial or summary trial with binding decision), they can set limits on the number of pages permitted for preliminary written submissions and the number of minutes allocated to each side for oral presentations. Parties should set forth the dates of the ADR process, along with the sequence of events to take place and the means by which the procedure will end. If parties have agreed to stay discovery or the accumulation of interest during the process, they should specify this in the agreement. Parties also may wish to determine in advance whom they will allow to participate and to attend. In some cases, a party may want to request the appearance of a specific individual on the other side if the party believes the presence of that individual will increase the likelihood of settlement. Parties also should record the amount of the mediator's fee and their agreement on how they will split it. The agreement may explain the role the parties expect the neutral to play (for example, whether facilitative or evaluative). The mediator and all parties should sign the agreement, and the mediator can make a valuable contribution toward its formulation.

Advocacy in Contract ADR

Because contract cases are different from other types of disputes, there are unique considerations in how to advocate effectively in this area.

Contract ADR proceedings can be comparatively formal processes, often taking place before board of contract appeals settlement judges or in other relatively evaluative contexts. Parties should provide the neutral with carefully drafted statements before the first ADR session, setting forth the facts and law in support of their case. They should be prepared to deliver an opening statement setting forth their arguments thoroughly. Parties should determine how to present their evidence most effectively. If clients are well-spoken and effective advocates, they can take the lead in presenting the case. In other cases, the lawyers should predominate. Some lawyers have used a question-and-answer format with their clients, similar to presenting live testimony at trial, although this can appear somewhat stilted. It is appropriate to bring exhibits and choose them carefully, as they can be very effective. Relevant contract language should be highlighted and presented to the neutral. It is often persuasive to compare "as planned" exhibits with "as built" exhibits.

Although emotions are present in every dispute, participants in contract cases often take a more business-oriented and factual approach (especially compared with workplace cases, where emotions can be paramount). Therefore, parties should be prepared to focus on the merits of their positions and expect to have extensive discussions of how the law should be applied to the facts of the case. In contract cases, considerable development of these issues is often necessary before the parties are willing to move toward discussions on how to resolve the matter. To use an analogy from trial practice, the liability phase of the proceeding generally must come before the damages phase. Nonetheless, parties in contract cases should not ignore emotional factors, which can be significant in some cases.

Neutrals in contract cases usually are more evaluative than in other types of cases. Parties often choose neutrals because of their expertise in the field and expect them to use their knowledge to provide predictions of what will happen if the case proceeds to a hearing. Therefore, it is particularly important in these cases for parties to persuade the neutral that their side of the case should prevail. Although a settlement judge's evaluation is generally nonbinding, it still can have a profound effect on the future of the case. For example, if a judge evaluates a case at a level that differs substantially from a party's settlement offer, the party will have a much harder time persuading the other side to accept the offer.

If parties reach a settlement agreement through ADR, they can agree to execute a bilateral modification of the contract. They can agree to settle the entire claim or any number of issues within it. The settlement must be justified, even though ADR was used. In appropriate cases, the government must arrange for an audit as well as require submission of certified cost or pricing information. If settlement occurs after the contractor has filed an appeal of the contracting officer's final decision, the contractor should agree to dismiss the appeal with prejudice. The government should insist that the contractor sign a release stating that the settlement extinguishes its claims.

If parties fail to reach an agreement, the case proceeds with adjudication along the same path that would have been followed if ADR had not been used. For example, if the ADR took place prior to the issuance of a contracting officer's final decision, the contracting officer will then reach a decision, and the contractor can file an appeal to a board of contract appeals or the U.S. Court of Claims. If the ADR occurred after the contractor had filed an appeal, the parties return to normal litigation.

Common options for settling claims cases are for the government to pay money for changes affecting the contract, alter delivery timetables, and substitute "termination for convenience" or "termination by agreement" for "termination by default." The last option, in appropriate cases, can assist a contractor by eliminating the negative effect of a default on past performance evaluations, improving its likelihood of receiving future contracts.

In bid protest settlements, parties have agreed, among other things, for the government to terminate the contract, hold a new competition for the contract, reevaluate the bids, revise the specifications and issue an amended solicitation, waive contract options after the first year to allow recompetition, permit the protestor to participate in the contract as a subcontractor (if the awardee agrees), and pay the costs of the bid. Bid protest resolutions through ADR also frequently take the form of withdrawal of the protest.

Chapter Eight

Confidentiality in Federal ADR

Confidentiality is generally not a problem in federal dispute resolution. In the thousands of ADR proceedings for cases in federal district court handled each year by the Justice Department, confidentiality problems have been very infrequent. In the tens of thousands of administrative ADR proceedings handled each year by other agencies, concerns in this area are equally unusual. Over the entire time that the Administrative Dispute Resolution Act (ADRA) has been in effect, there has been only a single reported federal case concerning administrative confidentiality.[1]

Nonetheless, confidentiality in government ADR is a subject that arouses considerable interest. Participants are understandably concerned about what use can be made of statements they make in ADR proceedings. To be sure, parties do not routinely make confessions in government ADR. There are no known examples of people admitting in a federal mediation that they embezzled millions of dollars or committed murder. Still, private parties may have reasonable concerns that the stakes are higher in an ADR proceeding where the other party represents the U.S. government. Furthermore, participants from the government know that their actions can face heightened scrutiny because important public interest issues are implicated in many settlements.

Federal statutes, regulations, and case law in this area recognize these competing interests. In the administrative arena, the ADRA sets the rules for confidentiality. In federal court, the Alternative Dispute Resolution Act of 1998 (ADR Act of 1998), local court rules, and case law define the bounds in this area. In both contexts, parties can bolster confidentiality protections through the use of a private contract or stipulated court order.[2]

The Importance of Confidentiality

Confidentiality is vital to dispute resolution for a number of reasons. First, parties feel freer to be candid with one another when they know their statements will not be used against them later. When participants feel secure, they are more willing to share detailed information about their interests and engage in the creative generation of options that can make settlement much more likely. Only when all parties have been forthright and thorough in expressing their interests can they craft a settlement that meets all of these interests as fully as possible. The Second Circuit Court of Appeals expressed the concept this way: "If participants cannot rely on the confidential treatment of everything that transpires during these sessions, then counsel of necessity will feel constrained to conduct themselves in a cautious, tight-lipped, noncommittal manner more suitable to poker players in a high stakes game than adversaries attempting to arrive at a just solution of a civil dispute."[3]

Confidentiality provides other benefits for parties as well. When proceedings are on the record, lawyers often engage in grandstanding that consumes considerable time and energy. Confidentiality removes the incentives to engage in this behavior. Lawyers posture somewhat less when there is no crowd to please and no transcript to record their words permanently.

Parties also are more candid when they know the neutral will not publicly take sides or disclose their statements after the proceedings are over. Without confidentiality protections, parties might be concerned that a neutral would reveal their confidential communications.

Neutrals also benefit from confidentiality. One of the most important qualities for a neutral is impartiality. If ADR were not confidential, parties could repeat statements by neutrals out of context in an attempt to shore up support for their case. These comments could compromise neutrals' reputations for impartiality, which would limit their effectiveness in future cases. Knowing that any of their statements could be repeated later, neutrals would feel greatly constrained in what they could say during an ADR proceeding.

The Ninth Circuit Court of Appeals noted the importance of confidentiality in this regard:

> To execute successfully their function of assisting in the settlement of labor disputes, the conciliators must maintain a reputation for impartiality. . . . If conciliators were permitted or required to testify about their activities, or if the production of notes or reports of their activities could be required, not even the strictest adherence to purely factual matters would prevent the evidence from favoring or seeming to favor one side or the other. The inevitable result would be that the usefulness of the [conciliators] in the settlement of future disputes would be seriously impaired, if not destroyed."[4]

The Limits of Confidentiality

At the same time, the values of confidentiality are not limitless. Whenever confidentiality is increased, the public's right to know is curtailed. This may have a serious cost in a democracy. It is a fundamental principle in law that the public is entitled to every person's evidence.[5]

Rules that provided for excessive confidentiality could allow bogus claims of privilege. For example, in one case, testimony in a racketeering trial concerned a "mediation" among criminal defendants conducted by another reportedly criminal group known as the "boys from New Jersey." If confidentiality were construed broadly, this type of evidence would be unavailable to convict lawbreakers who attempted to use ADR laws to shield their illegal conduct.[6] Conversely, ADR confidentiality should not extend so far that it prevents defendants from obtaining evidence necessary to establish their innocence. In one case, a defendant facing charges of attempted murder sought to introduce evidence that the victim had threatened his life during a mediation. Insisting on confidentiality in this case could send an innocent man to prison.[7]

The involvement of the government in federal dispute resolution also makes absolute confidentiality less appropriate. Citizens have a legitimate interest in knowing that government programs are using public funds appropriately. Federal dispute resolution in general would suffer a loss in reputation if participants were able to claim confidentiality as a shield for illegal activity or even gross inefficiency.

Fortunately, these situations are exceedingly unusual. Participants do not generally confess felonies in ADR proceedings where the government is involved. Even in the limited situations where untoward activity may have taken place, federal authorities usually have other avenues available to obtain necessary evidence. The use of ADR does not have any effect on evidence that existed before it began. For example, inspectors general or members of Congress can ask parties directly about possible illegal activity or obtain evidence from any of their traditional sources.

Federal Administrative Confidentiality

Congress balanced these competing concerns when it passed the ADRA.[8] This act provides for broad confidentiality for federal dispute resolution proceedings, along with a number of specific exemptions to ensure that protections are not unbounded. As an amendment to the Administrative Procedure Act, it applies to proceedings involving federal administrative programs. The Federal ADR Council, a group of high-level agency officials chaired by the attorney general, promulgated guidance on confidentiality under the ADRA, which is reproduced in Appendix F.

Confidentiality for Neutrals

Under the ADRA, a neutral is anyone who functions specifically to aid the parties in a federal administrative dispute resolution process.[9] This is a broad definition. It includes, for example, agency employees who participate in intake of cases and assembling of the parties for ADR processes.[10] There may be more than one neutral for a case, and a neutral may be from either the government or the private sector.[11] Confidentiality begins once a party contacts a neutral officially, and it ends when a final written agreement is reached or the neutral's dispute resolution work is completed.[12]

Neutrals must follow more stringent confidentiality rules than parties. Neutrals generally are prohibited from disclosing the contents of proceedings in which they participate.[13] The bar includes all oral statements made by the neutral, the parties, and other participants in the proceeding.[14] Similarly, neutrals may not disclose written documents prepared for the proceeding.[15] Neutrals may not voluntarily disclose these communications to anyone, and they cannot be compelled to do so through discovery or other legal process.[16] If something is improperly disclosed, it will not be admissible in any future proceeding relating to the issues originally being discussed.[17]

There are a number of exceptions to the confidentiality rule. The agreement to enter into an ADR proceeding and any settlement that results are not confidential.[18] Confidentiality for the neutral can be waived or limited if everyone, including the neutral, agrees in writing.[19] There is no protection for communications that are already public[20] or are required by statute to be made public.[21] However, in these cases, the neutral should make the disclosure only if no other person is reasonably available to do so.[22] The confidentiality rules permit the disclosure of information to document an agreement reached in an ADR proceeding[23] or resolve a dispute between a neutral and a party.[24] Information also may be used for research and educational purposes as long as specific parties and issues are not identifiable.[25]

Importantly, evidence that is otherwise discoverable does not become confidential merely because it was presented in an ADR proceeding.[26] If a key piece of evidence is discoverable, using it in ADR does not immunize it from the litigation process. This prevents parties from using ADR to block the admission of damaging evidence in court. A communication is not protected unless it was prepared specifically for the ADR proceeding. An example would be a medical report in a personal injury case that was prepared independent of the ADR and is otherwise discoverable. Introducing such a report in an ADR proceeding would not thereby render it confidential.

The ADRA also provides a judicial override provision allowing access to dispute resolution communications in limited circumstances. To use this provision, an individual must prove to a court that disclosure is necessary, on balance, to prevent a manifest injustice, help establish a violation of law, or prevent harm to the public health or safety.[27] The burden for establishing this necessity is a high one. The individual must prove that the need is sufficient to outweigh the damage that disclosure causes to the integrity of ADR proceedings in general.[28] This standard recognizes that any breach reduces the confidence of parties in future cases that their communications will be confidential.[29]

Confidentiality for Parties

Federal confidentiality rules are somewhat less stringent for parties than for neutrals. As a general matter, parties are prohibited from disclosing what happens in federal administrative ADR proceedings.[30] They generally may not disclose either oral statements or written communications prepared for the proceeding.[31] Nor may they be compelled to do so through discovery or other legal process.[32] If something is improperly disclosed, it will not be admissible in any future proceeding relating to the issues originally being discussed.[33]

However, the ADRA creates significant exceptions to confidentiality for parties. First, parties enjoy all of the confidentiality exceptions already noted for neutrals. Also, they are free to disclose their own communications to anyone.[34] Thus, parties may talk to their spouses or friends about what they said (though not about what the neutral said). If all the parties agree in writing, they may waive or limit confidentiality.[35] They do not need the neutral's consent to do this.[36] Parties also are permitted to disclose communications to establish the existence or meaning of an agreement resulting from an ADR proceeding.[37]

Confidentiality of Joint Sessions

Probably the most controversial exception to confidentiality in federal ADR is that parties are free to disclose communications (other than those from the neutral) that were available to all the parties in a proceeding.[38] Thus, statements that a party makes in a joint session with all other parties present may be disclosed by another party under the ADRA, as may documents that a party exchanges among all the other parties.[39] This is the most significant difference between federal and nonfederal ADR confidentiality. In the vast majority of private sector ADR proceedings, joint sessions are completely confidential. In federal ADR, they are not. This provision often comes as a surprise or even a shock to first-time participants in federal ADR.

The reason for this provision goes back to the fact that federal ADR involves taxpayer money and public employees. Parties to private ADR are free to agree to whatever confidentiality protections they desire, but the public's right to know may be stronger when public business is taking place. When Congress was considering what confidentiality provisions to include in the ADRA, some interest groups argued that the public should not be denied access to matters discussed in government ADR proceedings.

The compromise reached was that private caucuses between a party and a neutral would be confidential, but parties would be free to disclose what was said in joint sessions. This distinction builds on the traditional rule that routine, unassisted negotiations between government representatives and private parties over matters of public business are not confidential. Thus, these party-to-party negotiations remain public even when they take place in the presence of a neutral. In contrast, a unique feature of ADR is the opportunity to have private caucuses with a neutral. Because these types of private caucuses would not even occur without an ADR proceeding, making them confidential does not result in substantial harm to the public interest.

This rule has significant implications for confidentiality in federal ADR. Arbitration hearings, because they are conducted with all parties in the room, are not confidential. Some styles of mediation (for example, the transformative approach) take place almost entirely in joint session with all parties present. Thus, such proceedings are not confidential in the federal context either. Parties in a mediation who are particularly concerned about confidentiality may wish to consider a greater use of private caucuses, which are confidential. (Parties in an arbitration do not have this option.) Fortunately, there are ways to increase confidentiality through the use of a contract.

The rule does include an exception for communications "generated by the neutral."[40] Statements and documents from a neutral remain confidential, even when they are from a joint session. This exception was originally drafted to support the use of early neutral evaluation. Parties would be reluctant to submit a case for an evaluation by a neutral expert where the other side was permitted to use an unfavorable report against them later. Both sides are more inclined to participate at the outset if they know they are protected from this result. The exception also covers oral statements. This protects the parties when evaluations are given orally. It also protects the interest of the neutral in being seen as impartial. Neutrals will feel freer to talk openly with parties when they know these comments will not be publicized later to add support for one side or the other.

Disclosure Procedures

A neutral who receives a subpoena, Freedom of Information Act[41] request, or other formal demand for ADR communications cannot immediately supply the requested information. Rather, the neutral must make a reasonable effort to notify the parties of the request, even if the information apparently must be disclosed.[42] The purpose of this notice is to give the parties an opportunity to defend a refusal to disclose the information.

The neutral should send notice to the last address provided by the parties by a method that provides for certification of delivery.[43] Parties then have fifteen days to respond and offer to defend a refusal to disclose. If a party has no desire to suppress the information, it need not respond to the notice. If a party does want to prevent disclosure, it must notify the neutral and arrange to defend formally the refusal to disclose. A party who does not respond within fifteen days waives any objection to the disclosure.[44]

If none of the parties objects to the disclosure, the neutral has discretion on how to respond. The neutral may decide to provide the requested information or refuse to disclose and seek to quash the request.[45]

Inspectors General and Other Requesting Entities

Another area of potential tension between the desire for confidentiality in ADR and the limits caused by government involvement arises with inspectors general and other investigatory entities. This was the issue that attracted the most public comment on release of the confidentiality guidance from the Federal ADR Council in 2000.[46] The question is whether government investigatory agencies can have access to communications in federal ADR proceedings that otherwise would be confidential under the ADRA.

Some commenters believe that laws providing for investigatory access to government records do not take precedence over the ADRA.[47] An argument for this result is that Congress passed the

ADRA more recently than the investigatory statutes, and it more specifically covers the issues involved here: communications in ADR proceedings. Under this analysis, an inspector general or other authority could gain access to ADR communications only by obtaining a court order pursuant to the judicial override procedure set forth in the ADRA.

However, going to court is not a viable option in some government investigations. Under certain circumstances, an agency may not wish even to inform the parties of a request in order to avoid compromising a law enforcement investigation. Many agencies have express legislative authority to conduct investigations,[48] and it could be argued that these specific provisions override the general confidentiality protections of the ADRA.[49] Other laws and regulations provide that federal employees must disclose information about a felony;[50] evidence of waste, fraud, abuse, and corruption;[51] and information about crimes involving government officers and employees.[52]

There does not appear to be an easy reconciliation of these competing authorities. The legislative history of the ADRA sheds no light on these issues, as Congress does not appear to have formally discussed them when drafting the law. Resolution of these conflicting interpretations ultimately may require a court decision. The Federal ADR Council considered this issue when publishing its confidentiality guidance.[53] However, the council determined it did not have the authority to issue a binding resolution of the matter because it is an advisory body.[54]

The Federal ADR Council did issue a series of recommendations on how to handle this type of situation.[55] It stated that agency ADR programs and requesting entities should educate each other about their respective missions. ADR programs should freely provide nonconfidential information such as budgetary and statistical data about the number and types of cases, along with the different processes used. Both organizations then should jointly establish procedures to balance the competing interests involved, including processes to follow to resolve specific disagreements when they arise.

The Federal ADR Council stated that agency ADR programs and requesting entities should follow the judicial override standard in the ADRA whenever possible.[56] This standard acknowledges the need for access to information to prevent manifest injustice, establish violations of law, and prevent harm to the public health and safety. However, the standard also notes that this need must be balanced with the importance of protecting the integrity of dispute resolution proceedings in general and the consequences of breaching confidentiality. Finally, in a significant provision, the council stated that requesting entities should seek confidential information from an ADR proceeding only if the information is not available through other means.[57]

The inspector general community was actively involved in the drafting of the council's confidentiality guidance, and it submitted a letter recognizing the balance to be struck between investigatory needs and the need for ADR confidentiality. The following excerpt from that letter is noteworthy: "The Inspector General community considers the Report to reflect an effort to balance the need for confidentiality in alternate dispute resolution (ADR) proceedings with the need for access to information in order to protect the integrity of agency programs and activities. We also believe that the instances in which an Office of Inspector General would seek confidential information arising from an ADR proceeding would be rare."[58] Continued dialogue among the key players in this area will be beneficial to all participants.

Texas Tech Grand Jury Subpoena Case

One federal case decided prior to the issuance of the Federal ADR Council's confidentiality guidance has gained some notoriety: *In re Grand Jury Proceedings*.[59] In this case, the inspector general of the Department of Agriculture suspected criminal fraud was taking place during certain farm loan mediations. The mediations were conducted by Texas Tech University pursuant to a federal grant. When the university resisted administrative requests for evidence from the mediations, the U.S. Attorney in Dallas convened a federal grand jury, which issued subpoenas for the information. A motion was filed in the district court to quash the subpoenas, which the judge granted.

On appeal, the Fifth Circuit Court of Appeals ruled that the ADRA confidentiality protections did not apply in this case because there was no federal administrative "issue in controversy."[60] The ADRA requires "an issue which is material to a decision concerning an administrative program of an agency, and with which there is disagreement—(A) between an agency and persons who would be substantially affected by the decision; or (B) between persons who would be substantially affected by the decision."[61] The court holds in a single sentence, and without elaborating on the point, that the subpoena does not call for any such information.

The rationale for this holding is murky. Surely, neither of the parties to the appeal had even raised the issue. Although the ADRA's definition of "issue in controversy" is not as clear as it might be, both parties agreed that a federal issue was involved in the case. The Department of Agriculture was a party to most of the cases that were mediated, and the issues being mediated concerned actions and decisions of federal employees under the federal Agricultural Credit Act. Furthermore, the mediations were funded pursuant to a federal grant program. Indeed, the very reason the inspector general was involved was that the case involved federal issues.[62]

It is an open question whether the ADRA or the Inspector General Act must give way when both are applicable. However, the decision in this case that the ADRA did not even apply is puzzling. It is worth noting that the materials were provided only to the grand jury, whose proceedings are secret, at least until a public trial occurs.[63] The Fifth Circuit Court of Appeals explicitly noted the confidentiality of the grand jury in its opinion.[64]

Federal Court Confidentiality

Although federal administrative proceedings are governed by the ADRA, there is no comparable cross-cutting statute controlling proceedings in federal court. Confidentiality in federal court is determined by a series of sources, including the Federal Rules of Evidence, the ADR Act of 1998, local court rules, case law applying to federal mediation agencies, federal common law, and state privilege law.

Federal Rules of Evidence

Federal Rule of Evidence 408 addresses evidentiary admissibility of settlement discussions taking place in federal litigation (and some administrative adjudications).[65] Under the rule, "evidence of conduct or statements made in compromise negotiations" is not admissible to "prove liability for or invalidity of the claim or its amount."[66] There are several purposes behind the rule. First, statements made in settlement negotiations are unreliable because they may be motivated more by a desire for peace than by any weakness in litigation position.[67] Second, public policy favors compromise and settlement of disputes.[68] The rule encourages settlement negotiations because parties will be able to communicate more freely when they know their statements will not be used against them later. This rule provides a minimum level of protection for ADR participants because it is always in effect, whether parties contract for confidentiality or not.

However, there are substantial limitations to the protection afforded by Rule 408. First, it limits only the admissibility of statements at trial. Parties are free to file discovery requests to learn about statements made during negotiations, on the theory that this may lead to the discovery of other admissible evidence. Even further, parties are free to disclose statements made in settlement negotiations to anyone, and even to publicize them. The only prohibition is against using them in a court of law. Frequently, parties to ADR want their discussions to be completely private, and thus the rule provides little comfort, as communications can be used for almost any purpose as long as they are not used at trial.

Even the prohibition against use in trial has a number of exceptions. The rule applies only to evidence used to establish or disprove liability for a claim or its amount. Many other purposes exist for the admission of evidence, and clever trial lawyers often can introduce the evidence for another purpose. For example, statements made in an ADR proceeding may be used to impeach a witness by showing bias or prejudice. They also can be admitted to prove matters such as motive, knowledge, and intent, and they can be admissible as prior inconsistent statements.

Federal Rule of Evidence 403 may provide an additional source of confidentiality protection for settlement discussions in some circumstances. This rule states that evidence may be excluded if its value in proving the case is outweighed by the unfair prejudicial effect of admitting it. Courts have held that evidence from settlement discussions that might be admissible under Rule 408 sometimes may be excluded under Rule 403. The rationale is that in some cases, using settlement communications would be so unfairly prejudicial that it should be prohibited.[69]

Alternative Dispute Resolution Act of 1998

Congress explicitly provided for confidentiality in federal courts with the ADR Act of 1998.[70] The act requires every U.S. district court to "devise and implement its own alternative dispute resolution program" and to "provide for the confidentiality of the alternative dispute resolution processes and to prohibit disclosure of confidential dispute resolution communications."[71] This provision shows a clear federal policy in favor of confidentiality for ADR proceedings connected with federal court litigation.

The act does not specify, however, what is meant by confidentiality. For example, does the act prohibit only admissibility of ADR statements in trial, along the lines of federal Rule of Evidence 408? Or does the act contemplate additional safeguards, such as protection from discovery as well? Did Congress mean to provide for confidentiality outside the litigation process, preventing someone from disclosing ADR statements to a friend or spouse? What is the remedy for a breach? Are there any exceptions to confidentiality, such as for crimes or emergencies? These are all questions that Congress declined to answer in this act.

This act provides that confidentiality eventually will be set by national rules under Chapter 131 of title 28 of the U.S. Code. However, this process requires the involvement of the Supreme Court and Congress.[72] Because this could take a number of years, the act states that in the meantime, confidentiality will be set in each individual district by local rule.[73]

Local Court Rules

Until national rules are established, local court rules will play a major role in determining confidentiality in federal court.[74] These local rules vary enormously among districts.[75] Some merely mirror federal Rule of Evidence 408 or incorporate it by reference. Others expand on Rule 408 and provide that ADR statements are neither admissible nor discoverable. Still others prohibit parties from disclosing ADR statements to anyone not involved in the litigation. Because practice varies so widely among jurisdictions, it is vital to examine the local rules in the district where a case takes place. It can make a difference whether the ADR takes place in a court-annexed program or privately, because some local rules apply only to their own court programs. Not every district has yet responded to the ADR Act of 1998, so there will be more changes in this area in the future.

In federal circuit courts of appeal, local rules also determine confidentiality. Every regional circuit court has an ADR program in place, typically using neutrals who are court employees. The administration of these programs is wholly separate from the decision-making process in the court. Local rules of confidentiality generally prohibit participants from discussing what takes place in these programs with anyone, including judges and nonparties. Participants generally are permitted to discuss the fact that discussions took place and whether settlement occurred, along with any filing entered on the court's docket.[76]

Case Law Applying to Federal Mediation

Federal have held that confidentiality privileges exist for agencies with a statutory mediation function. For example, the Ninth Circuit Court of Appeals ruled that a neutral from the Federal Mediation and Conciliation Service (FMCS) was immune from testifying because of the importance of confidentiality to achieving the goals of the statute that created the agency.[77] The opinion mentioned FMCS regulations that provide for confidentiality.[78] Although the holding was limited to the FMCS, the court used language that could apply to other agencies by analogy: "The public interest in maintaining the perceived and actual impartiality of federal mediators does outweigh the benefits derivable from [the mediator's] testimony."[79] The court continued, "The parties to conciliation conferences must feel free to talk without any fear that the conciliator may subsequently make disclosures as a witness in some other proceeding."[80]

Courts found a similar privilege for federal Community Relations Service (CRS) mediators, who are statutorily charged with assisting in resolving civil rights disputes. In *Wilson v. Attaway* (1985), the court noted that the statute creating the CRS explicitly provides that their activities "shall be conducted in confidence and without publicity."[81] The trial court held that if the mediator were forced to testify, "the CRS would be substantially embarrassed and rendered less effective in the performance of their mission. . . . His testimony could taint the impartiality of CRS and thereby undermine its conciliation and mediation process."[82] Although these cases apply directly to only the limited number of agencies that exist explicitly to mediate disputes, the reasoning they employ may be helpful in other contexts as well.

Federal Common Law

A broader source of confidentiality protection may be developing in the direction of a federal common law mediation privilege. This is a new area, with a number of the leading cases in the past several years. It remains to be seen whether these cases will be the start of a trend in the federal courts. If the trend holds, common law may provide confidentiality for federal mediations in general, not just those involving specific mediation agencies such as the FMCS and CRS.

Federal common law is explicitly recognized as a source of privileges in the Federal Rules of Evidence. The rules state that the standard for privileges "shall be governed by the principles of the common law as they may be interpreted by the courts of the United States in the light of reason and experience."[83] In general, privileges are disfavored, under the axiom that the public is entitled to every person's evidence. However, the Supreme Court has ruled that privileges are appropriate when there is a "public good transcending the normally predominant principle of utilizing all rational means for ascertaining the truth."[84] The Court has held that this determination has four parts: (1) whether the privilege is rooted in the imperative need for confidence and trust, (2) whether it would serve public ends, (3) whether the evidentiary detriment caused by exercise of the privilege is modest, and (4) whether denial of the federal privilege would frustrate a parallel privilege adopted by the states.[85]

A privilege for mediation communications would seem to meet all four prongs of this test. The first federal case to so hold was *Folb* v. *Motion Picture Industry Pension and Health Plans*.[86] The *Folb* court worked through each of the four factors in this standard and determined that a new federal mediation privilege was necessary. As for the first factor, the court ruled that a mediation privilege is important to establish the public's confidence and trust by permitting people to speak candidly during the process.[87] The court held that the other three prongs of the test were satisfied as well. A mediation privilege serves public ends by promoting conciliatory relationships among parties and reducing the size of overcrowded court dockets.[88] It causes little evidentiary detriment because evidence from a mediation usually can be obtained directly from the parties.[89] Finally, it avoids frustrating parallel privileges that exist in nearly every state.[90]

Two years later, another federal court recognized a common law mediation privilege.[91] This court followed the same four-part analysis used in the *Folb* case. The opinion was bolstered by the passage of the ADR Act of 1998, which went into effect shortly after the *Folb* decision. Although this act speaks in terms of confidentiality rather than privilege, the court cited it as further evidence of the important federal interests served by a privilege.[92] Two years after that, a federal bankruptcy court also found a mediation privilege using the four-part analysis.[93]

Other courts have declined to find a federal common law mediation privilege, but they are distinguishable. The *In re Grand Jury Proceedings*[94] decision noted, "Because privileges are not lightly created, we will not infer one where Congress has not clearly manifested an intent to create one."[95] However, this case was decided several months prior to the passage of the ADR Act of 1998, which does clearly manifest a congressional intent to create a privilege. Similarly, the court in *In re March, 1994 Special Grand Jury* said, "Federal law does not recognize a mediator's privilege," but this case as well was decided prior to the ADR Act of 1998.[96] The court in *Olam* v. *Congress Mortgage Company* required a mediator to testify about mediation communications, but it did so only after determining that California state law applied because of the nature of the claims involved.[97] Therefore, this case makes no holding under federal common law. Nor was the federal government a party to the case. Finally, the court in *Federal Deposit Insurance Corporation* v. *White* permitted a party to testify about mediation communications, but only to the extent the communications pertained to the claim that they were coerced, during the mediation, into settling.[98] This limited exception does not go to the heart of the purposes of a mediation privilege.

The recent cases finding a federal mediation privilege do not by themselves constitute a trend, but the analysis they use seems sound.

The passage of the ADR Act of 1998 adds considerable support to this approach. If case law continues in this direction, a federal common law privilege eventually may become generally recognized.

State Privilege Law

In some limited cases, matters involving the federal government will be decided with reference to state law. Although federal common law applies in federal question cases, courts can choose to examine the law of the forum state in certain cases.[99] In one such case, *United States* v. *Gullo,* the court considered state privilege law because the mediation took place under the auspices of a state dispute resolution program.[100] The court found that a mediation privilege applied even though the matter was a criminal case. The opinion noted that the prosecution had not shown a particularized need for the evidence.[101] Furthermore, the state-promulgated privilege served a valuable function by encouraging "the resolution of disputes in an informal atmosphere without restraint and intimidation."[102]

Most states and the District of Columbia have adopted mediation privilege of some kind.[103] Some of these statutes apply only to specific mediation programs. Only about half have general application.[104] The variation in state laws resembles the variation in federal court local rules. Some prohibit only admissibility at trial, others block discovery as well, and others ban disclosure in general.[105]

The Uniform Mediation Act (UMA) will affect state privilege law in the future. The UMA was adopted by the National Conference of Commissioners on Uniform State Laws in 2001 and approved by the American Bar Association in 2002. States around the country are now in the process of considering passage of this act. The act provides for a mediation privilege that prevents the use of communications in proceedings including civil and criminal trials, arbitrations, and administrative hearings. Exceptions to the general privilege exist for threats of bodily harm, reports of abuse and neglect, and the use of mediation to further a crime. Under limited circumstances, a judge may order disclosure to establish fraud, duress, or professional malpractice in a mediation. As state legislatures continue to pass the UMA, mediation participants will need to follow closely the current practice in their jurisdictions.

Confidentiality in Practice

The following section includes a number of important practice pointers for parties who use ADR in cases involving the federal government. Special problems exist in government cases, and there are a number of possible solutions for these problems.

ADR Communications Can Be Discovered

No matter how much confidentiality is provided in laws and regulations, parties should be aware of what they say during ADR. Even if the law is clear that actual statements made in ADR cannot be disclosed, the underlying facts behind those statements may remain discoverable. Parties should consider these factors before discussing information that may be damaging to their case.

First, confidentiality in both administrative actions and federal court does not grant new protection to documents that are otherwise discoverable. Thus, if a party shows a document to the other side in an ADR proceeding, the other side can request a copy of the document in discovery. If the document was discoverable before the ADR proceeding, it remains so afterward as well. This rule is designed to prevent parties from "laundering" damaging evidence by using it in ADR. This can be a trap for the unwary if a party believes anything used in ADR is automatically immunized from discovery.

Even more disconcerting for some unprepared parties is the realization that statements made in ADR can become the subject of later discovery requests. For example, if a party confesses in ADR that he ran a stop sign, the other side may file a request for admission the next day on this issue. Although the fact that he made the statement in ADR is not admissible, the underlying fact that he ran the stop sign is admissible. The request thus puts the party in a difficult situation: the other side cannot force testimony about what was said in the ADR proceeding, but the party may not deny the truth of the request for admission if he did run the stop sign.

Following these lines, a federal court noted, "Evidence disclosed in mediation may be obtained directly from the parties to the mediation by using normal discovery channels. For example, a person's admission in mediation proceedings may, at least theoretically, be elicited in response to a request for admission or to questions in a deposition or in written interrogatories."[106]

Confidentiality Contracts

Although contracts cannot protect against every situation, they are a good way to provide for additional confidentiality in federal ADR. In federal court, parties are free to sign confidentiality contracts, and these follow the same rules of interpretation as any other contract. Parties may wish to note explicitly that they intend to invoke the protections of federal Rule of Evidence 408. They can supplement Rule 408 protections by agreeing to waive their right to discovery pertaining to ADR communications as well. In especially sensitive cases, they may wish to agree to prohibit disclosure to anyone outside the dispute as well.

In the administrative context, parties may use a contract to increase confidentiality protections.[107] They can agree to make joint sessions confidential, which otherwise would not be the case under the ADRA. However, there are several important caveats to the protection available through contract. First, a contract binds only those who sign it; its provisions may not affect third parties. Therefore, an outside party remains free to subpoena the participants in a federal ADR proceeding. Second, a contract cannot override the Freedom of Information Act (FOIA).[108] Thus, outside parties retain their statutory right under FOIA to request access to government documents that were exchanged among all the parties in an ADR proceeding.[109] Third, there is a chance a court might refuse to enforce such a contract for public policy reasons, particularly in a challenge to the enforceability of a subsequent settlement agreement the parties reached.[110]

Nonetheless, a contract still provides significant protection for federal ADR proceedings. Outside parties often have no knowledge that an ADR proceeding took place. Therefore, unless the parties tell them, they are unlikely to know that information exists in the first place. A contract can prevent participants from telling outside parties about the proceeding. Without this knowledge, outsiders will not be aware of any reason to issue subpoenas or FOIA requests.

Furthermore, FOIA applies only to documents. Thus, outside parties are unable to use it to obtain access to oral statements made in an ADR proceeding. If parties anticipate a possible FOIA request, they can limit their use of documents and confine any crucial communications to oral statements.

Stipulated Protective Orders

When a court or administrative board is involved in a case, parties have another option: a protective order. A protective order blocks third parties from access to ADR communications in subsequent cases. Courts and boards routinely issue protective orders, particularly when the need for confidentiality is significant and both sides stipulate to the order.[111] The importance of confidentiality for ADR to function effectively can support such an order. Parties who violate a protective order face contempt penalties.

Even protective orders do not provide absolute protection, because they may be challenged by other parties. There are two main grounds for overturning a protective order. The first is that it was granted improvidently.[112] To protect against this, parties should include in the order a detailed description of why confidentiality is necessary and should limit the order to materials for which it is required.[113]

The other way for a party to overturn a protective order is to show "extraordinary circumstances or compelling need."[114] In this situation, the court will weigh the competing interests of both sides. The reviewing court should recognize that litigants in our justice system must be able to rely on assurances of confidentiality given by trial judges.[115] The protection afforded is weakest when the parties seeking the information are involved in criminal cases, and sometimes courts have overturned protective orders in the light of "the sweeping power of the grand jury to compel the production of evidence."[116] However, other courts have upheld confidentiality even in criminal cases, noting "the need of our district courts and civil litigants to facilitate efficient resolution of disputes."[117]

Federal Records Act Issues

Another practical question is whether federal parties and mediators must preserve their notes pursuant to the Federal Records Act (FRA).[118] The FRA governs what documents must be kept in order to maintain an "accurate and complete documentation of the policies and transactions of the federal Government."[119] Under the FRA, the head of each federal agency is charged with defining which documents the agency will keep regarding its functions, policies, decisions, procedures, and essential transactions.[120] Each agency must keep records sufficient to protect the legal and financial rights of the government and of persons directly affected by the agency's activities.[121]

Because the FRA requires each agency to set its own records rules, practice in different parts of the government in this area may vary. Government employees who participate in an ADR proceeding should check with their own records offices to determine their course of action. If their agency rules cover ADR notes and documents, they must preserve these according to the agency's record retention schedule.

Neutrals who handle cases for the federal government also should check with the sponsoring agency. Private mediators may have no obligation to maintain their notes, while neutrals who work for the agency directly may have to maintain their records, especially if they serve in this function as part of their official job duties. Neutrals whose responsibilities are in another area and serve only on collateral duty are less likely to have to preserve their records. Again, however, these decisions are up to each individual agency. In workplace cases, the Equal Employment Opportunity Commission has stated that neutrals shall "ensure confidentiality, including destroying all written notes taken during the ADR proceeding or in preparation for the proceeding."[122]

The nature of the records at issue can be significant. Peripheral items such as notes reflecting personal impressions of a lower-level employee are less likely to be considered an agency record because they are not central to the policies and decisions of the agency. Documents from a senior official specifically reflecting the decision-making process are more likely to be considered records that must be preserved.

Finally, it is worth noting that public access to government records is governed by FOIA,[123] not the FRA. Thus, just because a document must be preserved does not mean the public will be able to obtain it. In federal court matters, the usual exemptions to disclosure under FOIA remain in effect. In administrative matters, the ADRA provides additional protection for confidential communications between a neutral and a party, making them explicitly immune from disclosure under FOIA.[124] To prevent inadvertent disclosure, it is good practice to mark ADR materials that are kept as federal records as follows: "Confidential ADR Documents—Do Not Disclose."

Statements by the Neutral About Confidentiality

A final issue that arises in this area is what a neutral in a federal ADR proceeding should tell the parties about confidentiality. When parties are sophisticated and represented by counsel, this is not a significant problem, because all sides will be aware of the issues involved. However, in many federal cases (such as workplace disputes), parties may be inexperienced with ADR. They may have little knowledge of the nuances in this area. In these cases, the neutral should explain confidentiality to the parties during the opening statement so that they understand what they can expect.

This can be a daunting task for the neutral. As we have seen, there are many complexities in this area. A neutral will want to explain as much as is necessary to ensure the parties have adequate notice of what will happen. It is important that they understand what is confidential in the proceeding as well as what is not. However, it can be equally important that the neutral does not burden the parties with excessive legal language and complicated hypothetical situations that are unlikely to arise. This is particularly significant at the beginning of a dispute resolution session, when a lengthy statement could discourage their participation. An exhaustive treatment of this issue would be enormously time-consuming and could raise more questions for the parties than it answered.

The Federal ADR Council wrestled with this issue when drafting its confidentiality guidance.[125] The council agreed that a neutral's opening statement should give parties adequate notice while not overloading them with unnecessary information. The guidance states that the opening should include the following components:

1. Application of the ADRA to administrative ADR processes.
2. Intent of the ADRA to provide confidentiality for communications between the parties and the neutral.
3. The ADRA's provisions for confidentiality between parties, as well as their limitations.

4. Exceptions to the ADRA's nondisclosure provisions pertinent to the particular dispute.
5. Option to argument confidentiality protections through a written agreement.
6. Possible application of authorities other than the ADRA.[126]

The council noted that neutrals should tailor their opening statements to the specific needs of the parties and the case. Statements would differ, for example, depending on the type of ADR used, the number of parties participating, and the issues involved. The council drafted the following general recommendation for a sample opening statement that covers the most important points:

> The confidentiality provisions of the Administrative Dispute Resolution Act apply to this mediation. The Act focuses primarily on protecting private communications between parties and the mediator. Generally speaking, if you tell me something during this process, I will keep it confidential. The same is true for written documents you prepare for this process and give only to me.
>
> There are exceptions to the confidentiality provisions in the act. For example, statements you make with all the other parties in the room or documents you provide to them are not confidential. Also, in unusual circumstances, a judge can order disclosure of information that would prevent a manifest injustice, help establish a violation of law, or prevent harm to public health and safety.
>
> You can agree to more confidentiality if you want to. For example, you can agree to keep statements you make or documents you share with the other parties confidential. If you want to do this, everyone will need to agree in writing. Outside parties may, however, still have access to statements or documents as provided by law.[127]

This statement provides a helpful example of an opening that highlights the key issues for the parties in plain language.

Chapter Nine

Federal ADR Program Design, Management, and Training

This chapter provides a broad overview of the considerations involved in designing and managing federal government ADR programs, as well as ideas on how to conduct ADR training.[1]

Federal ADR Program Design

The first step in designing a federal government ADR program is to conduct an assessment of how the agency is handling disputes. Important considerations include who the disputants are, the number of disputes, the different ways they are processed, the costs of each of these techniques, and the efficiency of the overall system. It also is important to explore all the reasons that the agency uses its current methods, including ones that may not be apparent at first. There may be important factors supporting the existing approaches that need to be considered when designing new ones. Designers should interview a wide range of people in examining these issues. This information can provide valuable clues into how ADR can be most helpful.

Designers can use this information to determine the goals of an ADR program. Sometimes agencies want the program to achieve specific improvements over the existing system, such as quicker and cheaper resolution of disputes, improved relationships among personnel, and more creative and satisfying agreements. They may implement ADR programs to fulfill legal obligations, such as the mandate to create employment mediation programs issued by the Equal Employment Opportunity Commission[2] or the general requirement promulgated by Congress and the president that the government promote the use of ADR.[3] The goals of the program will play a role in determining how to design it.[4]

An agency's mission, culture, and organizational structure are important to consider when designing an ADR program for it. The needs of larger agencies are different from those of smaller ones. Agencies that are centralized in one location operate differently from those that are spread throughout the country.

Change is often difficult for the government, and designers should recognize this fact. Indeed, the government is specifically designed, in part, not to change. Laws and regulations are created with the idea that they are permanent. To be sure, the government also is intended to evolve, but such evolution is sometimes halting and usually slow. Those seeking rapid transformation of an agency's dispute resolution systems are likely to be disappointed.

Barriers to ADR in the Federal Government

One of the most effective ways to foster change in the government is to reduce the sources of resistance to it. There are many barriers to the use of ADR in the federal government.[5]

The first barrier is the culture of competition in parts of the government. Many government employees (like employees everywhere else) are accustomed to the adversarial method of resolving disputes. There is a rich tradition in American culture of glorifying combat, from dramatic courtroom battle to war. Peacemakers typically receive far less celebration than combatants do. In parts of the government, attorneys who win trials are given awards and promotions, while those who settle cases merely receive new cases to handle. In order to address this barrier, agencies need to create new incentives that reward people for resolving disputes rather than fighting about them. For example, agencies have amended position descriptions to indicate that ADR is an important part of the job, have included successful use of ADR as a component of the evaluation process, and have created awards for effective use of ADR.

Another barrier is that some people in the government perceive new programs as fads. Career government employees see political appointees come and go, as do their new initiatives. Some perceive ADR as another in a long list of ideas that will pass quickly. To counter this sentiment, it should be noted that the government has been using these concepts for more than a century, and they have been growing rapidly for more than a decade.

Others in the government resist ADR because they have no experience with it and are afraid of what it might mean for them. Long-time government employees sometimes believe they know how to do their job best already, and they do not like the implication that there is some new method they should use instead. Research has shown that one of the best ways to overcome this resistance is to give people experience with ADR.[6] After trying it even once, most people are much more eager to use it again. Some agencies have gone even further and created goals for ADR use that have been effective in motivating employees. The Postal Service, for example, has a goal for parties to choose ADR in 70 percent of EEO cases. Every month, the agency distributes a report listing the performance of every district in meeting this target.

Some perverse incentives in the government encourage adversarial dispute resolution methods rather than consensual ones. For example, the Federal Tort Claims Act provides that private sector attorneys may receive fees of 20 percent of the damage award for administrative settlements, while they may receive 25 percent of the award for federal court settlements.[7] This incentive may encourage some lawyers to resist settling at the administrative level and proceed to federal litigation instead. Similarly, some agencies determine the size and budgets of various offices by the number of cases they have pending. If these offices settle cases more quickly, they may find their resources dwindle. ADR program designers should identify any of these circumstances and find ways to counteract them.

Some agencies have helped counter these disincentives by sponsoring government-wide awards for successful ADR programs. In the workplace arena, the Office of Personnel Management offers annual Director's Awards for Outstanding Alternative Dispute Resolution Programs. The Office of Management and Budget sponsors an annual award ceremony as well for outstanding contracting ADR programs. These awards serve an important function by granting recognition to agencies that have implemented successful ADR programs.

A final major barrier for any new government program is obtaining personnel and money. Most agencies are streamlining their operations and calling on programs to do more with less. In this climate, it can be difficult to get new programs established. ADR program designers should be ready to present documented evidence that ADR ultimately saves an agency far more than it costs, together with projected time lines showing when the payback should begin. (Chapters One and Ten include information that can be useful in this regard.)

ADR Program Design Working Groups

Forming a broad-based working group is a vital initial step in designing an ADR program at a government agency. The group should include representatives from every important type of stakeholder in the disputes that the program will address. For example, it could include people from the agency general counsel's office, relevant programmatic offices, policy offices, unions, and administrative judge staff. If the agency has a Washington office and regional field offices, both should be represented. If the ADR program will work with members of the private sector, such as contractors or the regulated community, it can be useful to have people from these constituencies participate.

It can be particularly helpful to enlist a high-level official as a member of the working group. Program managers should learn about top managers in the agency to determine if any is likely to be supportive of ADR. If so, managers should see if it is possible to persuade one of them to serve in the group. At a later stage in the program, high-level officials can assist with obtaining budgetary and personnel resources for an ADR program, and they can issue policy directives that require or encourage agency staff to consider ADR.

A working group has several important functions. First, it ensures that the ADR program will be designed with full understanding of the interests of all affected groups. Designers who do not consult with unions in workplace ADR programs, for example, may learn that their program conflicts with collective bargaining agreements in ways that could have been avoided. Similarly, outside companies may resist participating in agency contracting ADR programs when their interests were not accommodated during the design phase.

Another crucial reason to include a wide range of people in the design process is to enlist their support of the program. Those who help create a program are more likely to believe in its value. Conversely, people who are excluded from the development of a program are more likely to criticize it. Thus, it can be particularly important from the start to include representatives of groups that may seem likely to oppose an ADR program.

Finally, members of a design working group can assist with the ADR program after it has begun operating. They can play a vital role in training members of their respective groups, encouraging the use of the program. They can also coordinate record keeping and assist with research to evaluate and improve the program. The group should meet together periodically throughout the life of the program to report back on how it is working and suggest changes. With supporters throughout an agency, an ADR program is far more likely to be effective over the long term.

Staffing Federal ADR Programs

Agency program designers need to consider the resources necessary for an effective ADR program. Expenses can include office staff, training, marketing, travel, evaluation, neutral fees, and more. To justify creation of the program, designers should present estimates of the savings that the ADR program will realize. The government's experience has been that ADR programs pay for themselves many times over.

The location of the ADR office can be important. Placing it in the agency's office of general counsel can emphasize the legal aspects of the program and also may be consistent with the general counsel's role as a policy adviser and counselor. An independent office reporting directly to the head of the agency can emphasize the autonomy of the program. For disputes that take place before administrative tribunals, running the program from the office of administrative law judges can be most appropriate. Workplace programs run from the human relations or equal opportunity offices of the agency may make them seem more accessible to employees, who are accustomed to working with these offices. When an agency has offices throughout the country, it can be valuable to have programs available in different regions. In this situation, it is important to consider whether the programs should have decentralized leadership or be directed from agency headquarters. A related question is whether funding should come from each regional budget or from the headquarters.

At least one full-time professional should be in charge of each ADR program. The agency dispute resolution specialist, the person charged with the responsibility of implementing the Administrative Dispute Resolution Act (ADRA), can be a natural choice for this role.[8] In addition to coordinating the ADR program itself, the director can serve other functions, including advising agency management on ADR policy, providing training, consulting with others on how to use ADR, and evaluating the effectiveness of the agency's use of ADR. It is valuable to choose a director who is an effective and enthusiastic spokesperson for the program.

Other staff members in the office can play valuable roles as well. Some federal agencies have more than ten full-time ADR employees. Larger staffs enable a program to handle more cases and to take greater responsibility for agency dispute resolution in general. They also can assist with marketing the program inside and outside the agency.

Selecting Cases and Processes for Federal ADR Programs

Agencies can create ADR programs to handle different kinds of cases, and the government has found it beneficial in a wide variety of disputes. The ADRA requires each agency to consider using ADR for its formal and informal adjudications, rulemakings, enforcement actions, permit decisions, contract administration, litigation, and other actions.[9] The ADRA list is comprehensive, showing that Congress determined that ADR can be worthwhile for many things agencies do.

Some government disputes are particularly appropriate for ADR. (Chapter Two provides a detailed list of factors to use in choosing disputes where ADR is likely to be helpful.) For example, ADR works particularly well for matters where adversarial processes would be expensive and time-consuming. It is valuable when preserving the relationships between the parties is important. Parties also find it effective when they desire increased creativity or confidentiality in resolving their dispute.

Government ADR programs are especially common in the workplace and contracting areas. Parties with these disputes often must continue to work with each other while the complaint is processed, and even after it is resolved. Thus, it is particularly important for them to maintain cordial relationships with each other, and ADR processes are most effective in this regard. (Workplace disputes are covered in Chapter Six and contracting disputes in Chapter Seven.)

The government also frequently uses ADR in the enforcement, regulatory, and claims areas. When the government is taking an enforcement action against a private party, it often finds that ADR can assist in resolution of the dispute. These actions can be expensive and time-consuming, and ADR can save resources for both sides. When working with the regulated community, agencies find that ADR can smooth relations between the parties and also improve their communication, which can lead to more informed decisions. Finally, when private parties file claims against the government, they often report higher satisfaction levels when using ADR rather than adversarial processes.

Once agencies determine what subject matter their ADR program will cover, they need to decide how to select specific cases for it. In some situations, the agency may wish to refer all cases of a certain type to ADR. Another option is for ADR program staff to review cases and choose certain ones for ADR based on criteria specified in advance. Finally, parties may be given discretion to request ADR when they want it.

Agency ADR programs must be voluntary, because the ADRA provides that all parties must agree to the proceeding.[10] Nonetheless, agencies have different options in how to design the selection process, and these choices affect how often ADR is used. One approach is for the agency to assign cases to ADR but allow the parties to withdraw if they wish. As long as withdrawal is permitted under any circumstances, this approach meets the requirement that ADR be voluntary. It also often leads to a greater use of ADR, as parties must opt out in order to avoid ADR. Another option is to provide the parties with information and require that they affirmatively select ADR in order for it to occur. This may lead to a reduced use of ADR, but it will ensure that the parties truly want it in every case.

For cases involving private sector parties, the program can require that agency staff consider ADR. One way of ensuring that this happens is to mandate that agency personnel either offer ADR or document in the case file the reasons they did not do so. This ensures that employees seriously consider ADR in every appropriate matter.

Agencies must decide what ADR process to use. In the federal government, the parties choose mediation the vast majority of the time. However, there are some cases where other forms of ADR can be effective. (Chapter Two discusses these issues in detail.)

ADR program managers can select which ADR process to use in each case or allow the parties to make this decision. An advantage to the first approach is that ADR program staff usually have greater knowledge and experience in the field and may make more informed decisions. However, some programs allow the parties to choose, on the theory that they understand their dispute best. Giving the choice to the parties also may allow them to work together in reaching a joint decision, which can be a positive way to start their work on resolving their dispute. Agency staff should be available to assist the parties in this decision.

It is important to use ADR at an appropriate time in a dispute. (Timing issues are discussed in detail in Chapter Four.) As a general matter, ADR is most effective early in a case, when parties are not hardened in their positions and are more willing to compromise. However, in some government cases, parties do not know enough about their positions at the start to formulate appropriate settlement proposals. In these matters, the program should allow parties sufficient time to prepare themselves before ADR begins.

Selecting Neutrals for Federal ADR Programs

There are many different sources of neutrals for federal ADR programs. (Chapter Three covers these issues in detail.) As a general matter, agencies have found that private neutrals are often the most skilled but also the most expensive. Using collateral duty agency employees (who serve as neutrals in addition to their regular job assignments) is another option authorized by the ADRA, as long as all parties consent.[11] This approach can be cheaper, and these employees have personal knowledge of agency procedures, which often can be useful in government cases. To avoid a possible appearance of bias when employees serve as neutrals in cases involving their own agencies, shared neutrals programs allow agencies to swap neutrals to serve in each others' cases. However, collateral duty neutrals often do not have as much experience or time available to work on cases as private neutrals do. Some federal agencies, such as the Federal Mediation and Conciliation Service, provide full-time professional neutrals to other agencies for a fee. Agency administrative judges have been effective at providing ADR for cases in their jurisdiction, particularly when another judge takes over adjudication of the matter if it does not settle. This approach is most common in the government contracts area. Finally, some agencies hire neutrals as full-time agency employees to handle disputes.

Agency ADR program managers have a number of options for designing an approach for neutral selection and use. The simplest option is to serve as a clearinghouse. Under this approach, the program accepts applications from anyone interested in serving as a neutral. It merely acts as a conduit, providing all of this information to parties and allowing them to make their own selection. This is administratively easy for the agency but provides little assistance to the parties. If the parties have no experience with ADR, they may find it difficult to choose an appropriate neutral.

Therefore, many agencies find it valuable to screen neutrals for parties in their programs. The most common form of screening is to use criteria. Program managers can select neutrals based on many factors. Educational criteria can include neutrals' ADR training and legal training. Experiential criteria can include the number of hours neutrals have spent leading ADR processes and the number of cases they have handled. The types of cases also are relevant, including how complex they were, whether multiple parties were involved, how much money was at issue, and whether the government was involved. For disputes where subject matter expertise is important, agencies may wish to screen for it. Other factors to consider include neutrals' geographical location, fee, and style.

Developing appropriate criteria can be complicated. There is a tension between applying objective standards faithfully and yet retaining flexibility in the neutral selection process. No matter how carefully criteria are drawn, they often end up being both over- and underinclusive, approving some neutrals who are ineffective and rejecting others who would do a good job. For example, if an agency decides to require that neutrals have experience with at least ten complex disputes, it may find that some people who meet this criterion are nonetheless poor neutrals, while others with slightly less experience would be more effective.

To address this situation, some agencies have included a performance-based component in their neutral selection process.[12] This can be useful, but it also can introduce problems of its own. This approach requires program managers to observe neutrals personally, and it is time-consuming (and thus expensive) to observe large numbers of neutrals. If the agency uses several different people to conduct observation, they may have different standards for what constitutes an effective neutral. With trained observers, however, preliminary studies indicate that these disagreements are relatively minor.[13] Another problem is that neutrals may behave differently when they are being observed. If an agency keeps records of negative comments about neutrals, these documents may be subject to public scrutiny under the Freedom of Information Act.[14] Nonetheless, some agencies have found it worthwhile to use performance-based evaluation because it provides additional information to augment neutrals' paper qualifications.

There are different ways agencies can use rosters in choosing neutrals. Experienced parties may prefer to choose from the roster themselves. For inexperienced parties, hybrid approaches, with parties selecting neutrals under the guidance of program managers, are possible. Another option is for program managers to select neutrals randomly or sequentially from the roster. This ensures that every neutral has an equal opportunity to handle cases, but it does not attempt to find the best possible neutral for each specific dispute. Program managers also may decide to choose neutrals personally, on a case-by-case basis. However, in some agencies, neutrals who are not selected as frequently have complained of bias in the selection process.

Program managers should negotiate with private neutrals to obtain discounted government rates if possible. (Fees for private neutrals are discussed in detail in Chapter Three.) Many neutrals are willing to lower their fees for government cases, because they view the government as a potential source of repeat business or see government ADR as a public service. Generally, government and private parties each pay half of the neutral's fees (except for internal workplace disputes, where the government usually pays the entire cost at the administrative stage).

Pilot Programs

Agencies should consider using a pilot before rolling out their ADR program. If an agency is unsure about whether ADR will be beneficial, a pilot can be a way to learn more before committing to a permanent program. Beginning on a smaller scale also can allow agencies to learn about the effectiveness of their design before they make final decisions. If the design has problems, they can make necessary adjustments. If the pilot works well, it will provide success stories that can be useful when marketing the full program.

The scope of a pilot program can be limited in different ways. For example, if the final program is designed to cover a broad range of cases, the pilot could include only those involving a certain subject matter or maximum dollar amount. If the program is designed to be used throughout the country, the pilot could involve only one region. Programs that eventually will include multiple stages of a dispute (such as prefiling, postfiling, and appeal) could start by focusing on just one. Pilots also can be limited to certain types of ADR, such as mediation or early neutral evaluation.

Pilots can operate for various lengths of time. The pilot should last at least long enough to ensure it serves its purpose by providing sufficient information about program effectiveness. Managers need to know whether the full program is likely to be successful, and, if not, how they need to change it. Some agencies have maintained programs in pilot status for a number of years because of budgetary limitations.

Federal ADR Program Management

Active management is vital to the success of federal ADR programs. Once a program is designed, managers need to continue to work with parties, monitor how the program is operating, and make adjustments as necessary.

Managing Program Neutrals

Agencies should actively manage their rosters of neutrals. Program managers should develop procedures for adding new neutrals to the list. When appropriate, agencies should adapt their selection criteria based on experience. It can be valuable to keep records of everyone who uses a particular neutral. In this way, when people want to learn more about a specific neutral, they can find others in the agency to call for references.

Program managers should check for conflicts of interest before assigning neutrals. Agencies should ask all parties to provide information on any contacts, both professional and personal, they have had with the neutral. Similarly, the neutral should describe any contacts with the parties. In a few cases, parties have been willing to waive their objection to a neutral who has had prior dealings with their opponents. Program managers should review these situations to ensure that any waiver is appropriate under the circumstances.

Agencies should provide training to roster members. Initial training, before neutrals join the program, can teach them how to handle government cases.[15] It also allows program managers to observe neutrals, gaining insight into their effectiveness. In-service training, provided after neutrals have participated for some time, can keep them up-to-date on program developments and allow them to give feedback to program managers on possible improvements. It is particularly important to provide training for neutrals in the specific concerns applicable to government ADR. For example, even neutrals who have considerable private ADR experience may not understand the confidentiality rules involved in government ADR.

Ongoing evaluation can provide valuable feedback to the neutrals and the program managers. (Evaluation is discussed in detail in Chapter Ten.) Managers can observe neutrals, parties can report on their experiences, and neutrals can be asked to assess their own effectiveness. All of these sources can enable program managers to select the best neutrals for future cases and give feedback to neutrals to help them to improve their subsequent performance.

Complaint mechanisms are important in agency ADR programs. Parties should have a way to express dissatisfaction with any aspect of the program, either in writing or in person with a specifically designated individual. For complaints that refer to particular neutrals, agencies may wish to develop procedures by which a neutral can be disciplined or even removed from the program. Although the government has not enacted a specific code of conduct for neutrals, program managers may adapt one to their needs and require that neutrals follow it.[16] Parties also should be given the opportunity to provide feedback, both positive and negative, about general program administration issues. Complaints allow managers to learn how they can improve the program.

Managing Cases in ADR

Agency program managers can provide many helpful services to parties in ADR. At the beginning of a case, they can assist with the convening process. For example, a party may not be sure if ADR is a good idea. Program managers can answer the party's questions and encourage the use of ADR where appropriate. They also can provide logistical assistance by scheduling the sessions and arranging for conference space.

Sometimes program managers are called on to provide ADR consulting services. Parties may not know what type of ADR process they should use, and program managers can help select the best process. In appropriate cases, managers may even design a specialized approach.

Program managers should assist the parties with the agreement they sign before ADR begins. This agreement should describe items such as the process to be used, the role of the neutral, the neutral's fee and how it will be paid, whether parties will submit pre-ADR statements, who will attend, what confidentiality rules will apply, what timetable will be followed, and what will happen at the end of the ADR session. All parties and the neutral should sign the agreement before ADR begins.

As a case proceeds in ADR, program managers should monitor it. If parties request assistance, managers should provide whatever is necessary. If a case has been in ADR for an unusually long time, managers may inquire about its status. Confidentiality concerns may prevent participants from disclosing specific ADR communications, but calls from program managers may be helpful to prompt them to decide on their own how they should proceed. If the parties believe a change in the process or a new neutral might be helpful, program managers should work to accommodate these requests.

Program managers can assist parties at the end of ADR as well. Model settlement agreements can be useful to parties as they consider what to do. Program managers can draft models and suggest that parties tailor them as necessary. If a case settles in ADR, program managers can ensure the agreement is filed with the proper authorities. If the case does not settle, they can ensure that it is referred to an adjudicatory process if appropriate and advise the parties that they may consider ADR again later.

Tracking cases is another important part of program management. Records should be kept of each case considered for ADR, including whether ADR was used (and if not, the reasons for this decision), what type of ADR was used, who served as the neutral, what issues were involved in the case, the date ADR began, and the date it was concluded. This information is useful for analyzing the effectiveness of the program and drafting reports about it (see Chapter Ten for details).

Marketing

In order for a government ADR program to be successful, it must be marketed effectively. Marketing will ensure that the people in the agency for whom the program is designed will know that it exists and how they can use it. When a program is marketed effectively, people will use it more frequently and will be more enthusiastic when they do. Marketing is often thought of as a one-way street, as if it encompassed only selling and nothing more. However, it also should include a component of determining what the market is and what it needs. Keeping this in mind helps the program manager to use marketing partly as a way to explore where program changes may be needed. Responsiveness to the needs of potential users is a key element in making marketing effective.

The support of a high-level agency official can be extremely helpful in marketing. A single five-minute presentation from such an official at the beginning of a training program, in person or even on videotape, can send a powerful message that ADR is important to agency leadership. The government is hierarchical, and employees pay closer attention to programs that are sponsored by agency directors.

Program managers should assist with drafting memoranda and oral remarks for these officials. A memo or speech could start by describing the many benefits of ADR in the government, from time and money savings to increased satisfaction for the participants. The official should note how ADR can help people do their jobs more effectively. After that, it is helpful to refer to the government's overall commitment to ADR, as established by the ADRA[17] and the Presidential Memorandum of 1998.[18] Finally, the official can describe and endorse the agency's ADR program.

ADR supporters in specific components of the agency also can be useful. For example, public recommendations from leaders in the agency human relations office and employee unions can be invaluable for workplace ADR programs. Many times individuals on the working group that helped design the program can serve as champions or assist in identifying appropriate higher-level individuals to do so.

Written marketing materials can be effective. Program managers can work with agency graphics departments to design posters and brochures to publicize ADR. Some agencies mail documents to employees with their biweekly pay stubs, and this can be a way to reach everyone in the organization. Articles in agency publications can spread the word about an ADR program.

Program managers also can create their own ADR publications. Newsletters can describe the ADR program, set forth recent success stories, and tell employees how to learn more. Regular publications remind people about the ADR program and give public recognition to those who have used it effectively, encouraging more people to do the same.

Oral presentations by program managers also are valuable. In addition to training, brown bag discussions, open houses, and monthly group meetings can help increase awareness of the program. Videoconferencing and videotaped programs can reach people located in other parts of the country.

For ADR programs that involve private sector parties, it is important to market outside the agency as well. Sometimes ADR programs grow most quickly when private sector participants ask the government to use ADR more frequently. For example, if contractors request more ADR, this interest may prompt the government to respond by providing it more often.

In this regard, obtaining outside press coverage of ADR programs is helpful. An ADR settlement involving a significant case can be a good opportunity to gain press attention. Program managers should work with the agency's office of public affairs to distribute press releases, create press kits, and provide interviews. An increasing number of periodicals are dedicated to ADR, and they are interested in reporting on newsworthy events in the field. Program managers also should consider writing articles for law reviews and bar association publications.

A Web site is an important marketing resource. ADR program Web sites can include a description of the services offered, endorsements from agency officials, case study examples of successful ADR, and evaluations showing the effectiveness of the program. Managers also may wish to post program documents, such as ADR agreements, model settlement documents, and reporting forms on the Web site. In this way, program users will have easy access to important materials from anywhere in the agency. Agencies should provide Web links between their site and the main federal site (www.adr.gov).

Training

Training is a crucial component of a federal ADR program. Agencies have found that investments in training can pay substantial dividends. Training can increase awareness of ADR programs among agency employees, allow people to use ADR more effectively, and improve the performance of program neutrals.

When planning training, agencies should first consider the needs it will address. Training should focus on areas where a lack of knowledge is reducing the effectiveness of the program. Agencies should identify which audiences have the greatest need for training. The goals of a training program will determine the ways it should be designed and implemented.

Agencies must then decide who will conduct the training. If the agency has skilled trainers on staff, using them can be the easiest and least expensive option. If not, many quality private trainers are available throughout the country. They can be very experienced but also expensive. Agencies should ensure that private trainers will take the time to tailor their presentations to the specific needs of the government rather than provide a canned, generic program. Another approach is to hire private trainers for general topics and have in-house trainers cover topics specific to the agency. Agencies with large training needs have found it worthwhile to provide train-the-trainer courses. These programs allow the agency to cultivate large numbers of trainers, who can then run training programs on their own.

Using multiple trainers in a course can be advantageous, particularly with a large class size. Many ADR training techniques involve small group exercises, and having a faculty member work with each small group makes these methods more effective. Varying the presenters who lecture in a course also increases the audience's interest level. Of course, multiple trainers are more expensive as well.

It can be useful to begin courses by having the participants describe their experience with ADR and their expectations for the course. This information allows trainers to gauge the expertise of the audience and adjust the level of their presentations accordingly. It also gives trainers insight into what participants want from the training, permitting them to alter the content of the course if they wish. This approach does take time, and it may not be possible with shorter courses or larger class sizes.

Participants should be asked to complete evaluation forms on all ADR training. They should evaluate each individual segment of the training and provide overall comments about the program. This information will enable trainers to learn what they are doing that is most and least effective and to make appropriate changes to future courses.

Presentation Formats

There are several main teaching formats used in government ADR courses. Government employees often do not have extensive time available for training, so most programs are three days or less. Therefore, lectures are a common format, because they are an efficient way to present information. However, adult learners often find pure lecture courses to be boring. The effectiveness of lectures can be improved somewhat through the use of visual aids and interactive question-and-answer sessions.

To increase the audience's participation and interest level, some programs include group discussion segments. Trainers should ensure they actively moderate group discussions to keep them focused productively. Otherwise, these discussions may veer off-track when participants ask questions on topics of little interest to the group as a whole. Indeed, participants often do not know what issues are most important (which is why they are taking the course in the first place). Furthermore, without oversight, outspoken participants can dominate these discussions, and quiet ones may say little or nothing.

Demonstrations are often used in ADR courses. When audience members have never participated in ADR, they can benefit from watching experienced practitioners show how to use it effectively. This format is sometimes called a fishbowl presentation, because participants can observe the demonstrators as if they were in a fishbowl. One downside of this approach is that it does not involve audience participation and thus can become boring if used too long. For this reason, demonstrations can be more effective when broken into shorter segments, with opportunities for the audience to ask questions between segments. Some trainers have allowed more experienced members of the audience to substitute for demonstrators during a segment to increase interaction and variety.

Role plays are particularly valuable for ADR training. In a role play, audience members participate in simulated ADR sessions by playing the parts of people involved in a dispute. For example, the audience may divide into groups of three, with one person in each group playing the plaintiff in a case, another playing the defendant, and the third playing the neutral. Each participant receives written instructions describing the nature of the dispute. Through role plays, audience members can experience what it is like to participate in an ADR session. They can learn much more about ADR by taking part in it rather than simply hearing about it in a lecture. Evaluations that participants complete at the end of ADR programs often rate role-play segments as the highlight of the course.

It is important to use role plays carefully. Trainers should tell participants to take their roles seriously in order to make the exercise as authentic as possible. Otherwise, role plays may degenerate into casual, informal exchanges that are unrealistic and less useful. It is valuable to provide participants with their written instructions in advance so they have the opportunity to prepare before the exercise begins. Sometimes certain participants "fight the role play" by complaining that the instructions have ambiguities. Trainers should tell them that some uncertainties are inevitable in short role plays, and they should do the best they can.

One technique that is useful in some courses is to permit parties to stay in the room to observe when the neutral is meeting with the other side. For example, when the neutral is having a private caucus with the plaintiff, the defendant quietly can observe what happens. The disadvantage of this approach is that it sacrifices some realism, because a party would not normally be able to overhear what the other party discusses in a private caucus. Therefore, participants should be told to listen for educational purposes only, and not to use what they learn for strategic advantage in the role play. The benefit of allowing parties to stay in the room is that they are able to observe much more of the interaction, giving them greater insight into the ADR process. Trainers should decide on a case-by-case basis whether the advantages of this approach outweigh the disadvantages, which will depend on the nature of the program.

At the end of a role play, it is valuable for a trainer to facilitate a group discussion about what happened.[19] This discussion allows participants to reflect on what they encountered and learn about the experiences of others. An effective format is for the facilitator to ask general questions to stimulate discussion—for example: What worked well for you? What would you do differently next time? What surprised you about the experience? How would you advise someone else who had to play your role in the future? What did the others in your group do that was most and least effective?

Training Content

Federal government agencies provide three main types of ADR training. The first, awareness training, is designed to provide a basic introduction to ADR. It is useful to explain an ADR program to an inexperienced audience. The second, user training, provides guidance to participants who have already participated in ADR or are likely to do so in the future. It focuses on practical advice to assist people in using ADR more effectively. Finally, neutral training concentrates on improving the performance of those who serve as neutrals in agency ADR programs.

A good way to begin any training program is to discuss interest-based negotiation, because this is a fundamental part of ADR practice. Interest-based negotiation, popularized by the book *Getting to Yes,* encourages parties to focus on their underlying interests rather than argue about their positions.[20] For example, a plaintiff in a government workplace case may file a claim seeking $300,000 in damages, and the agency may respond that it will not pay a penny. These are their positions, and they could negotiate by arguing back and forth and exchanging counteroffers in an attempt to reach an agreeable dollar amount.

In contrast, the parties could instead examine their interests. Sometimes money demands serve mainly as a proxy for what plaintiffs believe they really deserve. The dynamics of the litigation process can deny them the respect and recognition that ultimately may be more important to them. Using this analysis, the parties may learn that the plaintiff actually wants to avoid a trial and would prefer an apology for what happened and a transfer to a different part of the agency. This type of interest-based discussion is the foundation of ADR. A major function of neutrals is to assist parties in identifying each others' underlying interests in order to develop creative options for resolution. A presentation on these ideas is a good way to show training participants how ADR can be valuable for them.

After covering interest-based negotiation, ADR courses can discuss the obstacles that sometimes prevent people from negotiating effectively without assistance. This can persuade participants that using a neutral third party can be invaluable in resolving disputes. A detailed overview of this topic is available in the book *Barriers to Conflict Resolution*.[21] An example of a barrier to unassisted negotiation is *reactive devaluation*. Research shows that when parties hear an offer from the other side, they react by immediately devaluing it. Imagine a plaintiff who enters a negotiation prepared to settle a case by accepting $50,000. If the defendant begins the negotiation by offering to pay $50,000, most of the time the plaintiff will not accept the offer and instead will ask for more. Neutrals can help parties avoid this phenomenon by having private discussions with each side. In this example, if the plaintiff privately tells the neutral that $50,000 is acceptable and the defendant does the same, the neutral can assist the parties in reaching a settlement at that amount even though they could not have done so without ADR. Trainers should discuss these types of situations with participants to persuade them that neutrals can help them settle cases they would be unable to resolve on their own. It also is effective to use interactive exercises that illustrate this point.[22]

Awareness Training

Awareness training is designed to introduce an inexperienced audience to ADR. Usually ADR program managers offer this kind of training to inform people in an agency about the availability of ADR and encourage them to use it. Therefore, these courses usually include both education and marketing components.

Telling participants how ADR can help them is a way to capture their interest. Discussions of interest-based negotiation and then barriers to unassisted negotiation provide a basic overview of the advantages ADR can provide. After that, it can be effective to give specific examples of how ADR has been successful in the agency. Participants typically appreciate stories of how others in situations like their own have benefited from ADR. Data showing how ADR has resolved cases more quickly and more cheaply than traditional adversarial processes can be useful. Research establishing that participants are more satisfied with ADR than with other processes is helpful as well.

The course should then tell participants how they can use the ADR program at the agency. It should describe the types of disputes that are appropriate for ADR and explain what will happen in an ADR process. Participants should learn how they can obtain ADR services and whom they can contact for further information.

If an agency has made awareness training mandatory for employees, trainers may find that some audience members will be skeptical about it. Experienced trainers welcome questions that indicate skepticism, because it is easiest to understand people's concerns when they are expressed. Trainers should listen closely to what participants ask and give positive yet candid answers. They should admit that ADR does not work in every case but describe how it can be useful in many situations.

Audience members often are most persuaded when they hear from one of their peers. Trainers may wish to locate someone in the group who has had a positive experience with ADR. Asking this person to describe a successful use of ADR to the other participants can be a very effective part of the training.

Awareness training can vary in length. Training given to an audience of upper-level executives should be relatively short. Because these participants appreciate respect for the limitations on their time, most of these trainings last from one to three hours. Trainings for a more general audience may last from one hour to several days.

Longer trainings allow greater use of interactive components such as role plays, which are often the most effective part of the course.

One role play that is effective in awareness courses is the Burning Sailboat Exercise, which allows participants to experience personally the difference between ADR and adjudication.[23] In this interactive exercise, the audience is divided into groups of three to resolve a simple dispute over a boat that was damaged while stored in a neighbor's garage. One party plays the boat owner, another plays the neighbor, and the third a judge. The judge listens to arguments from both sides and then issues a final decision. The exercise is then run a second time, and the judge becomes a mediator instead. Participants generally find the second approach, where the mediator works with the parties to achieve a voluntary resolution, is more satisfying than the first. This exercise shows them how ADR can be a better way to resolve disputes.

User Training

Training for those who are already using ADR (or will be doing so soon) is usually more in-depth than awareness training. This training should give participants a thorough understanding of ADR and how they can use it most effectively. It should take participants through the process step-by-step and include interactive exercises to give them an opportunity to practice what they have learned. User training programs in the government usually last from one to three days.

An introduction to interest-based negotiation is an appropriate way to start user training. Participants can benefit from a short exercise where they must negotiate with each other in an interest-based fashion in order to succeed. A classic example is the Ugli Orange Exercise, where participants are divided into groups of two to negotiate over a crop of oranges.[24] As the case is designed, the only way for the participants to complete the negotiation successfully is to work in a collaborative fashion in order to discover that one needs the rinds and the other needs the juice. This role play shows that in some situations, competitive positional negotiation will fail, while more cooperative, interest-based approaches (such as those used in ADR) will succeed.

In longer courses, more involved exercises can work well. Two examples are the Win as Much as You Can role play, which takes thirty to sixty minutes, and the Oil Pricing Exercise, which takes two to three hours.[25] Both simulations are engaging and entertaining for the participants, and they teach that cooperation can be essential for success, a vital lesson in an ADR course. Time spent on this topic is worthwhile because the competitive model of dispute resolution is so ingrained in the government. Starting with interest-based negotiation can set an effective tone for the rest of the program.

A presentation on the barriers to unassisted negotiation fits well after interest-based negotiation. This material provides a theoretical underpinning for ADR, showing participants how it can assist them in settling cases more effectively than they could on their own. The Burning Sailboat exercise can be useful at this point to demonstrate the differences between adjudication and ADR.

Next, user training should take participants through each of the stages of an ADR process: choosing cases and processes for ADR, selecting and hiring a neutral, ADR preparation, and ADR advocacy. Trainers should discuss these issues generally and also identify any concerns specific to the agency program.

A discussion of ethics is important in user training. Although the government has not adopted a specific ADR ethical code, general ethical principles can be discussed as they apply to ADR. Several private organizations have drafted ADR ethical guidelines that can be useful for discussions.[26]

With an experienced group, it can be useful to include a segment where participants can describe cases in which they have used ADR. Trainers can then provide their perspective on these examples. These case studies also can be useful springboards for discussion among the group as a whole.

It is particularly valuable in user training to have audience members participate in role-playing ADR sessions. Role plays give participants the opportunity to put the training into practice and can be the centerpiece of the course. For example, after the presentations on ADR preparation, participants can actually prepare with each other for the ADR they will conduct later in the course. They can discuss how to present their opening statements, what their overall strategy will be, and so forth. Because it is interactive, this experience can be far more effective than lectures alone.

For the ADR role plays, it is very helpful to use professional neutrals if possible. Some neutrals are willing to participate in government training sessions for free, both as a service to the community and to develop contacts that may result in business for them in the future. Others will agree to reduce their normal rates. If the agency has neutrals on staff, they can be used for training purposes. Agency trainers should do whatever they can to obtain skilled neutrals for the role plays, because this makes the program much more authentic and valuable to the participants.

If the training is using experienced neutrals, they can lead discussions with participants about what is happening during the role-play session. One natural point to have a discussion is after parties have made their opening statements. It works best not to have discussions during the ADR process itself, but rather to confine them to natural breaking points, such as when moving from a private caucus with one party to a caucus with the other party.

Neutrals should give participants critiques on how effectively they are using the process in the role play. Discussions can cover how to work with neutrals effectively, as well as how to persuade the other side. It can be illuminating to have parties comment on how they reacted to tactics employed by the other side. For example, neutrals can ask one side about the impact of a certain statement on them, and then ask the side that made the statement what their intent was. Comparing intent and impact can be revealing as people realize they are not always perceived the way they thought they were.

Neutral Training

Government agencies provide two main types of training for neutrals. One type is designed for experienced private sector neutrals who are selected to serve in government cases. This type of training is typically short, ranging from a half-day to a day. In these courses, neutrals learn administrative details about the program, such as how cases are assigned and where ADR will take place. If they will be handling specialized cases, such as complex contracting matters or environmental disputes, neutrals should receive training on these issues. Trainers also should inform private neutrals about special considerations involved in government ADR. Confidentiality is of particular importance in this regard, because the rules for government confidentiality are different from those in private practice. (Chapter Eight covers these issues in detail.)

Agencies also provide training for current government employees who will serve as neutrals on collateral duty. If the participants have no experience with ADR, this training must be thorough enough to enable them to serve effectively as neutrals. Thus, this type of training is often the most time-consuming in the government, usually lasting at least three to five days.

As with all other ADR training, introductory segments on interest-based negotiation and barriers to unassisted negotiation are worthwhile. After that, training can address each of the stages of ADR in sequence. It can be effective to use a combination of lectures, demonstrations, and participatory role-play exercises in neutral training.

For example, training on how to run an ADR opening session can begin with a lecture describing the process. Then trainers can present a demonstration of an opening session and answer questions about it. After that, participants can practice opening sessions in small-group role-play exercises.

Trainers can divide participants into groups of three, with one playing the neutral and the other two playing the disputants. The disputants should not be so cooperative that the dispute is unusually easy to resolve or so contentious that resolution is impossible. In order for every participant to have an opportunity to play the neutral, they should switch roles periodically.

After the opening session segment, trainers should focus on the later stages of ADR, such as identifying interests, generating options, examining alternatives, breaking impasse, reaching closure, and drafting settlement agreements. If the course is long enough, it can be worthwhile to cover each of these topics with lectures, demonstrations, and role plays, because different people respond better to different teaching methods. It also is useful to have participants serve as neutrals in complete role plays, from beginning to end. Ethics also should be covered.

Neutral training is more effective with a low student-faculty ratio. Optimally, an experienced trainer will work with each small-group role play to observe and offer critique to the participants. If necessary, a trainer can oversee several small groups by moving back and forth among them.

Chapter Ten

Evaluation of Federal ADR Programs

Evaluation is a vital element in every federal ADR program. The government is focusing more and more on rigorous evaluation of its activities to ensure that citizens are being well served. Congress has passed legislation requiring regular evaluation of program performance. The press reports frequently on the effectiveness (or ineffectiveness) of government initiatives. The public has a right to know whether its tax dollars are being spent wisely.

The leading law requiring the federal government to conduct evaluations is the Government Performance and Results Act.[1] It mandates that federal agencies measure and report on their effectiveness. Specifically, each agency must submit a strategic plan showing its goals, as well as an annual report on the performance of programs compared to the targets expressed in its performance plan. If the agency does not meet its targets, it must explain why and provide plans to improve performance in the future.

Federal ADR programs will benefit in a number of ways from evaluation of their effectiveness. Evaluation can show which parts of a system are working well and which are not. This information tells managers what they can change to make a program even more successful. Furthermore, agency budget decisions frequently are based on demonstrated benefits of specific programs. Program managers who are able to prove value will be able to obtain funding and personnel to develop their programs. Finally, statistics on participant satisfaction and savings of time and money can help persuade more people to use ADR in the future.

Preparing to Evaluate a Government ADR Program

It is important to take the time to prepare before undertaking an evaluation. Careful examination of the goals of the ADR program, the goals of the evaluation, the timing of the process, the background of those who will conduct the evaluation, and other issues will pay dividends down the road.

Goals of the ADR Program

The initial step in evaluating the effectiveness of an ADR program is to examine what the program is supposed to do. Why does the program exist? What interests does it serve? Several typical goals for a federal ADR program are set forth below.

First, an ADR program may be designed to resolve disputes in a manner that is more satisfying to the participants than non-ADR methods. Traditional dispute resolution methods often leave participants aggravated and upset. ADR may give people higher satisfaction levels with both the process and the results.

Second, ADR may be implemented in order to improve the efficiency of dispute resolution. Many agencies face backlogs in dispute processing from informal EEO complaints to federal court litigation. Reducing the delays in such systems can have far-reaching benefits.

Another goal may be to reduce the costs of dispute resolution. Settling disputes more quickly may itself reduce costs, and there may be other economic advantages to ADR as well. If parties can resolve their disagreements without extensive involvement of attorneys or with less use of formal litigation processes, both the government and private parties can save money.

Finally, an agency may use ADR because it is required to do so by law or regulation. The Administrative Dispute Resolution Act (ADRA) mandates that the federal government promote the use of ADR in appropriate cases.[2] The Equal Employment Opportunity Commission (EEOC) has issued regulations mandating that agencies offer ADR in EEO cases.[3] The Contract Disputes Act and Federal Acquisition Regulation call for ADR in procurement matters.[4] Other laws and agency policies require ADR as well.[5]

Goals of the Evaluation

The goals of the evaluation follow from the goals of the ADR program. The primary purpose for an evaluation is to measure how well the ADR program is accomplishing whatever it is designed to accomplish.

Evaluators should involve key stakeholders in the process from the beginning. It is best to avoid completing an evaluation, for example, only to find that the specific information that the agency budget staff really wanted was not captured. Agencies have avoided this problem by circulating draft evaluation plans widely and even publishing them in the *Federal Register*. This approach allows a broad audience of potentially affected people to comment on the plan. Experts from around the country can submit suggestions, and these can be useful in preparing an effective evaluation. Ultimately, these efforts are worthwhile because people are most persuaded by the results of an evaluation that they helped design themselves.

The evaluation should examine whether the ADR program is fulfilling its purposes (this is called *summative evaluation*). If the program is designed to increase satisfaction, are parties more satisfied than they would have been without it? If its role is to reduce time and cost, is it doing so? If the program exists to meet a statutory requirement, does it fulfill the conditions of the law? Is it reaching all of its intended beneficiaries?

Another important benefit of an evaluation is that it can provide a road map for how to improve the program (this is called *formative evaluation*). For example, an evaluation can show which types of neutrals lead to highest satisfaction rates among participants: internal agency staff or outside professionals; those with subject matter expertise or those with ADR expertise; those with an assertive, evaluative style, or those with a more informal, facilitative style. Perhaps certain forms of ADR (such as mediation) have higher settlement rates than others (such as arbitration). Timing issues may surface, showing that ADR is most cost-effective early or late in a case. It may be that voluntary ADR works better than mandatory, or vice versa. Interactions also may appear: certain types of ADR may work well in certain types of cases but not in others. Evaluation can show what an ADR program is doing wrong and how to correct problems. It also can show what the program is doing right and suggest how this can be duplicated and expanded.

Finally, evaluation can provide crucial data for promoting the program. Future parties may be more likely to participate in an ADR program when they learn that past parties were highly satisfied with it. Financial managers may be willing to provide additional funding and staff for a program that has saved time and money for the agency.

Timing of the Evaluation

There are a number of considerations in deciding when to conduct an evaluation. Early evaluations, done while the program is new, allow changes to be made quickly based on the findings. This timing ensures that bad designs do not become so ingrained that they are difficult to change. Early positive results can provide encouragement to participants in the program and help it to establish momentum.

Evaluations should not be conducted too early, however. The program must be in existence long enough for meaningful data to exist. It may be worthwhile to wait until the early problems of the program have been worked through. This way, the evaluation will take place after the program has had a chance to develop to its best potential.

The length of time to spend on data collection is another concern. The collection should last long enough to obtain a meaningful amount of data and ensure the results are accurate and representative. However, it should not continue so long that it becomes burdensome and unnecessarily expensive. Furthermore, beneficial results from an evaluation (such as suggestions for program improvement and positive data that will be useful for marketing) are more helpful the earlier they are obtained.

It can be helpful to begin with a limited pilot evaluation. This gives guidance for further evaluation down the line, allowing researchers to make tweaks before the full-scale evaluation gets too far along. For example, evaluators could conduct measurements at only one site in a multisite program. With this approach, it is important to choose the site carefully. Researchers may want to select a representative site (so that results can be generalized), a more successful site (to generate positive data for marketing), or a less successful site (to determine ways to improve the program). For a smaller program with only a single site, data could be collected for a short period of time at first, to give insights on how to proceed with a longer-term evaluation. Pilot-testing data collection instruments, to identify and minimize response errors, is also vital.

Evaluation need not be a one-time event. Multiple evaluations can provide helpful information to program managers, allowing them to measure the effects of changes they make to the program. Ongoing evaluations are another option, with programs continually collecting and analyzing data.

Selection of the Evaluator

A number of factors come into play when selecting an evaluator. Training, experience, and group affiliation can all play a role in the evaluator's effectiveness. Choosing wisely can make the evaluation more useful and more persuasive to its intended audience.

The academic training of the researcher often makes a difference. Economists, psychologists, political scientists, lawyers, and other professionals all have different orientations toward ADR. They tend to look at different elements of a program and use different methods to measure these elements. For example, evaluators with training in the law may focus on how ADR is affecting the legal rights and entitlements of participants. A psychologist may examine parties' emotions and subjective impressions. An economist will emphasize monetary effects. It can be problematic to ask evaluators to do things for which they are not trained.

An evaluator's experience also matters. The government is unique, and evaluators who have a background in this area can be more effective. It can also be useful to find someone who has conducted an ADR evaluation in the past. If an agency ADR program is involved with a specific subject matter (for example, government contracting or workplace), expertise in this area can be valuable. All of this can save time because the evaluator need not be brought up to speed on fundamental issues. The investigator will know what to look for and how to conduct the evaluation.

Good evaluators must be patient and willing to listen. They will need to spend a considerable amount of time talking to people at the outset to learn about the program and understand what the parties want from the evaluation. To maximize results, evaluators should distribute drafts of evaluation instruments in advance of the study, and they must be able to work with parties on multiple revisions.

Another key consideration is whether to use an evaluator from inside the agency or outside. Inside evaluators have several advantages. They are usually cheaper because the agency need not hire any outside personnel, and they generally have the greatest understanding of the unique issues of the agency as well as the government in general. ADR program managers can be uniquely qualified to conduct the evaluations of their own programs because they know these programs better than anyone else

The greatest strength of inside evaluators, their direct involvement with the program itself, also is their greatest weakness. By virtue of their position, inside evaluators are the least likely to be able to convince others that their evaluations are unbiased. Such evaluations are by definition not independent. Outside observers may suspect that the evaluation was conducted in such a way as to make the program look good. Furthermore, because they are so close to the program, they may overlook important questions that should be asked as part of the evaluation.

One compromise available at some agencies is to use agency employees who are not affiliated with the ADR program in any way to conduct the evaluation. This choice maintains the advantages of cost and knowledge of the agency while isolating the evaluation somewhat from the appearance of bias. Some agencies have specific program evaluation offices that enjoy a level of independence within the organization. Nonetheless, outside observers may note that everyone within the agency ultimately reports to the same upper management, and even evaluators in another component of the organization may be reluctant to be critical of the agency out of fear of retaliation.

Another compromise option is to hire an external consultant to design the evaluation and then use agency employees to administer it internally. With this approach, it can also be valuable to subject the data to external review periodically.

If Congress makes a request, the General Accounting Office (GAO) can conduct an evaluation of an agency ADR program. The GAO has experienced evaluators who understand the workings of the federal government and have established a reputation for independence that is recognized outside the government. Moreover, the GAO has already conducted a number of evaluations of ADR programs that have been useful in the development of the field.[6]

Another good option is to seek the assistance of a university for an evaluation. Research university professors have considerable experience with evaluation in general, and a number of them have worked with the government. They are generally reasonably affordable. Many professors have access to outside research grants that can help fund a study. Graduate students are often looking for opportunities to conduct and publish research, and they are eager to partner with a government agency in this regard. Other students can be enlisted to input data into a computer (an often painstaking part of the process) for a modest hourly wage as a work-study project. University evaluators are often grateful for the opportunity the government gives them to have inside access to significant data, as well as willing subjects with whom to conduct research.

Enlisting a university also makes the evaluation independent of the agency, a considerable credibility advantage. One example of such a partnership that has been extremely effective in the government ADR world is Indiana University's evaluation of the U.S. Postal Service's REDRESS ADR program.[7] Researchers at Indiana have published multiple articles based on their investigation of the Postal Service's program. This research has assisted the agency in understanding its ADR program and provided independent evidence of its success. This evidence of the value of ADR has been indispensable in persuading officials to increase funding for the ADR program.

A final option is to hire an outside commercial firm to conduct the evaluation. Talented evaluators are available in the private sector, and they can provide an independent assessment. However, this is almost always the most expensive approach.

An agency may wish to consider combining some of these options, using both inside and outside evaluators. For example, even though an ADR program manager may not be the best choice to conduct the evaluation because of bias concerns, this individual can be helpful to outside evaluators by providing background information about the program. A team of evaluators can combine the advantages of various approaches.

Evaluators and program managers should discuss at the outset what will be done with the results. It should be clear who controls the data and the findings of the evaluation. Where will research be published, who will be the authors, and who will have final control over the content of the publication? Parties also should consider what will be done if the results are negative. Problems have arisen for parties who did not reach agreement on these issues in advance.

What to Evaluate in a Government ADR Program

Once the goals of the evaluation are clear, the next step is to determine what to measure. The eight major evaluation categories for federal ADR are effectiveness, cost savings, time savings, relationship effects, outcome quality, program quality, quality of neutrals, and satisfaction.

Effectiveness

An evaluation should measure whether the ADR program is effectively resolving disputes. An initial way to examine this is to look at the settlement rate of the program. This is a relatively easy number to obtain: divide the total number of cases that go into ADR by the number that result in a settlement.[8]

Settlement rates are a part of almost all ADR evaluations, although the meaning of the result is not always clear. An ADR program with close to a 100 percent settlement rate may appear at first to be exceedingly effective, and this may be true. However, it also may be that the selection criteria for cases sent to ADR are so strict that many cases that could benefit from it are not receiving it. If only the cases that are certain to settle are using ADR, others that have a chance to benefit are missing out. Thus, an ADR program with a 60 percent settlement rate actually may be quite effective, as it is being used with success in a wide range of cases, even though not all of them settle every time.

Settlement rate evaluations also should consider whether ADR was effective even in cases that did not settle. ADR participants have reported numerous benefits in certain cases. Sometimes "unsuccessful" ADR nonetheless will help parties by narrowing the issues in a case and focusing their attention on what matters for future litigation. It may improve relationships between the parties, provide insight for parties into their opponents' positions, or assist parties in better understanding the strengths and weaknesses of their own position.

Evaluators can use a survey to measure the benefits of ADR when a case does not settle. Evaluators can ask parties if they experienced any of the advantages outlined and also provide a section where parties can note any other benefits. It is also worthwhile to ask parties if there were any disadvantages to the ADR, so that researchers will have a complete and balanced picture of its effectiveness.

Another measurement of effectiveness is how many matters ADR resolves before they become major disputes. In the workplace, for example, agencies offer ADR at the informal stage, before an employee has filed a formal complaint. One measure of the effectiveness of this type of program is the percentage of informal complaints that turn into formal complaints after ADR is used.[9] Researchers should compare this to the comparable figure when ADR is not used.[10]

Researchers should consider not only overall effectiveness, but also effectiveness for different types of disputes. It is possible to learn much about ADR programs by segregating the data in various ways. For example, if an ADR program handles more than one type of dispute, settlement rates may vary for each type.[11] It can be worthwhile to look at settlement rates for large versus small cases (case size can be analyzed, for example, in terms of the amount of damages requested in the complaint) or complex versus simple cases (complexity can be determined, for example, by surveying the parties).

Program design may make a difference in effectiveness. Examine whether ADR works better when it is voluntary or mandatory.[12] Look at whether ADR settles more cases when used early or late in a case.[13] Consider the significance of whether ADR takes the form of mediation, early neutral evaluation, minitrial, or another method.

Characteristics of the parties are another subject for study. It may be worthwhile to look at demographic issues such as race, national origin, gender, age, education, and income level. Whether the parties have used ADR before may make a difference in its effectiveness. Another issue is whether it matters if the parties attend ADR with a representative.

Cost Savings

An area of paramount importance for government programs is whether they save money. Congress often focuses explicitly on this issue, as do agency budget offices. In order to gain additional funding, a program frequently must demonstrate that it saves money for the agency and taxpayers. Objective measures of actual costs are most persuasive.

In order to examine whether an ADR program saves money, the first step is to determine what the program costs to operate. Administrative costs include all of the expenses the agency pays for the program, which are typically captured by the overall program budget. Costs for neutrals should be added, including any training expenses. If parties are represented by employees in another part of the agency (such as the general counsel's office), costs for the time they spend participating in ADR should be included. To calculate the per case cost of ADR, evaluators should divide the total cost of the program by the number of cases.

This figure should be compared to the costs of handling similar disputes without ADR. If the non-ADR option is litigation, evaluators should include the costs for the time that agency employees spend in litigation. If the agency general counsel's office handles the matter, the costs of their staff should be included. Litigation expenses such as deposition fees, travel costs, and expert witness fees should be added. Costs for the decision maker also should be examined. The agency must pay the cost of administrative law judges and associated staff to adjudicate matters that are not settled. Interest costs can be substantial in certain types of cases, such as contract disputes, and these should be calculated if litigation extends the average life of a case.[14]

It also is possible to measure cost effects subjectively. For a subjective evaluation, researchers can ask participants in ADR to estimate the costs of handling the case through litigation. It is important to remember that many cases would settle even without ADR. Thus, it is not appropriate to assume that all cases would go all the way to trial when calculating cost savings. Instead, participants should be asked to estimate what the costs would have been had ADR not been used, considering whether it would have settled prior to trial.[15]

As a general matter, the most rigorous way to obtain an unbiased evaluation is to use an experiment, assigning parties randomly to go to ADR or not and then comparing the costs of each approach. The experimental design controls for other factors that might cause cost differences. If an experiment is unavailable, a quasi-experimental design can be used. In this case, researchers need to ensure they control for all other variables that could cause differences in cost, including the type of case as well as its size and complexity.[16] Another approach is a before-and-after study, where the cost of handling a given set of complaints prior to the beginning of an ADR program is compared to the cost of handling analogous complaints after ADR. This approach requires the existence of detailed archival data on the cost of the cases prior to ADR.

In addition to measuring savings to the government, agencies may wish to survey private parties to determine if they save money with ADR. This information can help persuade Congress, the press, and other interested individuals that an ADR program is worthwhile. It also may encourage future private parties to select ADR for their cases with the government and to participate in ADR enthusiastically.

It is worthwhile to consider cost effects in different contexts, looking at the types of cases, the types of ADR used, the types of people who use the programs, and the types of providers.

Time Savings

Another important area for ADR research is whether the process saves time. The methods for measuring whether an ADR program saves time are similar to those for examining cost savings. Evaluators should first determine how much time ADR processes take. Participants should report the amount of time they spent preparing for ADR as well as the amount of time they spend in the ADR process itself.

Evaluators should then compare this figure with the amount of time that would have been required to resolve the dispute had ADR not been used.[17] Typically, the non-ADR process is litigation, which can require time for discovery, motions practice, trial, and appeal.

It is important to note that many cases that settle in ADR would have settled anyway before they reached trial. Therefore, researchers must examine time savings by comparing how long an ADR process took with the time that would have been required to resolve the case otherwise, considering whether trial would have taken place.

An experimental approach, where parties are randomly assigned to ADR or non-ADR methods, provides the most accurate evaluation of whether there are time savings. In a setting where an experiment is impossible, a quasi-experiment may be used. In studies of this type, researchers should work to control for all other variables that could cause a difference in the amount of time required to process a dispute. If this approach is used in a program established in multiple parts of the country, it is particularly important to control for time variations in the various regions, because different parts of the country can take substantially different amounts of time to resolve cases.[18] Before-and-after designs can work well, where researchers compare the amount of time required to handle cases prior to the introduction of the ADR program with the time required after.[19]

Finally, it is worthwhile to check whether time effects vary depending on the types of cases, the types of ADR used, the types of people who use the programs, and the types of providers.

Relationship Effects

ADR has the potential to have a more positive effect on relationships than adversarial processes do. ADR encourages more collaborative relationships than litigation, which often drives parties further apart by forcing them into combat with each other. The effects of this difference can extend beyond the ADR process itself. Parties may be able to avoid future disputes if they can establish a positive relationship. This is a worthwhile area for evaluation.

An evaluation should consider such relationship effects as morale, stress, and conflict levels of the participants. Disruption to others in the office may be worth examining in certain cases, particularly workplace disputes. These can be measured by surveying parties to get reports of their emotional states. These subjective reports can be augmented by objective measures such as levels of absenteeism, productivity, and turnover among parties to disputes. The experiences of parties participating in ADR should then be compared with those from parties participating in other non-ADR processes.

Evaluators can examine long-term effects by gathering data concerning parties after a dispute is over. Some forms of ADR are specifically designed to transform parties' relationships by increasing their recognition of each other's interests and empowering them for the future.[20] Parties can be asked through surveys to report on these effects.[21] Again, ADR participant responses should be compared to those who did not use ADR.

Another area for research is to examine whether the use of ADR improves relationships to the point where it helps change the culture of the organization and prevent future disputes. A number of studies have shown drops in the numbers of future complaints following the introduction of an ADR program.[22]

When examining whether ADR caused a drop in future disputes, it is important to consider whether other variables also could account for the result. Researchers will want to ensure there was not a significant change in law or agency policy, for example. A time-series analysis can work well for exploring this issue, particularly if the ADR program is large and can be rolled out in different regions at different times. If a drop in future complaints occurs in each region at roughly the same time interval after the introduction of the ADR program, the drop in complaints can reasonably be attributed to the ADR.[23]

As with all other ADR evaluation, it is worthwhile to check whether relationship effects vary depending on the types of cases, the types of ADR used, the types of people who use the programs, and the types of ADR providers.

Outcome Quality

Another essential consideration for an ADR program is the quality of the outcomes it generates. It is important to study the nature of these results. Are they different from the outcomes produced by non-ADR processes? If so, how are they different?

One key element in a settlement is the amount of money paid to the complaining party. Evaluators can compare the amounts paid in ADR and non-ADR processes to determine whether complainants receive more, less, or the same amount of money in ADR. With this type of analysis, it is vital to ensure that the cases being examined are truly comparable to one another. For example, if ADR is typically used in cases with larger damage amounts, it may appear that ADR settlements are larger than non-ADR settlements, even though the real explanation is that the underlying cases are different. Thus, researchers should use an approach that controls for all other relevant factors. One approach is to use ratios between the amount received in the settlement and the amount requested in the complaint. This method controls for the sizes of different cases and allows for a fair comparison. If the ratio between the amount requested and the amount received is similar for ADR and non-ADR cases, it is likely that neither of the processes is biased in favor of one party or the other.[24]

Nonmonetary interests also are very important in many settlements. ADR settlements may include nonmonetary relief that is tailored more closely to the needs of the parties because the parties themselves drafted the agreements. Furthermore, parties often believe that ADR leads to more creative settlements because the process allows and even encourages this approach. To measure these concepts, researchers can survey parties after both ADR and non-ADR resolutions to ask their opinions of the results. Parties can report how well the outcome meets their needs as well as how creative it is.

Durability is another important characteristic of settlements. If a settlement (or an adjudicated judgment) does not hold up well or leads to further disputes, it is much less effective. To evaluate settlement durability, evaluators should look at party behavior six months, one year, and longer after they reach agreement. Do the parties comply with the terms of a settlement? Do disputes recur between the parties despite the settlement? Did the settlement incorporate effective dispute resolution procedures to address future disputes? Evaluators can survey the parties on these issues and look at records of future complaint filings for additional data.

Evaluators should check whether outcomes vary depending on the types of cases, the types of ADR used, the types of people who use the programs, and the types of ADR providers.

Program Quality

Another purpose of evaluation is to explore how well an ADR program functions administratively. ADR program managers will want to know if they are providing services effectively and to pinpoint areas where they can improve. Evaluation is an excellent way to discover this information.

Evaluations of program quality should consider a number of substantive factors. Is ADR being used by the appropriate parties? Have barriers to ADR use been reduced, and is the program publicized sufficiently that everyone who could benefit from ADR is getting it? Is ADR being used in the appropriate disputes? Are all necessary subissues and related disputes included where appropriate? Is ADR taking place at a well-chosen time in the life span of disputes?

Research also should focus on the administrative aspects of the program. Participants can report whether they found the ADR program easy to use. Did program staff explain the process well, so that parties could make an informed decision whether to participate? Did parties have enough information to prepare for the ADR process and participate effectively? Did the ADR take place at a convenient time and location? Both parties and neutrals can be surveyed for their opinions on these issues. They also can provide comments on how to make the process work better.

Program managers should create a feedback loop, where the results of evaluations are considered in making changes to the program. After the changes have been in place for a sufficient period, the program should be evaluated again. With a continuous cycle of improvements followed by additional research, an ADR program can be greatly enhanced.

Quality of Neutrals

Evaluators should examine the effectiveness of neutrals in the program. With this information, they can give additional cases to neutrals who are working well and cut ineffective neutrals from their rosters. Knowledge of what makes a neutral effective in a government ADR program also can help a program manager determine whom to hire in the first place. The ability of the neutrals in a program may affect many aspects of its effectiveness, including cost and time savings, relationship effects, outcome quality, and settlement rates.

Determining the quality of neutrals can be a complicated undertaking. One measure of effectiveness is what percentage of cases involving particular neutrals settle. However, this is an imperfect indicator because some cases should not settle, and parties do not want a neutral who pressures them into doing something they prefer not to do. Another possibility is to examine how quickly cases settle with particular neutrals. However, unusually quick settlements might indicate that the neutral did not thoroughly explore a dispute or work to draft a careful agreement. Quality also could be measured by how high a satisfaction rate a neutral receives in surveys completed by the parties. However, some parties are inexperienced with ADR and can give unreliable impressions of the neutral. Yet another approach is for experienced ADR professionals to observe each neutral and provide evaluation reports. However, some parties do not want to be observed, and this process is time-consuming and expensive.[25]

Most government ADR evaluations have measured the quality of the neutral by surveying the participants. This approach is subjective and imperfect, but the opinions of the parties are nonetheless very important because they are the people the program primarily is designed to serve. Some programs have combined participant surveys with observations by program managers, a more comprehensive and reliable approach.

An evaluation should consider whether a neutral handles the parties to a dispute well. Does the neutral listen carefully, understand what the parties want, treat the parties with respect, show empathy when appropriate, improve the communication between the parties, and work to enhance the relationship of the parties?

Evaluations should examine whether a neutral handles the substance of a dispute effectively. Does the neutral understand the nature of the dispute? Is the neutral skilled at clarifying the underlying interests of the parties? Does the neutral generate creative options that meet the parties' interests? Is the neutral fair and impartial? Is the neutral effective in moving the parties toward closure when appropriate?

A good way to measure the general quality of the neutral is to ask the parties whether they would use this person again in the future and whether they would recommend the neutral to others. Parties also can be asked for their overall impression of the neutral.

Sharing the results of the evaluation with the neutrals themselves is important. Good neutrals welcome feedback, both positive and negative. Some questions that have been particularly helpful in this regard include asking parties what the neutral did well and less well. Some parties have given insightful answers when asked how the neutral could do better in the future. By learning how they are perceived by the parties they serve, neutrals can adjust their performance to be even more effective in the future.

Evaluators also will want to check for interaction effects. Does the quality of a neutral vary depending on the type of case, the type of ADR used, or the type of parties who participate? For example, some neutrals are much more effective with certain issues and certain parties. Understanding these effects will be valuable in selecting neutrals for future cases.

Participant Satisfaction

The final component of an evaluation is to measure how satisfied the parties are with the process.[26] The parties to a dispute often focus on criteria in addition to time and money savings when evaluating their experience with ADR. Ultimately, an ADR program must satisfy the parties who use it, or it will not succeed in the long run. This factor is especially important for a government agency, which exists to serve the public interest, not just to satisfy a bottom line.

One approach to measuring participant satisfaction centers on a concept called *procedural justice*.[27] The idea behind this theory is that there is more to justice than simply the outcome of a dispute. Parties often value the process used to resolve the dispute as much as or more than the result. Indeed, research has shown that parties prefer a process where they have an opportunity to participate actively and a measure of control over what happens, even when the outcome of this process is adverse to their interests.[28]

Procedural justice has two main elements. The first is that parties have an opportunity for self-expression. Traditional adversarial processes such as litigation largely silence the parties and permit them to participate, if at all, only in a narrowly circumscribed manner. In contrast, parties are sometimes the lead participants in an ADR process and almost always can speak more freely. Evaluators can measure this concept by asking the parties whether they felt they were able to participate in the ADR process, believed their comments were heard by the neutral and the other participants, believed they were treated with respect, and felt like an important part of the process.

The second element is the opportunity for self-determination. Adversarial processes typically place the decision-making power in the hands of a third party, such as a judge or jury. When parties participate in such a process, they relinquish control over the result. In contrast, parties in ADR processes retain control over the outcome.[29] Parties need not agree to any proposed settlement they do not like. To measure this aspect of party satisfaction, evaluators can ask parties if they believed they had control over the ADR process, their own decisions, and the ultimate outcome of the process.

There are other components to participant satisfaction as well. Researchers may want to measure whether parties understood what was happening in the process. Parties can describe whether they understood the reasons for the result. Questions can inquire whether the parties believed the process was fair.

Overall satisfaction can be measured well by asking parties if they would use an ADR process again to settle a future dispute or if they would recommend the ADR process to others. Another question is whether ADR is "the best way to handle a dispute like this." Parties also can give an assessment of their overall satisfaction level. Satisfaction levels measured by these questions have been very high in the federal government.[30]

Satisfaction surveys also should be given to participants in non-ADR processes. This allows a comparison of ADR with its alternatives, which is the best way to assess its value. Studies have shown much higher levels of party satisfaction at the end of ADR processes than adjudicatory processes in the government.[31] This evidence makes a compelling argument to outside parties, from agency budget staffs to congressional oversight committees, that ADR processes are valuable contributors to federal programs.

Finally, as with all other ADR research, it is important to look for possible interactions. Do satisfaction levels differ depending on the type of case, the nature of the ADR process used, the characteristics of the parties who participated, or the provider who served as the neutral? Answers to these questions will assist program managers in delivering the best possible ADR processes in each individual situation.

Methods for Evaluating a Government ADR Program

The next issue in designing an evaluation is determining how to collect the data. There are six major methods for data collection in federal ADR programs: archival sources, case studies, surveys, field experiments, quasi-experiments, and measurements over time.

Archival Data

The easiest and cheapest way to conduct an evaluation is to use existing (archival) data. Federal agencies keep considerable information that can be useful in an ADR evaluation. For example, in an ADR program for workplace EEO, an agency civil rights or personnel office may already record useful data, including the demographics of participants and costs of handling complaints. It will generally keep information on case filing and termination dates, which will allow the calculation of case processing time. For an ADR program designed to resolve administrative or federal court litigation, the general counsel's office may have a case tracking system that records this kind of information. Obtaining such data often requires little more than a request to the individual who runs the computer that keeps the information (though agreeing on protocols for how results will be released may be more complicated).

Case Studies

Another approach to evaluation is to examine a single case or small number of cases in depth, a method with a number of advantages. It is relatively easy to study individual cases, with no requirement of complicated data analysis or statistical formulas. A case study evaluation is also easy to explain to other people. It allows telling a story, which can be compelling to a reader or an audience. Because case studies typically involve only a small number of cases, in-depth exploration is possible with each one. Complex matters can be probed thoroughly, which may be necessary to understand them fully. Case studies also can include valuable historical perspectives, as a dispute can be examined from start to finish.

However, the nonstatistical quality of case studies can be a disadvantage. When only a small number of cases are examined, there is no way to be sure they are representative of what is happening in the vast majority of cases that are not studied. If the case studies are favorable, outside audiences may suspect that the researcher has chosen only the best ones to examine. If the results are negative, this may or may not mean that the program as a whole is ineffective.

There are ways to address these concerns. Evaluators can work to choose representative cases that are typical in carefully controlled ways. An evaluation can include multiple cases selected from a variety of different sources to cover a spectrum of situations. Qualitative case studies also can be combined with more quantitative forms of research discussed below. With this approach, the evaluation will include compelling, in-depth case examples along with statistical measures that cover the population as a whole. Finally, case studies are often useful for pilot evaluations, to give researchers insights into how to design more comprehensive evaluations in the future.

Surveys

Probably the most common form of ADR research in the federal government is the use of surveys. Survey research has both advantages and disadvantages, and there are a number of considerations to keep in mind when conducting an evaluation using this method.

Advantages

Surveys can be easier to design and administer than other forms of research. Most people have some familiarity with what is involved in putting together a survey. Rigorous survey question design requires careful attention from an expert, but most ADR program managers can consider what they want to measure and write questions that will capture it at least roughly. This can make survey research among the cheapest methods of evaluation. (With sufficient money to hire an expert, surveys can be even more valid and reliable.)

Another advantage of surveys is that people are familiar with them. Participants understand what is expected of them when they are asked to fill out a survey. Program managers find it easy to explain the results of an evaluation based on surveys because the audience will understand what is involved.

Surveys can be administered at different times during a dispute to capture different information. When administered at the beginning of a matter, surveys measure parties' attitudes and expectations before ADR is used. Surveys immediately after ADR examine what happened during the ADR process itself. Finally, surveys at the end of an entire case can evaluate ADR's overall effect on the dispute. Evaluators can use surveys at a specific time to pinpoint the information they want, or they can administer multiple surveys to gain a more broad-ranging perspective.

Disadvantages

Survey research is not perfect. For one thing, surveys do not necessarily measure what people really believe; they only measure what people *say* they believe. Social scientists have repeatedly demonstrated that these are not always the same thing. When people know others will be reading what they write, they tend to tailor their responses with this audience in mind.

Another major flaw of survey research is that response rates are usually low.[32] People do not always want to take the time to fill out a survey, so frequently researchers must work with response rates well under 100 percent. Sometimes responses to a mailed survey are only in the neighborhood of 20 percent. Even with repeated follow-up, evaluators may be fortunate if they have information from as many as half the people who used ADR.

The problem with low response rates is that people who take the time to return the survey may be different from those who do not. Perhaps they are more conscientious than those who are unwilling to fill out forms. Maybe they like ADR and thus are more favorably inclined to respond. It is also possible they liked the ADR less and want to make sure someone finds out their views. There is often no way to know whether any of these biases exist, or which way they cut, because researchers have no information from those who do not respond.

Finally, unless used as part of an experiment, surveys do not prove what causes things in ADR. Put more technically, surveys have internal validity problems because they do not prove a causal link. For example, consider a mediation program that allows participants to choose either a facilitative mediator (who allows the parties to take more of a lead in the mediation) or an evaluative mediator (who takes a more active role in providing opinions and telling the parties what to do). Assume that survey results show that parties who chose a facilitative mediator expressed higher satisfaction levels than those who chose an evaluative mediator. A novice researcher might be tempted to claim that the survey proved that facilitative mediation causes greater satisfaction among participants. Now this may be true, but it also may not. Indeed, the converse may be true instead: perhaps what is really going on is that people who are more satisfied with mediation choose facilitative mediators. This is easy enough to imagine. People who are happier with the way their case is going and are getting along agreeably with the other side may be willing to choose a mediator who will stay more in the background. In contrast, people who are frustrated with their case and angry with the other side may choose a mediator who will be evaluative, in hopes that the evaluation will go against their opponents. With this scenario, the happy parties are likely to report higher satisfaction than the angry parties. However, the type of mediation chosen did not cause their better mood; instead, their better mood caused them to select the type of mediation. This type of situation is common enough that survey research by itself does not reliably prove causation.

It is possible to use surveys as part of an experiment to learn about causation. In the above situation, a researcher could assign people randomly to either a facilitative or evaluative mediator rather than allowing them to choose. Then differences in satisfaction reported in surveys at the end of mediation could not be due to parties' choice of the mediator.

Surveys Distributed at the End of ADR

Encouraging parties to complete their surveys at the end of their ADR experience and while they are still in the room yields a much higher response rate. Once the parties disperse at the end of ADR, they tend to go on to other things and have less interest in filling out and returning a survey. Often they never get around to filling it out. Another advantage is that participants' memories are fresher right when they finish the ADR, which can make the data more accurate.

One method that has worked well is for the ADR neutral to distribute the surveys to the parties.[33] The neutral will always be present at the end of an ADR process and is in a perfect position to provide survey forms to the participants. The neutral also can ensure that the forms are filled out completely and collect them from the parties before they depart.

Of course, some parties are in a hurry to leave at the end of an ADR session and resist completing surveys. Agencies may wish to make returning the survey voluntary, to avoid a coercive atmosphere, in which case parties can take the survey home with them and fill it out at their leisure. This approach also can make people feel that their answers are more confidential than if they hand their surveys to the neutral. Furthermore, participants may have more time later to complete a survey more thoroughly, and the added reflection from time away from the ADR may give them greater perspective. However, evaluators can expect to receive fewer survey responses from people who leave before filling them out.

Surveys Mailed Out After ADR Is Completed

Some programs choose to mail evaluations to participants after ADR is completed. One advantage is that this allows people to complete the surveys anonymously. Some participants may prefer this, and an evaluation could theoretically be more accurate when respondents are not concerned that their answers can be traced back to them. Also, conducting a survey by mail can be easier administratively. Evaluation forms do not need to be provided in advance to parties and mediators who may misplace them. Program managers are not always present at the exact end of an ADR process to provide surveys themselves.

One problem with this method is that response rates from mailed surveys are notoriously low. There are many reasons for this. Address information can be inaccurate. An agency may not have an address for every ADR participant. People move without providing an updated address. It is surprising how often addresses provided by participants are incomplete or illegible.

Even if they do receive the form, many ADR participants never get around to filling it out and mailing it back in. Others may refuse outright to complete the form; they may want nothing further to do with the case.

Among participants who do fill out the forms, some do not fill them out completely. This creates missing data, which can cause invalid conclusions. For example, if unsatisfied participants consistently leave certain questions blank and satisfied participants do not answer other questions, there will be an overall bias in the data.

Some methods can boost response rates. One is to send the survey with a cover letter signed by an important, respected person. Parties are more likely to respond when they know that someone they hold in esteem (or someone who is a high-level official in their agency) values their response. Providing a postage-paid, self-addressed return envelope can help. This makes it easier to respond, which means more people will do so. It also is valuable to follow up with those who do not respond. Additional letters sent after an appropriate period of time can gather data from those who forgot to respond or misplaced the original survey. Telephone call reminders also can help. Of course, in order to follow up, an agency must know who has responded and who has not. This requires being able to identify who filled out each survey, which removes confidentiality. It is possible to use identifying numbers on each survey rather than require participants to supply their names, but these numbers must still be traceable to the individual participants. Numbering systems can appear more anonymous, but they do not provide complete confidentiality.

Surveys Using the Computer

Technology provides a number of useful tools to the survey researcher. E-mail can be a very effective way to distribute a survey. It avoids costs for stationery or postage and can be extremely easy to administer, because a single survey can be mailed to thousands of participants at one time.

A major advantage of electronic surveys is that the results automatically come in a machine-readable format. Most statistical research requires data to be in a form that a computer can use to analyze the results. Coding data into a computer from paper forms can be an extremely laborious process, both time-consuming and expensive. It can introduce errors if done imperfectly. Receiving results in a ready-made computer format minimizes all of these problems.

Nevertheless, e-mail surveys do have disadvantages. Agencies may not have e-mail addresses for everyone who participates in their ADR program. Moreover, e-mail addresses can change even more frequently than home addresses. Some participants may not have access to a computer. Furthermore, providing a response by e-mail automatically links it to a participant's name, which destroys anonymity.

One approach is to have participants fill out surveys on a Web site. This approach preserves the advantages of e-mail surveys while also allowing anonymity. Agencies also can give participants a choice of completing the survey on-line or in traditional paper form.

Surveys Conducted Through Personal Interviews

Conducting survey research in person, rather than with a form, is another option. This approach tends to increase response rates: participants find it easier to respond to questions orally than write out their responses, and it is more difficult to refuse a request from a live person than it is to neglect to return a form. A human interviewer can overcome the problems of written surveys that are not completely filled out by ensuring that participants answer all questions.

A unique advantage of personal interview surveys is the opportunity for personal interaction. If interviewers do not understand responses, they can follow up with clarifying questions. Equally important, respondents can provide information not specifically requested on the form. Often this information would never have been obtained if participants had been limited to checking specific boxes on a document. Responses from interview surveys are generally richer and more detailed than from paper surveys. This can be useful to provide researchers with in-depth examples and illustrations for reports.

These qualities make personal interviews particularly valuable for a pilot evaluation. Talking with participants directly will give evaluators insights into what questions they should ask on their formal evaluation. Even if the eventual evaluation will be in the form of a written survey, researchers should consider conducting personal interviews first to learn about the program.

There are two main protocols for conducting interview surveys. The first is the in-depth interview: researchers use a planned format in asking questions but are allowed to make deviations to cover a broader range of issues that arise during the process. The second is the structured questionnaire: interviewers must follow a specific, predetermined schedule of questions, with no deviations permitted. The first approach allows more flexibility, while the second makes interview responses easier to code and evaluate.

These advantages of personal interviews come at a cost: this is the most expensive and time-consuming form of survey research. A program must have staff to interview each participant individually.

Furthermore, personal interviews can introduce biases. Some participants may try to answer questions the way they expect the interviewer wants them to. Because the interviewer is a live person, this effect can be stronger than with a paper survey. Also, interviewers must be careful to ask questions in the same way with each participant. If the form of questions differs, this can affect the results. It is important to develop an interview protocol listing each question specifically. Finally, personal interviews are by their nature not anonymous.

Designing Survey Questions

A fundamental general concern in creating a survey is reliability. In its technical sense, reliability means that an instrument yields consistent results whenever it is used again under the same circumstances. In other words, if the same ADR participants filled out the same form later, they would fill it out the same way. A survey that is ambiguous, for example, may not be reliable because participants might answer questions differently later because they misunderstood them. It is essential that surveys be reliable in order to be accurate.

The second concern is validity. In research, internal validity means that an evaluation measures what it is designed to measure. For example, it is important to know whether surveys of satisfaction levels really represent participants' actual satisfaction with ADR. Many things can interfere with a survey's validity, and this compromises the value of the evaluation.

The wording of questions and even their sequencing can have unexpectedly profound effects on their validity. For example, people shown a videotape of a car accident described as a "crash" give higher estimates of the speed of the vehicles than people shown the same videotape when it is described as a "collision." Relatedly, people estimate that "$8 \times 7 \times 6 \times 5 \times 4 \times 3 \times 2 \times 1$" is a much larger figure than "$1 \times 2 \times 3 \times 4 \times 5 \times 6 \times 7 \times 8$," even though the results are actually identical.[34] These issues can make it valuable to consult with a survey expert before conducting this type of research.

There are also different ways to structure questions. The most straightforward approach to survey research is to ask closed-end questions: respondents must choose from a limited number of possible answers to each question. This method yields uniform results that can easily be compared and combined among surveys.

A special case of the closed-end survey question is the Likert scale. In this type of question, respondents are asked to rate something on a numerical scale (typically 1–5, 1–7, or 1–9). For example, the survey may ask, "Please rate your satisfaction with the mediation from 1 to 5, where 1 is very unsatisfied, 2 is somewhat unsatisfied, 3 is neither satisfied nor unsatisfied, 4 is somewhat satisfied, and 5 is very satisfied." This scale allows evaluators to report the average level of satisfaction by taking the mean of all the responses.

Open-ended survey questions provide respondents with more flexibility in their answers. This type of question can be more useful when an evaluator does not want to limit responses to fixed categories decided in advance. For example, a survey may ask, "Why did your case not settle in mediation?" in order to obtain the broadest possible spectrum of explanations.

One difficulty of open-ended questions is that responses must be coded to be analyzed statistically. For example, one participant may answer the question by saying, "The case did not settle because the other side had unrealistic expectations." Another may respond, "The case did not settle because the other side stubbornly asked for too much money." These answers are closely related but not exactly the same. Usually answers to open-ended questions will not quite be identical, making analysis difficult. It is possible to address this problem by creating categories for responses. In this example, evaluators could code both responses in the category, "Respondent believed the case did not settle because of the behavior of the other side."

In all survey research, it is vital to pretest the instrument. Typographical errors such as leaving out the word *not* can change the meaning of questions completely. Questions can be ambiguous or otherwise hard to understand. It can be difficult to know how much writing space to leave on the form for open-ended questions without testing them first. It is much easier to solve these problems at the beginning, before hundreds or thousands of forms have been printed and distributed.

Evaluators should consider how burdensome a form is to fill out. To be sure, the survey must be complete enough to be useful. However, there are real costs to using a form that is time-consuming to complete. Parties are less likely to fill out a lengthy form, or they may not fill it out completely. If they are required to spend a long time working on the survey, they may feel upset about this, which could affect the results. They may feel more negatively about their entire ADR experience if their last memory of it is an annoyingly long form.

Sampling

If researchers are not going to provide surveys to every participant, they must be careful in how they determine who will be asked to complete a survey and who will not. This issue is called *sampling*. Evaluations using sampling must follow certain procedures, or the research may not be valid. Specifically, evaluators must ensure that their samples adequately represent the different types of people who participate in ADR, the different places where it is used, and the different times when it is used. The goal of sampling is to ensure that the research on a limited group of participants will be generalizable to the entire population that uses ADR.

Random sampling is designed to help ensure that the group being examined is representative of the overall population. For example, perhaps the population of those who use ADR in a given program is 1,000 but the researchers wish to study only 100 of them. In this case, the researchers can use a computer to randomly select those who will be studied. The process is analogous to putting all 1,000 names into a hat and randomly drawing 100 of them. Random selection ensures that no bias is introduced into the process. If enough people are studied, it is likely that any differences between the people, places, and times in the sample group and the overall population will average out.

If researchers want to ensure that they adequately cover certain specific groups, they can use a stratified random sample. This method involves dividing the population into the selected groups (for example, males and females, or those who have used ADR before and those who have not) and then taking random samples of people within each group. In this way, the key groups are sure to be represented in large enough numbers to allow a comparison between them.

Sampling is a complex subject, and decisions in this area can have important consequences for the validity of research. It is worthwhile engaging an expert when conducting evaluations using this method.

The Paperwork Reduction Act

Federal evaluations that use surveys must comply with the Paperwork Reduction Act.[35] This act is designed to reduce the paperwork burden on the public from filling out government forms. Under certain circumstances, an agency must follow procedures and obtain clearance from the Office of Management and Budget (OMB) before requiring members of the public to answer questions.

Obtaining OMB approval can be a time-consuming process, and agencies should plan in advance if conducting evaluation that will require it. The process involves publishing a notice in the *Federal Register* soliciting public comment on the proposed survey. The notice must include a summary of the data to be collected, an estimate of the time burden in completing the survey, and a description of the need for the data, among other information. The public has sixty days to respond with comments. Then the agency submits a report including all public comments to the Office of Information and Regulatory Affairs at OMB, which decides whether to approve the survey. In making this decision, OMB weighs the burden to the public in completing the survey with the benefit in terms of practical utility for the agency. OMB approval lasts only a maximum of three years, after which additional approval must be sought.

Fortunately, the act does not apply to most evaluations of ADR in the federal government. No approval is necessary in order to ask questions of federal employees acting in the scope of their employment.[36] Nor must an agency seek approval for information collected during the conduct of a civil or administrative action to which the agency is a party.[37] These exceptions cover the great majority of situations where ADR is used in the government. To ensure compliance with the act, evaluators may consult with the agency chief information officer, who is charged with responsibility in this area.[38]

Confidentiality

Participants are more likely to give accurate information to researchers if they know their comments will be kept confidential. Without such assurances, they may believe their supervisors or others in the agency may learn about their comments. This could lead them to give undeserved positive feedback (hoping it could benefit them professionally) or to avoid giving deserved negative feedback (fearing it could harm them professionally).

At the same time, evaluators want to be able to publicize their findings. An evaluation that cannot be distributed to managers and others in an agency is of little value. This creates a tension around the issue of confidentiality in ADR evaluation.

A good general compromise is to tell participants that their names and other identifying information will not be revealed. Thus, although participant comments may be disclosed, they cannot be linked to a particular person. This allows researchers to issue a thorough report without compromising participants' anonymity. Most of the time, this will satisfy all sides.

This is the approach taken in the ADRA. The ADRA permits "gathering of information for research or educational purposes, in cooperation with other agencies, governmental entities, or dispute resolution programs, so long as the parties and the specific issues in controversy are not identifiable."[39]

Field Experiments

Without using an experiment, it can be impossible to know what caused what in ADR. For example, if a researcher wants to measure whether ADR saves money, nonexperimental designs may not provide an accurate answer. Other factors besides ADR can affect how much a case costs to resolve. The complexity of a case is one such factor: more complicated cases are generally more expensive to resolve. If parties with complicated cases tend to select ADR more often than parties with easier cases, this would affect the results of the research. This *selection bias* may make it appear that cases going to ADR are more expensive to resolve, when the reality is that the observed cost difference is due to the complexity of the case. Without controlling for this possibility, an evaluator has no way of knowing for sure what is going on.

Experiments address this problem through a process called *random assignment:* every participant is assigned to either a test group or a control group. Typically, one group is required to use ADR, and the other group is prohibited from doing so. Assignment to the groups is done completely randomly, to avoid introducing any bias.

The process works by having effects caused by things other than ADR cancel each other out. Complicated cases and simple cases will be distributed randomly between ADR and non-ADR approaches. With enough cases, things will balance out, and roughly equal numbers of all types of case will be found in each experimental group. The only consistent difference between the groups will be whether ADR was used. Thus, any differences in results between the groups will be due to ADR.

The importance of this design becomes clear when considering how many different variables can affect the outcome of a case. The relationship between the parties is significant, as is the greediness of the plaintiff or the stubbornness of the defendant. The attitudes of the lawyers make a difference. The race, gender, or national origin of the participants may have an effect in certain situations. The subject matter of the case where ADR is used plays a role. Other personal factors, such as age, income level, and education, may be relevant in some cases. Without random assignment, different interactions of all of these characteristics can affect the results of a study. With random assignment, they all will be more or less equally distributed between ADR and non-ADR approaches, permitting the researcher to conclude that ADR did or did not cause the results.

The rigor of the experimental design does not come without costs. This approach can be administratively difficult. Program managers must insist that the assignment of parties to ADR and non-ADR be done strictly randomly. This requires that the managers have control over the program, which may not be possible in some government agencies. In many offices, the attorney handling a case has control over how to proceed, and the attorney may not want to be told whether to use ADR. Clients as well may resist being forced to use ADR or being prohibited from doing so.

In some government contexts, an experimental design may be ill advised. If ADR is a beneficial process (as many believe), it may not be appropriate to prevent a party from using it just because the party happened to be randomly assigned to the non-ADR group. Conversely, if a case is simply not appropriate for ADR, it may be a waste of taxpayer resources to require the parties to use ADR just to follow an experimental protocol.

In other government contexts, an experimental approach is unavailable. For example, the EEOC has mandated that agencies make ADR available for workplace discrimination cases.[40] In these programs, an agency must offer ADR to anyone who wants it and cannot withhold it in order to conduct research. In litigation, a judge may order a case to litigation, and an agency will be unable to refuse.

It is possible that an experimental design will alter the data it is supposed to measure. In the absence of an experiment, parties choose whether to use ADR. With the experiment, this choice is taken from them, which changes things. Thus, the type of ADR the experiment measures is different from the type of ADR that occurs in the real world. This is an example of the Heisenberg uncertainty principle, which states that it is impossible to measure all aspects of a system without changing that system.[41]

It is also important with this type of research to have the guidance of an experienced professional. Experimental evaluation must follow strict standards in design, application, and data interpretation. A knowledge of statistics is required to analyze the results accurately. This is not work that can be done by a novice.

Finally, research involving experiments in the federal government must follow guidelines covering the protection of human subjects.[42] Because researchers determine who uses ADR and who does not, they change what would be occurring in the absence of the research. Under these circumstances, regulations require that an agency institutional review board review the research plans.[43] The board's function is to examine proposed research to determine that any risks to participants are minimized and are reasonable in relation to anticipated benefits, to confirm that participants give informed consent, and to ensure that the rights and welfare of the participants are maintained.[44] Fortunately, ADR research generally can be conducted in accord with these guidelines. The risks of ADR are negligible (unlike, for example, the risks of new medicines tested under these provisions). Because of this, review boards can exempt ADR research from the requirement of informed consent in appropriate circumstances.[45] It is a good idea to consult with officials in the agency's review board while designing the research in order to incorporate their suggestions and ensure approval of the final plan.

Quasi-Experiments

If an agency cannot use a true experimental design, a quasi-experiment is often the next best thing. With this method, parties are not randomly assigned to ADR and non-ADR groups. Rather, researchers compare the cases where ADR was selected with those where it was not. This approach also is called the *nonequivalent control group design,* because the ADR cases are not completely equivalent to the control group cases. Important differences may exist that complicate the analysis. Nonetheless, researchers can control for these differences as much as possible.

Suppose an agency wishes to examine the effectiveness of its contracting ADR program. It decides not to assign cases to ADR and non-ADR groups randomly, but instead to compare the cases that naturally go to ADR with those that do not. In order to ensure that differences between the two groups are due to ADR and not other factors, it must consider what other factors could be playing a role and account for them.

Such factors may include the subject matter of the claim, the amount of money involved, the location of the claim (some parts of the country differ from others), the demographics of the participants, and other variables. Whatever the evaluators think may make a difference in the outcome of the case should be considered, so that the true contribution of ADR can be measured accurately.

Once the important variables are identified, researchers can control for them in several ways. One method is the matched-pairs analysis. With this approach, researchers compare an ADR case to a non-ADR case matched as closely as possible with it on all other relevant factors. For example, if a contracting ADR case involved a defective pricing claim for $1 million between the government and a Fortune 100 company in a western state, researchers will attempt to find a non-ADR case with as close to the same characteristics as they can. If all of the other variables have been controlled for, any differences between two cases will be due to whether ADR was used.

It is also possible to use a regression analysis to examine these cases. With this approach, all of the characteristics of every case, both those using ADR and those not using it, are fed into a computer statistical program. The computer analyzes the effect of all variables mathematically, in an attempt to isolate the parts each plays in the result.

One problem with these methods is that it is difficult to be certain whether all other relevant variables have been controlled for. It may be that a "missing variable," other than ADR, is causing the difference between the ADR and non-ADR cases. In the true experimental design, random assignment helps ensure that all missing variables cancel each other out. Absent an experimental design, the human role in selecting which cases go to ADR means that a researcher never can be completely certain of the results of the analysis. Nonetheless, careful research that controls for variables known to affect dispute resolution can give considerable insight into the effectiveness of an ADR program.

Observations over Time

Another way that researchers can evaluate an ADR program is to take advantage of the effects of time. By looking at the same case or the same types of cases at different times, it is possible to isolate the impact of ADR. This approach relies on the fact that causes can come only before effects, never after.

The most basic example of this design is the before-and-after analysis. A researcher can look at a government program before ADR was implemented and compare it to what happened afterward. For example, evaluators can examine the time required to resolve each case, the cost for each case, and the satisfaction levels of the parties, both before and after the start date of the ADR program. The researchers also should check whether other changes during this same time period might account for the difference, such as a shift in the law or agency policy. If no other changes appear to account for the differences before and after ADR was implemented, any differences may be due to the ADR.

If an agency does not have historical data on the performance of a program prior to the introduction of ADR, other approaches are possible. Evaluators can measure such variables as cost and satisfaction within the life of each individual case. If party satisfaction levels increase immediately after ADR is used, ADR may be the cause of the increase.

Some agencies have used a *time series design* to measure the effect of an ADR program as it is rolled out in various parts of the country. The U.S. Postal Service, for example, implemented a workplace ADR program in different regions at different times. It measured the number of new cases filed in each region over several years. The number of new disputes filed in each region dropped after the introduction of the ADR program.[46] This appears to indicate that ADR led to a reduction in new cases, perhaps because it encouraged employees to communicate better with each other.

One weakness of this design is that other factors may account for the difference apart from ADR. A party may report a higher satisfaction level right after ADR because something else happened that had nothing to do with the case. Or, in the Postal Service example, perhaps other things occurring at the same time as the introduction of ADR account for the difference, such as unrelated changes to personnel rules. Without a true experimental design, it is impossible to be sure what is happening.

With enough data, the possibility of outside factors can be reduced to a negligible level. If party satisfaction levels increase right after ADR in a large number of cases, it is unlikely that all of these people independently had outside influences that account for the difference.

Reporting the Results

Once an evaluation is complete, the final consideration is how to report the results. The answer to this question will depend on the audience for which the report is intended. It may be advisable to prepare individually tailored versions of the report to address the different needs of each group that has an interest in the ADR program.

Evaluations can be presented in several different formats. A written presentation allows for a detailed explanation of results and permits readers to look at different sections, picking and choosing the parts that are most interesting to them. Reports should begin with an executive summary to give an overview of their contents. This allows a busy reader to get the highlights without having to work through pages of detailed analysis.

Oral presentations have different advantages. One is that they give the audience an opportunity to ask questions of the researchers. A written report may not anticipate all of the questions a particular audience may have. Oral interaction also can be more stimulating than reading a printed page. If the evaluators can get the opportunity to meet with high-level decision makers, an oral presentation may be more effective than simply supplying them with a written report.

It is important in all cases to present a transparent report. Most evaluations have both positive and negative findings, and providing both will strengthen the credibility of the research. Negative results also can be presented in terms of what the program managers learned and how they will change the program in the future.

It may be valuable to make the results as publicly available as possible. Publishing the report in a journal or on a Web site is helpful in this regard. Rigorous evaluation is relatively new in ADR, and it is important for the advancement of the field to publicize good research. In this way, the public, the press, agency managers, employees, and all other interested parties can learn more about the value of ADR.

Finally, once an evaluation is complete, program managers should use the results to determine how to improve the program. Lessons learned from evaluation can provide many insights into how programs can be made more effective. Once changes are implemented, additional evaluation may be appropriate to see how well they worked. Programs can use a feedback loop in this fashion to continue evolving, building on the experience of the past to provide the best possible ADR for the future.

Appendix A: Administrative Dispute Resolution Act of 1996

Sec. 1. Short Title

This Act may be cited as the "Administrative Dispute Resolution Act of 1996."

Sec. 2. Findings

The Congress finds that—

(1) administrative procedure, as embodied in chapter 5 of title 5, United States Code, and other statutes, is intended to offer a prompt, expert, and inexpensive means of resolving disputes as an alternative to litigation in the Federal courts;

(2) administrative proceedings have become increasingly formal, costly, and lengthy resulting in unnecessary expenditures of time and in a decreased likelihood of achieving consensual resolution of disputes;

(3) alternative means of dispute resolution have been used in the private sector for many years and, in appropriate circumstances, have yielded decisions that are faster, less expensive, and less contentious;

(4) such alternative means can lead to more creative, efficient, and sensible outcomes;

(5) such alternative means may be used advantageously in a wide variety of administrative programs;

Public Law 104–320 (1996), *Statutes at Large of the United States*, 110:3,870.

(6) explicit authorization of the use of well-tested dispute resolution techniques will eliminate ambiguity of agency authority under existing law;

(7) Federal agencies may not only receive the benefit of techniques that were developed in the private sector, but may also take the lead in the further development and refinement of such techniques; and

(8) the availability of a wide range of dispute resolution procedures, and an increased understanding of the most effective use of such procedures, will enhance the operation of the Government and better serve the public.

Sec. 3. Promotion of Alternative Means of Dispute Resolution

(a) Promulgation of Agency Policy.—

Each agency shall adopt a policy that addresses the use of alternative means of dispute resolution and case management. In developing such a policy, each agency shall—

(1) consult with the agency designated by, or the interagency committee designated or established by, the President under section 573 of title 5, United States Code, to facilitate and encourage agency use of alternative dispute resolution under subchapter IV of chapter 5 of such title; and

(2) examine alternative means of resolving disputes in connection with—

(A) formal and informal adjudications;

(B) rulemakings;

(C) enforcement actions;

(D) issuing and revoking licenses or permits;

(E) contract administration;

(F) litigation brought by or against the agency; and

(G) other agency actions.

(b) Dispute Resolution Specialists.—The head of each agency shall designate a senior official to be the dispute resolution specialist of the agency. Such official shall be responsible for the implementation of—

(1) the provisions of this Act and the amendments made by this Act; and

(2) the agency policy developed under subsection (a)

(c) Training.—Each agency shall provide for training on a regular basis for the dispute resolution specialist of the agency and other employees involved in implementing the policy of the agency developed under subsection (a). Such training should encompass the theory and practice of negotiation, mediation, arbitration, or related techniques. The dispute resolution specialist shall periodically recommend to the agency head agency employees who would benefit from similar training.

(d) Procedures for Grants and Contracts.

(1) Each agency shall review each of its standard agreements for contracts, grants, and other assistance and shall determine whether to amend any such standard agreements to authorize and encourage the use of alternative means of dispute resolution.

(2) (A) Within 1 year after the date of the enactment of this Act, the Federal Acquisition Regulation shall be amended, as necessary, to carry out this Act and the amendments made by this Act.

(B) For purposes of this section, the term "Federal Acquisition Regulation" means the single system of Government-wide procurement regulation referred to in section 6(a) of the Office of Federal Procurement Policy Act (41 U.S.C. 405(a)).

Sec. 4. Administrative Procedures

(a) Administrative Hearings.—Section 556(c) of title 5, United States Code, is amended—

(1) in paragraph (6) by inserting before the semicolon at the end thereof the following: "or by the use of alternative means of dispute resolution as provided in subchapter IV of this chapter"; and

(2) by redesignating paragraphs (7) through (9) as paragraphs (9) through (11), respectively, and inserting after paragraph (6) the following new paragraphs:

(7) inform the parties as to the availability of one or more alternative means of dispute resolution, and encourage use of such methods;

(8) require the attendance at any conference held pursuant to paragraph (6) of at least one representative of each party who has authority to negotiate concerning resolution of issues in controversy.

    (b) Alternative Means of Dispute Resolution.—Chapter 5 of title 5, United States Code, is amended by adding at the end the following new subchapter:

Subchapter IV Alternative Means of Dispute Resolution in the Administrative Process

§571. Definitions.
§572. General authority.
§573. Neutrals.
§574. Confidentiality.
§575. Authorization of arbitration.
§576. Enforcement of arbitration agreements.
§577. Arbitrators.
§578. Authority of the arbitrator.
§579. Arbitration proceedings.
§580. Arbitration awards.
§581. Judicial review.
§582. Compilation of Information (Repealed).
§583. Support services.
§584. Authorization of appropriations (New).

§571. Definitions

For the purposes of this subchapter, the term—

(1) "agency" has the same meaning as in section 551(1) of this title;
(2) "administrative program" includes a Federal function which involves protection of the public interest and the determination of rights, privileges, and obligations of private persons

through rule making, adjudication, licensing, or investigation, as those terms are used in subchapter II of this chapter;

(3) "alternative means of dispute resolution" means any procedure that is used to resolve issues in controversy, including, but not limited to, conciliation, facilitation, mediation, fact finding, minitrials, arbitration, and use of ombuds, or any combination thereof;

(4) "award" means any decision by an arbitrator resolving the issues in controversy;

(5) "dispute resolution communication" means any oral or written communication prepared for the purposes of a dispute resolution proceeding, including any memoranda, notes or work product of the neutral, parties or nonparty participant; except that a written agreement to enter into a dispute resolution proceeding, or final written agreement or arbitral award reached as a result of a dispute resolution proceeding, is not a dispute resolution communication;

(6) "dispute resolution proceeding" means any process in which an alternative means of dispute resolution is used to resolve an issue in controversy in which a neutral is appointed and specified parties participate;

(7) "in confidence" means, with respect to information, that the information is provided—
   (A) with the expressed intent of the source that it not be disclosed; or
   (B) under circumstances that would create the reasonable expectation on behalf of the source that the information will not be disclosed;

(8) "issue in controversy" means an issue which is material to a decision concerning an administrative program of an agency, and with which there is disagreement—
   (A) between an agency and persons who would be substantially affected by the decision; or
   (B) between persons who would be substantially affected by the decision;

(9) "neutral" means an individual who, with respect to an issue in controversy, functions specifically to aid the parties in resolving the controversy;

(10) "party" means—
    (A) for a proceeding with named parties, the same as in section 551(3) of this title; and
    (B) for a proceeding without named parties, a person who will be significantly affected by the decision in the proceeding and who participates in the proceeding;
(11) "person" has the same meaning as in section 551(2) of this title; and
(12) "roster" means a list of persons qualified to provide services as neutrals.

§572. General Authority

(a) An agency may use a dispute resolution proceeding for the resolution of an issue in controversy that relates to an administrative program, if the parties agree to such proceeding.

    (b) An agency shall consider not using a dispute resolution proceeding if—

(1) a definitive or authoritative resolution of the matter is required for precedential value, and such a proceeding is not likely to be accepted generally as an authoritative precedent;
(2) the matter involves or may bear upon significant questions of Government policy that require additional procedures before a final resolution may be made, and such a proceeding would not likely serve to develop a recommended policy for the agency;
(3) maintaining established policies is of special importance, so that variations among individual decisions are not increased and such a proceeding would not likely reach consistent results among individual decisions;
(4) the matter significantly affects persons or organizations who are not parties to the proceeding;
(5) a full public record of the proceeding is important, and a dispute resolution proceeding cannot provide such a record; and
(6) the agency must maintain continuing jurisdiction over the matter with authority to alter the disposition of the matter in the light of changed circumstances, and a dispute resolution

proceeding would interfere with the agency's fulfilling that requirement.

(c) Alternative means of dispute resolution authorized under this subchapter are voluntary procedures which supplement rather than limit other available agency dispute resolution techniques.

§573. Neutrals

(a) A neutral may be a permanent or temporary officer or employee of the Federal Government or any other individual who is acceptable to the parties to a dispute resolution proceeding. A neutral shall have no official, financial, or personal conflict of interest with respect to the issues in controversy, unless such interest is fully disclosed in writing to all parties and all parties agree that the neutral may serve.

(b) A neutral who serves as a conciliator, facilitator, or mediator serves at the will of the parties.

(c) The President shall designate an agency or designate or establish an interagency committee to facilitate and encourage agency use of dispute resolution under this subchapter. Such agency or interagency committee, in consultation with other appropriate Federal agencies and professional organizations experienced in matters concerning dispute resolution, shall—

(1) encourage and facilitate agency use of alternative means of dispute resolution; and

(2) develop procedures that permit agencies to obtain the services of neutrals on an expedited basis.

(d) An agency may use the services of one or more employees of other agencies to serve as neutrals in dispute resolution proceedings. The agencies may enter into an interagency agreement that provides for the reimbursement by the user agency or the parties of the full or partial cost of the services of such an employee.

(e) Any agency may enter into a contract with any person for services as a neutral, or for training in connection with alternative means of dispute resolution. The parties in a dispute resolution proceeding shall agree on compensation for the neutral that is fair and reasonable to the Government.

§574. Confidentiality

(a) Except as provided in subsections (d) and (e), a neutral in a dispute resolution proceeding shall not voluntarily disclose or through discovery or compulsory process be required to disclose any dispute resolution communication or any communication provided in confidence to the neutral, unless—

(1) all parties to the dispute resolution proceeding and the neutral consent in writing, and, if the dispute resolution communication was provided by a nonparty participant, that participant also consents in writing;

(2) the dispute resolution communication has already been made public;

(3) the dispute resolution communication is required by statute to be made public, but a neutral should make such communication public only if no other person is reasonably available to disclose the communication; or

(4) a court determines that such testimony or disclosure is necessary to—

(A) prevent a manifest injustice;

(B) help establish a violation of law; or

(C) prevent harm to the public health or safety,
of sufficient magnitude in the particular case to outweigh the integrity of dispute resolution proceedings in general by reducing the confidence of parties in future cases that their communications will remain confidential;

(b) A party to a dispute resolution proceeding shall not voluntarily disclose or through discovery or compulsory process be required to disclose any dispute resolution communication, unless—

(1) the communication was prepared by the party seeking disclosure;

(2) all parties to the dispute resolution proceeding consent in writing;

(3) the dispute resolution communication has already been made public;

(4) the dispute resolution communication is required by statute to be made public;

(5) a court determines that such testimony or disclosure is necessary to—

    (A) prevent a manifest injustice;

    (B) help establish a violation of law; or

    (C) prevent harm to the public health and safety,
of sufficient magnitude in the particular case to outweigh the integrity of dispute resolution proceedings in general by reducing the confidence of parties in future cases that their communications will remain confidential;

(6) the dispute resolution communication is relevant to determining the existence or meaning of an agreement or award that resulted from the dispute resolution proceeding or to the enforcement of such an agreement or award; or

(7) except for dispute resolution communications generated by the neutral, the dispute resolution communication was provided to or was available to all parties to the dispute resolution proceeding.

(c) Any dispute resolution communication that is disclosed in violation of subsection (a) or (b), shall not be admissible in any proceeding relating to the issues in controversy with respect to which the communication was made.

(d)(1) The parties may agree to alternative confidential procedures for disclosures by a neutral. Upon such agreement the parties shall inform the neutral before the commencement of the dispute resolution proceeding of any modifications to the provisions of subsection (a) that will govern the confidentiality of the dispute resolution proceeding. If the parties do not so inform the neutral, subsection (a) shall apply.

(2) To qualify for the exemption established under subsection (j), an alternative confidential procedure under this subsection may not provide for less disclosure than the confidential procedures otherwise provided under this section.

(e) If a demand for disclosure, by way of discovery request or other legal process, is made upon a neutral regarding a dispute resolution communication, the neutral shall make reasonable efforts to notify the parties and any affected nonparty participants of the demand. Any party or affected nonparty participant who receives such notice and within 15 calendar days does not offer to defend a refusal of the neutral to disclose the requested information shall have waived any objection to such disclosure.

(f) Nothing in this section shall prevent the discovery or admissibility of any evidence that is otherwise discoverable, merely because the evidence was presented in the course of a dispute resolution proceeding.

(g) Subsections (a) and (b) shall have no effect on the information and data that are necessary to document an agreement reached or order issued pursuant to a dispute resolution proceeding.

(h) Subsections (a) and (b) shall not prevent the gathering of information for research or educational purposes, in cooperation with other agencies, governmental entities, or dispute resolution programs, so long as the parties and the specific issues in controversy are not identifiable.

(i) Subsections (a) and (b) shall not prevent use of a dispute resolution communication to resolve a dispute between the neutral in a dispute resolution proceeding and a party to or participant in such proceeding, so long as such dispute resolution communication is disclosed only to the extent necessary to resolve such dispute.

(j) A dispute resolution communication which is between a neutral and a party and which may not be disclosed under this section shall also be exempt from disclosure under section 552(b)(3).

§575. Authorization of Arbitration

(a) (1) Arbitration may be used as an alternative means of dispute resolution whenever all parties consent. Consent may be obtained either before or after an issue in controversy has arisen. A party may agree to—

(A) submit only certain issues in controversy to arbitration; or
(B) arbitration on the condition that the award must be within a range of possible outcomes.

(2) The arbitration agreement that sets forth the subject matter submitted to the arbitrator shall be in writing. Each such arbitration agreement shall specify a maximum award that may be issued by the arbitrator and may specify other conditions limiting the range of possible outcomes.

(3) An agency may not require any person to consent to arbitration as a condition of entering into a contract or obtaining a benefit.

(b) An officer or employee of an agency shall not offer to use arbitration for the resolution of issues in controversy unless such officer or employee—

(1) would otherwise have authority to enter into a settlement concerning the matter; or
(2) is otherwise specifically authorized by the agency to consent to the use of arbitration.

(c) Prior to using binding arbitration under this subchapter, the head of an agency, in consultation with the Attorney General and after taking into account the factors in section 572(b), shall issue guidance on the appropriate use of binding arbitration and when an officer or employee of the agency has authority to settle an issue in controversy through binding arbitration.

§576. Enforcement of Arbitration Agreements

An agreement to arbitrate a matter to which this subchapter applies is enforceable pursuant to section 4 of title 9, and no action brought to enforce such an agreement shall be dismissed nor shall relief therein be denied on the grounds that it is against the United States or that the United States is an indispensable party.

§577. Arbitrators

(a) The parties to an arbitration proceeding shall be entitled to participate in the selection of the arbitrator.

(b) The arbitrator shall be a neutral who meets the criteria of section 573 of this title.

§578. Authority of the Arbitrator

An arbitrator to whom a dispute is referred under this subchapter may—

(1) regulate the course of and conduct arbitral hearings;
(2) administer oaths and affirmations;
(3) compel the attendance of witnesses and production of evidence at the hearing under the provisions of section 7 of title 9 only to the extent the agency involved is otherwise authorized by law to do so; and
(4) make awards.

§579. Arbitration Proceedings

(a) The arbitrator shall set a time and place for the hearing on the dispute and shall notify the parties not less than 5 days before the hearing.

(b) Any party wishing a record of the hearing shall—

(1) be responsible for the preparation of such record other parties and the arbitrator of the preparation of such record;
(2) notify the other parties and the arbitrator of the preparation of such record;
(3) furnish copies to all identified parties and the arbitrator; and
(4) pay all costs for such record, unless the parties agree otherwise or the arbitrator determines that the costs should be apportioned.

(c) (1) The parties to the arbitration are entitled to be heard, to present evidence material to the controversy, and to cross-examine witnesses appearing at the hearing.

(2) The arbitrator may, with the consent of the parties, conduct all or part of the hearing by telephone, television, computer, or other electronic means, if each party has an opportunity to participate.

(3) The hearing shall be conducted expeditiously and in an informal manner.

(4) The arbitrator may receive any oral or documentary evidence, except that irrelevant, immaterial, unduly repetitious, or privileged evidence may be excluded by the arbitrator.

(5) The arbitrator shall interpret and apply relevant statutory and regulatory requirements, legal precedents, and policy directives.

(d) No interested person shall make or knowingly cause to be made to the arbitrator an unauthorized ex parte communication relevant to the merits of the proceeding, unless the parties agree otherwise. If a communication is made in violation of this subsection, the arbitrator shall ensure that a memorandum of the communication is prepared and made a part of the record, and that an opportunity for rebuttal is allowed. Upon receipt of a communication made in violation of this subsection, the arbitrator may, to the extent consistent with the interests of justice and the policies underlying this subchapter, require the offending party to show cause why the claim of such party should not be resolved against such party as a result of the improper conduct.

(e) The arbitrator shall make the award within 30 days after the close of the hearing, or the date of the filing of any briefs authorized by the arbitrator, whichever date is later, unless—

(1) the parties agree to some other time limit; or

(2) the agency provides by rule for some other time limit.

§580. Arbitration Awards

(a) (1)   Unless the agency provides otherwise by rule, the award in an arbitration proceeding under this subchapter shall include a brief, informal discussion of the factual and legal basis for the award, but formal findings of fact or conclusions of law shall not be required.

(2) The prevailing parties shall file the award with all relevant agencies, along with proof of service on all parties.

(b) The award in an arbitration proceeding shall become final 30 days after it is served on all parties. Any agency that is a party to the proceeding may extend this 30-day period for an additional 30-day period by serving a notice of such extension on all other parties before the end of the first 30-day period.

(c) A final award is binding on the parties to the arbitration proceeding, and may be enforced pursuant to sections 9 through 13 of title 9. No action brought to enforce such an award shall be dismissed nor shall relief therein be denied on the grounds that it is against the United States or that the United States is an indispensable party.

(d) An award entered under this subchapter in an arbitration proceeding may not serve as an estoppel in any other proceeding for any issue that was resolved in the proceeding. Such an award also may not be used as precedent or otherwise be considered in any factually unrelated proceeding, whether conducted under this subchapter, by an agency, or in a court, or in any other arbitration proceeding.

§581. Judicial Review

(a) Notwithstanding any other provision of law, any person adversely affected or aggrieved by an award made in an arbitration proceeding conducted under this subchapter may bring an action for review of such award only pursuant to the provisions of sections 9 through 13 of title 9.

(b) A decision by an agency to use or not to use a dispute resolution proceeding under this subchapter shall be committed to the discretion of the agency and shall not be subject to judicial review, except that arbitration shall be subject to judicial review under section 10(b) of title 9.

§582. Compilation of Information (Repealed)

§583. Support Services

For the purposes of this subchapter, an agency may use (with or without reimbursement) the services and facilities of other Federal agencies, State, local, and tribal governments, public and private organizations and agencies, and individuals, with the consent of such agencies, organizations, and individuals. An agency may accept voluntary and uncompensated services for purposes of this subchapter without regard to the provisions of section 1342 of title 31.

§584. Authorization of Appropriations

There are authorized to be appropriated such sums as may be necessary to carry out the purposes of this subchapter.

Sec. 5. Judicial Review of Arbitration Awards

Section 10 of title 9, United States Code, is amended—

(1) by designating subsections (a) through (e) as paragraphs (1) through (5), respectively;

(2) by striking out "In either" and inserting in lieu thereof "(a) in any"; and

(3) by adding at the end thereof the following:

(b) The United States district court for the district wherein an award was made that was issued pursuant to section 580 of title 5 may make an order vacating the award upon the application of a person, other than a party to the arbitration, who is adversely affected or aggrieved by the award, if the use of arbitration or the award is clearly inconsistent with the factors set forth in section 572 of title 5.

Sec. 6. Government Contract Claims

(a) Alternative Means of Dispute Resolution.—
Section 6 of the Contract Disputes Act of 1978 (41 U.S.C. 605) is amended by adding at the end the following new subsections:

(d) Notwithstanding any other provision of this Act, a contractor and a contracting officer may use any alternative means of dispute resolution under subchapter IV of chapter 5 of title 5, United States Code, or other mutually agreeable procedures, for resolving claims. The contractor shall certify the claim when required to do so as provided under subsection (c)(1) or as otherwise required by law. All provisions of subchapter IV of chapter 5 of title 5, United States Code, shall apply to such alternative means of dispute resolution.

(b) Judicial Review of Arbitral Awards.—
Section 8(g) of the Contract Disputes Act of 1978 (41 U.S.C. 607(g)) is amended by adding at the end the following new paragraph:

(3) An award by an arbitrator under this Act shall be reviewed pursuant to sections 9 through 13 of title 9, United States Code,

except that the court may set aside or limit any award that is found to violate limitations imposed by Federal statute.

Sec. 7. Federal Mediation and Conciliation Service

Section 203 of the Labor Management Relations Act, 1947 (29 U.S.C. 173) is amended by adding at the end the following new subsection:

> (f) The Service may make its services available to Federal agencies to aid in the resolution of disputes under the provisions of subchapter IV of chapter 5 of title 5, United States Code. Functions performed by the Service may include assisting parties to disputes related to administrative programs, training persons in skills and procedures employed in alternative means of dispute resolution, and furnishing officers and employees of the Service to act as neutrals. Only officers and employees who are qualified in accordance with section 573 of title 5, United States Code, may be assigned to act as neutrals. The Service shall consult with the agency designated by, or the interagency committee designated or established by, the President under section 573 of title 5, United States Code, in maintaining rosters of neutrals and arbitrators, and to adopt such procedures and rules as are necessary to carry out the services authorized in this subsection.

Sec. 8. Government Tort and Other Claims

(a) Federal Tort Claims.—Section 2672 of title 28, United States Code, is amended by adding at the end of the first paragraph the following: "Notwithstanding the proviso contained in the preceding sentence, any award, compromise, or settlement may be effected without the prior written approval of the Attorney General or his or her designee, to the extent that the Attorney General delegates to the head of the agency the authority to make such award, compromise, or settlement. Such delegations may not exceed the authority delegated by the Attorney General to the United States attorneys to settle claims for money damages against the United States. Each Federal agency may use arbitration, or other alternative means of dispute resolution under the provisions of subchapter IV of chapter 5 of title 5, to settle any tort claim against the

United States, to the extent of the agency's authority to award, compromise, or settle such claim without the prior written approval of the Attorney General or his or her designee."

(b) Claims of the Government.—Section 3711(a)(2) of title 31, United States Code, is amended by striking out "$20,000 (excluding interest)" and inserting in lieu thereof "$100,000 (excluding interest) or such higher amount as the Attorney General may from time to time prescribe."

Sec. 9. Use of Nonattorneys

(a) Representation of Parties.—Each agency, in developing a policy on the use of alternative means of dispute resolution under this Act, shall develop a policy with regard to the representation by persons other than attorneys of parties in alternative dispute resolution proceedings and shall identify any of its administrative programs with numerous claims or disputes before the agency and determine

(b)(1) the extent to which individuals are represented or assisted by attorneys or by persons who are not attorneys; and

(2) whether the subject areas of the applicable proceedings or the procedures are so complex or specialized that only attorneys may adequately provide such representation or assistance.

(c) Representation and Assistance by Nonattorneys.—A person who is not an attorney may provide representation or assistance to any individual in a claim or dispute with an agency, if—

(1) such claim or dispute concerns an administrative program identified under subsection (a);
(2) such agency determines that the proceeding or procedure does not necessitate representation or assistance by an attorney under subsection (a)(2); and
(3) such person meets any requirement of the agency to provide representation or assistance in such a claim or dispute.

(d) Disqualification of Representation or Assistance.—Any agency that adopts regulations under subchapter IV of chapter 5 of title 5, United States Code, to permit representation or assistance by persons who are not attorneys shall review the rules of practice before such agency to—

(1) ensure that any rules pertaining to disqualification of attorneys from practicing before the agency shall also apply, as appropriate, to other persons who provide representation or assistance; and
(2) establish effective agency procedures for enforcing such rules of practice and for receiving complaints from affected persons.

Sec. 10. Definitions

As used in this Act, the terms 'agency', 'administrative program', and 'alternative means of dispute resolution' have the meanings given such terms in section 571 of title 5, United States Code (enacted as section 581 of title 5, United States Code, by section 4(b) of this Act, and redesignated as section 571 of such title by section 3(b) of the Administrative Procedure Technical Amendments Act of 1991).

Sec. 11. Reauthorization of Negotiated Rulemaking Act of 1990

(a) Permanent Reauthorization.—Section 5 of the Negotiated Rulemaking Act of 1990 (Public Law 101–648; 5 U.S.C. 561 note) is repealed.

Sec. 12. Jurisdiction of the United States Court of Federal Claims and the District Courts of the United States: Bid Protests

(a) Bid Protests—Section 1491 of title 28, United States Code, is amended—

(1) by redesignating subsection (b) as subsection (c);
(2) in subsection (a) by striking out paragraph (3); and
(3) by inserting after subsection (a), the following new subsection:

(b)(1) Both the United States Court of Federal Claims and the district courts of the United States shall have jurisdiction to render judgment on an action by an interested party objecting to a solicitation by a Federal agency for bids or proposals for a proposed contract or to a proposed award or the award of a contract or any alleged violation of statute or regulation in connection with a procurement or a proposed procurement. Both the United States Court of Federal Claims and the district courts of the United States shall have jurisdiction to entertain such an action without regard to whether suit is instituted before or after the contract is awarded.

(2) To afford relief in such an action, the courts may award any relief that the court considers proper, including declaratory and injunctive relief except that any monetary relief shall be limited to bid preparation and proposal costs.

(3) In exercising jurisdiction under this subsection, the courts shall give due regard to the interests of national defense and national security and the need for expeditious resolution of the action.

(4) In any action under this subsection, the courts shall review the agency's decision pursuant to the standards set forth in section 706 of title 5.

(b) Effective Date—This section and the amendments made by this section shall take effect on December 31, 1996 and shall apply to all actions filed on or after that date.

(c) Study—No earlier than 2 years after the effective date of this section, the United States General Accounting Office shall undertake a study regarding the concurrent jurisdiction of the district courts of the United States and the Court of Federal Claims over bid protests to determine whether concurrent jurisdiction is necessary. Such a study shall be completed no later than December 31, 1999, and shall specifically consider the effect of any proposed change on the ability of small businesses to challenge violations of Federal procurement law.

(d) Sunset—The jurisdiction of the district courts of the United States over the actions described in section 1491(b)(1) of title 28, United States Code (as amended by subsection (a) of this section) shall terminate on January 1, 2001 unless extended by Congress. The savings provisions in subsection (e) shall apply if the bid protest jurisdiction of the district courts of the United States terminates under this subsection.

(e) Savings Provisions—(1) Orders—A termination under subsection (d) shall not terminate the effectiveness of orders that have been issued by a court in connection with an action within the jurisdiction of that court on or before December 31, 2000. Such orders shall continue in effect according to their terms until modified, terminated, superseded, set aside, or revoked by a court of competent jurisdiction or by operation of law.

(2) Proceedings and Applications—

(A) A termination under subsection (d) shall not affect the jurisdiction of a court of the United States to continue with any proceeding that is pending before the court on December 31, 2000.

(B) Orders may be issued in any such proceeding, appeals may be taken therefrom, and payments may be made pursuant to such orders, as if such termination had not occurred. An order issued in any such proceeding shall continue in effect until modified, terminated, superseded, set aside, or revoked by a court of competent jurisdiction or by operation of law.

(C) Nothing in this paragraph prohibits the discontinuance or modification of any such proceeding under the same terms and conditions and to the same extent that proceeding could have been discontinued or modified absent such termination.

(f) Nonexclusivity of GAO Remedies—In the event that the bid protest jurisdiction of the district courts of the United States is terminated pursuant to subsection (d), then section 3556 of title 31, United States Code, shall be amended by striking 'a court of the United States or' in the first sentence.

Appendix B:
United States Department of Justice, Attorney General Order Promoting the Broader Appropriate Use of Alternative Dispute Resolution Techniques, April 6, 1995

1. PURPOSE. The purpose of this order is to promote the broader use of alternative dispute resolution (ADR) in appropriate cases to improve access to justice for all citizens and to lead to more effective resolution of disputes involving the government.

2. SCOPE. The provisions of this order shall apply to all Departmental litigating divisions and to all U.S. Attorneys. This order is applicable to civil matters only. It is not intended to affect criminal matters, including enforcement of criminal fines or judgments of forfeiture.

3. MODIFICATION. This order expands upon but does not otherwise modify the Department of Justice's Memorandum of Guidance on Implementation of the Litigation Reforms of Executive Order No. 12778, notice of which was published at 58 Fed. Reg. 6015–03.

4. AUTHORITY. In addition to the general authority conferred upon the Attorney General by law, specific authority to provide ADR guidance is provided by section 3 of the Administrative Dispute Resolution Act of 1990, Pub. Law 101–552, 104 Stat. 2736–37.

5. DEFINITION. As used in this order, "formal ADR techniques" include, but are not limited to, arbitration, mediation, early neutral evaluation, neutral expert evaluation, mini-trials and summary jury trials.

6. CREATION OF POSITION OF SENIOR COUNSEL FOR ALTERNATIVE DISPUTE RESOLUTION. There shall be created within the Department of Justice, the position of "Senior Counsel for Alternative Dispute Resolution." The Associate Attorney General shall designate a career employee of the Department of Justice at the Senior Executive Service level to fill this position. The Senior Counsel shall develop policy on, and promote aspects of ADR, and in furtherance of that goal shall:

1. Assist senior management in developing policies for the use of ADR, including revising the Department Guidance on the Use of Alternative Dispute Resolution for Litigation in the Federal Courts.
2. Assist with the design and execution of ADR-related training, recordkeeping, program evaluation and reporting functions.
3. Provide advice and assistance to Department supervisors and employees on selecting appropriate cases for using ADR and on the application of particular ADR techniques.
4. Report regularly to the Attorney General, through the Associate Attorney General, on the status of the Department's ADR activities.
5. Represent the Department in government-wide ADR activities, including programs and projects with the Administrative Conference of the United States, the Office of Management and Budget, the National Performance Review, and the federal courts.
6. Advise senior management on legislation, rulemaking, and other policy matters relating to ADR.
7. Serve as the Dispute Resolution Specialist for the Department of Justice as defined in Section 3(b) of the Administrative Dispute Resolution Act, 104 Stat. at 2737.
8. Perform such other duties and functions related to the promotion of ADR as may be assigned by the Attorney General, the Deputy Attorney General and the Associate Attorney General.

7. COMPONENT ADR GUIDANCE. By September 11, 1995, each litigating division and the Executive Office for United States At-

torneys acting on behalf of the United States Attorneys shall provide its attorneys with ADR guidance containing the following provisions:

1. A policy statement by the head of the component indicating that attorneys are expected to use ADR in appropriate cases as an alternative to litigation and are to cooperate with court-annexed or court-sponsored ADR programs and with efforts to develop and evaluate such programs.
2. A set of criteria to be used in identifying specific cases appropriate for resolution through settlement negotiations or the use of a formal ADR technique. The component guidance should also identify ADR methods most suitable to resolving certain categories of cases, and criteria for the selection of ADR providers.
3. A requirement that any attorneys whose practices are substantially civil attend a comprehensive basic training program in negotiation and ADR and that all experienced attorneys handling civil matters be required to participate in periodic supplemental ADR training. The content and nature of such training shall be determined by the Senior Counsel for Alternative Dispute Resolution in consultation with the Department's training components.
4. A complete explanation of the internal procedures attorneys should follow in obtaining authorization and funding for the use of formal ADR techniques.

8. FURTHER RESPONSIBILITIES OF PERFORMING COMPONENTS.

1. The components subject to this order shall coordinate with the Senior Counsel for Alternative Dispute Resolution the development of the ADR guidance, as well as their performance of related recordkeeping, program evaluation and reporting functions.
2. The components subject to this order shall review their ADR guidance at least annually and, in conjunction with the Senior Counsel for Alternative Dispute Resolution, shall make any necessary changes.
3. The components subject to this order, in consultation with the Senior Counsel for ADR, shall designate a person or persons with primary responsibility for coordinating the component's ADR efforts so that a network of individuals with ADR expertise

is established throughout the Department. This network shall assist the Senior Counsel for ADR in developing and implementing Department ADR policies.

4. The components subject to this order shall maintain statistics regarding its use of ADR and report those statistics annually to the Associate Attorney General. These statistics should demonstrate both the component's compliance with this order and the full extent of its overall use of informal and formal ADR techniques.

9. NO PRIVATE RIGHTS CREATED. This order is intended only to improve the internal management of the Justice Department in resolving disputes and conducting litigation. This order shall not be construed as creating any right or benefit, substantive or procedural, enforceable at law or in equity, by a party against the United States, its agencies, its officers, or any other person. This order shall not be construed to create any right to judicial review involving the compliance or noncompliance of the United States, the Justice Department, its officers, or any other person with this order. Nothing in this order shall be construed to obligate the United States to offer funds to settle any case, accept a particular settlement or resolution of a dispute, to alter its standards for accepting settlements, to submit to binding arbitration or to alter any existing delegation of settlement or litigating authority.

10. FURTHER GUIDANCE. The Associate Attorney General shall have the authority to issue further guidance regarding the scope of this order, consistent with the purposes of this order.

Appendix C:
Alternative Dispute
Resolution Act of 1998

Sec. 1. Short Title

This Act may be cited as the "Alternative Dispute Resolution Act of 1998."

Sec. 2. Findings and Declaration of Policy

Congress finds that—

(1) alternative dispute resolution, when supported by the bench and bar, and utilizing properly trained neutrals in a program adequately administered by the court, has the potential to provide a variety of benefits, including greater satisfaction of the parties, innovative methods of resolving disputes, and greater efficiency in achieving settlements;

(2) certain forms of alternative dispute resolution, including mediation, early neutral evaluation, minitrials, and voluntary arbitration, may have potential to reduce the large backlog of cases now pending in some Federal courts throughout the United States, thereby allowing the courts to process their remaining cases more efficiently; and

(3) the continued growth of Federal appellate court-annexed mediation programs suggests that this form of alternative dispute resolution can be equally effective in resolving disputes in the Federal trial courts; therefore, the district courts should consider

Public Law 105–315 (1998), *Statutes at Large of the United States,* 112:2,993.

including mediation in their local alternative dispute resolution programs.

Sec. 3. Alternative Dispute Resolution Processes to Be Authorized in All District Courts

Section 651 of title 28, United States Code, is amended to read as follows:

Sec. 651. Authorization of alternative dispute resolution

(a) Definition.—For purposes of this chapter, an alternative dispute resolution process includes any process or procedure, other than an adjudication by a presiding judge, in which a neutral third party participates to assist in the resolution of issues in controversy, through processes such as early neutral evaluation, mediation, minitrial, and arbitration as provided in sections 654 through 658.

(b) Authority.—Each United States district court shall authorize, by local rule adopted under section 2071(a), the use of alternative dispute resolution processes in all civil actions, including adversary proceedings in bankruptcy, in accordance with this chapter, except that the use of arbitration may be authorized only as provided in section 654. Each United States district court shall devise and implement its own alternative dispute resolution program, by local rule adopted under section 2071(a), to encourage and promote the use of alternative dispute resolution in its district.

(c) Existing Alternative Dispute Resolution Programs.— In those courts where an alternative dispute resolution program is in place on the date of the enactment of the Alternative Dispute Resolution Act of 1998, the court shall examine the effectiveness of that program and adopt such improvements to the program as are consistent with the provisions and purposes of this chapter.

(d) Administration of Alternative Dispute Resolution Programs.—Each United States district court shall designate an employee, or a judicial officer, who is knowledgeable in alternative dispute resolution practices and processes to implement, administer, oversee, and evaluate the court's alternative dispute resolution program. Such person may also be responsible for recruiting, screening, and training attorneys to serve as neutrals and arbitrators in the court's alternative dispute resolution program.

(e) Title 9 Not Affected.—This chapter shall not affect title 9, United States Code.

(f) Program Support.—The Federal Judicial Center and the Administrative Office of the United States Courts are authorized to assist the district courts in the establishment and improvement of alternative dispute resolution programs by identifying particular practices employed in successful programs and providing additional assistance as needed and appropriate.

Sec. 4. Jurisdiction

Section 652 of title 28, United States Code, is amended to read as follows:

Sec. 652. Jurisdiction

(a) Consideration of Alternative Dispute Resolution in Appropriate Cases.—Notwithstanding any provision of law to the contrary and except as provided in subsections (b) and (c), each district court shall, by local rule adopted under section 2071(a), require that litigants in all civil cases consider the use of an alternative dispute resolution process at an appropriate stage in the litigation. Each district court shall provide litigants in all civil cases with at least one alternative dispute resolution process, including, but not limited to, mediation, early neutral evaluation, minitrial, and arbitration as authorized in sections 654 through 658. Any district court that elects to require the use of alternative dispute resolution in certain cases may do so only with respect to mediation, early neutral evaluation, and, if the parties consent, arbitration.

(b) Actions Exempted from Consideration of Alternative Dispute Resolution.—Each district court may exempt from the requirements of this section specific cases or categories of cases in which use of alternative dispute resolution would not be appropriate. In defining these exemptions, each district court shall consult with members of the bar, including the United States Attorney for that district.

(c) Authority of the Attorney General.—Nothing in this section shall alter or conflict with the authority of the Attorney General to conduct litigation on behalf of the United States, with the authority of any Federal agency authorized to conduct litigation in the United States courts, or with any delegation of litigation authority by the Attorney General.

(d) Confidentiality Provisions.—Until such time as rules are adopted under chapter 131 of this title providing for the confidentiality of alternative dispute resolution processes under this chapter, each district court shall, by local rule adopted under section 2071(a), provide for the confidentiality of the alternative dispute resolution processes and to prohibit disclosure of confidential dispute resolution communications.

Sec. 5. Mediators and Neutral Evaluators

Section 653 of title 28, United States Code, is amended to read as follows:

Sec. 653. Neutrals

(a) Panel of Neutrals.—Each district court that authorizes the use of alternative dispute resolution processes shall adopt appropriate processes for making neutrals available for use by the parties for each category of process offered. Each district court shall promulgate its own procedures and criteria for the selection of neutrals on its panels.

(b) Qualifications and Training.—Each person serving as a neutral in an alternative dispute resolution process should be qualified and trained to serve as a neutral in the appropriate alternative dispute resolution process. For this purpose, the district court may use, among others, magistrate judges who have been trained to serve as neutrals in alternative dispute resolution processes, professional neutrals from the private sector, and persons who have been trained to serve as neutrals in alternative dispute resolution processes. Until such time as rules are adopted under chapter 131 of this title relating to the disqualification of neutrals, each district court shall issue rules under section 2071(a) relating to the disqualification of neutrals (including, where appropriate, disqualification under section 455 of this title, other applicable law, and professional responsibility standards).

Sec. 6. Actions Referred to Arbitration

Section 654 of title 28, United States Code, is amended to read as follows:

Sec. 654. Arbitration

(a) Referral of Actions to Arbitration.—Notwithstanding any provision of law to the contrary and except as provided in subsections (a), (b), and (c) of section 652 and subsection (d) of this section, a district court may allow the referral to arbitration of any civil action (including any adversary proceeding in bankruptcy) pending before it when the parties consent, except that referral to arbitration may not be made where—

(1) the action is based on an alleged violation of a right secured by the Constitution of the United States;
(2) jurisdiction is based in whole or in part on section 1343 of this title; or
(3) the relief sought consists of money damages in an amount greater than $150,000.

    (b) Safeguards in Consent Cases.—Until such time as rules are adopted under chapter 131 of this title relating to procedures described in this subsection, the district court shall, by local rule adopted under section 2071(a), establish procedures to ensure that any civil action in which arbitration by consent is allowed under subsection (a)

(1) consent to arbitration is freely and knowingly obtained; and
(2) no party or attorney is prejudiced for refusing to participate in arbitration.

    (c) Presumptions.—For purposes of subsection (a)(3), a district court may presume damages are not in excess of $150,000 unless counsel certifies that damages exceed such amount.
    (d) Existing Programs.—Nothing in this chapter is deemed to affect any program in which arbitration is conducted pursuant to section title IX of the Judicial Improvements and Access to Justice Act (Public Law 100–702), as amended by section 1 of Public Law 105–53.

Sec. 7. Arbitrators

Section 655 of title 28, United States Code, is amended to read as follows:

Sec. 655. Arbitrators

(a) Powers of Arbitrators.—An arbitrator to whom an action is referred under section 654 shall have the power, within the judicial district of the district court which referred the action to arbitration—

(1) to conduct arbitration hearings;

(2) to administer oaths and affirmations; and

(3) to make awards.

(b) Standards for Certification.—Each district court that authorizes arbitration shall establish standards for the certification of arbitrators and shall certify arbitrators to perform services in accordance with such standards and this chapter. The standards shall include provisions requiring that any arbitrator—

(1) shall take the oath or affirmation described in section 453; and

(2) shall be subject to the disqualification rules under section 455.

(c) Immunity.—All individuals serving as arbitrators in an alternative dispute resolution program under this chapter are performing quasi-judicial functions and are entitled to the immunities and protections that the law accords to persons serving in such capacity.

Sec. 8. Subpoenas

Section 656 of title 28, United States Code, is amended to read as follows:

Sec. 656. Subpoenas

Rule 45 of the Federal Rules of Civil Procedure (relating to subpoenas) applies to subpoenas for the attendance of witnesses and the production of documentary evidence at an arbitration hearing under this chapter.

Sec. 9. Arbitration Award and Judgment

Section 657 of title 28, United States Code, is amended to read as follows:

Sec. 657. Arbitration award and judgment

(a) Filing and Effect of Arbitration Award.—An arbitration award made by an arbitrator under this chapter, along with proof of service of such award on the other party by the prevailing party or by the plaintiff, shall be filed promptly after the arbitration hearing is concluded with the clerk of the district court that referred the case to arbitration. Such award shall be entered as the judgment of the court after the time has expired for requesting a trial de novo. The judgment so entered shall be subject to the same provisions of law and shall have the same force and effect as a judgment of the court in a civil action, except that the judgment shall not be subject to review in any other court by appeal or otherwise.

(b) Sealing of Arbitration Award.—The district court shall provide, by local rule adopted under section 2071(a), that the contents of any arbitration award made under this chapter shall not be made known to any judge who might be assigned to the case until the district court has entered final judgment in the action or the action has otherwise terminated.

(c) Trial de Novo of Arbitration Awards.—

(1) Time for filing demand.—Within 30 days after the filing of an arbitration award with a district court under subsection (a), any party may file a written demand for a trial de novo in the district court.

(2) Action restored to court docket.—Upon a demand for a trial de novo, the action shall be restored to the docket of the court and treated for all purposes as if it had not been referred to arbitration.

(3) Exclusion of evidence of arbitration.—The court shall not admit at the trial de novo any evidence that there has been an arbitration proceeding, the nature or amount of any award, or any other matter concerning the conduct of the arbitration proceeding, unless—

(A) the evidence would otherwise be admissible in the court underthe Federal Rules of Evidence; or

(B) the parties have otherwise stipulated.

Sec. 10. Compensation of Arbitrators and Neutrals

Section 658 of title 28, United States Code, is amended to read as follows:

Sec. 658. Compensation of arbitrators and neutrals

(a) Compensation.—The district court shall, subject to regulations approved by the Judicial Conference of the United States, establish the amount of compensation, if any, that each arbitrator or neutral shall receive for services rendered in each case under this chapter.

(b) Transportation Allowances.—Under regulations prescribed by the Director of the Administrative Office of the United

States Courts, a district court may reimburse arbitrators and other neutrals for actual transportation expenses necessarily incurred in the performance of duties under this chapter.

Sec. 11. Authorization of Appropriations

There are authorized to be appropriated for each fiscal year such sums as may be necessary to carry out chapter 44 of title 28, United States Code, as amended by this Act.

Sec. 12. Conforming Amendments

(a) Limitation on Money Damages.—Section 901 of the Judicial Improvements and Access to Justice Act (28 U.S.C. 652 note), is amended by striking subsection (c).

(b) Other Conforming Amendments.—

(1) The chapter heading for chapter 44 of title 28, United States Code, is amended to read as follows: "CHAPTER 44—ALTERNATIVE DISPUTE RESOLUTION".

(2) The table of contents for chapter 44 of title 28, United States Code, is amended to read as follows:

Sec.
651. Authorization of alternative dispute resolution.
652. Jurisdiction.
653. Neutrals.
654. Arbitration.
655. Arbitrators.
656. Subpoenas.
657. Arbitration award and judgment.
658. Compensation of arbitrators and neutrals.

(3) The item relating to chapter 44 in the table of chapters for Part III of title 28, United States Code, is amended to read as follows:

44. Alternative Dispute Resolution . . . . 651.

Appendix D: Presidential Memorandum on ADR, May 1, 1998

As part of an effort to make the Federal Government operate in a more efficient and effective manner, and to encourage, where possible, consensual resolution of disputes and issues in controversy involving the United States, including the prevention and avoidance of disputes, I have determined that each Federal agency must take steps to:

1. promote greater use of mediation, arbitration, early neutral evaluation, agency ombuds, and other alternative dispute resolution techniques, and
2. promote greater use of negotiated rulemaking.

By the authority vested in me as President by the Constitution and laws of the United States including sections 569(a) and 573(c) of title 5, United States Code, as amended by the Administrative Dispute Resolution Act of 1996 (Public Law 104–320), I hereby direct as follows:

An Alternative Dispute Resolution Working Group, comprised of the Cabinet Departments and, as determined by the Attorney General, such other agencies with a significant interest in dispute resolution, shall be convened and is designated under 5 U.S.C. 573(c) as the interagency committee to facilitate and encourage agency use of alternative means of dispute resolution. The Working Group shall consist of representatives of the heads of all participating agencies, and may meet as a whole or in subgroups of agencies with an interest in particular issues or subject areas, such as disputes involving personnel, procurement, and claims. The Working Group shall be convened by the Attorney General, who may designate a representative to convene and facilitate meetings of the subgroups. The Working Group shall facilitate, encourage, and provide coordination for agencies in such areas as:

1. development of programs that employ alternative means of dispute resolution,
2. training of agency personnel to recognize when and how to use alternative means of dispute resolution,
3. development of procedures that permit agencies to obtain the services of neutrals on an expedited basis, and
4. recordkeeping to ascertain the benefits of alternative means of dispute resolution.

The Working Group shall also periodically advise the President, through the Director of the Office of Management and Budget, on its activities.

The Regulatory Working Group established under section 4(d) of Executive Order 12866 is designated under 5 U.S.C. 569(a) as the interagency committee to facilitate and encourage agency use of negotiated rulemaking.

This directive is for the internal management of the executive branch and does not create any right or benefit, substantive or procedural, enforceable by a party against the United States, its agencies or instrumentalities, its officers or employees, or any other person.

Appendix E:
Federal ADR Council, Confidentiality in Federal Alternative Dispute Resolution Programs, December 29, 2000

SUMMARY: This notice publishes a document entitled "Confidentiality in Federal Alternative Dispute Resolution Programs," which provides guidance to assist Federal agencies in developing ADR programs. The document was created by a subcommittee of the Federal ADR Steering Committee, a group of subject matter experts from federal agencies with ADR programs. It was approved by the Federal ADR Council, a group of high-level government officials chaired by the Attorney General. The document contains detailed guidance on the nature and limits of confidentiality in Federal ADR programs and also includes guidelines for a statement on these issues that Federal neutrals may use in ADR proceedings.

Interested persons have been afforded an opportunity to participate in the making of this guidance. A draft was submitted for public comment in the Federal Register, and due consideration has been given to the comments received. Comments were provided by private sector organizations and government agencies from around the country.

Federal Register, Dec. 29, 2000, 83,085.

Authority

The Administrative Dispute Resolution Act of 1996 (ADR Act), 5 U.S.C. secs. 571–584, requires each Federal agency to promote the use of ADR and calls for the establishment of an interagency committee to assist agencies in the use of ADR. Pursuant to this Act, a Presidential Memorandum dated May 1, 1998, created the Interagency ADR Working Group, chaired by the Attorney General, to "facilitate, encourage, and provide coordination" for Federal agencies. In the Memorandum, the President charged the Working Group with assisting agencies with training in "how to use alternative means of dispute resolution." The following document is designed to serve this goal.

Introduction

The subject of the document is confidentiality, which is a critical component of a successful ADR process. Guarantees of confidentiality allow parties to freely engage in candid, informal discussions of their interests in order to reach the best possible settlement of their claims. A promise of confidentiality allows parties to speak openly without fear that statements made during an ADR process will be used against them later. Confidentiality can reduce posturing and destructive dialogue among parties during the settlement process.

Public comment was solicited on a draft of this document that was published in the *Federal Register* at 65 FR 59200, October 4, 2000. The draft was revised to incorporate many suggestions on the draft received from the following private sector organizations, government agencies, and individuals from around the country:

American Bar Association, Section of Administrative Law and Regulatory Practice

American Bar Association, Section of Dispute Resolution

Association of the Bar of the City of New York, Committee on Alternative Dispute Resolution

Executive Council on Integrity and Efficiency

Federal Mediation and Conciliation Service

Martin J. Harty

Lawrence A. Huerta

Oregon Department of Agriculture Farm Mediation Program

Margaret Porter, Administrator, Federal Sharing Neutrals Program

Karen D. Powell

President's Council on Integrity and Efficiency

Texas Center for Public Policy Dispute Resolution

United States Department of Agriculture, Office of Inspector General

United States Department of Energy, Chicago Operations Office

United States Department of Transportation, Federal Aviation Administration

United States Institute for Environmental Conflict Resolution

Richard C. Walters

Major comments fell primarily into three categories. The first is the interplay of the ADR Act confidentiality provisions with federal "access" statutes that provide Federal entities authority to seek access to certain classes of information. The second is the extent of confidentiality protection for statements of parties made in joint session. The third is the model statement on confidentiality for neutrals to read to parties at the beginning of a mediation.

The ADR Council believes that the understanding of these issues will benefit from experience and further collaboration with a broader community. The Council recognizes that its timetable for comments to this document was limited and wants to make clear that it anticipates further discussion of these issues. Future research, analysis, and practical experience in the field are certain to have a continuing impact on these important areas, and this Guidance may need to be revised or updated. We look forward to cooperation with interested parties in this work.

The Relationship Between the ADR Act and Other Authorities

The largest number of comments concerned the relationship between ADR Act confidentiality guarantees and other laws or regulations that authorize access to certain classes of information. Some commenters suggested that confidentiality should be narrower than provided under the draft Guidance. For example, some commenters believed that threats of physical harm and statements concerning ongoing or future criminal activity should not be confidential. Other commenters stated that Federal statutes providing access for government investigatory agencies should override the ADR Act's confidentiality guarantees.

In sharp contrast, other commenters believed that the confidentiality guarantees in the draft should be much broader. Several commenters argued that the ADR Act prohibitions on disclosure take precedence over any other Federal statute. These commenters argue that the ADR Act allows Inspectors General and other investigators to obtain confidential communications only through a court order obtained pursuant to the Act.

The Federal ADR Council acknowledges the points of view expressed in these comments but does not concur with them. There does not appear to be an easy answer to the tension between these authorities. While the ADR Act's confidentiality provisions are clear, the access provisions of other statutes are equally clear.

Standard techniques for resolving statutory conflicts do not provide a ready answer in this situation. For example, arguments have been made on both sides as to which statute is more specific. While the ADR Act specifically addresses the types of processes to which it applies, some have argued that other acts, such as the Inspector General Act, do the same by specifically describing the types of information that may be requested and the purposes for which a request can be made. Nor does the legislative history of the ADR Act provide an apparent solution, as it does not appear to contain any mention of this conflict.

A further problem is that the Federal ADR Council is not the appropriate body to provide a final decision on this question. The Council is an advisory body created by the Attorney General to issue guidance, but it is not authorized to promulgate binding interpretations in the manner of a court.

While it is, of course, appropriate to give this matter careful attention, we note that the circumstances when confidentiality might be challenged are, based on our experience, rare. The Council believes that there are opportunities for ADR programs and Federal requesting entities to establish good working relationships such that disputes over demands for disclosure of confidential communications can be minimized. This report continues to endorse a cooperative approach of this nature.

In addition, the revised report endorses use of the standards in the ADR Act's judicial override provision, sections 574(a)(4) and (b)(5), stating that they should be used both formally, when available, and informally to resolve the rare instances where requesting entities seek access to communications protected by the ADR Act.

The Confidentiality of Statements Made in Joint Session

Many comments were also received concerning the extent of confidentiality protection for statements made by parties in joint session. The draft report stated that there is no confidentiality protection for a party's dispute resolution communications that are available to all other parties, such as comments made or documents shared in joint session. Commenters noted that the guidance on this issue differs from traditional ADR practices and party expectations regarding confidentiality, and said this interpretation could reduce the utility of joint sessions. One commenter suggested that the report's interpretation of section 574(b)(7), the key provision on this point, would render sections 574(b)(1)–(6) superfluous. Further, this commenter noted that comments by several legislators and a Senate report indicate 574(b)(7) was intended to cover only documents, not oral statements.

The Federal ADR Council acknowledges that the ADR Act's treatment of this issue is different from the practice in many ADR processes that do not involve the government, but notes that the language of the statute is difficult to overcome. The Act states that there is no confidentiality protection if "the dispute resolution communication was provided to or was available to all parties in the dispute resolution proceeding." 5 U.S.C. 574(b)(7). Communications in a joint session with all parties present fit squarely within this provision. Further, the Act's definition of dispute resolution communication contains no exception for oral statements. Indeed, it explicitly includes "any *oral* or written communication prepared for the purposes of a dispute resolution proceeding" (emphasis added).

Despite the language of (b)(7), it appears that the remaining provisions of 574(b) provide protection for limited types of communications. These other sections continue to protect, for example, a party who is asked what a mediator said at any time, or a party who is asked what another party said in a multi-party case when not all parties were present. With regard to legislative history, an indicator of Congressional intent is the report of the final Conference Committee in 1996, when the current statute was enacted. It states, "A dispute resolution communication originating from a party to a party or parties is not protected from disclosure by the ADR Act." H.R. Rep. No. 104–841, 142 Cong. Rec. H11,110 (September 25, 1996). The Committee could have used the word "document" if it wanted to exclude oral statements, but it chose to use the term "dispute resolution communication," which is explicitly defined in the statute to include oral statements.

The Council does recognize that this provision could hinder a party's candor in a joint session, and therefore the Guidance suggests that parties address this issue through the use of a contract. Confidentiality agreements are a standard practice in many ADR contexts, and their use is encouraged in Federal dispute resolution processes where confidentiality of party-to-party communications is desired. It is important to note that confidentiality agreements do not bind anyone who is not a signatory. Further, such agreements will not protect against disclosure of documents through the Freedom of Information Act (FOIA). Nevertheless, the majority of problems caused by the plain language reading of section 574(b)(7) can be rectified through a well-drafted confidentiality agreement.

The Model Confidentiality Statement for Use by Neutrals

Finally, many commenters made suggestions regarding the Model Confidentiality Statement for Use by Neutrals that appeared at the end of the draft report. Some commenters argued that provisions should be added to the statement to ensure parties were made aware of additional possible confidentiality exceptions. Others stated that the statement was already too complex and potentially chilling. The Council appreciates the difficulty in making an opening statement complete enough to put parties on notice of important issues, while not making it so exhaustive that it discourages participation in ADR.

The Council acknowledges that a well-drafted statement should accommodate all of these concerns as well as possible.

Other commenters noted that the statement may not be appropriate for all types of proceedings or all types of neutrals. The Federal ADR Council agrees that the model statement may not fit all situations and all ADR processes, or even all stages of a single ADR process. In response to these comments, the Guidance now includes a set of guidelines for neutrals to use in developing their own statements on confidentiality, appropriate to the situation. It is the neutral's responsibility to address confidentiality with the parties. Neutrals and agency ADR programs may want to develop a standard confidentiality statement, consistent with the guidelines presented in this report, that is appropriate to a particular ADR process.

The Guidance also includes an example of one possible confidentiality statement. It is important to note that this statement should be tailored, as necessary, to fit the needs of each particular case. This statement refers to a mediation, because mediation is the most common ADR process in the Federal government.

Conclusion

The balance of this revised report follows the same format as the draft report. Section I is a reprint of the confidentiality provisions of the ADR Act. Section II is a section-by-section analysis of the confidentiality provisions of the Act. Section III contains the revised questions and answers on confidentiality issues likely to arise in practice. Section IV contains the new guidelines for use in developing confidentiality statements. In addition, as assistance for neutrals and agencies drafting confidentiality statements, Section IV contains an example of one possible confidentiality statement.

Nothing in these guidance documents shall be construed to create any right or benefit, substantive or procedural, enforceable at law or in equity, by a party against the United States, its agencies, its officers or any other person.

The Federal ADR Council

Chair: Janet Reno, Attorney General, Department of Justice

Vice Chair: Erica Cooper, Deputy General Counsel, Federal Deposit Insurance Corporation

Members: Leigh A. Bradley, General Counsel, Department of
Veterans Affairs; Meyer Eisenberg, Deputy General Counsel,
Securities and Exchange Commission; Mary Anne Gibbons,
General Counsel, U.S. Postal Service; Gary S. Guzy, General
Counsel, Environmental Protection Agency; Jeh C. Johnson,
General Counsel, Department of the Air Force; Stewart Aly,
Acting Deputy General Counsel, Department of Defense;
Rosalind Knapp, Acting General Counsel, Department of
Transportation; Anthony N. Palladino, Director, Office of Dis-
pute Resolution, Federal Aviation Administration, Department
of Transportation; Janet S. Potts, Counsel to the Secretary,
Department of Agriculture; Harriett S. Rabb, General Counsel,
Department of Health and Human Services; Henry L. Solano,
Solicitor, Department of Labor; John Sparks, Acting General
Counsel, Department of the Navy; Peter R. Steenland, Jr.,
Senior Counsel for Dispute Resolution, U.S. Department of
Justice; Mary Ann Sullivan, General Counsel, Department
of Energy; Robert Ward, Senior Counsel for Dispute Resolu-
tion, Environmental Protection Agency.

Report on the Reasonable Expectations
of Confidentiality Under the Administrative
Dispute Resolution Act of 1996

· · ·

II. Section-by-Section Analysis of
Confidentiality Provisions (5 U.S.C. 574)

Section 574(a)

In general, a neutral in a dispute resolution proceeding is prohibited from disclosing any dispute resolution communication or any
communication provided to him or her in confidence. Unless the
communication falls within one of the exceptions listed below, the
neutral cannot voluntarily disclose a communication and cannot
be forced to disclose a communication through a discovery request
or by any other compulsory process.

The exceptions to this general rule are found in subsections 574(a)(1)–(4), 574(d) and 574(e).

Section 574(a)(1)

A neutral may disclose a dispute resolution communication if all parties *and* the neutral agree in writing to the disclosure. If a nonparty provided the dispute resolution communication, then the nonparty must also agree in writing to the disclosure.

Section 574(a)(2)

A neutral may disclose a dispute resolution communication if the communication has already been made public.

Section 574(a)(3)

A neutral may disclose a dispute resolution communication if there is a statute which requires it to be made public. However, the neutral should not disclose the communication unless there is no other person available to make the disclosure.

Section 574(a)(4)

A neutral may disclose a dispute resolution communication or a communication provided in confidence to the neutral if a court finds that the neutral's testimony, or the disclosure, is necessary to:

A. prevent a manifest injustice;
B. help establish a violation of law; or
C. prevent harm to the public health and safety.

In order to require disclosure, a court must determine that the need for disclosure is of sufficient magnitude to outweigh the detrimental impact on the integrity of dispute resolution proceedings in general. The need for the information must be so great that it outweighs a loss of confidence among other potential parties that their dispute resolution communications or communications provided in confidence to the neutral will remain confidential in future proceedings.

Section 574(b)

Unless a dispute resolution communication falls within one of the exceptions listed below, a party cannot voluntarily disclose the communication and cannot be forced to disclose a communication through a discovery request or by any other compulsory process.

Section 574(b)(1)

The party who prepared the dispute resolution communication is free to disclose it.

Section 574(b)(2)

A party may disclose a dispute resolution communication if all the parties agree in writing to the disclosure.

Section 574(b)(3)

A party may disclose a dispute resolution communication if the dispute resolution communication has already been made public.

Section 574(b)(4)

A party may disclose a dispute resolution communication if there is a statute which requires it to be made public.

Section 574(b)(5)

A party may be required to disclose a dispute resolution communication if a court finds that the party's testimony, or the disclosure, is necessary to:

A. prevent a manifest injustice;
B. help establish a violation of law; or
C. prevent harm to the public health and safety.

In order to require disclosure, a court must determine that the need for disclosure is of sufficient magnitude to outweigh the detrimental impact on the integrity of dispute resolution proceedings in general. The need for the information must be so great that it outweighs a loss of confidence among other potential parties that their dispute resolution communications will remain confidential in future proceedings.

Section 574(b)(6)

1. Parties may use dispute resolution communications to show that a settlement agreement was in fact reached or to show what the terms of this agreement mean.

2. Parties may also use dispute resolution communications in connection with later issues regarding enforcing the agreement.

Section 574(b)(7)

1. A party is not prohibited from disclosing another party's dispute resolution communication that was available to all parties in the proceeding. For example, in a joint mediation session with all parties present, statements made and documents provided by parties are not confidential.

2. Dispute resolution communications coming from the neutral are nonetheless confidential.

Section 574(c)

No one may use any dispute resolution communication in a related proceeding, if that communication was disclosed in violation of Section 574(a) or (b).

Section 574(d)(1)

1. Parties may agree to alternative confidentiality procedures for disclosures by a neutral.

2. Parties must inform the neutral of the alternative procedures before the dispute resolution proceeding begins.

3. If parties do not inform the neutral of the alternative procedures, the procedures outlined in Section 574(a) will apply.

Section 574(d)(2)

1. Dispute resolution communications covered by alternative confidentiality procedures may be protected from disclosure under FOIA.

2. To qualify for this protection, the alternative procedures must provide for as much, or more, disclosure than the procedures provided in Section 574.

3. Dispute resolution communications covered by alternative confidentiality procedures do not qualify for protection from disclosure under FOIA if the alternative procedures provide for less disclosure than those outlined in Section 574.

Section 574(e)

1. A neutral who receives a demand for disclosure, in the form of a discovery request or other legal process, must make reasonable efforts to notify the parties and any affected non-party participants of the demand.

2. Parties and non-party participants who receive a notice of a demand for disclosure from a neutral:

a. must respond within 15 calendar days and offer to defend a refusal to disclose the information; or
b. if they do not respond within 15 calendar days, they will be deemed to have waived their objections to disclosure of the information.

Section 574(f)

Evidence that is otherwise discoverable or admissible is not protected from disclosure under this Section merely because the evidence was presented during a dispute resolution proceeding.

Section 574(g)

The provisions of Section 574 (a) and (b) do not affect information and data that are necessary to document agreements or orders resulting from dispute resolution proceedings.

Section 574(h)

Information from and about dispute resolution proceedings may be used for educational and research purposes as long as the parties and specific issues in controversy are not identifiable.

Section 574(i)

Dispute resolution communications may be used to resolve disputes between the neutral in a dispute resolution proceeding and a party or participant, but only to the extent necessary to resolve a dispute between a neutral and party or participant.

Section 574(j)

A dispute resolution communication between a neutral and a party that is protected from disclosure under this section is also protected from disclosure under FOIA (Section 552(b)(3)).

III. Questions and Answers on Confidentiality Under the Administrative Dispute Resolution Act of 1996 (ADR Act)

General Confidentiality Rules

1. What types of communications are confidential?
Subject to certain exceptions, the following two types of communications are potentially confidential under the ADR Act:

A. A dispute resolution communication.
A dispute resolution communication is any oral statement made or writing presented by a party, nonparty participant or neutral during a dispute resolution proceeding prepared specifically for the purposes of a dispute resolution proceeding. However, written agreements to enter into a dispute resolution proceeding and any written final agreement reached as a result of the proceeding are not dispute resolution communications. *Citation: 5 USC 571(5).*

Example: At the outset of the mediation conference, the parties sign an agreement to mediate. During private meetings with the mediator, they each make oral statements and give the mediator documents prepared specifically for use in the mediation. At the conclusion of the mediation, the parties sign a settlement agreement resolving the matter.

The oral statements and written documents prepared specifically for use in the mediation are dispute resolution communications. The agreement to mediate and the settlement agreement are not dispute resolution communications.

B. A "communication provided in confidence to the neutral." A "communication provided in confidence to the neutral" is any oral statement or written document provided to a neutral during a dispute resolution proceeding. The communication must be: (1) made with the express intent that it not be disclosed or (2) provided under circumstances that would create a reasonable expectation that it not be disclosed. *Citation: 5 USC 571(7) and 574 (a).*

Example: During private meetings, counsel for the contractor and for the agency separately give the mediator different documents prepared before mediation which contain highly sensitive information. Counsel for the contractor expressly asks the mediator to keep his document confidential; counsel for the agency says nothing about keeping her document confidential. Both documents are "communications provided in confidence to the neutral." The contractor's documents are communications provided in confidence because counsel for the contractor expressly asked the neutral to keep it confidential. The agency's documents are communications provided in confidence because they were provided under circumstances which create a reasonable expectation that they should not be disclosed.

Example: An employee during a caucus in a mediation session tells the neutral that he might appear inattentive during the joint session because he has been diagnosed recently with cancer and is taking medicine. He tells the mediator not to share that information with the other party, his supervisor. The information is a communication provided in confidence because the employee provided it to the neutral with the expressed intent that it not be disclosed.

2. What confidentiality protection is provided for dispute resolution communications?

Generally, neutrals and parties may not voluntarily disclose or be compelled to disclose dispute resolution communications. The ADR Act contains specific exceptions to the general rule. (See Question 11.) *Citation: 5 USC 574(a), (b).*

> *Example:* A party resolves his EEO complaint through mediation and signs a written agreement settling all issues. The mediator subsequently receives a phone call from another employee asking 1) what was management's position in the mediation, and, 2) what relief was obtained. The mediator, as a neutral, may not disclose to the employee any communications made by management in the dispute resolution proceeding. However, the neutral may provide the employee with a copy of the final agreement which sets forth the relief obtained.

> *Example:* During a mediation involving ten parties, two meet in caucus with the mediator and discuss their common interests. Later, a person contacts one of the two parties asking about what the other party said during the caucus with the mediator. The first party may not disclose what the other party said during the caucus.

3. What confidentiality protection applies to a "communication provided in confidence" by a party to a neutral?

Generally, neutrals may not disclose any communication provided to them in confidence. The ADR Act contains specific exceptions to the general rule. (See Question 11.) *Citation: 5 USC 574(a).*

> *Example:* A government contractor during a caucus in a mediation session tells the neutral the details of his proposed "bid" for a government contract. The neutral may not disclose the information because the program participant would have a reasonable expectation that the information would not be shared.

4. What is a dispute resolution proceeding?

A dispute resolution proceeding is an alternative means of resolving an issue in controversy arising from an agency's program, operations or actions. The ADR Act supports a broad reading of the term "dispute resolution proceeding." The ADR Act broadly incorporates all

ADR forms and techniques, including any combination of ADR forms or techniques. In defining an issue in controversy, the ADR Act incorporates disagreements between an agency and parties or between parties. This indicates a legislative intent to provide for the use of ADR processes in an inclusive manner to assist the wide range of situations where disagreements may arise in the conduct of an agency's programs, operations, or actions. A dispute resolution proceeding includes intake and convening stages as well as more formal stages, such as mediation. *Citation: 5 USC 571(3), (6), and (8).*

> *Example:* A neutral is engaged to help resolve a dispute between an agency and one of its contractors. The process managed by the neutral (i.e., mediation, arbitration, or another technique) is a dispute resolution proceeding.

> *Example:* A dispute exists between an agency and several other parties with regard to the agency's interpretation of a regulation. The work of a neutral to convene the parties (i.e., to bring them together for purposes of conducting a negotiated settlement) is a dispute resolution proceeding.

5. *Who is a neutral?*

A neutral is anyone who functions specifically to aid the parties during a dispute resolution process. A neutral may be a private person or a federal government employee who is acceptable to the parties. There may be more than one neutral during the course of a dispute resolution process (e.g., an "intake" neutral, a "convener" neutral, as well as the neutral who facilitates a face-to-face proceeding). It is important that agencies clearly identify neutrals to avoid misunderstanding.

The ADR Act supports a broad reading of the term neutral. In defining neutral, the ADR Act refers to the services of an individual who functions to aid parties in the resolution of an issue in controversy. This indicates the intent of the ADR Act to support the use of neutrals to aid parties during all stages of the resolution of a disagreement, from the convening of participants and design of effective dispute resolution procedures to the conduct of settlement discussions.

The ADR Act provides that a neutral should be acceptable to the parties. In light of the broad variety of ADR services and types of disagreements encompassed by the ADR Act, this requirement must be considered on a case by case basis to provide flexibility in how individual parties "accept" a neutral. If an agency clearly identifies an individual as an intake or convening neutral, an agency or private party who contacts the neutral for the purpose of seeking aid in resolving a disagreement indicates an acceptance of the neutral for that purpose. Likewise, the voluntary participation of a party in an ADR process conducted by a neutral indicates an acceptance of the neutral. *Citation: 5 USC 571(3), (6), (8), and (9) & 573(a).*

> *Example:* An employee contacts an agency ADR program seeking assistance in resolving a dispute and describes a dispute to an intake person. The conversation is confidential only if the intake person has been appropriately identified as a neutral by the agency to aid parties in resolving such disputes.

> *Example:* An EEO office automatically assigns, on a rotating basis, a trained neutral from within the agency, without consulting the parties. The parties can be deemed to have agreed to the neutral by virtue of their participation.

6. Who is a party?

A party is any person or entity who participates in a dispute resolution proceeding and is named in an agency proceeding or will be affected significantly by the outcome of an agency proceeding. Consistent with common legal practice, the obligations of parties extend to their representatives and agents. *Citation: 5 USC 571(10).*

> *Example:* An agency convenes a mediation of all affected stakeholders to resolve an environmental dispute. Every person, business entity, state or local government, and non-profit organization that will be significantly affected by the outcome of the process and agrees to participate is a party to the mediation.

7. What constitutes disclosure?

Disclosure is not defined in the ADR Act. Disclosure occurs when a neutral, a party, or a non-party participant makes a communication available to some other person or entity by any method.

> *Example:* A federal employee is mediating a workplace dispute as a collateral duty. The mediator's supervisor asks for a briefing on the case.

Telling the supervisor "dispute resolution communications" or "communications provided in confidence" would constitute disclosure.

8. May a party or neutral disclose dispute resolution communications in response to discovery or compulsory process?

In general, neither a neutral nor a party can be required to disclose dispute resolution communications through discovery or compulsory process. Compulsory processes include any administrative, judicial or regulatory process that compels action by an individual. *Citation: 5 USC 574(a) and (b).*

> *Example:* A neutral receives a notice of deposition from an attorney in a lawsuit regarding a matter which the neutral mediated. The attorney informs her that she will be asked about the statements by the complainant made during the mediation. In the deposition, the neutral may not disclose the complainant's statements because they are dispute resolution communications.

9. What confidentiality protection is provided for communications by a nonparty participant in a dispute resolution proceeding?

The term "nonparty participant" is not defined in the ADR Act. However, common usage suggests that a nonparty participant is an individual present during a dispute resolution proceeding other than a party, an agent or representative of a party, or the neutral. This could be an individual who is asked by the neutral to present information for use of the neutral or parties. Dispute resolution communications made by nonparty participants are subject to the same protections and exceptions as are all other dispute resolution communications. A neutral needs to obtain the written consent of all parties and the nonparty participant to disclose such communications. *Citation: 5 USC 574(a)(1).*

> *Example:* An expert talks about inflation and wages she prepared for mediation. The communication is confidential and cannot be disclosed by the neutral without the consent of all the parties and the expert.

> *Example:* An expert retained by the neutral discusses his environmental impact research and participates in subsequent discussions with the parties. The expert is not prohibited from disclosing any

communications from those discussions, absent a signed agreement to that effect.

10. In an ADR process do the confidentiality protections of the ADR Act apply?

Confidentiality applies to communications when a person seeking ADR services contacts an appropriate neutral. A communication made by a party to a neutral is covered even if made prior to a face-to-face ADR proceeding. Confidentiality does not apply to communications made after a final written agreement is reached or after resolution efforts aided by the neutral have otherwise ended. *Citation: 5 USC 571(6), 574(a) and (b).*

> *Example:* Two parties have agreed to use an ADR process to try to resolve a dispute and have selected a neutral. Prior to the first session between the parties and the neutral, the neutral communicates independently with each of the parties. The confidentiality provisions of the ADR Act apply to these discussions.

> *Example:* The parties to an ADR process have completed a dispute resolution proceeding and signed a settlement agreement. One of the parties subsequently calls the neutral to discuss how the settlement is being implemented. This discussion is not confidential under the ADR Act because the dispute resolution proceeding has already ended.

Exceptions to Confidentiality Protection

11. Under what circumstances may communications be disclosed under the ADR Act?

1. A party's own communications during a dispute resolution proceeding.

A party may disclose any oral or written communication which the party makes or prepares for a dispute resolution proceeding. *Citation: 5 USC 574(b)(1).*

> *Example:* During a separate caucus, the contractor drafts a document showing the financial impact of his breach of contract. The mediation is unsuccessful. The government subpoenas the contractor to produce the document for an administrative hearing. The

contractor cannot be compelled to produce the document. She may, however, voluntarily produce it.

2. A dispute resolution communication that has "already been made public."

The ADR Act's confidentiality protections do not apply to communications that have already been made public. Although the ADR Act does not define the term, examples of communications that have "already been made public" could include, for example, the following:

1. The communication has been discussed in an open Congressional hearing;
2. The communication has been placed in a court filing or testified about in a court in a proceeding not under seal;
3. The communication has been discussed in a meeting which is open to the public;
4. The communication has been released under FOIA.
   Citation: 5 USC 574(a)(2) & 574(b)(3).

3. Communications required by statute to be made public.

There are a handful of statutes which require certain classes of information to be made public. To the extent that such information is shared during a dispute resolution proceeding the information is not confidential. *Citation: 5 USC 574(a)(3), 574(b)(4).*

> *Example:* Section 114(c) of the Clean Air Act states that certain records, reports or information obtained from regulated entities "shall be made available to the public." These communications are not subject to the ADR Act prohibitions on disclosure by a neutral or a party.

4. When a court orders disclosure.

A court may override the confidentiality protections of the ADR Act in three limited situations. In order to override the confidentiality protections, a court must determine that testimony or disclosure of a communication is necessary to either (1) prevent a manifest injustice, (2) help establish a violation of law, or (3) prevent harm to the public health or safety. The court must also determine, by applying a balancing test, that the need for the information is of a sufficient magnitude in the particular case to outweigh the integrity of dispute resolution proceedings in general by reducing the confidence of parties in future cases that their communications will remain confidential. *Citation: 5 USC 574(a)(4) and (b)(5)*.

> *Example (to prevent a manifest injustice):* During a separate caucus in a Federal Tort Claims Act mediation, a husband tells the mediator that his wife's claims to have been paralyzed in an accident were false. Mediation terminates, and the case proceeds to trial. Information about the wife's statements comes to the attention of the insurance company which seeks an order to compel testimony from the mediator. The court, in applying the balancing test in 574(a)(4), may order the mediator to disclose information if it finds that a failure to disclose the information would result in a manifest injustice to the moving party.

> *Example (help establish a violation of law):* During a mediation regrading the dismissal of a federal employee, the employee divulges to the mediator that he charged personal goods to his government credit card. In a later action against the employee for misuse of government funds, the neutral is asked to testify about what he learned in the mediation. The court, in applying the balancing test in 574(a)(4), may require the neutral to testify if it determines that the neutral's testimony is necessary to help establish a violation of law.

> *Example (prevent harm to the public health or safety):* During mediation of a tort claim, an engineer discloses to the neutral that her structural evaluation indicated serious defects in a building, but that her supervisor refused to accept the report as written and threatened her job security if she did not alter the report. When the case comes to trial, the plaintiff subpoenas the neutral to testify. The court, in applying the balancing test in 574(a)(4), may require the neutral to testify if it determines that the neutral's testimony is necessary to prevent harm to the public safety.

5. In order to resolve a dispute over the existence or meaning of a settlement arrived at through a dispute resolution proceeding. The ADR Act creates an exception to the general rule of nondisclosure by a party for the limited purpose of determining the existence or meaning of an agreement arrived at through a dispute resolution proceeding. Parties may also disclose communications

as required to enforce an agreement arrived at through a dispute resolution proceeding. *Citation: 5 USC 574(b)(6).*

> *Example:* Parties may disclose dispute resolution communications as required to show that a settlement agreement was reached or explore the meaning of the terms of this agreement.

6. Parties' communications in joint session, with all parties present.

A neutral may not disclose dispute resolution communications made in joint session. However, except for communications by a neutral, there is no prohibition against a party disclosing communications available to all other parties in the proceeding. *Citation: 5 USC 574(b)(7).*

> *Example:* In a joint session, with all parties present, a party admits that she was unaware of the defect in question. The other parties may disclose the information without violating the ADR Act.

7. Information sought for specific purposes.

The ADR Act allows for the disclosure of information for educational and research purposes, in cooperation with agencies, governmental entities, or dispute resolution programs. However, it is required that the parties and specific issues in controversy not be identifiable. *Citation: 5 USC 574(h).*

> *Example:* An individual who has served as a neutral in a number of agency ADR proceedings may share collected experiences when participating in a training program, provided that the parties and specific issues are not identifiable.

> *Example:* An ADR program administrator may provide statistical information to an auditor or inspector who is evaluating the efficiency and effectiveness of an ADR program, provided that the parties and specific issues are not identifiable.

8. Communications required to resolve disputes that arise between the neutral and a party.

If there is a dispute between a neutral and a party regarding the conduct of a dispute resolution proceeding, both may disclose dispute resolution communications to the extent necessary to resolve the dispute. *Citation: 5 U.S.C. 574(I)*

> *Example:* If a party refuses to pay the neutral for services, the neutral can disclose dispute resolution communications to the extent necessary to establish that payment is due.

12. Are a neutral's communications to parties in joint session or otherwise provided to all parties confidential?

Yes. The ADR Act protects communications by a neutral. A party, however, may not use this provision to gain protection for a communication by providing it to the neutral who then provides it to another party. The ADR Act provides that the communication must be "generated" by the neutral, not just passed along by the neutral. *Citation: 5 USC 574 (b)(7). (See* H. Rept. 104–841,142 Cong. Rec. H11108–11 (September 25, 1996).

> *Example:* Early neutral evaluations or settlement proposals provided to the parties by a neutral are protected from disclosure by either the neutral or the parties.

13. Can confidentiality attach to communications that are provided to or available to fewer than all of the parties?

Yes. The ADR Act does not prohibit parties from disclosing dispute resolution communications that are "provided to or . . . available to all parties to the dispute resolution proceeding." Under a plain reading of the statute, communications are not protected when provided to, or available to, *all* parties; thus, they remain protected if they are provided to, or are available to, some (but not all) of the parties in a dispute.

The legislative history states, "A dispute resolution communication originating from a party to a party or parties is not protected from disclosure by the ADR Act." H.R. Rep. No. 104–841, 142 Cong. Rec. H11110 (Sept. 25, 1996). The plain language of the statute is not inconsistent with this piece of legislative history, in that it can be interpreted to mean both parties in a two-party ("party to the other party") or all parties in a multi-party dispute ("party to all other parties"). *Citation: 5 U.S.C. 574(b)(7).*

Example: Six parties participate in a mediation. The mediator initially convenes a day-long meeting with all parties together in a joint session. The mediator believes that four have similar interests and convenes a separate meeting with just those four. Confidentiality attaches to communications which take place at the separate meeting, since fewer than all parties are present. Only if all six were present, or the information was available to all six, would disclosure be permissible under the (b)(7) exception.

14. Does the ADR Act prevent the discovery or admissibility of all information presented in a dispute resolution proceeding?

No. Information presented in a dispute resolution proceeding that is not protected by the ADR Act may be subject to discovery or admissibility as evidence in a subsequent legal action. *Citation: 5 USC 574(f).*

Example: During a mediation proceeding in a dispute over a promotion, the complainant produces notes she made during an interview with the selecting official. She shares her interview notes with the neutral and management representative. In private caucus with the neutral, complainant prepares handwritten notes of the neutral's comments regarding the case. When the case goes to litigation, the agency requests discovery of complainant's interview notes, as well as the notes reflecting the neutral's assessment of the case.

The agency would not be prohibited from seeking complainant's notes of the interview with the selecting official. The interview notes are not dispute resolution communications because they were not prepared for purposes of the dispute resolution proceeding. However, the complainant's notes reflecting the neutral's assessment of her case constitute a dispute resolution communication because they were prepared for the purpose of the dispute resolution proceeding.

15. Does the ADR Act protect against the disclosure of dispute resolution communications in response to requests by federal entities for such information?

Section 574 of the ADR Act prohibits a neutral or a party from disclosing, voluntarily or in response to discovery or compulsory process, any protected communication. The ADR Act further states that neutrals and parties shall not "be required" to disclose such communications.

A number of federal entities have statutory authority to request disclosure of documents from federal agencies and employees. Examples of such statutes include, but are not limited to, the Inspector General Act (5 USC App.) and the Whistleblower Protection Act (5 USC Section 1212(b)(2)). Further, certain statutes may be read to impose an affirmative obligation to disclose certain classes of information. These include, 18 USC Section 4 (knowledge relating to the commission of a felony) and 28 USC Section 535 (investigation of crimes involving Government officers and employees).

None of the exceptions to the ADR Act's confidentiality provisions directly applies to the above-mentioned authorities. For example, none of the authorities cited above constitutes a requirement that information be "made public" pursuant to ADR Act section 574 (a)(3) and (b)(4). In addition, the judicial override procedure outlined in Section 574 (a)(4) and (b)(5) will not always be available when a conflict between the ADR Act and disclosure statute arises.

In summary a tension among these authorities exists. The issues of statutory interpretation between these differing authorities have not yet been considered in an appropriate forum. Although we do not anticipate that direct conflicts between the ADR Act and one of the disclosure statutes will be common, it is important for agencies, neutrals, and participants to be aware of the potential issue.

The ADR Act's judicial override provision contains a standard for determining if disclosure is necessary despite the Act's general prohibition on disclosure. The judicial override procedure should be followed whenever possible by requesting entities. Use of this statutorily authorized procedure will provide the best guidance to both the ADR community and requesting entities. Even when the override procedure is not available (because of jurisdictional limitations, for example), this standard should be used in determining whether to disclose an otherwise protected communication. The override provision, at section 574(a)(4) & (b)(5), takes into account the need for access to information to prevent manifest injustice, establish violations of law, and prevent harm to public health and safety, while considering the integrity of dispute resolution proceedings in general and the consequences breaching confidentiality.

There are also several practical steps that agencies can take to minimize the likelihood of a dispute over a demand for disclosure of confidential communications. Agency ADR programs and potential requesting entities should enter into a dialogue to establish a framework for how potential demands for disclosure will be handled. The following principles should be included in such a framework:

- Agency ADR programs and requesting entities should educate each other about their respective missions.
- Procedures should be established for access to information that balance the need to prevent manifest injustice, help establish a violation of law, and prevent harm to the public health and safety against the need to protect the integrity of the agency's dispute resolution proceedings.
- ADR programs should identify classes of information that are not confidential, such as budgetary and statistical information regarding the number and types of cases and processes used.
- Requesting entities should use non-confidential information as a basis for information requests.
- Requesting entities should seek confidential information only if the information is not available through other means.
- Requesting entities should seek information from a neutral only if the information is not otherwise available.
- The ADR program and requesting entities should agree to procedures to resolve specific disagreements that arise with regard to the disclosure of information.

Alternative Procedures to Establish Confidentiality Protection

16. *May parties agree to confidentiality procedures which are different from those contained in the ADR Act?*

Yes. Parties may agree to more, or less, confidentiality protection for disclosure by the neutral or themselves than is provided for in the Act.

The ADR Act provides that parties may agree to alternative confidential procedures for disclosures by a neutral. While there is no parallel provision for parties, the exclusive wording of this subsection should not be construed as limiting parties' ability to agree to alternative confidentiality procedures. Parties have a general right to sign confidentiality agreements, and there is no reason this should change in a mediation context.

If the parties agree to alternative confidentiality procedures regarding disclosure by a neutral, they must so inform the neutral before the dispute resolution proceeding begins or the confidentiality procedures in the ADR Act will apply. An agreement providing for alternative confidentiality procedures is binding on anyone who signs the agreement. On the other hand, such an agreement will not be binding on third parties and may not guarantee that dispute resolution communications will be protected by the ADR Act from disclosure to such parties. Consistent with prudent practice, it is recommended that any such agreements be documented in writing. (See Questions 23 and 24 for potential FOIA implications.) *Citation: 5 USC 574(d)(1).*

> *Example:* Parties to an ADR proceeding can agree to authorize the neutral to use his or her judgment about whether to voluntarily disclose a protected communication, as long as the neutral is informed of this agreement before the ADR proceeding commences.

> *Example:* Parties to an ADR proceeding can agree that they, and the neutral, will keep everything they say to each other in joint session confidential. A third party expert who overhears their discussions is not bound by their agreement unless she also signs it.

Issues Regarding the Disclosure of Protected Communications

17. What restrictions are put on the use of confidential communications disclosed in violation of the ADR Act?

If the neutral or any participant discloses a confidential communication in violation of Sections 574(a) or (b), that communication is not admissible in any proceeding that is related to the subject of the dispute resolution proceeding in which the protected communication was made. A dispute resolution communication that was improperly disclosed may not be protected from use in an unrelated proceeding. *Citation: 5 U.S.C. 574(c).*

> *Example:* A supervisor and employee are engaged in a very bitter dispute regarding allegations of sexual harassment. They try mediation with a well respected mediator who is considered an expert in federal sexual harassment law. During a separate caucus between

the mediator and the supervisor (alleged harasser) the mediator pointedly questioned the strength of the supervisor's defense.

The mediation is unsuccessful, and the EEOC issues a decision finding that the supervisor did not sexually harass his employee. The supervisor is ecstatic and talks to his friends about the situation, mocking some of the "wrong" comments the mediator made.

The employee appeals the case. She learns of the supervisor's reaction to the mediator's comments and wants to use the information in her brief. She will not be able to use the information because (1) the supervisor improperly disclosed information generated by the neutral, and (2) the appeal is a related proceeding.

Example: A federal agency and two contractors are mediating a dispute over an alleged breach of contract. During a caucus with the mediator, the two contractors share confidential information about their financial status. After completing mediation, Contractor 1, in violation of the ADR Act, tells Company X about Contractor 2's financial status.

A year later, Company X and Contractor 2 are in a dispute over a different contract in which Contractor 2's financial status is in dispute. Company X wants to use the information disclosed by Contractor 1. Company X would not be precluded by the ADR Act from using the information disclosed by Contractor 1, because the subject of the current proceeding is not related to that of the prior mediation.

18. What is the penalty for disclosing confidential communications in violation of the statute?

The ADR Act does not specify any civil or criminal penalty for the disclosure of a protected communication in violation of the Act. However, such disclosure may violate other laws, regulations or agreements of the parties.

Example: The parties agree in writing to keep confidential all statements they make in joint session. The agreement includes a provision that anyone disclosing statements made in joint session will be liable for damages. A party issues a press release disclosing statements made in joint session. The other parties may proceed against him in a suit for damages.

19. What must a neutral do when he or she receives a "demand for disclosure" of dispute resolution communications?

Although the ADR Act does not define the term, a "demand for disclosure" may be understood as a formal request for confidential information. The demand must be made by a discovery request or some other legal process.

Upon receiving a demand for disclosure of a dispute resolution communication, a neutral must make a reasonable effort to notify the parties and any affected non-party participants of the demand. Notice must be provided even if the neutral believes that there is no basis for refusing to disclose the communication.

Notice should be delivered to the last address provided by a party. Parties have fifteen calendar days, from the date they receive the notice, in which to offer to defend the neutral against disclosure. Therefore, notice should be sent by a process that provides certification of delivery. For example, delivery could be by registered mail, courier, or by any other carrier that provides tracking and certification of delivery. Use of telephone or email communications as notice could be problematic. Since the parties must respond within 15 calendar days or waive their right to object to disclosure, there should be a written record of when the notice was sent and when it was received. In certain rare circumstances, such as a criminal investigation, a neutral may be asked not to notify parties and others (e.g., program administrators) of a request for information. Under such circumstances, the neutral should seek the advice of counsel. *Citation: 5 USC 574(e).*

> *Example:* A colleague asks a neutral what happened in a mediation. The neutral must simply refuse to discuss the matter. The neutral does not need to notify the parties of the request since the demand was not a formal request for information.

> *Example:* A neutral receives a formal discovery request for information on what happened in a mediation. Despite the fact that the neutral believes that the requested information could be disclosed under the ADR Act, the neutral must notify the parties of this demand for disclosure using the procedures described above.

20. What can/must parties do when they receive notice of a demand for disclosure from the neutral?

If a party has no objection to the disclosure of confidential communications, it need not respond to the notice. On the other hand, if a party believes that the sought-after communications should not be disclosed, the party should notify the neutral within 15 calendar days and make arrangements to defend the neutral from the demand for disclosure. Federal agencies should develop departmental procedures for responding to such notices.

> *Example:* A party receives notice from a neutral that she has been served with a subpoena from the agency to produce documents and testify in a court proceeding. The party fulfills his responsibility under the Act by notifying the neutral within 15 calendar days that he objects to the demand for disclosure and that he will obtain counsel to defend the neutral.

21. What responsibilities do agencies have for ensuring that the notification requirement is met?

An agency does not have a notification requirement under the ADR Act. However, in some Federal ADR programs the neutral may be a Federal employee performing collateral duty. Requiring these neutrals to keep records of parties to dispute resolution proceedings may be unduly onerous and ineffective. Agencies should develop administrative procedures to ensure that the necessary records are retained. It is ultimately the neutral's responsibility to ensure that the notice is sent to the parties.

> *Example:* A Federal employee who serves on collateral duty as a mediator for the ADR program of another agency receives a demand for disclosure but does not know how to locate the parties. She approaches the ADR program manager of the other agency for assistance. The program manager provides the neutral with sufficient information to deliver notice as required under the ADR Act.

22. May a neutral refuse to disclose communications even when the parties have failed to agree to defend the neutral?

Yes. The ADR Act permits, but does not compel, a neutral to disclose if the parties have waived objections to disclosure under Section 574(e). While the statute is clear that a neutral "shall not" disclose where a party objects, the statute does not say that a neutral must disclose if a party does not object.

The effectiveness and integrity of mediation and other ADR processes is largely dependent on the credibility and trustworthiness of neutrals. In order to safeguard the integrity of ADR programs and to eliminate the potential for eroding confidence in future ADR proceedings, neutrals should be allowed to rely on established codes of ethics and confidentiality standards to support a decision not to disclose. *Citation: 5 USC 574(a) and (e).*

> *Example:* A neutral receives a subpoena requesting disclosure of confidential communications from a dispute resolution process. The parties do not object to the disclosure and have not offered to defend the neutral against the subpoena. The neutral may still, at his or her own expense, resist the subpoena if the neutral objects to the disclosure.

Issues Related to the Freedom of Information Act (FOIA)

23. *What dispute resolution communications are protected from disclosure under FOIA?*

Dispute resolution communications between a neutral and a party that may not be disclosed under the ADR Act are specifically exempted from disclosure under section 552(b)(3) of the Freedom of Information Act. This could include communications that are generated by a neutral and provided to all parties, such as an Early Neutral Evaluation. In addition, other FOIA exemptions may apply.

Since only Federal records are subject to FOIA, dispute resolution communications that are not Federal records are not subject to the disclosure requirements of FOIA. Therefore, this subsection would not apply to oral dispute resolution communications because they are not records. *Citation: 5 USC 574(j).*

> *Example:* During mediation of a contract claim, the parties (a contractor and the agency) request a neutral to provide an evaluation of the merits of their respective cases. The neutral agrees, reviews the evidence, and presents each party separately with a written assessment of their respective cases. The contractor submits a FOIA request to obtain a copy of the neutral's written evaluation of the agency's case. The FOIA request can be denied under section 574(j) because the document is a dispute resolution communication generated by a neutral and may not be disclosed under the ADR Act.

24. *If parties agree to alternative confidentiality procedures, are dispute resolution communications subject to FOIA?*

Parties may agree to confidentiality procedures that differ from those otherwise provided in the Act. Parties should be aware, however, that the FOIA exemption might not apply to all the communications that are protected under their agreement to use alternative confidentiality procedures.

If the alternative confidentiality procedures agreed to by the parties provide for less disclosure than the ADR Act permits, those dispute resolution communications that would not be protected under the ADR Act are also not protected by the FOIA exemption in section 574(j). Parties cannot contract for more FOIA protection than the ADR Act provides. *Citation: 5 USC 574(d) and (j).*

> *Example:* Parties enter into a confidentiality agreement as part of an agreement to mediate. The parties agree to keep statements made and documents presented during joint session confidential. Documents that are made available by the parties during joint session are not protected by the FOIA exemption in 574(j), even though they are provided by contract to be kept confidential.

Other Considerations

25. *Do the ADR Act's confidentiality provisions apply differently to government and private sector neutrals?*

No. There are, however, certain circumstances in which the choice of neutral may affect disclosure related to ADR processes. For example, because a private neutral's records are likely not deemed "agency records," they likely will not be subject to FOIA or to record retention requirements. Additionally, the IG Act authorizes an IG to subpoena a private neutral, but not a government neutral. Finally, a private neutral is not subject to some of the statutory provisions that create a tension with the ADR Act's non-disclosure requirements (See Question 15).

IV. Guidance on Confidentiality Statements for Use by Neutrals

Neutrals should make introductory remarks at the outset of a dispute resolution process explaining applicable ADR Act confidentiality provisions. Which provisions apply will vary, depending on

such things as the type of ADR used, the number of parties participating, and the issues involved. In addition, agencies may choose
to highlight or supplement ADR Act provisions to meet specific programmatic needs. We provide guidelines below to assist neutrals in
crafting appropriate introductory confidentiality statements.

An introductory confidentiality statement should address the
following topics:

1. Application of the ADR Act to administrative ADR processes;
2. The intent of the ADR Act to provide confidentiality assurances
   for communications between the parties and the neutral occurring during an ADR proceeding;
3. Confidentiality between and among parties, consistent with this
   Guidance;
4. Exceptions to the Act's nondisclosure provisions pertinent to
   the particular dispute;
5. Availability of alternative confidentiality protections through
   written agreement and applicable limitations; and
6. Authorities other than the ADR Act that may also apply.

Example: The confidentiality provisions of the Administrative Dispute Resolution Act apply to this mediation. The Act focuses primarily on protecting private communications between parties and
the mediator. Generally speaking, if you tell me something during
this process, I will keep it confidential. The same is true for written
documents you prepare for this process and give only to me.

There are exceptions to the confidentiality provisions in the
Act. For example, statements you make with all the other parties in
the room or documents you provide to them are not confidential.
Also, in unusual circumstances, a judge can order disclosure of information that would prevent a manifest injustice, help establish a
violation of law, or prevent harm to public health and safety.

You can agree to more confidentiality if you want to. For example, you can agree to keep statements you make or documents you
share with the other parties confidential. If you want to do this,
everyone will need to agree in writing. Outside parties may, however,
still have access to statements or documents as provided by law.

[This is only an example of one possible confidentiality statement.
It is important that this statement be tailored to fit the needs of
each particular case.]

Appendix F:
Report to the President on the Interagency ADR Working Group, May 8, 2000

The President
The White House
Washington, DC 20500

Dear Mr. President:

The Report of the Interagency Alternative Dispute Resolution (ADR) Working Group, which is hereby submitted, marks the end of the first year of this government-wide effort to promote more collaborative ways to handle disputes. The report, prepared pursuant to your Memorandum creating the Working Group, was written jointly by the Department of Justice and officials from more than ten agencies, including the Environmental Protection Agency, the Federal Deposit Insurance Corporation, the U.S. Postal Service, and the Department of the Air Force, whose staff served as chairs of individual sections of the group. As you will see from the report, there has been a great deal accomplished during the past year, and we plan to do much more in the months ahead.

In the past, the government has relied heavily upon traditional, adversarial processes to resolve both internal matters and disputes involving the public. Experience teaches us, however, that there are many costs to this approach. Even when the government

wins a case, it can find that victory has come at too
high a price. Litigation can destroy the underlying
relationships between the parties, and this can be far
more harmful in the long run. In the workplace area,
for example, formal complaints often force employees
working in the same office to take sides against one
another. During the months or years required to
process a complaint, and even long after it is over, the
dispute can be extremely corrosive to the productivity
of the office and the morale of its employees. Similarly,
when contract and other disputes arise involving
outside parties, previously healthy and productive
relationships can be damaged if formal, adversarial
processes are used.

Our experience has shown that ADR can resolve
disputes in a manner that is quicker, cheaper, and less
adversarial. For that reason, I call it "appropriate"
dispute resolution, rather than "alternative" dispute
resolution. In ADR, parties meet with each other
directly, under the guidance of a neutral professional
who is trained and experienced in handling disputes.
They talk about the problems that led to the complaint
and the resolution that will work best for them in the
future. With the assistance of the neutral professional,
they are able to retain control over their own dispute
and work collaboratively to find creative, effective
solutions that are agreeable to all sides.

We believe that every well-run agency should have
at least one ADR program. Over the past year, the
Working Group has worked to make this a reality.
The Group has sponsored programs in the following
areas: workplace, contracts and procurement, claims
against the government, and civil enforcement. There
have been more than 50 training sessions, meetings,
and colloquia on all aspects of ADR. More than 500
representatives from across the government have been
participating. We have created a Federal ADR website
that has received tens of thousands of requests for
information from across the country.

We have found many specific examples of time
and money saved through the use of ADR. The U.S.
Postal Service, for example, has one of the leading

workplace mediation programs in the country. It has
mediated more than 12,000 EEO complaints under
this program. Its average mediation takes just 4 hours,
and 81 percent of mediated cases are closed without
a formal complaint being filed. Participants in the
mediation are twice as satisfied with the amount of
control, respect, and fairness in the ADR process
compared with the traditional adversarial process
(88 percent satisfaction rate versus 44 percent). The
mediation program has also increased communication
in the workplace, creating lasting and beneficial
changes that help prevent future complaints. In the
first year after full implementation of this ADR
program, the number of new complaints filed by
U.S. Postal Service employees dropped by 24 percent
compared with the previous year. This translates
into thousands of fewer complaints per year, which
represents a huge cost savings, not to mention savings
in morale and productivity.

In the contracting arena, the Department of
the Air Force has used ADR to resolve more than
$1 billion in recent procurement disputes. It has used
mediation in more than 100 cases, and more than
93 percent have settled. Relations with contractors
have improved, and parties on all sides are very
pleased with the results. Due to the success of these
programs, the Secretary of the Department of the Air
Force has now committed to include ADR provisions
in its contracts and ordered employees to use ADR
"to the maximum extent practicable."

In addition to these savings in time and money,
agencies have reported other important benefits.
By emphasizing consensual resolution of disputes,
these processes allow the participants to retain control
over the outcome of the conflict. By moving away from
winning and losing, and focusing instead on problem
solving, these programs encourage the parties to
identify what they really need to get the controversy
resolved. We often see parties jointly engaged in
finding creative, mutually acceptable solutions to
disputes that no board, judge, or court would have
the authority or the knowledge to impose.

Over the coming year, we will also work with individual agencies to assist them in developing ADR programs. While our first year was devoted to offering a broad-based introduction to ADR, we see our second year as requiring work with agencies on a more individually tailored basis. We hope to draw upon the expertise of agencies that have already been using ADR successfully to persuade and assist agencies that are not as well developed in this field.

As I wrote to you when I accepted the position of chair of this Working Group, I believe that ADR has the potential to transform significantly the way that Federal departments and agencies resolve disputes. We look forward to a continuing growth in the use of ADR and the establishment of new programs that can provide our citizens with a maximum amount of respect and a minimum amount of adversity. With your continued support, we look forward to a future where all government employees facing conflict will be able to act as peacemakers and problem-solvers.

Respectfully,
Janet Reno

Report to the President on the Interagency ADR Working Group

I. Introduction

Disputes are inevitable. They arise in the course of doing our jobs as public servants and are part of life itself. Unfortunately, existing administrative systems to handle conflict are often overburdened and ineffective. They are clogged with delay, which often exacerbates the disputes, making negative feelings fester and grow. The formalistic procedures used tend to divide people rather than unite them. The parties involved in the dispute are often silenced by the process and rarely meet with each other directly. When a court or administrative body makes the final decision, parties have given up control over their own dispute. Even if the government wins a case, the relationship involved may be destroyed, and this can be far more costly in the long run.

The goal of Alternative Dispute Resolution (ADR), is to ensure that communication comes first and litigation comes last, if at all. Parties meet with a neutral third party who is trained and experienced in handling disputes, and they seek a resolution of their problem directly. Participants report that the opportunity to talk with each other, under the guidance of a dispute resolution professional, is often far more satisfying and effective than having their lawyers fight against each other before a tribunal.

The Interagency Alternative Dispute Resolution Working Group was created by Presidential Memorandum dated May 1, 1998, to assist agencies in utilizing these more effective ways to handle conflict. This Report sets forth the activities and successes of the Working Group thus far.

II. Benefits of ADR

In the Memorandum directing all Federal agencies to promote greater use of ADR, the President recognized that ADR can "make the Federal Government operate in a more efficient and effective manner." Indeed, the Working Group has found numerous examples of advantages that ADR provides. The following [list] sets forth the ten most common benefits of ADR that agencies reported to us:

Ten Common Benefits of ADR

Complaints are processed more quickly and resolved earlier.

Litigation and other costs are lower.

Future complaints are avoided as parties learn to communicate better with each other.

Parties are more satisfied with the problem solving process and with the results.

Relations with contractors and other outside parties are improved.

The process leads to more creative solutions.

Internal morale is improved.

Turnover is low.

Parties comply better with their settlement agreements.

Productivity is improved.

These benefits are demonstrated in the following specific examples from agencies that have participated in the Working Group.

United States Postal Service

The U.S. Postal Service has one of the nation's leading ADR programs in the workplace area. The average mediation takes just four hours, and the parties successfully resolve 61 percent of the cases at the mediation table. Overall, 81 percent of mediated cases are eventually closed without a formal complaint being filed. Satisfaction with the program is extremely high. Exit surveys completed anonymously by 26,000 participants show that 88 percent of employees are highly satisfied or satisfied with the amount of control, respect, and fairness in the ADR process. This figure is very significant because the satisfaction rate for the Postal Service's traditional adversarial workplace process is only 44 percent. Moreover, both employees and supervisors are equally satisfied with ADR.

Another benefit of the Postal Service program has been that mediation seems to be changing the behavior of people in the workplace. With the increased communication that mediation provides, employees and supervisors appear to be learning to get along better. In the first year after full implementation of the program, the number of complaints dropped by 24 percent as compared to the previous year. Formal complaints have continued to drop in FY 2000, by an additional 20 percent. In an agency as large as the Postal Service, this reduction of several thousand complaints per year leads to huge cost savings. Processing a simple workplace case can cost the government $5,000 in administrative expenses alone, and a more complicated case that reaches a formal adjudication can cost up to $77,000. Thus the Postal Service program saves millions of dollars each year, in addition to improving morale and productivity.

Department of the Air Force

The Air Force has found ADR very effective in the government contracts area, where it has used ADR in more than 100 cases, and more than 93 percent have settled. Of particular note is the agency's recent successful use of ADR to resolve a $785 million contract claim with the Boeing company that had been unresolved, prior to the use of ADR, for more than ten years. This is one of the largest contract claims ever settled through an alternative dispute resolution process. In another recent major case with the Northrop Grumman Corporation, the agency settled a $195 million contract claim. Litigating either of these extremely large and complex cases through trial would have been enormously expensive and uncertain in outcome. Litigation could also have damaged relationships with some of the military's most important suppliers. The Secretary of the Air Force has recognized the success of these programs and codified them in formal agency procedures. It is now official Air Force policy to use ADR "to the maximum extent practicable."

The Air Force has also used ADR in more than 7,000 workplace disputes in the last three years, with a successful resolution rate exceeding 70 percent. This ADR program has helped make the agency's EEO process one of the most efficient in the Federal government. While Federal agencies require an average of 404 days to settle an EEO complaint, Air Force settlements require an average of only 258 days, a 37 percent difference.

Another measure of the impact of ADR at the Air Force is its EEO complaint flow-through rate, which is the rate at which employees who receive counseling (including ADR) nevertheless file formal complaints. In a recent typical year, this figure was only 23 percent, which is approximately half the Federal government average. The Air Force believes its aggressive use of ADR is a major component of this success.

Department of Health and Human Services

Before using ADR, the Provider Reimbursement Review Board at the Department of Health and Human Services (HHS) had a backlog of 10,000 pending cases. Although HHS had been able to settle 90 percent of its cases without assistance, most of these settlements occurred on the eve of the hearing, after three years of delay. HHS instituted an ADR program that has saved all parties both time and money. ADR resulted in settlements of 44 of the first 48 cases where it was used. Since then, use of ADR has increased. In 1999, the Office of Hearings and Appeals completed mediation of 81 cases and had mediation underway in an additional 53 cases. ADR has also reduced the time required to resolve these disputes from three years to six months.

HHS has also used ADR successfully to resolve state government challenges involving Food Stamp and Medicaid claim adjustments. All of the forty-one states that elected mediation under the Departmental Appeals Board's mediation program have successfully negotiated settlements. ADR has resolved more than $500 million in disputed funds in each of the past five years, and HHS estimates that it has saved the Federal government $600,000 in potential adjudication costs. In addition, the process saved considerable time, because administrative appeals could have taken two years, while mediation took an average of nine months. Finally, by the parties' own assessment, mediation allowed for a fairer and less acrimonious settlement of differences, preserving ongoing relationships between state and Federal officials involved.

Department of Energy

Ombuds staff at the Sandia National Laboratories assisted employees in more than 400 cases during FY 1999. Ombuds personnel counseled employees on available options for handling their disputes and advised them on how to proceed. Most of the work was with agency employees, but agency suppliers and technology transfer partners also used the ombuds services in some cases. Benefits of the program included improved productivity, lower turnover, and higher decision quality. The agency believes that a conservative estimate of the program's savings last year is $600,000 (50% more than the program cost). The program also generated considerable improvements in morale. Litigation and EEOC charges against Sandia have dropped well below the levels experienced prior to the creation of the program.

Federal Emergency Management Agency

After Hurricane Georges wreaked havoc on the Island of Puerto Rico in September 1998, a local community had disputes regarding a debris removal contract, including disagreements as to which company actually performed the work, the total amount of debris, and the amounts of money owed to the companies. This difficult situation was further complicated by an FBI criminal investigation, the incarceration of the community mayor, litigation filed against the community by a subcontractor, allegations of fraud and conspiracy by all parties, death threats, and bankruptcy petitions. Without a consensual resolution, expensive and time consuming litigation involving all parties to the seven relevant contracts was virtually inevitable.

FEMA suggested mediation. The Governor, the local community, and the three contractors agreed. The mediation was very difficult, but the mediators were able to craft an acceptable agreement. The principal contractor later wrote a letter to FEMA saying the following: "I write this letter to praise certain individuals who have gone above and beyond the call of duty in representing FEMA and the people of the United States. Through [FEMA's] initiative and good judgment, mediation was arranged. . . . Had [FEMA] not pursued the matter with uncommon vigor, it would probably be wrapped up in court for many years."

Federal Labor Relations Authority

The FLRA has instituted an ADR program that encourages agencies and unions to resolve their problems before an unfair labor practice charge is filed. Following implementation of this program, the number of charges filed has fallen sharply, from 8,764 in 1993 to 5,686 in 1999. Even in instances where charges are not resolved and complaints are issued, these disputes as well are settling through the use of ADR. For example, 12.4 percent of all complaints went to trial in 1993. In 1999, only 9.2 percent of complaints went to trial. Significantly, cases are settling more quickly as well. The number of expensive, last-minute "courthouse steps" settlements (settlements reached immediately prior to hearing) have declined to just 1.9 percent of all settlements as parties have used ADR to settle their cases earlier in the process. In earlier years, these costly late settlements comprised as many as 15 percent of all settled matters.

Environmental Protection Agency

The Environmental Protection Agency (EPA) used a variety of ADR processes to facilitate settlement of the GE Pittsfield case, involving the cleanup of widespread contamination of the Housatonic River in Massachusetts. The agency used mediation to facilitate settlement discussions between eleven parties including EPA, GE, and other state and Federal regulatory agencies. The team of mediators assisted the parties in reaching agreement on a wide range of difficult issues including the cleanup of contaminated sediments and restoration of natural resources. EPA values the work to be accomplished by GE pursuant to this settlement at upwards of $200 million. Without the use of ADR, according to the EPA, negotiations among this large group of parties would have been very difficult. ADR has also permitted the parties to fashion their own remedy, including elements that a court would not have been able to order on its own. For example, in order to ensure meaningful public input, a neutral facilitator organized and is facilitating meetings of a Citizens Coordinating Council. The Council is composed of representatives of local communities affected by the cleanup. Finally, the parties established a neutral peer review process to resolve conflicts regarding technical aspects of the required remedial activities.

The EPA has also used three different types of ADR to resolve the Helen Kramer Landfill Federal and state litigation, concerning contamination at a hazardous waste site in New Jersey. EPA provided an internal convening professional to help the parties organize settlement efforts and retain a mediator. The efforts of the convener enabled a large group of defendants to coalesce and enter into a mediation agreement. Two experienced mediators then assisted the parties in reaching an agreement on the allocation of costs associated with remedial activities at the site. Finally, the parties entered into mediated discussions with EPA to resolve their liability for site contamination. The complex convening and mediations involved more than 200 parties and third-party defendants, including forty-four municipalities. The resulting settlement totaled more than $95 million. The agency believes that this case would have been enormously time-consuming and expensive to litigate if ADR had not been used.

III. Accomplishments of the Working Group

The Working Group expects that success stories such as those described above will continue across the government as more agencies use ADR in the future. Our major goal for this first year was to assist every agency in creating at least one new ADR program or substantially enhancing an existing program. We are pleased to report that every cabinet agency and most administrative agencies met this goal.

The Working Group has built upon earlier government initiatives to increase the use of ADR. In 1996, Congress permanently enacted the Administrative Dispute Resolution Act, 5 U.S.C. secs. 571–584, which requires all executive agencies to promote the use of ADR. Specifically, this Act directs each agency to do the following:

- Adopt a policy that addresses the use of alternative means of dispute resolution;
- Designate a senior official to be the dispute resolution specialist of the agency;
- Provide ADR training on a regular basis; and
- Review each of its standard agreements for contracts, grants, and other assistance to encourage the use of alternative means of dispute resolution.

All agencies now have a senior official designated as their dispute resolution specialist. All cabinet agencies and most administrative agencies now have adopted ADR policy statements. Most agencies provide ADR training, and many have been taking advantage of the resources of the Working Group in this regard. With the assistance of the Contracts Section of the Working Group, agencies are increasing their use of ADR in the contracting arena as well.

In preparing this report, we conducted the first government-wide tabulation of Federal ADR resources. We learned that some 410 employees now work full time on ADR in the Federal government. Agency ADR programs now receive $36 million annually in dedicated budgets. Moreover, many agencies staff ADR programs through the use of collateral duty employees and fund these operations from their general budgets. Counting these resources, the government's total commitment is even higher than the figures mentioned above.

Working Group Activities

The Working Group began on September 14, 1998, with an initial organizing meeting hosted by the Attorney General and the Deputy Director for Management at the Office of Management and Budget.

More than one hundred high-level representatives from nearly sixty Federal agencies attended this meeting. At this meeting, the Attorney General gave all agencies the goal of creating at least one new ADR program or substantially increasing an existing program by the end of 1999.

To assist agencies in developing specific programs to meet this goal, the Working Group created four Sections, organized by subject matter, to provide technical assistance and guidance on best practices in ADR program development. Sections have operated simultaneously to cover disputes in the following areas: civil enforcement, claims against the government, contracts and procurement, and workplace.

The Sections have conducted more than fifty training sessions, meetings, and colloquia on all aspects of ADR. Representatives from across the government have been participating. Topics have included incentives for Federal employees to use ADR, finding quality neutrals, designing an ADR training program, dispute systems design, evaluation of ADR programs, obtaining resources for ADR programs, overcoming barriers to ADR, ethics, confidentiality, and conflict assessment/case selection.

Materials Created by the Working Group

The Working Group has produced substantial materials to assist agencies in developing ADR programs. Most noteworthy are two resource books covering best practices in ADR. The *Federal ADR Program Manager's Resource Manual* is more than 200 pages long, and it is a comprehensive guide to creating and operating an ADR program in the Federal government. It includes relevant laws and regulations, links to Federal and private websites, and an extensive bibliography. *The Electronic Guide to Federal Procurement ADR* is an exhaustive manual covering procurement ADR programs, managing the process, training, neutrals, and resources. The guide includes hyperlinks to ADR-related materials, a listing of Federal ADR mentors, detailed profiles of existing procurement ADR programs, success stories, and sample ADR agreements. Both of these manuals are available on the website for all Federal employees and interested members of the public.

The Group created a website at www.financenet.gov/iadrwg that has had tens of thousands of requests for information in the year it has been in existence. The website includes agendas and minutes from Working Group meetings. A number of key ADR-related documents are available on the site, including the Administrative Dispute Resolution Act, the Presidential Memorandum creating the Working Group, a model Policy Statement on ADR, and a statement of key elements of a successful ADR program. The site includes additional links to other Federal agency ADR programs and private sector ADR organizations.

The Forums section of the website provides an opportunity for users to exchange information electronically (via e-mail) and to tap into the ADR-related expertise of hundreds of others around the country who are involved in government ADR programs. This feature of the website has facilitated productive discussions on such topics as recommendations of qualified neutrals, the availability and development of ADR training courses, and establishment of ADR policy.

To capture the current state of ADR in the Federal government, the Working Group asked each participating agency to complete an ADR survey on its activities. These surveys include contact information for each agency's dispute resolution specialist and ADR staff, data on its dedicated ADR budget and employees, a description of its ADR programs, success stories from these programs, and a statement of its ADR goals for the future. All of these surveys are available on the Working Group website.

Accomplishments of the Sections

The Civil Enforcement Section has provided participating agencies with information, training, and support to enable them to develop ADR programs in enforcement and compliance activities. Twenty-six agencies with unique statutory and regulatory missions, requirements, and regulated communities have participated in Section activities. Section consultation teams provided personalized assistance to agencies in a wide variety of areas, from dispute system design to training. Robert Ward of the EPA served as chair of the Section, with the assistance of David Batson and Lee Scharf of the EPA.

The Claims Against the Government Section has worked with agencies to use dispute resolution techniques to supplement traditional administrative adjudication of claims for money that are filed against the government. More than forty representatives from twenty different agencies have participated in the work of the Section, which was chaired by Peter Steenland of the Justice Department, with the assistance of Jeff Senger of the Justice Department.

The Contracts and Procurement Section has focused on assisting agencies with developing and operating ADR programs in the contracting arena. More than thirty agencies participated in the work of the Section. In addition to holding meetings on program design, ADR process, training, and neutrals, the Section produced the Electronic Guide to Federal Procurement ADR described above. The Section was chaired by Brigadier General Frank Anderson of the Air Force, with the assistance of Joseph McDade and Major Becky Weirick of the Air Force, as well as Tony Palladino and Rich Walters of the Federal Aviation Administration.

The Workplace Section, which was the largest in the Working Group, covered a broad range of workplace issues, including Equal Employment Opportunity, Federal Labor Relations Act, and Merit Systems Protection Board cases as well as grievances. Total attendance at the twenty-six programs the Section sponsored totaled more than 1,000 participants. Section mentoring programs resulted in the formation of the Small Agency Caucus, an organization devoted to addressing the unique ADR program and resource needs of small Federal agencies. The Workplace Section was chaired by Erica Cooper of the Federal Deposit Insurance Corporation (FDIC) and Mary Elcano of the United States Postal Service (USPS), with the assistance of Cathy Costantino and Martha McClellan of the FDIC, and Cindy Hallberlin and Kim Brown of the USPS.

Further information about these accomplishments is provided in the Reports from the Sections to the Attorney General attached at the end of this report.

Plans for the Future

During the second year of its existence, the Working Group plans to offer additional seminars and discussions that are open to all government employees. We also plan to focus on mentoring agencies that desire to create new programs or improve existing ones. We will continue to offer consultation teams of experienced ADR professionals to assist agencies with their ADR efforts on an individualized basis.

The Working Group will also coordinate with the newly created ADR Council, a group of senior executives who will develop ADR policy guidance for the executive branch. This Council will focus on issues that cut across ADR programs at all agencies, such as confidentiality, best practices, and procedures for the use of arbitration.

IV. Conclusion

Congress effectively summarized the problems with traditional administrative approaches to conflict and the benefits of ADR when it passed the Administrative Dispute Resolution Act of 1990:

> [A]dministrative proceedings have become increasingly formal, costly, and lengthy resulting in unnecessary expenditures of time and in a decreased likelihood of achieving consensual resolution of disputes; alternative means of dispute resolution . . . in appropriate circumstances, have yielded decisions that are faster, less expensive, and less contentious; such alternative means can lead to more creative, efficient, and sensible outcomes.

> With the continued assistance and support of the President, the Office of Management and Budget, and all participating agencies, we look forward to working together to use these processes to enhance the operation of the Government and better serve the public.

Notes

Preface

1. ADR touches so many other fields that it is not possible to cover them all in a book of manageable size. For example, this book does not directly address the use of ADR to resolve matters of public policy, such as developing government regulations or deciding where to locate an airport runway. Readers interested in this field can consult L. Susskind, S. McKearnan, and J. Thomas-Larmer, *Consensus Building Handbook* (Thousand Oaks, Calif.: Sage, 1999), and review the Negotiated Rulemaking Act, U.S. Code, Title 5, sec. 561–570a. Nor does this book address ADR in the criminal context, which has been used only sparingly at the federal level. Readers can learn more by consulting M. S. Umreit, *The Handbook of Victim Offender Mediation: An Essential Guide to Practice and Research* (San Francisco: Jossey-Bass, 2001). The book also does not cover ethics. Although this is a vital field, the government has not yet adopted an ethical code specifically applying to ADR. Instead, ethical rules applying to government ADR can vary depending on the subject matter of the case and the jurisdiction where it is located. Readers interested in this topic can consult CPR-Georgetown Commission on Ethics and Standards in ADR, *Proposed Model Rule of Professional Conduct for the Lawyer as Third Party Neutral* (New York: CPR Institute for Dispute Resolution, 1999); American Arbitration Association, American Bar Association, and Society of Professionals in Dispute Resolution, *Model Standards of Conduct for Mediators* (New York: American Arbitration Association, 1995); and R.A.B. Bush, "The Dilemmas of Mediation Practice: A Study of Ethical Dilemmas and Policy Implications," *Journal of Dispute Resolution* 1 (1994): 1–55.

Chapter One

1. The dominant form of ADR in the federal government is mediation, with parties choosing it about 95 percent of the time they use ADR. Therefore, the terms *ADR* and *neutral* in this book will refer

mainly to mediation and mediators, following the terminology used in the government. However, the government does use other processes, particularly in certain subject areas, which will be covered separately where appropriate.

2. *U.S. Code,* Title. 5, sec. 571 and note (Congressional Findings).

3. W. Burger, "Our Vicious Legal Spiral," *Judges Journal* 16 (1977): 49.

4. J. Reno, Address at the Meeting of the American Judicature Society Chicago Bar Association Standard Club, Feb. 5, 1998.

5. Federal Interagency ADR Working Group, *Report of the Interagency Alternative Dispute Resolution Working Group to the President of the United States* (Washington, D.C.: Federal Interagency ADR Working Group, 2000), 6.

6. Ibid.

7. Administrative Office of the United States Courts, *U.S. District Court Judicial Caseload Profile* (Washington, D.C.: Administrative Office of the United States Courts, 2001); W. Burger, "Remarks to the American Bar Association," *ABA Journal* 68 (1982): 274.

8. The Executive Office for United States Attorneys reports that 79,854 civil cases were filed or responded to by U.S. attorneys in fiscal year 2001. U.S. Department of Justice, *U.S. Attorney Annual Statistical Report* (Washington, D.C.: U.S. Department of Justice, 2001). The Administrative Office of the United States Courts reports that 250,907 civil cases were filed in U.S. district courts in fiscal year 2001. Administrative Office of the United States Courts, *Judicial Business of the U.S. Courts: 1999 Annual Report of the Director* (Washington, D.C.: Administrative Office of the United States Courts, 2001).

9. In fiscal year 2001, for example, U.S. Attorneys' Offices took 1,266 civil cases to trial out of a total of 74,558 civil cases that were terminated during that period. U.S. Department of Justice, *U.S. Attorney Annual Statistical Report* (Washington, D.C.: U.S. Department of Justice, 2002).

10. A. P. Lofaro, "ADR in the Federal Workplace: Why It Is Needed, How It Can Help, and Some Cautions to Observe," in M. Breger, G. Schatz, and D. Laufer (eds.), *Federal Administrative Dispute Resolution Deskbook* (Chicago: American Bar Association, 2001), 407.

11. Ibid.

12. Office of Special Counsel, *Application for Office of Personnel Management Director's Award for Outstanding Alternative Dispute Resolution Program* (Washington, D.C.: Office of Special Counsel, 2002).

13. Federal Aviation Administration Office of Dispute Resolution for Acquisition, *Case Management Statistics* (Washington, D.C.: Federal Aviation Administration, 2001).

14. J. M. Senger, "Evaluation of ADR in United States Attorney Cases," *United States Attorneys' Bulletin* 48 (2000): 26.

15. U.S. Department of the Air Force, *Nomination for the Office of Federal Procurement Policy's ADR Award* (Washington, D.C.: U.S. Department of the Air Force, 2001), 3.

16. Senger, "Evaluation of ADR in United States Attorney Cases," 26.

17. Office of Special Counsel, *Application for Office of Personnel Management Director's Award for Outstanding Alternative Dispute Resolution Program.*

18. Federal Interagency ADR Working Group, *Report of the Interagency Alternative Dispute Resolution Working Group to the President,* 3.

19. U.S. Equal Employment Opportunity Commission, *Annual Report on the Federal Work Force* (Washington, D.C.: U.S. Equal Employment Opportunity Commission, 2001).

20. Senger, "Evaluation of ADR in United States Attorney Cases," 26.

21. Office of Special Counsel, *Application for Office of Personnel Management Director's Award for Outstanding Alternative Dispute Resolution Program.*

22. U.S. Department of the Air Force, *Nomination for the Office of Federal Procurement Policy's ADR Award,* 2.

23. B. Saxton, "How Well Do Jurors Understand Jury Instructions? A Field Test Using Real Juries and Real Trials in Wyoming," *Land and Water Law Review* 33 (1998): 59.

24. Ibid.

25. Dwight Golann conducted empirical research and found that mediation can assist parties in creating integrative settlements, but that full reconciliation between the parties is relatively rare. D. Golann, "Is Legal Mediation a Process of Repair—or Separation? An Empirical Study and Its Implications," *Harvard Negotiation Law Review* 7 (2002): 301–336.

26. Federal Interagency ADR Working Group, *Report of the Interagency Alternative Dispute Resolution Working Group to the President of the United States,* 2–3.

27. Ibid.

28. U.S. Department of the Air Force, *Nomination for the Office of Personnel Management Director's Award,* 6.

29. Federal Interagency ADR Working Group, *Report of the Interagency Alternative Dispute Resolution Working Group,* 2.

30. Ibid.

31. Ibid.

32. E. P. McDermott, R. Obar, A. Jose, and M. Bowers, *An Evaluation of the EEOC Mediation Program* 1 (Washington, D.C.: U.S. Equal Employment Opportunity Commission, 2000), 1.

33. "2001: A Timeline," *Cincinnati Enquirer,* Dec. 30, 2001.

34. Federal Interagency ADR Working Group, *Report of the Interagency Alternative Dispute Resolution Working Group*, 3.
35. Ibid.
36. Policy Directive from the Secretary of the Air Force to the U.S. Department of the Air Force, Apr. 1, 1999.
37. For a discussion of ways to use ADR effectively in cases involving government principles, see D. Golann, "If You're Willing to Experiment, 'Principle' Cases Can Be Mediated," *Alternatives to the High Cost of Litigation* 16 (1998): 50–51.
38. See S. B. Goldberg, F.E.A. Sander, and N. H. Rogers, *Dispute Resolution, Negotiation, Mediation, and Other Processes,* 3rd ed. (New York: Aspen Law and Business, 1999), 6–7.
39. *Statutes at Large of the United States* (1888), 25:501.
40. Ibid. (1898), 30:424.
41. Ibid. (1913), 38:103.
42. *U.S. Code,* Title 45, sec. 154.
43. *Statutes at Large of the United States* (1913), 37:736.
44. Ibid. (1947), 61:153.
45. Ibid. (1925), 42:883, codified as amended at *U.S. Code,* Title 9, sec. 1–16.
46. See C. A. Wright, A. R. Miller, and M. K. Kane, *Federal Practice and Procedure Civil,* 2nd ed. (St. Paul, Minn.: West, 1990), 6A, 1522.
47. *Statutes at Large of the United States* (1946), 60:237, (codified as amended at *U.S. Code,* Title 5, sec. 701 et seq.)
48. 42 *U.S. Code,* Title 42, sec. 2000g et seq.
49. F.E.A. Sander, "Varieties of Dispute Processing," *Federal Rules Decisions* 70 (1976): 111.
50. Ibid.
51. Ibid.
52. G. B. Bell, "The Pound Conference Follow-Up: A Response from the United States Department of Justice," *Federal Rules Decisions* 76 (1978): 321.
53. See L. B. Solum, "2020 Vision: A Plan for the Future of California's Courts," *Southern California Law Review* 66 (1993): 2162–2164.
54. *U.S. Code,* Title 5, sec. 7101 et seq.
55. *Statutes at Large of the United States* (1980), 94:17.
56. *U.S. Code,* Title 28, secs. 471–482.
57. U.S. Senate, Judiciary Committee, *Judicial Improvements Act of 1990,* S. Rept. 416, 101st Cong., 2nd sess., 1990, 28.
58. For additional information on the early implementation of this act, see Administrative Conference of the United States, *Implementing the ADR Act: Guidance for Agency Dispute Resolution Specialists* (Washing-

ton, D.C.: Administrative Office of the United States Courts, 1992), and Administrative Conference of the United States, *Toward Improved Agency Dispute Resolution: Implementing the ADR Act* (Washington, D.C.: Administrative Office of the United States Courts, 1995).

59. *U.S. Code,* Title 5, sec. 571 and note (Congressional Findings).
60. Ibid. (Promotion of Alternative Means of Dispute Resolution).
61. Ibid.
62. Ibid.
63. Ibid.
64. Ibid.
65. Ibid., secs. 575, 580–581.
66. Ibid., sec. 552; see also P. J. Harter, "Neither Cop nor Collection Agent: Encouraging Administrative Settlements by Ensuring Mediator Confidentiality," *Administrative Law Review* 41 (1989): 335–337.
67. For a summary of the legislative history of the 1990 and 1996 acts, see W. F. Funk, J. S. Lubbers, and C. Pou Jr., *Federal Administrative Procedure Sourcebook,* 3rd ed. (Chicago: American Bar Association, 2000), 297–300.
68. *U.S. Code,* Title 5, secs. 575, 580–581.
69. Ibid., sec. 574(j).
70. Ibid., Title 28, sec. 651 note (Findings and Declaration of Policy)
71. Ibid., secs. 651–658.
72. Executive Order 12,778, *Federal Register,* Oct. 23, 1991, 55,195–55,196.
73. Ibid.
74. Executive Order 12,988, *Federal Register,* Feb. 5, 1996, 4,729.
75. Memorandum from the President of the United States to the Heads of Executive Departments and Agencies, May 1, 1998.
76. Ibid.
77. Memorandum from the Attorney General to All Offices, Boards, and Divisions, Apr. 6, 1995.
78. Notices: Department of Justice, Policy on the Use of Alternative Dispute Resolution, and Case Identification Criteria for Alternative Dispute Resolution, *Federal Register,* July 15, 1996, 36,895.
79. Ibid., 36,896.
80. Executive Order 9646, *Federal Register,* Oct. 25, 1945, 13,391.

Chapter Two

1. The U.S. Department of Justice has issued guidelines for the types of cases it believes are appropriate for ADR. *Federal Register,* July 15, 1996, 36,895. In these guidelines, each of the components of the Justice Department that uses ADR sets forth the criteria it uses to select cases for these processes.

2. See generally K. Arrow and others (eds.), *Barriers to Conflict Resolution* (New York: Norton, 1995).

3. See L. Ross, "Reactive Devaluation in Negotiation and Conflict Resolution," in ibid., 26–42.

4. See D. Lax and J. Sebenius, *The Manager as Negotiator* (New York: Free Press, 1987), 29–45.

5. See I. Ayres and B. J. Nalebuff, "Common Knowledge as a Barrier to Negotiation," *U.C.L.A. Law Review* 44 (1997): 1631.

6. Under the Administrative Dispute Resolution Act, the final written agreement reached as a result of a dispute resolution proceeding is not confidential. See *U.S. Code,* Title 5, sec. 571(5). In federal court litigation, Justice Department policy generally requires that settlement documents be available to the public.

7. The Administrative Dispute Resolution Act sets forth six situations where ADR may not be appropriate: (1) a definitive or authoritative resolution of the matter is required for precedential value, and such a proceeding is not likely to be accepted generally as an authoritative precedent; (2) the matter involves or may bear on significant questions of government policy that require additional procedures before a final resolution may be made, and such a proceeding would not likely serve to develop a recommended policy for the agency; (3) maintaining established policies is of special importance, so that variations among individual decisions are not increased and such a proceeding would not likely reach consistent results among individual decisions; (4) the matter significantly affects persons or organizations who are not parties to the proceeding; (5) a full public record of the proceeding is important, and a dispute resolution proceeding cannot provide such a record; and (6) the agency must maintain continuing jurisdiction over the matter with authority to alter the disposition in the light of changed circumstances, and a dispute resolution proceeding would interfere with the agency's fulfilling that requirement. *U.S. Code,* Title 5, sec. 572(b).

8. For example, criminal grand jury evidence is secret, and disclosing it to outside parties can constitute contempt of court. *Federal Rule of Criminal Procedure* 6(e).

9. See U.S. Department of Justice, "No Compromise of Civil Liability When Criminal Case Pending," in *United States Attorneys' Manual,* secs. 6–6.200, 2003.

10. The Eastern District of Virginia, for example, is known as the "rocket docket" because civil trials take place an average of ten months after the complaint is filed, an unusually short period of time. Administrative Office of the U.S. Courts, *Federal Court Management Statistics*

(Washington, D.C.: Administrative Office of the U.S. Courts, 2001).

11. J. Reno, address at the Meeting of the American Judicature Society and Chicago Bar Association, Feb. 5, 1998.

12. A. F. Acland, *Resolving Disputes Without Going to Court* (New York: Random House 1995), 29.

13. R. Cudjoe, address at United States Agency for International Development, Abuja, Nigeria, Apr. 5, 2001.

14. *U.S. Code,* Title 28, secs. 471–482.

15. Ibid., Title 5, secs. 571 and note (Congressional Findings).

16. Ibid., Title 28, secs. 651–652.

17. Executive Order No. 12,988, *Federal Register,* Feb. 5, 1996, 4,729.

18. The Administrative Dispute Resolution Act requires every agency to "adopt a policy that addresses the use of alternative means of dispute resolution." *U.S. Code,* Title 5, secs. 571–584.

19. It also is worth noting that offering ADR can be seen as a sign of strength, not weakness. Suggesting ADR implies that a party is confident enough of its positions that it is willing to discuss the case openly with a neutral party.

20. Binding arbitration is the only ADR process where the parties surrender final control to an outside party.

21. For the definitive analysis of the advantages and disadvantages of the different types of ADR, see F. Sander and S. Goldberg, "Fitting the Forum to the Fuss: A User-Friendly Guide to Selecting an ADR Procedure," *Negotiation Journal* 10 (1994): 49.

22. See M. Irvine, "Serving Two Masters: The Obligation Under the Rules of Professional Conduct to Report Attorney Misconduct in a Confidential Mediation," *Rutgers Law Journal* 26 (1994): 158 n. 13.

23. Research establishing the benefits of ADR in the federal government is described in Chapter Ten.

24. See E. Plapinger and D. Stienstra, *ADR and Settlement in the Federal District Courts* (Washington, D.C.: Federal Judicial Center, 1996), 99–102.

25. See Administrative Dispute Resolution Act, *U.S. Code,* Title 5, sec. 574.

26. See J. W. Cooley, *Mediation Advocacy* (Notre Dame, Ind.: National Institute of Trial Advocacy, 2002), 211–213; Plapinger and Stienstra, *ADR and Settlement in the Federal District Courts,* 67–69.

27. One difference between these processes is that early neutral evaluation is generally more informal than nonbinding arbitration, which tends to follow a carefully prescribed format.

28. The original Administrative Dispute Resolution Act included an "opt-out" provision, whereby an agency head could choose to nullify the award of an arbitrator. Private litigants were understandably reluctant

to agree to arbitration knowing that they were bound by the result but the government was not. In 1995, the Justice Department issued an opinion that the U.S. Constitution did not prohibit arbitration. Memorandum of Assistant Attorney General Walter Dellinger to Associate Attorney General John Schmidt, Sept. 7, 1995. Congress amended the Administrative Dispute Resolution Act in 1996 to remove the opt-out provision, permitting the government to participate fully in arbitration.

29. *U.S. Code,* Title 5, sec. 575(a)(1).
30. Ibid., sec. 575(a)(2).
31. Ibid., sec. 575(a)(3).
32. Ibid., sec. 572(b).
33. A useful guide for agencies in developing arbitration programs is Federal ADR Council, "Developing Guidance for Binding Arbitration—A Handbook for Federal Agencies," *Federal Register,* Aug. 16, 2000, 50,005–50,014.
34. Thus far, the only agencies to issue arbitration guidance are the Federal Deposit Insurance Corporation, *Federal Register,* Apr. 10, 2001, 18,632–18,633; the Federal Aviation Administration, *Federal Register,* Oct. 15, 2001, 52,475; and the Federal Motor Carrier Safety Administration (Attorney General Memorandum, Mar. 6, 2003).
35. *U.S. Code,* Title 5, sec. 575(a)(2).
36. Ibid., sec. 575(b).
37. Ibid., sec. 578.
38. Ibid., sec. 579(c)(5).
39. Ibid., sec. 580(a)(1).
40. Ibid., sec. 580(d).
41. Ibid., Title 9, sec. 10.
42. Ibid., sec. 11.
43. Ibid., Title 26, sec. 7123(b)(2).
44. Ibid., Title 42, sec. 9622(h)(2); *Code of Federal Regulations,* Title 40, sec. 304.
45. *Statutes at Large of the United States* (1978), 92:1111, Civil Service Reform Act of 1978 (codified as amended in various sections of *U.S. Code,* Title 5); Executive Order 11,491, *Federal Register,* Oct. 29, 1969, 17,605.
46. The ADRA provides that parties "shall be entitled to participate in the selection of the arbitrator." *U.S. Code,* Title 5, sec. 577(a).
47. The ADRA does not provide for confidentiality of the final arbitral award. *U.S. Code,* Title 5, sec. 571(5). Many agencies have policies that the outcome of claims must be public.
48. Some critics have claimed that the word *arbitrator* comes from a combination of the word *arbitrary* and the word *traitor.*

49. For example, the doctrine of sovereign immunity and defenses involving discretionary functions apply only to the government.

50. Because the process takes place with all parties present, the ADRA does not provide for general confidentiality of parties' arbitration communications. *U.S. Code,* Title 5, sec. 574(b)(7).

Chapter Three

1. 5 *U.S. Code,* Title 5, sec. 573(a).

2. Ibid., sec. 573(d). This section also provides that an agency may choose whether to agree to reimburse another agency for all or part of the cost of a collateral duty neutral.

3. The Sharing Neutrals Program received the 2002 Office of Personnel Management Director's Award for Outstanding Alternative Dispute Resolution Programs.

4. *U.S. Code,* Title 42, secs. 2000g–2000g-3.

5. See J. J. Alfini, "Risk of Coercion Too Great: Judges Should Not Mediate Cases Assigned to Them for Trial," *Dispute Resolution Magazine* 5 (1999): 13; F.E.A. Sander, "A Friendly Amendment," *Dispute Resolution Magazine* 5 (1999): 22. The Federal Judicial Conference's Committee on Codes of Conduct recognizes some of the concerns raised by this practice: "Judges must be mindful of the effect settlement discussions can have not only on their own objectivity and impartiality but also on the appearance of their objectivity and impartiality. Despite a judge's best efforts there may be instances where information obtained during settlement discussions could influence a judge's decision-making during trial. Parties who have confronted deficiencies in their cases, or who have negotiated candidly as to the value of their claims, may question whether the judge can set aside this knowledge in a case tried to the judge, whereas in a case tried to a jury, there may be less reason to question the judge's impartiality." Administrative Office of the United States Courts, Advisory Opinion No. 95, Judges Acting in a Settlement Capacity (Washington, D.C.: Administrative Office of the U.S. Courts, 1999).

6. See generally R.A.B. Bush and J. P. Folger, *The Promise of Mediation* (San Francisco: Jossey-Bass, 1994).

7. See C. Honeyman, "Patterns of Bias in Mediation," *Journal of Dispute Resolution* 1985 (1985): 141–149.

8. Neutrals paid by the case receive their fee at the conclusion of the ADR, regardless of whether the case settles. Contingent fee arrangements, where neutrals receive fees only when they settle a case, are almost universally forbidden in ADR contexts, out of concern that neutrals might coerce parties into inappropriate settlements in order to get paid.

9. Depending on the terms of the arbitration agreement, all three arbitrators can be neutral, or the arbitrators chosen by the parties can be expected to represent the interests of the party that selected them.

10. In some cases, private parties that preferred to use a particularly expensive neutral have agreed to pay more than half of the fee. In rare cases, the government has agreed to pay more than half of the fee when private parties would have been unable to participate otherwise. However, the government has found that ADR is much more effective when both sides pay for it, as this increases their motivation to participate fully.

11. The Federal Acquisition Streamlining Act provides that full and open competitive procedures are not required "to procure the services of [a] neutral for use in any part of an alternative resolution or negotiated rulemaking process." *U.S. Code,* Title 10, sec. 2304(c)(3).

12. Ibid., Title 5, secs. 571–584.

13. Ibid., sec. 574.

Chapter Four

1. J. M. Senger, T. Nabatchi, and L. B. Bingham, unpublished research. The study used a regression model, finding an R^2 of .595 and an adjusted R^2 of .591. This indicates that the model explained almost 60 percent of the variance in time to disposition for cases where ADR was used. The probability that this result is due to chance is less than .000.

2. Federal Interagency ADR Working Group, *Report of the Interagency Alternative Dispute Resolution Working Group to the President of the United States* (Washington, D.C.: Federal Interagency ADR Working Group, 2000), 3.

3. Ibid., 4.

4. J. M. Senger, "Evaluation of ADR in United States Attorneys' Cases," *United States Attorneys' Bulletin* 48 (2000): 25–26.

5. Another factor may be that cases that are easy to settle already would have been resolved at the administrative stage and would never reach federal court.

6. Senger, "Evaluation of ADR," 25.

7. T. Arnold, "Twenty Common Errors in Mediation Advocacy," *Alternatives to the High Cost of Litigation* 15 (1995): 70.

8. See R. Fisher, W. Ury, and B. Patton, *Getting to Yes: Negotiating Agreement Without Giving In,* 2nd ed. (New York: Penguin Books, 1991).

9. Ibid., 95–106.

10. See *U.S. Code,* Title 28, sec. 515.

11. See U.S. Department of Justice, *U.S. Attorney Annual Statistical Report* (Washington, D.C.: U.S. Department of Justice, 1999), 76.

12. *Code of Federal Regulations,* Title 28, sec. 0.160–0.172.

13. See "Memorandum of Guidance on Implementation of the Litigation Reforms of Executive Order 12,998," *Federal Register,* July 22, 1997, 39,252: "Litigation counsel . . . should not be expected to have the authority to bind the government finally. . . . Final settlement authority is governed by regulations and may be exercised only by the officials designated in those regulations."

14. 42 *U.S. Code,* Title 42, secs. 9622(d)(2) and (i), 7413(g); *Code of Federal Regulations,* Title 28, sec. 50.7.

15. Federal Rules of Civil Procedure, Advisory Committee Notes to Rule 16(c) (1993).

16. U.S. Senate, Judiciary Committee, *Report on the Judicial Improvements Act of 1990,* S. Rept. 416, 101st Cong., 2nd sess., 1990, 124; U.S. House, Judiciary Committee, *Report on the Judicial Improvements Act of 1990,* H.R. 416, 101st Cong., 2nd sess., 1990, 44.

17. *In re M.P.W. Stone,* 986 F.2d 898, 904 (5th Circuit 1993).

18. Ibid., 905.

19. Ibid.

20. *In re United States,* 149 F.3d 332, 334 (5th Cir. 1998).

21. *U.S. Code,* Title 5, sec. 574(b)(7).

Chapter Five

1. For useful general resources on ADR advocacy, see J. W. Cooley, *Mediation Advocacy,* 2nd ed. (Notre Dame, Ind.: National Institute of Trial Advocacy, 2002); D. Golann, *Mediating Legal Disputes: Effective Strategies for Lawyers and Mediators* (New York: Aspen Law and Business, 2001); and J. W. Cooley and S. Lubet, *Arbitration Advocacy* (Notre Dame, Ind.: National Institute of Trial Advocacy, 1997).

2. See N. A. Welsh, "Making Deals in Court-Connected Mediation: What's Justice Got to Do with It?" *Washington University Law Quarterly* 79 (2001): 787.

3. See J. R. Cohen, "Advising Clients to Apologize," *Southern California Law Review* 79 (1999): 1009.

4. See R. E. Creo, "A Pie Chart Tool to Resolve MultiParty, Multi-Issue Conflicts," *Alternatives to the High Cost of Litigation* 18 (2000): 90.

5. See C. Honeyman, "Confidential, More or Less," *Dispute Resolution Magazine* 5 (1999): 12–13.

6. See, for example, L. Ross, "Reactive Devaluation in Negotiation and Conflict Resolution," in K. J. Arrow and others (eds.), *Barriers to Conflict Resolution* (New York: Norton, 1995), 27.

7. See J. M. Senger and C. Honeyman, "Cracking the Hard-Boiled Student: Some Ways to Turn Research Findings into Interactive Exercises," *Conflict Resolution Practitioner* 1 (2001): 31.

8. See R. H. Mnookin, S. R. Peppet, and A. S. Tulumello, *Beyond Winning: Negotiating to Create Value in Deals and Disputes* (Cambridge, Mass.: Harvard University Press, 2000), for a discussion of the tension between empathy and assertiveness in negotiation.

9. See D. P. Hoffer, "Decision Analysis as a Mediator's Tool," *Harvard Negotiation Law Review* 1 (1996): 113.

10. For a discussion of advocacy considerations involved with evaluation, see D. Golann, "Benefits and Dangers of Mediation Evaluation," *Alternatives to the High Cost of Litigation* 15 (1997): 35–38, and D. Golann, "Planning for Mediation Evaluation," *Alternatives to the High Cost of Litigation* 15 (1997): 56–58.

11. *Notification and Federal Employee Anti-Retaliation Act of 2002*, U.S. Public Law 107–174, 107th Cong., 2nd sess., 2002.

12. See, for example, A. Tversky and D. Kahneman, "Judgments Under Uncertainty: Heuristics and Biases," *Science* 185 (1974): 1124–1131.

13. See, for example, R. S. Adler and E. M. Silverstein, "When David Meets Goliath: Dealing with Power Differentials in Negotiations," *Harvard Negotiation Law Review* 5 (2000): 75–76.

14. See T. Arnold, "Twenty Common Errors in Mediation Advocacy," *Alternatives to the High Cost of Litigation* 13 (May 1995): 69, 71.

15. See, for example, Adler and Silverstein, "When David Meets Goliath," 76–77.

16. *U.S. Code*, Title 28, sec. 2678.

Chapter Six

1. U.S. Equal Employment Opportunity Commission, *Annual Report on the Federal Work Force* (Washington, D.C.: U.S. Equal Employment Opportunity Commission, 2001).

2. Ibid.

3. Administrative Office of the United States Courts, *Annual Report of the Director* (Washington, D.C.: Administrative Office of the United States Courts, 2001), Table C-2A.

4. Ibid.

5. U.S. Equal Employment Opportunity Commission, *Annual Report on the Federal Work Force* (Washington, D.C.: U.S. Equal Employment Opportunity Commission, 2001).

6. Ibid.

7. J. M. Senger, "Evaluation of ADR in United States Attorney Cases," *United States Attorneys' Bulletin* 48 (2000): 25.

8. A. P. Lofaro, "ADR in the Federal Workplace: Why It Is Needed, How It Can Help, and Some Cautions to Observe," in M. Breger, G. Schatz,

and D. Laufer (eds.), *Federal Administrative Dispute Resolution Deskbook* (Chicago: American Bar Association, 2001), 407.

9. Ibid.

10. Ibid.

11. U.S. General Accounting Office, *Equal Employment Opportunity: Rising Trends in EEO Complaint Caseloads in the Federal Sector 42–43* (Washington, D.C.: U.S. General Accounting Office, 1998).

12. *U.S. Code,* Title 42, sec. 1981a.

13 Ibid., secs. 12101–12213.

14. See *Code of Federal Regulations,* Title 24, Part 1614.

15. U.S. General Accounting Office, *Equal Employment Opportunity: Rising Trends in EEO Complaint Caseloads in the Federal Sector* (Washington, D.C.: U.S. General Accounting Office, 1998), 6.

16. The median time from date of filing to date of trial is 21.6 months. Administrative Office of the United States Courts, *Federal Court Management Statistics* (Washington, D.C.: Administrative Office of the United States Courts, 2001).

17. Lofaro, "ADR in the Federal Workplace," 408. More recent data indicate a slight reduction in backlogs and delays, perhaps due to increased ADR use, among other factors.

18. Federal Interagency ADR Working Group, *Report of the Interagency Alternative Dispute Resolution Working Group to the President of the United States* (Washington, D.C.: Federal Interagency ADR Working Group, 2000), 3.

19. Ibid., 2.

20. Senger, "Evaluation of ADR in United States Attorney Cases," 25.

21. Federal Interagency ADR Working Group, *Report of the Interagency Alternative Dispute Resolution Working Group to the President of the United States,* 3.

22. Senger, "Evaluation of ADR in United States Attorney Cases," 25.

23. Ibid.

24. M. B. Richardson, "The Department of the Navy's Equal Employment Opportunity Complaint Dispute Resolution Process Pilot Program: A Bold Experiment That Deserves Further Exploration," *Military Law Review* 169 (2001): 1.

25. Federal Interagency ADR Working Group, *Report of the Interagency Alternative Dispute Resolution Working Group to the President of the United States,* 2.

26. E. P. McDermott, R. Obar, A. Jose, and M. Bowers, *An Evaluation of the EEOC Mediation Program* (Washington, D.C.: U.S. Equal Employment Opportunity Commission, 2000), 1.

27. U.S. General Accounting Office, *Equal Employment Opportunity*, 6.
28. Ibid.
29. Federal Interagency ADR Working Group, *Report of the Interagency Alternative Dispute Resolution Working Group to the President of the United States*, 2–3.
30. Ibid.
31. U.S. Department of the Air Force, *Nomination for the Office of Personnel Management Director's Award for Outstanding Alternative Dispute Resolution Programs* (Washington, D.C.: U.S. Department of the Air Force, 2001), 6.
32. See Title VII of the Civil Rights Act of 1964, *U.S. Code*, Title 42, sec. 2000e et seq.; Age Discrimination in Employment Act of 1967, *U.S. Code*, Title 29, sec. 621 et seq.; Rehabilitation Act of 1973, *U.S. Code*, Title 29, sec. 791 et seq.; Equal Pay Act of 1963, *U.S. Code*, Title 29, sec. 206(d).
33. *Code of Federal Regulations*, Title 29, sec. 1614.105(a)(1).
34. Ibid., sec. 1614.301. The regulations also explain the procedures for handling a "mixed case" that could be presented to either the agency or the Merit Systems Protection Board. Ibid., sec. 1614.302.
35. Ibid., sec. 1614.105(b)(1).
36. Ibid., sec. 105(d).
37. Ibid., sec. 105(e).
38. Ibid., sec. 105(d).
39. Ibid., sec. 1614.107. A complainant may appeal such a dismissal to the EEOC under sec. 1614.404, and ultimately to federal court under secs. 1614.407–408.
40. Ibid., secs. 1614.106(e)(2) and 1614.108(e), which also provide that both parties can agree in writing to extend this time period.
41. Ibid., sec. 1614.108(b).
42. Ibid., secs. 1614.108(f) and (g).
43. Ibid., sec. 1614.110(b).
44. Ibid., sec. 1614.109(a).
45. Ibid., sec. 1614.109(i).
46. Ibid., sec. 1614.404.
47. Ibid., sec. 1614.405.
48. Ibid., secs. 1614.407–408, which also provide that if an EEOC administrative judge denied the claim, the complainant may appeal directly to federal court.
49. Ibid.
50. *U.S. Code*, Title 42, secs. 1981 note, 1981a note, 1988 note, 2000e note, 2000e-1 note, 2000e-2 note, 2000e-4 note, 2000e-5 note, 2000e-16 note, 12111 note, and 12112 note.

51. *Code of Federal Regulations,* Title 29, secs. 1614.108(b), 1614.603.
52. U.S. Equal Employment Opportunity Commission, Management Directive EEO MD-110, Federal Sector Complaint Processing Manual, Chap. 3, sec. I.
53. *Code of Federal Regulations,* Title 29, sec. 102(b)(2).
54. U.S. Equal Employment Opportunity Commission, *Management Directive EEO MD-110, Federal Sector Complaint Processing Manual* (Washington, D.C.: U.S. Equal Employment Opportunity Commission, 1999), Chap. 3, sec. II(A)(5).
55. *Code of Federal Regulations,* Title 29, sec. 105(b)(2).
56. Ibid., sec. 1614.105(f).
57. U.S. Equal Employment Opportunity Commission, *Management Directive EEO MD-110,* Chap. 3, sec. VII. See also Federal ADR Council, "Core Principles for Federal Non-Binding Workplace ADR Programs," *Federal Register,* Aug. 16, 2000, 50,005–50,006.
58. U.S. Equal Employment Opportunity Commission, *Management Directive EEO MD-110,* Chap. 3, sec. VII.
59. Ibid.
60. Ibid.
61. Ibid.
62. Ibid., sec. VII(A)(1).
63. Ibid.
64. Ibid., sec. VII(A)(1).
65. Ibid.
66. Ibid.
67. See, for example, U.S. Department of Justice, Human Resources Order 1200.1 C(11), July 6, 2000: "Once a complainant accepts the option of entering into the ADR process, management is required to enter into good faith discussions to resolve the dispute."
68. U.S. Equal Employment Opportunity Commission, *Management Directive EEO MD-110,* Chap. 3, sec. II(A)(5).
69. Ibid., sec. IV(a).
70. Ibid.
71. Ibid.
72. Ibid., sec. VII(a)(2).
73. Ibid.
74. See *U.S. Code,* Title 5, sec. 574.
75. Ibid.
76. *Code of Federal Regulations,* Title 29, sec. 1614.504.
77. Ibid.
78. Ibid.
79. Ibid.

80. Ibid.
81. U.S. Equal Employment Opportunity Commission, *Management Directive EEO MD-110,* Chap. 3, sec. VII(B) (1999).
82. Ibid.
83. See *U.S. Code,* Title 5, sec. 572(b).
84. B. S. Murphy, "Mediation of Federal Employment Discrimination Charges," in Breger, Schatz, and Laufer (eds.), *Federal Administrative Dispute Resolution Deskbook,* 421.
85. U.S. Equal Employment Opportunity Commission, *Facts About Mediation* (Washington, D.C.: U.S. Equal Employment Opportunity Commission, 1999).
86. Ibid.
87. Ibid.
88. U.S. Equal Employment Opportunity Commission, *Questions and Answers About Mediation* (Washington, D.C.: U.S. Equal Employment Opportunity Commission, 1999).
89. Ibid.
90. Ibid.
91. Ibid.
92. Ibid.
93. Ibid.
94. Ibid.
95. U.S. Equal Employment Opportunity Commission, *Annual Report on the Federal Work Force* (Washington, D.C.: U.S. Equal Employment Opportunity Commission, 2001), pt. IV.
96. Ibid.
97. Of course, the relationship between the parties is less important in EEO cases where they are unlikely to see each other again—for example, in nonselection disputes or matters where the complainant has already moved on to other employment.
98. Ibid.
99. See R.A.B. Bush and J. P. Folger, *The Promise of Mediation: Responding to Conflict Through Empowerment and Recognition* (San Francisco: Jossey-Bass, 1994).
100. U.S. Equal Employment Opportunity Commission, *Annual Report on the Federal Work Force,* pt. IV.
101. Ibid.
102. Ibid.
103. See U.S. Department of the Air Force, *Common Interests of the Parties* (Washington, D.C.: U.S. Department of the Air Force, 2002).
104. U.S. Equal Employment Opportunity Commission, *Annual Report on the Federal Work Force,* pt. II.

105. The U.S. Department of the Air Force has produced an excellent guide to these options, on which the following section is based, in Appendixes 9 and 10 of U.S. Department of the Air Force, *Mediation Compendium: How to Mediate Civilian Personnel Workplace Dispute,* 2nd ed. (Washington, D.C.: U.S. Department of the Air Force, 2000).

106. See Memorandum from Randolph D. Moss, Acting Assistant Attorney General, Office of Legal Counsel, United States Department of Justice, to Harriet S. Rabb, General Counsel, United States Department of Health and Human Services, Dec. 4, 1998.

107. *U.S. Code,* Title 42, secs. 2000e-5(g)(1).

108. Franks v. Bowman, 424 U.S. 747, 770–771 (1976). See Selgas v. American Airlines, Inc., 104 F.3d 9, 13 (1st Cir. 1997): "Trial courts have discretion to fashion the awards in Title VII cases so as to fully compensate a plaintiff in a manner that suits the specific facts of the case; this discretion includes the selection of the elements which comprise the remedial recovery."

109. Matter of Equal Employment Opportunity Commission, Informal Settlement of Discrimination Complaints, 62 Comp. Gen. 239, 242 (1983).

110. U.S. Equal Employment Opportunity Commission, *Management Directive EEO MD-110,* Chap. 12.

111. Ibid.

112. Ibid.

113. The following are useful guides on this topic: U.S. Equal Employment Opportunity Commission, *Management Directive EEO MD-110,* Chap. 12, and Office of Personnel Management, *Guidelines for Settlement of Federal Personnel Actions Involving Civil Service Retirement Benefits* (Washington, D.C.: Office of Personnel Management, 2000).

114. *U.S. Code,* Title 5, sec. 7114(a)(2).

115. Certain U.S. Postal Service employees may be able to proceed on both tracks simultaneously, pursuant to contract.

116. *Code of Federal Regulations,* Title 5, sec. 1201.3.

117. 5 *U.S. Code,* Title 5, sec. 7702.

118. Office of Personnel Management, *Alternative Dispute Resolution: A Resource Guide* (Washington, D.C.: Office of Personnel Management, 1999), 130.

119. Ibid.

120. *Federal Register* 64 (1999): 27,899.

121. *U.S. Code,* Title 5, secs. 7321–7326.

122. Ibid., Title 38, secs. 4301–4333.

123. Office of Special Counsel, *The OSC Mediation Program* (Washington, D.C.: Office of Special Counsel, 2001); Office of Personnel Management, *Alternative Dispute Resolution,* 130.

124. Federal Labor Relations Authority, *About the FLRA* (Washington, D.C.: Federal Labor Relations Authority, 2002); Office of Personnel Management, *Alternative Dispute Resolution*, 127.
125. *U.S. Code*, Title 5, secs. 7101–7135.
126. See ibid., sec. 2423.1(a).
127. See *Code of Federal Regulations*, Title 5, sec. 2423.25(d).
128. Ibid., sec. 7119.
129. See sec. 7119(a).
130. Office of Personnel Management, *Alternative Dispute Resolution*, 128.
131. *U.S. Code*, Title 5, sec. 571(3).
132. While ombuds offices can deal with many different issues, workplace disputes usually make up the great majority of their work, and thus they are covered in this chapter.
133. See D. L. Meltzer, "Can a Federal Ombuds Help You?" in Breger, Schatz, and Laufer, *Federal Administrative Dispute Resolution Deskbook.*
134. *U.S. Code*, Title 48, sec. 4806(d).
135. Ibid.
136. *U.S. Code*, Title 15, sec. 657.
137. *U.S. Code*, Title 22, sec. 2664a(a)(c).
138. U.S. General Accounting Office, *The Role of Ombudsmen in Dispute Resolution* (Washington, D.C.: U.S. General Accounting Office, 2001), 3–4.
139. Ibid., 42–43.
140. See American Bar Association, *Standards for the Establishment and Operation of Ombuds Offices* (Chicago: American Bar Association, 2001).
141. See *U.S. Code*, Title 5, sec. 574.
142. Ibid., sec. 571(8) requires a "disagreement" involving an agency and/or individuals; secs. 573 and 574 require "parties" to a dispute.
143. Ibid., Title 18, sec. 4.
144. *Code of Federal Regulations*, Title 5, sec. 2635.101(b)(11).
145. *U.S. Code*, Title 28, sec. 535(b).

Chapter Seven

1. *Code of Federal Regulations*, Title 48, sec. 33.204
2. 5 *U.S. Code*, Title 5, secs. 571–584 (1996)
3. Ibid., sec. 3(a)(2).
4. Ibid., sec. 3(d)(1).
5. Ibid., Title 41, secs. 601–613 (1978).
6. Ibid., sec. 605(d).
7. Ibid., sec. 605(e).
8. See ibid., Title 5, sec. 572(b).
9. Ibid., Title 41, sec. 607(e).

10. *Code of Federal Regulations,* Title 48, sec. 33.204.

11. Ibid.

12. Ibid., sec. 33.201.

13. Ibid., sec. 33.204.

14. Ibid., sec. 33.201.

15. Ibid., sec. 33.214(a).

16. Ibid., sec. 33.214(c).

17. Ibid.

18. Ibid., sec. 33.214(f)(1).

19. Ibid.

20. "Agency Procurement Protests," *Federal Register,* Oct. 27, 1995, 55,171–55,172.

21. *Code of Federal Regulations,* Title 48, sec. 33.201.

22. If the claim exceeds $100,000, the contractor must certify that it is made in good faith, that the supporting data are accurate and complete, that the amount requested accurately reflects the contract adjustment for which the contractor believes the government is liable, and that the signer is authorized to certify the claim on behalf of the contractor. Ibid., sec. 33.207.

23. Ibid., sec. 33.211.

24. Ibid.

25. See U.S. Department of Justice, "Policy on the Use of Alternative Dispute Resolution, and Case Identification Criteria for Alternative Dispute Resolution," *Federal Register,* July 15, 1996, 36,895–36,913.

26. See ibid.

27. *U.S. Code,* Title 41, sec. 605(a) and *Code of Federal Regulations,* Title 48, sec. 33.210(b).

28. *Code of Federal Regulations,* Title 48, sec. 33.209.

29. Ibid.

30. Executive Order 12,979, *Federal Register,* Oct. 25, 1995, 55,171.

31. *Code of Federal Regulations,* Title 48, sec. 33.204.

32. Ibid.

33. Ibid., sec. 33.214(c).

34. The U.S. Air Force follows this practice for all contracting officer final decisions over $50,000.

35. The FAA uses dispute resolution officers for this function.

36. This approach contrasts with that of the GAO, where the neutral who provides outcome prediction is the same individual who ultimately will adjudicate a bid protest.

37. C. P. Conroy and M. J. Harty, "Alternative Dispute Resolution at the ASBCA," *Briefing Papers* 00-07 (2000): 1.

38. Under the FAA process, parties may choose among FAA dispute resolution officers, GSA board judges, or private compensated neutrals.

39. Conroy and Harty, "Alternative Dispute Resolution at the ASBCA," 5.
40. *U.S. Code*, Title 5, sec. 575(a)(2).
41. Ibid.
42. Ibid., sec. 575(c).
43. See Federal Deposit Insurance Corporation, "Statement of Policy Regarding Arbitration," *Federal Register*, Apr. 10, 2001, 18,632–18,633; Federal Aviation Administration, "Final Guidance for the Use of Binding Arbitration Under the Administrative Dispute Resolution Act of 1996," *Federal Register*, Oct. 15, 2001, 52,475; Federal Motor Carrier Safety Administration, Guidance for the Use of Binding Arbitration Under the Administrative Dispute Resolution Act of 1996, Nov. 4, 2002.
44. Some boards permit parties to indicate a preference for the settlement judge they would like, but the boards retain the power to make the final selection.
45. Rules of the United States Court of Federal Claims, Appendix A, Case Management Procedure, II(3)(e) (2002).
46. Ibid., III(4)(i).
47. Ibid., Appendix H, 3(b).
48. *Code of Federal Regulations*, Title 48, sec. 33.208.
49. Public Law 96-481 (1980); *Statutes at Large of the United States* 94: 2325, codified at U.S. Code, Title 5, sec. 504 and Title 28, sec. 2412.
50. *U.S. Code*, Title 5, sec. 504.
51. Public Law 98-369 (1984); *Statutes at Large of the United States* 98:1175 (codified at various sections of U.S. Code, Titles 31, 41).

Chapter Eight

1. Administrative Dispute Resolution Act of 1990, *U.S. Code*, Title 5, secs. 571–584.
2. This chapter focuses on mediation, the most common form of ADR in the government. Typically, party expectations of confidentiality are more limited in arbitration than in mediation. The statutory law developing in the states has been focusing on mediation rather than arbitration. Similarly, the nascent federal common law privilege applies only to mediation, and not to arbitration. Nonetheless, the protections described in the chapter from the Federal Rules of Evidence, the ADR Act of 1998, and local court rules do apply to arbitration. Furthermore, parties can use private contracts and stipulated court orders to increase arbitration confidentiality.
3. Lake Utopia Paper Ltd. v. Connelly Containers, Inc., 608 F.2d 928, 930 (2d Cir. 1979), cert. denied, 555 U.S. 1076 (1980). See also U.S. Senate, *Administrative Dispute Resolution Act*, S. Rept. 101–543, 101st Cong.,

2nd sess., 1990, 3,941: "[Confidentiality] protections are created to enable parties to ADR proceedings to be forthcoming and candid, without fear that frank statements may later be used against them."

4. National Labor Relations Board v. Macaluso, 618 F.2d 51, 55 (9th Cir. 1980), quoting Tomlinson v. High Point, Inc., 74 N.L.R.B. 681, 688 (1947).

5. Branzburg v. Hayes, 408 U.S. 665, 688 (1972), J. H. Wigmore, *Evidence in Trials at Common Law,* rev. by J. McNaughton (New York: Little, Brown, 1961), Vol. 8, sec. 2192, p. 70.

6. "'Jersey Boys' Mediate a Dixie Mob Dispute," *Newark Star Ledger,* July 22, 1987; N. H. Rogers and C. A. McEwen, *Mediation: Law, Policy, Practice,* 2nd ed. (Deerfield, Ill.: Clark Boardman Callaghan, 1994), sec. 9:10.

7. State v. Castellano, 460 So. 2d 480, 481–2 (Fla. App. 1984); Rogers and McEwen, *Mediation,* sec. 9:02.

8. 5 *U.S. Code,* Title 5, sec. 571–584.

9. Ibid., sec. 571(9).

10. Federal ADR Council, "Confidentiality in Federal Alternative Dispute Resolution Programs," *Federal Register,* Dec. 29, 2000, 83,085.

11. Ibid.

12. Ibid., 13,091.

13. *U.S. Code,* Title 5, sec. 574(a). Disclosure means making a communication available to another person or entity by any method. Federal ADR Council, "Confidentiality in Federal Alternative Dispute Resolution Programs," 83,091.

14. *U.S. Code,* Title 5, sec. 571(5).

15. Ibid.

16. Ibid., sec. 574(a).

17. Ibid., sec. 574(c). Note that it may be admissible, however, in an unrelated proceeding.

18. Ibid., sec. 571(5).

19. Ibid., sec. 574(a)(1).

20. Ibid., sec. 574(a)(2). This section applies, for example, to statements made at a congressional hearing, a public trial, or a meeting open to the public, as well as statements released through FOIA. Federal ADR Council, "Confidentiality in Federal Alternative Dispute Resolution Programs," 83,091.

21. *U.S. Code,* Title 5, sec. 574(a)(3). This section applies, for example, to the Clean Air Act, which states that certain records, reports, or information obtained from regulated entities "shall be made available to the public." Ibid., Title 42, sec. 7414(c).

22. Ibid., Title 5, sec. 574(a)/3).

23. Ibid., sec. 574(g).

24. Ibid., sec. 574(i). In this case, information may be disclosed only to the extent necessary to resolve the dispute.

25. Ibid., sec. 574(h).

26. Ibid., sec. 574(f) provides: "Nothing in this section shall prevent the discovery or admissibility of any evidence that is otherwise discoverable, merely because the evidence was presented in the course of a dispute resolution proceeding."

27. Ibid., sec. 574(a)(4).

28. Ibid.

29. Ibid.

30. Ibid., sec. 574(b). The term *parties* includes parties named in an agency proceeding, those who participate in the ADR proceeding, and those who will be affected significantly by the results. Federal ADR Council, "Confidentiality in Federal Alternative Dispute Resolution Programs," 83,091.

31. *U.S. Code,* Title 5, sec. 571(5).

32. Ibid., sec. 574(b).

33. Ibid., sec. 574(c).

34. Ibid., sec. 574(b)(1). Note that although this section provides that parties may choose to disclose, they still may not be compelled to do so.

35. Ibid., sec. 574(b)(2).

36. Ibid.

37. Ibid., sec.574(b)(6).

38. Ibid., sec. 574(b)(7).

39. However, documents generated by the neutral, such as early neutral evaluations, are still protected, even if they are exchanged among all the parties. Ibid., sec. 574(b)(7). Also, other protections exist, such as Federal Rule of Evidence 408, which makes settlement discussions generally inadmissible at trial.

40. *U.S. Code,* Title 5, sec. 574(b)(7).

41. Ibid., sec. 552.

42. Ibid., sec. 574(e).

43. Federal ADR Council, "Confidentiality in Federal Alternative Dispute Resolution Programs," 83,094.

44. *U.S. Code,* Title 5, sec. 574(e).

45. Federal ADR Council, "Confidentiality in Federal Alternative Dispute Resolution Programs, 83,094–83,095.

46. Ibid., 83,086.

47. See, for example, C. Pou, Jr., "Gandhi Meets Elliot Ness: Fifth Circuit Ruling Raises Concerns About Confidentiality in Federal Agency ADR," *Dispute Resolution Magazine* 5 (1998): 9–11.

48. See, e.g., Inspector General Act, *U.S. Code,* Title 5 App.; U.S. Constitution amendment V (providing for Grand Jury investigations); Labor Management-Relations Act, *U.S. Code,* Title 5, sec. 7114(4); Merit Systems Protection Act, *U.S. Code,* Title 5, sec. 1204(2)(A); Whistleblower Protection Act, *U.S. Code,* Title 5, sec. 12112(b)(2); Equal Employment Opportunities Act, 42 *U.S. Code,* Title 42, sec. 2000e–4.

49. Of course, it could be as easily argued that the specific provisions of the ADR Act governing dispute resolution proceedings override these general investigatory provisions.

50. 18 *U.S. Code,* Title 18, sec. 4.

51. *Code of Federal Regulations,* Title 5, sec. 2635.101(b)(11).

52. 28 *U.S. Code,* Title 28, sec. 535(b).

53. Federal ADR Council, "Confidentiality in Federal Alternative Dispute Resolution Programs," 83,086.

54. Ibid.

55. Ibid., 83,093.

56. Ibid.

57. Ibid.

58. Letter from G. L. Gianni, Jr., Vice Chair of the President's Council on Integrity and Efficiency, and B. R. Snyder, Vice Chair of the Executive Council on Integrity and Efficiency, to D. Marcus, Associate Attorney General, U.S. Department of Justice, Oct. 31, 2000.

59. In re Grand Jury Proceedings, 148 F.3d 487 (5th Cir. 1998).

60. Ibid., 492.

61. *U.S. Code,* Title 5, sec. 571(8).

62. See Pou, "Gandhi Meets Elliot Ness," 9.

63. Federal Rule of Criminal Procedure 6(e).

64. In re Grand Jury Proceedings, 148 F.3d at 493.

65. Some administrative tribunals look to the principles of Federal Rule of Evidence 408 when making decisions. See, for example, Ateron Corp., ASBCA Nos. 46,352, 46,867, 94–3 BCA para. 27,229.

66. Federal Rule of Evidence 408.

67. Ibid., advisory committee's note (1972).

68. Ibid.

69. See Weir v. Federal Insurance Company, 811 F.2d 1387, 1395–1396 (10th Cir. 1987); John McShain, Inc. v. Cessna Aircraft Co., 563 F.2d 632, 635 (3d Cir. 1977); R. J. Niemic, D. Stienstra, and R. E. Ravitz, *Guide to Judicial Management of Cases in ADR* (Washington, D.C.: Federal Judicial Center, 2001), 169.

70. *U.S. Code,* Title 28, secs. 651–658.

71. Ibid., secs. 651(b), 652(d).
72. Ibid., sec. 652(d).
73. Ibid. For a discussion of problems with this approach, see G. Litt, "No Confidence: The Problem of Confidentiality by Local Rule in the Alternative Dispute Resolution Act of 1998," *Texas Law Review* 78 (2000): 1015–1036.
74. See, for example, In re Anonymous, 283 F.3d 627 (4th Cir. 2002), for a detailed discussion of confidentiality under a local rule.
75. See Niemic, Stienstra, and Ravitz, *Guide to Judicial Management of Cases in ADR;* K. M. Scanlon, "Primer on Recent Developments in Mediation Confidentiality," *Alternatives to the High Cost of Litigation* 19 (2001): 1–2.
76. R. J. Niemic, *Mediation and Conference Programs in the Federal Courts of Appeals* (Washington, D.C.: Federal Judicial Center, 1997), 9–20.
77. National Labor Relations Board v. Macaluso, 618 F.2d 51, 54–55 (9th Cir. 1980).
78. Ibid., citing *Code of Federal Regulations,* Title 29, secs. 1401.2(a),(b).
79. Ibid., 54.
80. Ibid., 55.
81. Wilson v. Attaway, 757 F.2d 1227, 1245 (11th Cir. 1985), rehearing denied, 764 F.2d 1411 (11th Cir. 1985), citing *U.S. Code,* Title 42, secs. 2000g–2(b).
82. Ibid. (internal quotation marks omitted). Other cases finding confidentiality for CRS mediators are Port Arthur v. United States, 517 F. Supp. 987, n.105 (D.D.C. 1981) aff'd, 459 U.S. 159 (1982), and People v. Reyes, 816 F. Supp. 619 (E.D. Cal. 1992). See A. Kirtley, "The Mediation Privilege's Transition from Theory to Implementation: Designing a Mediation Privilege Standard to Protect Mediation Participants, the Process and the Public Interest," *Journal of Dispute Resolution* 1995 (1995): n.84.
83. Federal Rule of Evidence 501.
84. Trammel v. United States, 445 U.S. 40, 50 (1980).
85. Jaffee v. Redmond, 518 U.S. 1, 9–13 (1996).
86. Folb v. Motion Picture Industry Pension and Health Plans, 16 F. Supp. 2d 1164 (C.D. Cal. 1998).
87. Ibid., 1171–1176.
88. Ibid., 1176–1177.
89. Ibid., 1177–1178.
90. Ibid., 1178–1180.
91. Sheldone v. Pennsylvania Turnpike Commission, 104 F. Supp. 2d 511 (W.D. Pa. 2000).
92. Ibid., 513.

93. In re RDM Sports Group, Inc., 277 B.R. 415 (N.D. Ga. 2002).
94. 148 F.3d 487 (5th Cir. 1998).
95. Ibid., 493 (citation omitted).
96. 897 F. Supp. 1170 (S. D. Ind. 1995).
97. 58 F. Supp. 2d 1110 (N.D. Cal. 1999).
98. 76 F. Supp. 2d 736, 738 (N.D. Tex. 1999).
99. Federal Rule of Evidence 501, advisory committee's note (1974): "A federal court sitting in a non-diversity case such as this does not sit as a local tribunal. In some cases it may see fit for special reasons to give the law of a particular state highly persuasive or even controlling effect, but in the last analysis its decision turns upon the law of the United States, not that of any state." D'Oench, Dhume & Co. v. Federal Deposit Insurance Corp., 315 U.S. 447, 471 (1942) (Jackson, J., concurring).
100. United States v. Gullo, 672 F. Supp. 99 (W.D.N.Y. 1987).
101. Ibid., 104.
102. Ibid. (internal quotation marks omitted).
103. P. A. Kentra, "Hear No Evil, See No Evil, Speak No Evil: The Intolerable Conflict for Attorney-Mediators Between the Duty to Maintain Mediation Confidentiality and the Duty to Report Fellow Attorney Misconduct," *Brigham Young University Law Review,* 1977 (1977): 715–757.
104. Niemic, Stienstra, and E. Ravitz, *Guide to Judicial Management of Cases in ADR,* 177.
105. Rogers and McEwen, *Mediation,* Appendix A.
106. Folb v. Motion Picture Industry Pension and Health Plans, 16 F. Supp. 2d 1164, 1178 (C.D. Cal. 1998).
107. Federal ADR Council, "Confidentiality in Federal Alternative Dispute Resolution Programs," 83,093.
108. *U.S. Code,* Title 5, sec. 552.
109. The ADR Act does block access under FOIA to documents that were exchanged privately between a party and a neutral. Ibid., sec. 574(j).
110. See W. D. Brazil, "Protecting the Confidentiality of Settlement Negotiations," *Hastings Law Journal* 39 (1998): 1026–1027.
111. Federal court authority for these orders comes from Federal Rule of Civil Procedure 26(c).
112. Martindell v. International Telephone & Telegraph, 594 F.2d 291, 296 (2d Cir. 1979)
113. See Rogers and McEwen, *Mediation,* sec. 9:21.
114. Martindell v. International Telephone & Telegraph, 594 F.2d 291, 296 (2d Cir. 1979).
115. Palmieri v. State of New York, 779 F.2d 861, 865 (2d Cir. 1985).

116. In re Grand Jury Subpoena, 836 F.2d 1468, 1470 (4th Cir. 1988).
117. Palmieri v. State of New York, 779 F.2d 861, 864 (2d Cir. 1985).
118. *U.S. Code,* Title 44, secs. 2101–2118, 2901–2910, 3101–3107, 3301–3324.
119. Ibid., sec. 2902(1).
120. Ibid., sec. 3101.
121. Ibid.
122. U.S. Equal Employment Opportunity Commission, *Management Directive EEO MD-110, Federal Sector Complaint Processing Manual* (Washington, D.C.: U.S. Equal Employment Opportunity Commission, 1999), Chap. 3, sec. IV(c)(5).
123. *U.S. Code,* Title 5, sec. 552.
124. Ibid., 574(j).
125. Federal ADR Council, "Confidentiality in Federal Alternative Dispute Resolution Programs," 83,085.
126. Ibid., 83,095.
127. Ibid., 83,085.

Chapter Nine
1. Readers who desire a more in-depth treatment of these topics can consult a number of books. See, for example, W. L. Ury, J. M. Brett, and S. B. Goldberg, *Getting Disputes Resolved: Designing Systems to Cut the Costs of Conflict* (San Francisco: Jossey-Bass, 1988); C. Costantino and C. S. Merchant, *Designing Conflict Management Systems: A Guide to Creating Productive and Healthy Organizations* (San Francisco: Jossey-Bass, 1996); N. H. Rogers and C. A. McEwen, *Mediation: Law, Policy, Practice,* 2nd ed. (Deerfield, Ill.: Clark Boardman Callaghan, 1994), Chapter 11.
2. *Code of Federal Regulations,* Title 29, sec. 102(b)(2).
3. See Administrative Dispute Resolution Act of 1996, *U.S. Code,* Title 5, secs. 571–584; Memorandum from the President of the United States to the Heads of Executive Departments and Agencies, May 1, 1998.
4. See generally Federal Interagency ADR Working Group, *Federal ADR Program Manager's Resource Manual* (Washington, D.C.: Federal Interagency ADR Working Group, 1999).
5. See J. M. Senger, "Turning the Ship of State," *Journal of Dispute Resolution* 2000 (2000): 87–95.
6. See Frank E.A. Sander, "The Future of ADR," *Journal of Dispute Resolution* 2000 (2000): 6.
7. *U.S. Code,* Title 28, sec. 2678.
8. Ibid., Title 5, sec. 571 note (Promotion of Alternative Means of Dispute Resolution).

9. Ibid.
10. Ibid., sec. 572(a). Note, however, that agencies may require management employees to participate in workplace ADR because the agency is considered to be the party making the voluntary decision to participate, not the employees themselves. U.S. Equal Employment Opportunity Commission, *Management Directive EEO MD-110, Federal Sector Complaint Processing Manual* (Washington, D.C.: U.S. Equal Employment Opportunity Commission, 1999), Chap. 3, sec. II(A)(5).
11. *U.S. Code,* Title 5, sec. 573(a).
12. For descriptions of subjective evaluation approaches, see C. Honeyman, "On Evaluating Mediators," *Negotiation Journal* 6 (1990): 23–36; C. Honeyman and others, *Performance-Based Assessment: A Methodology for Use in Selecting, Training and Evaluation Mediators* (Washington, D.C.: National Institute of Dispute Resolution, 1995); and E. Waldman, "Credentialling Approaches: The Slow Movement Toward Skills-Based Testing Continues," *Dispute Resolution Magazine* 8 (2001): 13–21.
13. See C. Honeyman, K. Miezio, and W. Houlihan, "In the Mind's Eye? Consistency and Variation in Evaluating Mediators," Working Paper 90–21, Program on Negotiation at Harvard Law School, 1990.
14. *U.S. Code,* Title 5, sec. 552.
15. For a discussion of how a program can develop an apprentice system for senior neutrals to train beginners, see J. J. Upchurch, "Florida Firm Trains and Leverages Its New Mediation Associates," *Alternatives to the High Cost of Litigation* 20 (2002): 1, 15.
16. See, for example, CPR-Georgetown Commission on Ethics and Standards in ADR, *Proposed Model Rule of Professional Conduct for the Lawyer as Third Party Neutral* (New York: CPR Institute for Dispute Resolution, 1999), and American Arbitration Association, American Bar Association, and Society for Professionals in Dispute Resolution, *Model Standards of Conduct for Mediators* (New York: American Arbitration Association, 1995).
17. *U.S. Code,* Title 5, secs. 571–584.
18. Memorandum from the President of the United States to the Heads of Executive Departments and Agencies, May 1, 1998.
19. See S. Heen and D. Stone, *Facilitation Handbook* (Cambridge, Mass.: Program on Negotiation at Harvard Law School, 1994).
20. R. Fisher, W. Ury, and B. Patton, *Getting to Yes: Negotiating Agreement Without Giving In,* 2nd ed. (New York: Penguin Books, 1991).
21. K. Arrow and others (eds.), *Barriers to Conflict Resolution* (New York: Norton, 1995). R. Mnookin provides a useful overview of this subject in "Why Negotiations Fail: An Exploration of Barriers to the Resolution of Conflict," *Ohio State Journal on Dispute Resolution* 8 (1993): 235–249.

22. See J. M. Senger and C. Honeyman, "Cracking the Hard-Boiled Student: Some Ways to Turn Research Findings into Interactive Exercises," *Conflict Resolution Practitioner* 1 (2001): 31–42.
23. The Burning Sailboat Exercise was created by N. Laughrey and is available in L. L. Riskin, J. E. Westbrook, and J. H. Levin, *Instructor's Manual with Simulation and Problem Materials to Accompany Dispute Resolution and Lawyers* (St. Paul, Minn.: West 1998), 93–99.
24. A thorough discussion of ways to use this exercise is given by J. Barkai in "Teaching Negotiation and ADR: The Savvy Samurai Meets the Devil," *Nebraska Law Review* 75 (1996): 711–723.
25. Win as Much as You Can was created by G. R. Williams, and the Oil Pricing Exercise was created by R. Fisher and revised by A. Clarkson and B. Patton. Both exercises are available at modest cost from the Program on Negotiation at Harvard Law School, 513 Pound Hall, Cambridge, MA, 02138, (800) 258–4406.
26. See CPR-Georgetown Commission on Ethics and Standards in ADR, *Proposed Model Rule of Professional Conduct for the Lawyer as Third Party Neutral* (1999); and American Arbitration Association, American Bar Association, and Society of Professionals in Dispute Resolution, *Model Standards of Conduct for Mediators*. See also R.A.B. Bush, "The Dilemmas of Mediation Practice: A Study of Ethical Dilemmas and Policy Implications," *Journal of Dispute Resolution* 1994 (1994): 1–55.

Chapter Ten

1. Public Law 103–62 (1993); *Statutes at Large of the United States* 107:285 (codified in various sections of *U.S. Code,* Title 31).
2. *U.S. Code,* Title 5, secs. 571–584.
3. *Code of Federal Regulations,* Title 29, sec. 1614.102(b)(2).
4. *U.S. Code,* Title 41, sec. 605(d); *Code of Federal Regulations,* Title 48, sec. 33.204.
5. See, for example, U.S. Department of Justice, "Policy on the Use of Alternative Dispute Resolution and Case Identification Criteria for Alternative Dispute Resolution," *Federal Register,* July 15, 1996, 36,895–36,913.
6. See U.S. General Accounting Office, *Alternative Dispute Resolution: Employers' Experiences with ADR in the Workplace* (Washington, D.C.: U.S. General Accounting Office, 1997); U.S. General Accounting Office, *Employment Discrimination: Most Private-Sector Employers Use Alternative Dispute Resolution* (Washington, D.C.: U.S. General Accounting Office, 1995); U.S. General Accounting Office, *The Role of Ombudsmen in Dispute Resolution* (Washington, D.C.: U.S. General Accounting Office, 2001).

7. This research has been led by L. B. Bingham of the Indiana University School of Public and Environmental Affairs.

8. Some evaluators believe it is appropriate to include not only cases that settle during the ADR process but also those that settle immediately after. The rationale is that the ADR process probably facilitated the settlement if the two events occurred close in time. Following this theory, it is possible to include settlements up to one month after the ADR closed. If using this approach, it is advisable to explain it when presenting the results.

9. The U.S. Postal Service found that the introduction of ADR caused a drop in the number of informal complaints that became formal from 43 percent to only 22 percent. General Accounting Office, *Alternative Dispute Resolution*, 67.

10. The U.S. Air Force has realized substantial cost savings by resolving more equal employment opportunity cases at the informal stage. Its audit agency reported that an informal complaint costs only $1,795 to resolve, while a formal complaint costs $16,372. U.S. Department of the Air Force, *Nomination for the Office of Personnel Management Director's Award for Outstanding Alternative Dispute Resolution Programs* (Washington, D.C.: U.S. Department of the Air Force, 2001), 5.

11. At the Justice Department, for example, the settlement rate for medical malpractice cases was 74 percent, while the settlement rate for employment discrimination cases was only 53 percent. J. M. Senger, "Evaluation of ADR in United States Attorney Cases," *United States Attorneys' Bulletin* 48 (2000): 25.

12. The Justice Department found settlement rates were 71 percent for voluntary ADR and only 50 percent for mandatory ADR. Ibid., 27. Other studies have not found substantial differences between voluntary and mandatory ADR. See S. B. Goldberg and J. M. Brett, "Disputants' Perspectives on the Differences Between Mediation and Arbitration," *Negotiation Journal* 6 (1990): 249–256; C. A. McEwen and R. J. Maiman, "Mediation in Small Claims Court: Consensual Processes and Outcomes," in K. Kressel and D. G. Pruitt (eds.), *Mediation Research* (San Francisco: Jossey-Bass, 1989); and J. Pearson and N. Thoennes, "Divorce Mediation: Reflections on a Decade of Research," in Kressel and Pruitt (eds.), *Mediation Research*.

13. The Justice Department found settlement rates of 72 percent for ADR used fewer than ninety days before trial and 53 percent for ADR used ninety or more days before trial. Senger, "Evaluation of ADR in United States Attorney Cases," 28.

14. The U.S. Air Force estimates saving $1.15 million in interest costs in 2000 because ADR enabled the agency to settle its contracting

claims more quickly. U.S. Department of the Air Force, *Nomination for the Office of Federal Procurement Policy's ADR Award* (Washington, D.C.: U.S. Department of the Air Force, 2001), 2.

15. Justice Department attorneys estimated that the use of ADR in their cases saved $10,700 per case in litigation costs alone (deposition fees, expert witness fees, and others). Senger, "Evaluation of ADR in United States Attorney Cases," 26.

   A study by the Office of Special Counsel found that average hourly salaries are $37 for an investigator, $44 for an attorney, $50 for a supervisor, and $40 for an ADR specialist. The average ADR case takes 24 hours, while the average non-ADR case takes 260 hours (160 hours for an investigator, 80 for the attorney, and 20 for the supervisor). Thus, the average ADR cost is $1,000, and the average non-ADR cost is $10,500. Office of Special Counsel, *Application for OPM Director's Award for Outstanding Alternative Dispute Resolution Program* (Washington, D.C.: Office of Special Counsel, 2002).

16. In a quasi-experimental study examining travel costs and staff costs for base engineers, inspectors, contracting officers, pricers, auditors, and experts, the U.S. Air Force determined ADR saved $40,000 per case for contract cases involving less than $1 million and $250,000 for cases over $1 million. U.S. Department of the Air Force, *Nomination for the Office of Federal Procurement Policy's ADR Award,* 2.

17. In contract cases, the Federal Aviation Administration found that bid protests resolved in an average of 25 days with ADR compared to 61 days when going to a final agency decision, and contract disputes resolved in an average of 65 days with ADR compared with 123 days when going to a final agency decision. Federal Aviation Administration Office of Dispute Resolution for Acquisition, *Case Management Statistics* (Washington, D.C.: Federal Aviation Administration, 2001), 2–3.

   In workplace cases, the Office of Special Counsel found that ADR resolved complaints in an average of 115 days, while non-ADR investigation, review, and resolution required an average of 465 days. Office of Special Counsel, *Application for OPM Director's Award for Outstanding Alternative Dispute Resolution Program.*

   In workplace cases, air force use of ADR allows that agency to settle EEO complaints in an average of 258 days, compared to the federal agency average of 404 days. Federal Interagency ADR Working Group, *Report of the Interagency Alternative Dispute Resolution Working Group to the President of the United States* (Washington, D.C.: Federal Interagency ADR Working Group, 2000), 3.

   In workplace cases, the U.S. Navy found the average time to close all EEO administrative cases (formal and informal) was 576 days, while ADR required only 75 days on average for similar cases. U.S. Department of the Navy, *DON ADR Statistics for FY 01* (Washington, D.C.: U.S. Department of the Navy, 2002).

In federal court civil cases (mostly torts and employment discrimination actions), Justice Department assistant U.S. Attorneys estimated time savings averaging six months per case where ADR was used. Senger, "Evaluation of ADR in United States Attorney Cases," 26.

18. In the federal district courts, for example, some districts take more than twice as much time to resolve cases as other districts. See Administrative Office of the United States Courts, *Federal Court Management Statistics* (Washington, D.C.: Administrative Office of the United States Courts, 2001). In order to accurately compare time required for ADR with time required for litigation, these differences must be taken into account.

19. The U.S. Air Force used a before-and-after design to measure time savings in an ADR program for appeals pending before the Armed Services Board of Contract Appeals. After the agency began an ADR program, the amount of time required to process a case dropped by 50 percent. Department of the Air Force, *Nomination for the Office of Federal Procurement Policy's ADR Award*, 3.

20. R.A.B. Bush and J. P. Folger, *The Promise of Mediation: Responding to Conflict Through Empowerment and Recognition* (San Francisco: Jossey-Bass 1994).

21. The Postal Service has reported considerable success in achieving empowerment and recognition through transformative mediation. J. F. Anderson and L. B. Bingham, "Upstream Effects from Mediation of Workplace Disputes: Some Preliminary Evidence from the USPS," *Labor Law Journal* 48 (1997): 601–615.

22. At the Postal Service, in the first year after full implementation of ADR, the number of complaints dropped by 24 percent compared to the previous year. Formal complaints continued to drop during the following year by an additional 20 percent. Federal Interagency ADR Working Group, *Report of the Interagency Alternative Dispute Resolution Working Group to the President*, 2–3.

Similarly, during a three-year period at the U.S. Air Force, the number of EEO complaints that were mediated increased by 36 percent, and the number of total complaints (measured as a percentage of the workforce) dropped by 39 percent. U.S. Department of the Air Force, *Nomination for the Office of Personnel Management Director's Award for Outstanding Alternative Dispute Resolution Programs*, 6.

23. The Postal Service used this method in its research showing a drop in future complaints. L. B. Bingham and M. C. Novac, "Mediation's Impact on Formal Complaint Filing: Before and After the REDRESS

Program at the United States Postal Service," *Review of Public Personnel Administration* 21 (2001): 308–331.

24. The Justice Department used this approach and found no significant difference in the ratio between amount requested and amount granted for almost one thousand cases around the country. J. M. Senger, T. Nabatchi, and L. B. Bingham, unpublished research, 2002.

25. Further discussion of these issues is available in a number of publications. One of the best treatises on evaluating mediators, which was the work of a wide-ranging group of scholars and practitioners, is C. Honeyman and others, *Performance-Based Assessment: A Methodology for Use in Selecting, Training, and Evaluating Mediators* (Washington, D.C.: National Institute of Dispute Resolution 1995).

26. See C. Guthrie and J. S. Levin, "A 'Party Satisfaction'—Perspective on a Comprehensive Mediation Statute," *Ohio State Journal on Dispute Resolution* 13 (1998): 885–907.

27. See N. A. Welsh, "Making Deals in Court-Connected Mediation: What's Justice Got to Do with It?" *Washington University Law Quarterly* 79 (2001): 787–861.

28. See R.A.B. Bush, "'What Do We Need a Mediator For?' Mediation's 'Value-Added' for Negotiators," *Ohio State Journal on Dispute Resolution* 12 (1996): 18–21.

29. The sole ADR process where parties do not have ultimate control over the outcome is binding arbitration, which is rare in the federal government.

30. For example, the Equal Employment Opportunity Commission asked both charging parties and respondents who had mediated EEO cases whether they would be willing to participate in mediation again if they were a party to a similar case in the future. Overwhelming majorities said they would: 91 percent of charging parties and 96 percent of respondents. E. P. McDermott, R. Obar, A. Jose, and M. Bowers, *An Evaluation of the EEOC Mediation Program* (Washington, D.C.: U.S. Equal Employment Opportunity Commission, 2000), 1.

31. The Postal Service, for example, surveyed 26,000 participants in mediation and found that 88 percent of employees were highly satisfied or satisfied with the amount of control, respect, and fairness in the ADR process. In contrast, the satisfaction rate for the Postal Service's traditional adversarial workplace process was only 44 percent. Federal Interagency ADR Working Group, *Report of the Interagency Alternative Dispute Resolution Working Group to the President*, 2.

32. For advice on reducing nonresponse error, see D. A. Dillman, *Mail and Telephone Surveys: The Total Design Method* (New York: Wiley, 1978).

33. The U.S. Postal Service has used this approach with great success in its programs.

34. A. Tversky and D. Kahneman, "Judgments Under Uncertainty: Heuristics and Biases," *Science* 185 (1974): 1124–1131.

35. *U.S. Code,* Title 44, secs. 3501–3518; see *Code of Federal Regulations,* Title 5, secs. 1320.1–1320.18.

36. *Code of Federal Regulations,* Title 5, sec. 1320.3(c)(4).

37. 44 *U.S. Code,* Title 44, sec. 3518(c)(1)(B).

38. Ibid., sec. 3506(a)(2).

39. Ibid., Title 5, sec. 574(h).

40. *Code of Federal Regulations,* Title 29, secs. 1614 et seq.

41. W. Heisenberg, *The Physical Principles of the Quantum Theory* (New York: Dover, 1930).

42. See U.S. Department of Agriculture and others, "Federal Policy for the Protection of Human Subjects," *Federal Register,* June 18, 1991, 28,003.

43. See ibid., model policy, secs. 102(f), 109.

44. See ibid., model policy, sec. 111.

45. To receive a waiver from the requirement of informed consent, research must involve no more than minimal risk to the subjects; the waiver must not adversely affect the rights and welfare of the subjects; the research must be impractical to carry out without the waiver; and the subjects must be provided with additional pertinent information after the participation wherever appropriate. See ibid., model policy, sec. 114.

46. Bingham and Novac, "Mediation's Impact on Formal Complaint Filing," 308–331.

References

Acland, A. *Resolving Disputes Without Going to Court.* New York: Random House, 1995.

Adler, R. S., and Silverstein, E. M. "When David Meets Goliath: Dealing with Power Differentials in Negotiations." *Harvard Negotiation Law Review,* 2000, *5,* 75–76.

Administrative Conference of the United States. *Alternatives for Resolving Government Contract Disputes.* Washington, D.C.: Administrative Conference of the United States, 1987.

Administrative Conference of the United States. *An Introduction to ADR and the Roster of Neutrals.* Washington, D.C.: Administrative Conference of the United States, 1989.

Administrative Conference of the United States. *Implementing the ADR Act: Guidance for Agency Dispute Resolution Specialists.* Washington, D.C.: Administrative Conference of the United States, 1992.

Administrative Conference of the United States. *Dispute Systems Design Pre-Design Organizational Checklist.* Washington, D.C.: Administrative Conference of the United States, 1993.

Administrative Conference of the United States, *Performance Indicators for ADR Program Evaluation.* Washington, D.C.: Administrative Conference of the United States, 1993.

Administrative Conference of the United States. *Operational Aspects of Designing Dispute Resolution Systems.* Washington, D.C.: Administrative Conference of the United States, 1994.

Administrative Conference of the United States. *Evaluating ADR Programs.* Washington, D.C.: Administrative Conference of the United States, 1995.

Administrative Conference of the United States. *Toward Improved Agency Dispute Resolution: Implementing the ADR Act.* Washington, D.C.: Administrative Conference of the United States, 1995.

Administrative Office of the United States Courts. *Advisory Opinion No. 95, Judges Acting in a Settlement Capacity.* Washington, D.C.: Administrative Office of the United States Courts, 1999.

Administrative Office of the United States Courts. *Annual Report of the Director.* Washington, D.C.: Administrative Office of the United States Courts, 2001.

Administrative Office of the United States Courts. *Federal Court Management Statistics.* Washington, D.C.: Administrative Office of the United States Courts, 2001.

Administrative Office of the United States Courts. *U.S. District Court Judicial Caseload Profile.* Washington, D.C.: Administrative Office of the United States Courts, 2001.

Alfini, James J. "Risk of Coercion Too Great: Judges Should Not Mediate Cases Assigned to Them for Trial." *Dispute Resolution Magazine,* 1999, *5,* 11.

American Arbitration Association, American Bar Association, and Society of Professionals in Dispute Resolution. *Model Standards of Conduct for Mediators.* New York: American Arbitration Association, 1995.

American Bar Association. *Standards for the Establishment and Operation of Ombuds Offices.* Chicago: American Bar Association, 2001.

Anderson, D. R., and Hill, L. B. "The Ombudsman: A Primer for Federal Agencies." In J. H. Young (ed.), *Practicing Law Before Federal Agencies in a New World of ADR.* New York: Aspen Law and Business, 1995.

Anderson, F. J., Jr. and others (eds.). *Electronic Guide to Federal Procurement ADR.* Washington, D.C.: Federal Interagency ADR Working Group, 2000.

Anderson, J. F., and Bingham, L. B. "Upstream Effects from Mediation of Workplace Disputes: Some Preliminary Evidence from the USPS." *Labor Law Journal,* 1997, *48,* 601–615.

Arnold, T. "Twenty Common Errors in Mediation Advocacy." *Alternatives to the High Cost of Litigation,* 1995, *13,* 69–70.

Arrow, K., and others (eds.). *Barriers to Conflict Resolution.* New York: Norton, 1995.

Ayres, I., and Nalebuff, B. J. "Common Knowledge as a Barrier to Negotiation." *U.C.L.A. Law Review,* 1997, *44,* 1631–1659.

Barkai, J. "Teaching Negotiation and ADR: The Savvy Samurai Meets the Devil." *Nebraska Law Review,* 1996, *75,* 704–751.

Barkat, J. S. "Blueprint for Success: How to Effectively Design an Organizational Ombuds Department." Unpublished manuscript, 2002.

Bell, G. B. "The Pound Conference Follow-Up: A Response from the United States Department of Justice." *Federal Rules Decisions,* 1978, *76,* 320–337.

Bingham, L. B., and Napoli, L.-M. "Employment Dispute Resolution and Workplace Culture: The REDRESS Program at the United States Postal Service." In M. Breger, G. Schatz, and D. Laufer (eds.), *Fed-*

eral Administrative Dispute Resolution Deskbook. Chicago: American Bar Association, 2001.

Bingham, L. B., and Novac, M. C. "Mediation's Impact on Formal Complaint Filing: Before and After the REDRESS Program at the United States Postal Service." *Review of Public Personnel Administration,* 2001, *21,* 308–331

Brazil, D. "Protecting the Confidentiality of Settlement Negotiations." *Hastings Law Journal,* 1998, *39,* 955–1029.

Brazil, W. D. "Comparing Structures for the Delivery of ADR Services by Courts: Critical Values and Concerns." *Ohio State Journal on Dispute Resolution,* 1999, *14,* 715–811.

Breger, M., Schatz, G., and Lavter, D. (eds.). *Federal Administrative Dispute Resolution Deskbook.* Chicago: American Bar Association, 2001.

Brunet, E. "Questioning the Quality of Alternative Dispute Resolution." *Tulane Law Review,* 1987, *62,* 1–56.

Burger, W. "Our Vicious Legal Spiral." *Judges Journal,* 1977, *16,* 22–49.

Burger, W. "Remarks to the American Bar Association." *American Bar Association Journal,* 1982, *68,* 274–275.

Bush, R.A.B. "The Dilemmas of Mediation Practice: A Study of Ethical Dilemmas and Policy Implications." *Journal of Dispute Resolution,* 1994, *1994,* 1–55.

Bush, R.A.B. "'What Do We Need a Mediator For?' Mediation's `Value-Added' for Negotiators." *Ohio State Journal on Dispute Resolution,* 1996, *12,* 1–36.

Bush, R.A.B., and Folger, J. P. *The Promise of Mediation: Responding to Conflict Through Empowerment and Recognition.* San Francisco: Jossey-Bass, 1994.

Carr, F. "How to Design a Dispute Resolution Program." *Alternatives to the High Cost of Litigation,* 1994, *12,* 36–38.

Carr, F. "Alternative Means of Dispute Resolution in Federal Contract Disputes." In M. Breger, G. Schatz, and D. Laufer (eds.), *Federal Administrative Dispute Resolution Deskbook.* Chicago: American Bar Association, 2001.

Clarke, S. H., Ellen, E. D., and McCormick, K. *Court-Ordered Civil Case Mediation in North Carolina: An Evaluation of Its Effects.* Chapel Hill: Institute of Government, University of North Carolina, 1995.

Cohen, J. R. "Advising Clients to Apologize." *Southern California Law Review,* 1999, *79,* 1009–1069.

Conroy, C. P., and Harty, M. J. "Alternative Dispute Resolution at the ASBCA." *Briefing Papers,* 2000, *00-07,* 1–24.

Cooley, J. W. *The Mediator's Handbook.* Notre Dame, Ind.: National Institute of Trial Advocacy, 2000.

Cooley, J. W. *Mediation Advocacy.* (2nd ed.) Notre Dame, Ind.: National Institute of Trial Advocacy, 2002.

Cooley, J. W., and Lubet, S. *Arbitration Advocacy.* Notre Dame, Ind.: National Institute of Trial Advocacy, 1997.

Costantino, C., and Sickles-Merchant, C. *Designing Conflict Management Systems: A Guide to Creating Productive and Healthy Organizations.* San Francisco: Jossey-Bass, 1996.

CPR-Georgetown Commission on Ethics and Standards in ADR. *Proposed Model Rule of Professional Conduct for the Lawyer as Third Party Neutral.* New York: CPR Institute for Dispute Resolution, 1999.

CPR Institute for Dispute Resolution. *Arbitration.* New York: CPR Institute for Dispute Resolution, 1995.

CPR Institute for Dispute Resolution. *Confidentiality.* New York: CPR Institute for Dispute Resolution, 1998.

CPR Institute for Dispute Resolution. *Mediation.* New York: CPR Institute for Dispute Resolution, 1998.

CPR Institute for Dispute Resolution. *Systems Design for the Law Department.* New York: CPR Institute for Dispute Resolution, 1998.

CPR Institute for Dispute Resolution. *ADR Suitability Guide.* New York: CPR Institute for Dispute Resolution, 2001.

Creo, R. E. "A Pie Chart Tool to Resolve Multi-Party, Multi-Issue Conflicts." *Alternatives to the High Cost of Litigation,* 2000, *18,* 89–99.

Deason, E. E. "Predictable Mediation Confidentiality in the U.S. System." *Ohio State Journal on Dispute Resolution,* 2002, *17,* 239–319.

"Developments in the Law—The Paths of Civil Litigation." *Harvard Law Review,* 2000, *113,* 1851–1875.

Dillman, D. A. *Mail and Telephone Surveys: The Total Design Method.* New York: Wiley, 1978.

Ehrhardt, C. W. "U.S. Courts Will Likely Give Mediation Confidentiality Some Protection, But the Question Remains Open." *Dispute Resolution Magazine,* 1998, *5,* 17–19.

Federal ADR Council. "ADR Program Evaluation Recommendations." *Federal Register,* Oct. 4, 2000, p. 59,200.

Federal ADR Council. "Confidentiality in Federal Alternative Dispute Resolution Programs." *Federal Register,* Dec. 29, 2000, p. 83,085.

Federal ADR Council. "Core Principles for Federal Non-Binding Workplace ADR Programs." *Federal Register,* Aug. 16, 2000, p. 50,005.

Federal ADR Council. "Developing Guidance for Binding Arbitration—A Handbook for Federal Agencies." *Federal Register,* Aug. 16, 2000, p. 50,005.

Federal Aviation Administration Office of Dispute Resolution for Acquisition. *Case Management Statistics.* Washington, D.C.: Federal Aviation Administration Office of Dispute Resolution for Acquisition, 2001.

Federal Interagency ADR Working Group. *Federal ADR Program Manager's Resource Manual.* Washington, D.C.: Federal Interagency ADR Working Group, 1999.

Federal Interagency ADR Working Group. *Report of the Interagency Alternative Dispute Resolution Working Group to the President of the United States.* Washington, D.C.: Federal Interagency ADR Working Group, 2000.

Federal Judicial Center. *Experimentation in the Law: Report of the Federal Judicial Center Advisory Committee on Experimentation in the Law.* Washington, D.C.: Federal Judicial Center, 1981.

Federal Labor Relations Authority. *About the FLRA.* Washington, D.C.: Federal Labor Relations Authority, 2002.

Fisher, R., Ury, W., and Patton, B. *Getting to Yes: Negotiating Agreement Without Giving In.* (2nd ed.) New York: Penguin Books, 1991.

Funk, W. F., Lubbers, J. S., and Pou, C., Jr. *Federal Administrative Procedure Sourcebook.* (3rd ed.) Chicago: American Bar Association, 2000.

Galanter, M., and Cahill, M. "'Most Cases Settle': Judicial Promotion and Regulation of Settlements." *Stanford Law Review,* 1994, *46,* 1339–1391.

Golann, D. "Benefits and Dangers of Mediation Evaluation." *Alternatives to the High Cost of Litigation,* 1997, *15,* 35–38.

Golann, D. "Planning for Mediation Evaluation." *Alternatives to the High Cost of Litigation,* 1997, *15,* 56–58.

Golann, D. "If You're Willing to Experiment, 'Principle' Cases Can Be Mediated." *Alternatives to the High Cost of Litigation,* 1997, *16,* 37, 50–51.

Golann, D. *Representing Clients in Mediation: How Advocates Can Share a Mediator's Powers.* Chicago: American Bar Association, 2000.

Golann, D. *Mediating Legal Disputes: Effective Strategies for Lawyers and Mediators.* New York: Aspen Law and Business, 2001.

Golann, D. "Is Legal Mediation a Process of Repair—or Separation? An Empirical Study, and Its Implications." *Harvard Negotiation Law Review,* 2002, 7, 301–336.

Goldberg, S. B., and Brett, J. M. "Disputants' Perspectives on the Differences Between Mediation and Arbitration." *Negotiation Journal,* 1990, *6,* 249–256.

Goldberg, S. B., Sander, F.E.A., and Rogers, N. H. *Dispute Resolution, Negotiation, Mediation, and Other Processes.* (3rd ed.) New York: Aspen Law and Business, 1999.

Goodman, A. H. *Alternative Dispute Resolution at the General Services Board of Contract Appeals.* [http://users.erols.com/arbmed/article.htm]. 1997

Gordon, D. I. "GAO's Use of 'Negotiation Assistance' and 'Outcome Prediction' as ADR Techniques." *Federal Contracts Report*, 1999, *71*, 72–73.

Green, E. D. "A Heretical View of the Mediation Privilege." *2 Ohio State Journal on Dispute Resolution*, 1986, *2*, 1–36.

Guthrie, C., and Levin, J. "A 'Party Satisfaction' Perspective on a Comprehensive Mediation Statute." *Ohio State Journal on Dispute Resolution*, 1998, *13*, 885–907.

Harter, P. J. "Neither Cop nor Collection Agent: Encouraging Administrative Settlements by Ensuring Mediator Confidentiality." *Administrative Law Review*, 1989, *41*, 315–364.

Harty, M. J. "Results of Survey of Boards of Contract Appeals (BCA) Judges' Attitudes Towards Alternative Dispute Resolution (ADR)." Unpublished manuscript, 1996.

Harty, M. J., McDade, J. M., Jr., and Walters, R. C. (eds.). *Alternative Dispute Resolution: A Practical Guide for Resolving Government Contract Controversies*. Chicago: American Bar Association, 1999.

Heen, S., and Stone, D. *Facilitation Handbook*. Cambridge, Mass.: Program on Negotiation, Harvard Law School, 1994.

Hensler, D. R. "Puzzling over ADR: Drawing Meaning from the RAND Report." *Dispute Resolution Magazine*, 1997, *3*, 8–9.

Hodges, A. *Dispute Resolution Under the Americans with Disabilities Act*. Washington, D.C.: Administrative Conference of the United States, 1995.

Hoffer, D. P. "Decision Analysis as a Mediator's Tool." *Harvard Negotiation Law Review*, 1996, *1*, 113–137.

Honeyman, C. "Confidential, More or Less." *Dispute Resolution Magazine*, 1999, *5*, 12–13.

Honeyman, C. "Patterns of Bias in Mediation." *Journal of Dispute Resolution*, 1985, *1985*, 141–149.

Honeyman, C. "Five Elements of Mediation." *Negotiation Journal*, 1988, *4*, 149–158.

Honeyman, C. "On Evaluating Mediators." *Negotiation Journal*, 1990, *6*, 23–36.

Honeyman, C., and others. *Finding and Hiring Quality Neutrals: What Every Government Official Needs to Know*. Washington, D.C.: U.S. Environmental Protection Agency, 1996.

Honeyman, C., and others. *Performance-Based Assessment: A Methodology for Use in Selecting, Training, and Evaluating Mediators*. Washington, D.C.: National Institute of Dispute Resolution, 1995.

Honeyman, C., Miezio, K., and Houlihan, W. "In the Mind's Eye? Consistency and Variation in Evaluating Mediators." Working Paper 90–21, Program on Negotiation at Harvard Law School, 1990.

Irvine, M. "Serving Two Masters: The Obligation Under the Rules of Professional Conduct to Report Attorney Misconduct in a Confidential Mediation." *Rutgers Law Journal,* 1994, *26,* 155–185.

Kakalik, J. S., and others. *An Evaluation of Mediation and Early Neutral Evaluation Under the Civil Justice Reform Act.* Santa Monica, Calif.: Rand, 1996.

Kakalik, J. S., and others. *Just, Speedy, and Inexpensive? An Evaluation of Judicial Case Management Under the Civil Justice Reform Act.* Santa Monica, Calif.: Rand, 1996.

Kelly, J. "Court of Federal Claims to Test ENE with Settlement Judges." *adrworld.com,* Mar. 26, 2001.

Kentra, P. A. "Hear No Evil, See No Evil, Speak No Evil: The Intolerable Conflict for Attorney-Mediators Between the Duty to Maintain Mediation Confidentiality and the Duty to Report Fellow Attorney Misconduct." *Brigham Young University Law Review,* 1977, *1977,* 715–757.

Kichaven, J. G. "ADR Does Not Save Time or Money? Great News!" *Dispute Resolution Magazine,* 1997, *3,* 15.

Kirtley, A. "The Mediation Privilege's Transition from Theory to Implementation: Designing a Mediation Privilege Standard to Protect Mediation Participants, the Process and the Public Interest." *Journal of Dispute Resolution,* 1995, *1995,* 1–53.

Kochan, T. A., Lautsch, B. A., and Bendersky, C. "An Evaluation of the Massachusetts Commission Against Discrimination Alternative Dispute Resolution Program." *Harvard Negotiation Law Review,* 2000, *5,* 233–278.

Lax, D., and Sebenius, J. *The Manager as Negotiator.* New York: Free Press, 1987.

Lipsky, D. B., and Seeber, R. L. *The Appropriate Resolution of Corporate Disputes: A Report on the Growing Use of ADR by U.S. Companies.* Ithaca, N.Y.: Cornell/PERC Institute on Conflict Resolution, 1998.

Litt, G. "No Confidence: The Problem of Confidentiality by Local Rule in the Alternative Dispute Resolution Act of 1998." *Texas Law Review,* 2000, *78,* 1015–1036.

Loewen, J. W. *Social Science in the Courtroom.* San Francisco: New Lexington Press, 1982.

Lofaro, A. P. "ADR in the Federal Workplace: Why It Is Needed, How It Can Help, and Some Cautions to Observe." In M. Breger, G. Schatz, and D. Laufer (eds.), *Federal Administrative Dispute Resolution Deskbook.* Chicago: American Bar Association, 2001.

Manos, K. L. "The Antideficiency Act Without an M Account: Reasserting Constitutional Control." *Public Contract Law Journal,* 1994, *23,* 337–377.

Marcus, D., and Senger, J. M. "ADR and the Federal Government: Not Such Strange Bedfellows After All." *Missouri Law Review,* 2001, *66,* 709–723.

Mazadoorian, H. "Institutionalizing ADR: Few Risks, Many Benefits: Some Guidelines for System Design." *Alternatives to the High Cost of Litigation,* 1994, *12,* 45–46.

Mazadoorian, H. (ed.). *Mediation Practice Book, Critical Tools, Techniques and Forms.* New Britain, Conn.: LawFirst Publishing, 2002.

McDade, J. M. *Guidelines for Using Alternative Dispute Resolution Techniques to Resolve Contract Disputes.* Washington, D.C.: U.S. Department of the Air Force, 1994.

McDade, J. M. *Air Force Alternative Dispute Resolution (ADR) Reference Book (Acquisition).* Washington, D.C.: U.S. Department of the Air Force, 2001.

McDade, J. M. *The Administrative Dispute Resolution Act of 1996: What You Need to Know to Make It Work for You.* Washington, D.C.: U.S. Department of the Air Force, 1999.

McDermott, E. P., Obar, R., Jose, A., and Bowers, M. *An Evaluation of the EEOC Mediation Program.* Washington, D.C.: U.S. Equal Employment Opportunity Commission, 2000.

McEwen, C. A., and Maiman, R. J. "Mediation in Small Claims Court: Consensual Processes and Outcomes." In K. Kressel and D. G. Pruitt (eds.), *Mediation Research.* San Francisco: Jossey-Bass, 1989.

McEwen, C. A., and Plapinger, E. "RAND Report Points Way to Next Generation of ADR Research." *Dispute Resolution Magazine,* 1997, *3,* 10–11.

McGovern, F. E. "Beyond Efficiency: A Bevy of ADR Justifications." *Dispute Resolution Magazine,* 1997, *3,* 12–13.

Meece, M. "Companies Adopting Postal Service Grievance Process." *New York Times,* Sept. 6, 2000, p. C1.

Meltzer, D. L. "The Federal Workplace Ombuds." *Ohio State Journal on Dispute Resolution,* 1998, *13,* 549–609.

Meltzer, D. L. "Can a Federal Ombuds Help You?" In M. Breger, G. Schatz, and D. Laufer (eds.), *Federal Administrative Dispute Resolution Deskbook.* Chicago: American Bar Association, 2001.

Menkel-Meadow, C. "Ethics in ADR: The Many 'C's' of Professional Responsibility and Dispute Resolution." *Fordham Urban Law Journal,* 2001, *28,* 979–990.

Miller, B. *A Practical Guide to GAO's Alternative Dispute Resolution Techniques.* Washington, D.C.: U.S. General Accounting Office, n.d.

Mnookin, R. H. "Why Negotiations Fail: An Exploration of Barriers to the Resolution of Conflict." *Ohio State Journal on Dispute Resolution,* 1993, *8,* 235–249.

Mnookin, R. H., Peppet, S. R., and Tulumello, A. S. *Beyond Winning: Negotiating to Create Value in Deals and Disputes.* Cambridge, Mass.: Harvard University Press, 2000.

Murphy, B. S. "Mediation of Federal Employment Discrimination Charges." In M. Breger, G. Schatz, and D. Laufer (eds.), *Federal Administrative Dispute Resolution Deskbook.* Chicago: American Bar Association, 2001.

Niemic, R. J. *Mediation and Conference Programs in the Federal Courts of Appeals.* Washington, D.C.: Federal Judicial Center, 1997.

Niemic, R. J., Stienstra, D., and Ravitz, R. E. *Guide to Judicial Management of Cases in ADR.* Washington, D.C.: Federal Judicial Center, 2001.

Office of Personnel Management. *Alternative Dispute Resolution: A Resource Guide.* Washington, D.C.: Office of Personnel Management, 1999.

Office of Personnel Management. *Guidelines for Settlement of Federal Personnel Actions Involving Civil Service Retirement Benefits.* Washington, D.C.: Office of Personnel Management, 2000.

Office of Special Counsel. *The OSC Mediation Program.* Washington, D.C.: Office of Special Counsel, 2001.

Office of Special Counsel. *Application for OPM Director's Award for Outstanding Alternative Dispute Resolution Program.* Washington, D.C.: Office of Special Counsel, 2002.

Palladino, A. N., and Sheehan, W. R. "Acquisition ADR at the Federal Aviation Administration." In M. Breger, G. Schatz, and D. Laufer (eds.), *Federal Administrative Dispute Resolution Deskbook.* Chicago: American Bar Association, 2001.

Pearson, J., and Thoennes, N. "Divorce Mediation: Reflections on a Decade of Research." In K. Kressel and D. G. Pruitt (eds.), *Mediation Research.* San Francisco: Jossey-Bass, 1989.

Plapinger, E., and Stienstra, D. *ADR and Settlement in the Federal District Courts, A Sourcebook for Judges and Lawyers.* Washington, D.C.: Federal Judicial Center, 1996.

Pou, C., Jr. "'Wheel of Fortune' or 'Singled Out'? How Rosters 'Matchmake' Mediators." *Dispute Resolution Magazine,* 1997, *3,* 10–13.

Pou, C., Jr. "Gandhi Meets Elliot Ness: Fifth Circuit Ruling Raises Concerns About Confidentiality in Federal Agency ADR." *Dispute Resolution Magazine,* 1998, *5,* 9–11.

Purcell, S. "Funding Court ADR: Advice from the Trenches." *Dispute Resolution Magazine,* 2003, *9,* 19–21, 37.

Reno, J. Address at the Meeting of the American Judicature Society and Chicago Bar Association, Feb. 5, 1998.

Retson, N. P. *Alternative Disputes Resolution, Policies and Procedures Guide for Trial Attorneys.* Washington, D.C.: U.S. Department of the Army, 1997.

Richardson, M. B. "The Department of the Navy's Equal Employment Opportunity Complaint Dispute Resolution Process Pilot Program: A Bold Experiment That Deserves Further Exploration." *Military Law Review,* 2001, *169,* 1–69.

Riskin, L. L. "Understanding Mediators' Orientations, Strategies, and Techniques: A Grid for the Perplexed." *Harvard Negotiation Law Review,* 1996, *1,* 7–51.

Riskin, L. L., and Westbrook, J. E. *Dispute Resolution and Lawyers.* (2nd ed.) Minneapolis: West, 1998.

Riskin, L. L., Westbrook, J. E., and Levin, J. H. *Instructor's Manual with Simulation and Problem Materials to Accompany Dispute Resolution and Lawyers.* Minneapolis: West, 1998.

Rogers N. H., and McEwen, C. A. *Mediation: Law, Policy, Practice.* (2nd ed.) Deerfield, Ill.: Clark Boardman Callaghan, 1994.

Ross, L. "Reactive Devaluation in Negotiation and Conflict Resolution." In K. Arrow and others (eds.), *Barriers to Conflict Resolution.* New York: Norton, 1995.

Rowe, M. P. "The Corporate Ombudsman: An Overview and Analysis." *Negotiation Journal,* 1987, *3,* 127–140.

Rowe, M. P., and Bendersky, C. "Workplace Justice, Zero Tolerance and Zero Barriers: Getting People to Come Forward in Conflict Management Systems." In T. Kochan and R. Locke (eds.), *Negotiations and Change: From the Workplace to Society.* Ithaca, N.Y.: Cornell University Press, 2000.

Sander, F.E.A. "Varieties of Dispute Processing." *Federal Rule Decisions,* 1976, *70,* 111–133.

Sander, F.E.A. "A Friendly Amendment." *Dispute Resolution Magazine,* 1999, *6,* 11–24.

Sander, F.E.A. "The Future of ADR." *Journal of Dispute Resolution,* 2000, *2000,* 3–10.

Sander, F.E.A., and Goldberg, S, "Fitting the Forum to the Fuss: A User-Friendly Guide to Selecting an ADR Procedure." *Negotiation Journal,* 1994, *10,* 49–68.

Saxton, B. "How Well Do Jurors Understand Jury Instructions? A Field Test Using Real Juries and Real Trials in Wyoming." *Land and Water Law Review,* 1998, *33,* 59–189.

Scanlon, K. M. "Primer on Recent Developments in Mediation Confidentiality." *Alternatives to the High Cost of Litigation,* 2001, *19,* 1–2.

Senger, J. M. "Evaluation of ADR in United States Attorney Cases." *United States Attorneys' Bulletin,* 2000, *48,* 25–29.

Senger, J. M. "Frequently Asked Questions About ADR." *United States Attorneys' Bulletin,* 2000, *48,* 9–15.

Senger, J. M. "Turning the Ship of State." *Journal of Dispute Resolution,* 2000, *2000,* 79–95.

Senger, J. M., and Honeyman, C. "Cracking the Hard-Boiled Student: Some Ways to Turn Research Findings into Interactive Exercises." *Conflict Resolution Practitioner,* 2001, *1,* 31–42.

Shack, J. E. "Saves What? A Survey of Pace, Cost and Satisfaction Studies of Court-Related Mediation Programs." Materials for American Bar Association Conference presentation, Apr. 4, 2002.

Sheridan, P. J. "Board of Contract Appeal Judges: Sharing a Common Vision." In M. Breger, G. Schatz, and D. Laufer (eds.), *Federal Administrative Dispute Resolution Deskbook.* Chicago: American Bar Association, 2001.

Singer, L. A. *Settling Disputes.* (2nd ed.) Boulder, Colo.: Westview Press, 1994.

Society for Professionals in Dispute Resolution. *Best Practices for Government Agencies: Guidelines for Using Collaborative Agreement-Seeking Processes.* Washington, D.C.: Society for Professionals in Dispute Resolution, 1997.

Society for Professionals in Dispute Resolution. *Guidelines for the Design of Integrated Conflict Management Systems Within Organizations.* Washington, D.C.: Society for Professionals in Dispute Resolution, 2000.

Solum, L. B. "2020 Vision: A Plan for the Future of California's Courts." *Southern California Law Review,* 1993, 2162–64 (1993), 66, 2162–2182.

Spiegelman, P. J. "Certifying Mediators: Using Selection Criteria to Include the Qualified: Lessons from the San Diego Experience." *University of San Francisco Law Review,* 1996, *30,* 677–721.

Stienstra, D. "Evaluating and Monitoring ADR Procedures." *FJC Directions,* 1994, *7,* 24–25.

Stienstra, D. *Rules of Thumb for Designing and Administering Mailed Questionnaires.* Washington, D.C.: Federal Judicial Center, 2000.

Susskind, L. E., Babbitt, E. F., and Segal, P. N. "When ADR Becomes the Law: A Review of Federal Practice." *Negotiation Journal,* 1993, *9,* 59–75.

Susskind, L., McKearnan, S., and Thomas-Larmer, J. *Consensus Building Handbook.* Thousand Oaks, Calif.: Sage, 1999.

Tolan, P. E., Jr. "Using ADR to Resolve Contract Disputes Between Government Contractors and the Air Force." In M. Breger, G. Schatz, and D. Laufer (eds.), *Federal Administrative Dispute Resolution Deskbook.* Chicago: American Bar Association, 2001.

Trochim, W. M. *Research Methods Knowledge Base.* (2nd ed.) Cincinnati, Ohio: Atomic Dog Publishing, 2000.

Tversky, A., and Kahneman, D. "Judgments Under Uncertainty: Heuristics and Biases." *Science,* 1974, *185,* 1124–1131.

"2001: A Timeline." *Cincinnati Enquirer,* Dec. 30, 2001. [www.enquirer. com/unrest2001/timeline.html].

Umbreit, M. S. *The Handbook of Victim Offender Mediation: An Essential Guide to Practice and Research.* San Francisco: Jossey-Bass, 2001.

U.S. Department of the Air Force. *Mediation Compendium: How to Mediate Civilian Personnel Workplace Dispute.* (2nd ed.) Washington, D.C.: U.S. Department of the Air Force, 2000.

U.S. Department of the Air Force. *Nomination for the Office of Federal Procurement Policy's ADR Award.* Washington, D.C.: U.S. Department of the Air Force, 2001.

U.S. Department of the Air Force. *Nomination for the Office of Personnel Management Director's Award for Outstanding Alternative Dispute Resolution Programs.* Washington, D.C.: U.S. Department of the Air Force, 2001.

U.S. Department of the Air Force. *Common Interests of the Parties.* Washington, D.C.: U.S. Department of the Air Force, 2002.

U.S. Department of Justice. "No Compromise of Civil Liability When Criminal Case Pending." In *United States Attorneys' Manual.* Washington, D.C.: U.S. Department of Justice, 2003.

U.S. Department of Justice. *U.S. Attorney Annual Statistical Report.* Washington, D.C.: U.S. Department of Justice, 1999.

U.S. Equal Employment Opportunity Commission. *Facts About Mediation.* Washington, D.C.: U.S. Equal Employment Opportunity Commission, 1999.

U.S. Equal Employment Opportunity Commission. *Management Directive EEO MD-110: Federal Sector Complaint Processing Manual.* Washington, D.C.: U.S. Equal Employment Opportunity Commission, 1999.

U.S. Equal Employment Opportunity Commission. *Questions and Answers About Mediation.* Washington, D.C.: U.S. Equal Employment Opportunity Commission, 1999.

U.S. Equal Employment Opportunity Commission. *Annual Report on the Federal Work Force.* Washington, D.C.: U.S. Equal Employment Opportunity Commission, 2001.

U.S. General Accounting Office. *Designing Evaluations.* Washington, D.C.: U.S. General Accounting Office, 1991.

U.S. General Accounting Office. *Employment Discrimination: Most Private-Sector Employers Use Alternative Dispute Resolution.* Washington, D.C.: U.S. General Accounting Office, 1995.

U.S. General Accounting Office. *Bid Protests at GAO: A Descriptive Guide.* Washington, D.C.: U.S. General Accounting Office, 1996.

U.S. General Accounting Office. *Alternative Dispute Resolution, Employers— Experiences with ADR in the Workplace.* Washington, D.C.: U.S. General Accounting Office, 1997.

U.S. General Accounting Office. *Equal Employment Opportunity: Rising Trends in EEO Complaint Caseloads in the Federal Sector.* Washington, D.C.: U.S. General Accounting Office, 1998.

U.S. General Accounting Office. *The Role of Ombudsmen in Dispute Resolution.* Washington, D.C.: U.S. General Accounting Office, 2001.

U.S. Institute for Environmental Conflict Resolution. *Program Evaluation System at the U.S. Institute for Environmental Conflict Resolution.* Tucson, Ariz.: U.S. Institute for Environmental Conflict Resolution, 2002.

Upchurch, J. J. "Florida Firm Trains and Leverages Its New Mediation Associates." *Alternatives to the High Cost of Litigation,* 2002, *20,* 1, 15.

Ury, W. L., Brett, J. M., and Goldberg, S. B. *Getting Disputes Resolved: Designing Systems to Cut the Costs of Conflict.* San Francisco: Jossey-Bass, 1988.

Van Doren, B., Gilmore, B. S., and McCann, R. A. *Energy Board of Contract Appeals ADR Handbook.* Washington, D.C.: U.S. Department of Energy, 1999.

Waldman, E. "Credentialling Approaches: The Slow Movement Toward Skills-Based Testing Continues." *Dispute Resolution Magazine,* 2001, *8,* 13–21.

Weckstein, D. T. "Mediator Certification: Why and How." *University of San Francisco Law Review,* 1996, *30,* 757–801.

Welsh, Nancy N. A. "Making Deals in Court-Connected Mediation: What's Justice Got to Do with It?" *Washington University Law Quarterly,* 2001, *79,* 787–861.

Wissler, R. L. "Court-Connected Mediation in General Civil Cases: What We Know from Empirical Research." *Ohio State Journal on Dispute Resolution,* 2002, *17,* 641–703.

Yates, S. M., and Shack, J. E. *An Evaluation of the Lanham Act Mediation Program, U.S. District Court for the Northern District of Illinois.* Chicago: Center for the Analysis of Alternative Dispute Resolution Systems, 2000.

Young, J. H. "Private Perspectives on ADR in Federal Contract Disputes." In M. Breger, G. Schatz, and D. Laufer (eds.), *Federal Administrative Dispute Resolution Deskbook.* Chicago: American Bar Association, 2001.

Zamke, R., and Zamke, S. "Thirty Things We Know for Sure About Adult Learning." *Training,* 1981, *18,* 45–52.

Index

About the Author

JEFFREY M. SENGER is senior counsel in the Office of Dispute Resolution at the U.S. Department of Justice. He advises and trains federal lawyers around the country in alternative dispute resolution and negotiation. He has served as a federal mediator for the U.S. District Court; a civil, family, and criminal misdemeanor mediator for the Superior Court in Washington, D.C.; and an arbitrator for the Better Business Bureau and the District of Columbia Bar Association. In previous experience at the Justice Department, he directed civil and appellate training at the Attorney General's Advocacy Institute, litigated discrimination cases around the country as a senior trial attorney in the civil rights division, and prosecuted crimes as a special assistant U.S. Attorney. He began his career as a judicial law clerk for U.S. District Court Judge Earl B. Gilliam. A well-known educator in the field, he teaches with Harvard Law School's Program on Negotiation, the National Institute of Trial Advocacy, and Harvard's trial advocacy program. His international ADR experience includes trips to India, Turkey, Israel, Nigeria, Jordan, Egypt, and Argentina to speak to judges and political leaders. He has published numerous articles in the field, and the U.S. Congress has asked him to testify as an expert witness on ADR. He is a graduate of Harvard College and Harvard Law School.